DIS

NONVERBAL
LEARNING
DISABILITIES

NONVERBAL LEARNING DISABILITIES

A Clinical Perspective

Joseph Palombo

W. W. NORTON & COMPANY
New York • London

For information about permission to reproduce selections from this
book, write to Permissions, W. W. Norton & Company, Inc.,
500 Fifth Avenue, New York, NY 10110

Composition by PennSet, Inc.
Production Manager: Benjamin Reynolds
Manufacturing by Quebecor World—Fairfield, PA Division

Library of Congress Cataloging-in-Publication Data

Palombo, Joseph, 1928-
    Nonverbal learning disabilities : a clinical perspective /
Joseph Palombo.
        p.   cm.
    "A Norton professional book."
    Includes bibliographical references and index.
    ISBN 0-393-70478-5
    ISBN 978-0-393-70478-5
    1. Learning disabled children—Education. 2. Nonverbal learning
disabilities. 3. Personality disorders in children. I. Title.

LC4704.5.P354 2006
371.9—dc22   2005049539

W. W. Norton & Company, Inc., 500 Fifth Avenue, New York, N.Y. 10110
www.wwnorton.com

W. W. Norton & Company Ltd., Castle House, 75/76 Wells St.,
London W1T 3QT

1   3   5   7   9   0   8   6   4   2

To the children and their families,
the staff (past and present), and
Meryl Lipton, the founder and director
of the
Rush Neurobehavioral Center

Contents

PART IV: TREATMENT

Preface

In September 1992 Meryl Lipton, a pediatric neurologist with a Ph.D. in learning disabilities, convened a multidisciplinary study group of colleagues that included Pearl Rieger, a psychoeducational diagnostician, Karen Pierce, a child psychiatrist, Warren Rosen, a developmental neuropsychologist, and myself, a clinical social worker. The charge we set ourselves was to think about and discuss the issues of children with nonverbal learning disabilities. At the time, there was little public or professional awareness of the disorder, in spite of the fact that Rourke's publications were widely available.

We asked ourselves, "Is there such an entity as a *nonverbal learning disability*?" If there is such an entity, "What are its specific behavioral markers?" If there were such markers, "What specific brain dysfunctions would undergird these behaviors?" And . . .

> "Is this entity a syndrome or simply a set of unrelated symptoms?"
> "What of the children themselves, how does the disorder affect their development?"
> "Why do some of the children appear less impaired by their learning difficulties while others are deeply affected?"
> "How do the children's parents cope with the difficulties that accompany living with a child with such a disability?"
> "How are schools managing these children?"

We asked these and many more questions. Of importance to me, as a clinician, were the questions related to the effects of the disorder on the children's development, the contribution the disorder made to their social adjustment, and the implications of our understanding of these children's problems for their psychotherapy.

The outcome of our discussions was twofold. First, I published a paper on "The Psychodynamic and Relational Problems of Children with Nonverbal Learning Disabilities" (Palombo, 1995). Later, my colleague Anne

H. Berenberg and I published two more papers, one on the treatment of these children (Palombo & Berenberg, 1997) and another on working with the parents (Palombo & Berenberg, 1999). A second outcome of our group's discussion was the establishment of a clinic in which we could conduct research on the topic of nonverbal learning disabilities. With the encouragement of Dr. Samuel Gottoff, who was then Chair of the Department of Pediatrics, Rush–Presbyterian–St. Luke's Medical Center, and with the help of an active advisory board that helped raise the necessary funds, the Rush Neurobehavioral Center was opened in January 1997. A substantial grant from the women's board of the Rush–Presbyterian–St. Luke's Medical Center helped launch our first research program.

These developments gave me the impetus to draw together materials I had collected over the years into this book. Writing about the social and emotional problems of children with nonverbal learning disabilities provides an opportunity to present some of the current controversies regarding these children prevalent in the field. Constructing a theoretical framework through which to understand these problems is a prerequisite for planning and implementing appropriate interventions in this domain. I therefore set myself the task of formulating a developmental perspective that might account specifically for the social and emotional problems these children experience. Because my orientation is broadly psychoanalytic, self psychology, in particular, has heavily influenced my thinking. The framework I present lies squarely in this tradition. Enriching this orientation is a major emphasis on the role of endowment and constitutional factors in every aspect of normal development as well as psychopathology. I also provide a summary of social–emotional symptoms in Appendix 1.

This book is addressed to clinicians, psychiatrists, psychologists, clinical social workers, and other psychotherapists who work with children. Those who are familiar with learning disabilities may find its perspective particularly useful in their work. Pediatric neuropsychologists and educational psychologists involved in the assessment of children may also find this work of interest to them. Although the book is not specifically addressed to the caregivers of children with nonverbal learning disabilities, these caregivers may find some sections of the book helpful. I suggest that caregivers skip those sections that are overly technical (for their purposes) and go directly to the summaries and conclusions.

This work is primarily devoted to the problems of children and adolescents. The data are lacking as to the specific expression of the disorder in older adolescents and adult. Increasingly, practitioners who have become more knowledgeable of the literature are identifying adults with the disorder. My clinical impression is that without intervention, the neurobehavioral symptoms in those patients become more severe with age. Often, some of these adults were not diagnosed previously or were misdiagnosed. A benefit of practitioners' and caregivers' increasing familiarity with the disorder is the identification of older adolescents and adults and the shift in attitude toward the problems they present. However, much remains to be learned about the condition in these populations.

Acknowledgments

I owe an enormous debt to the many people who have contributed to the formulation of the ideas in this work:

My first debt is to the families and children who gave me the privilege of consulting with them about their problems. The insights they provided into their difficulties and the kind of assistance they found most valuable deeply enriched my understanding of the disorder.

Among my colleagues, I would like to thank the members of the original study group: Meryl Lipton, Pearl Rieger, Karen Pierce, and Warren Rosen. The members of my Los Angeles neuropsychoanalysis study group, which includes (or has included in past years) Justin Call, Lou Cozollino, Francine Inbinder, David Meltzer, Hans Miller, Regina Pally, Renee Schwartz, Sandy Shapiro, John Watkins, and Jeff Weinberg, significantly enlarged my knowledge of modern developments in neurobiology. My Chicago study group on neurobiology and psychoanalysis, which includes Anne Berenberg, Lynn Bornstein, William Gieseke, Gloria Levin, Susan Lipton, Mike McNulty, Judith Feigon Schiffman, Erika Schmidt, and Rita Sussman, helped me focus on the clinical relevance of the ideas that I was struggling to formulate. I specially want to express my gratitude to Jeffrey Weinberg, with whom, in our weekly telephone conversations, I covered a broad range of topics and discussed various aspects of this work as it progressed. John Watkins has been particularly helpful in clarifying difficult aspects of the theories and definition of nonverbal learning disabilities. I thank my colleague, Francine Inbinder, who, during our commute to our study group in Los Angeles, challenged me to clarify and at times modify my position. Karen Pierce read some of the beginning chapters in their early form and provided me with valuable feedback. Many of the brief illustrative case vignettes are drawn from neuropsychological reports written by Warren Rosen. The data for these vignettes are derived from a qualitative study of 25 children assessed by Dr. Rosen and diagnosed with a nonverbal learning disability. I am grateful to Joshua Mark for contributing the case in Chapters 1 and 12. All case material was disguised for purposes of confidentiality and to protect the identity of subjects or patients. In some instances case illustrations are composites of one or more subjects or patients.

I thank the people at Norton Professional Books—Deborah Malmud, my editor, Michael J. McGandy, for his comments, and Margaret Ryan for her skillful copyediting. They helped me bring greater coherence to the work than my original effort.

Portions of Chapter 13 were published as an article titled "Working with Parents of Children with Nonverbal Learning Disabilities: A Conceptual and Intervention model" (Palombo & Berenberg, 1999) in *Understanding, Diagnosing, and Treating ADHD in Children and Adolescents: An Integrative Approach* (Incorvia, Mark-Goldstein, & Tessmer, 1999, pp. 398–441). I wish to thank Rowman and Little Publishing Group for permission to use this previously published material. I thank American Psychiatric Publishing, Inc. for permission to use the chart titled: Diagnostic criteria for 299.80 Asperger's Disorder. p. 77. *DSM-IV* (1994), American Psychiatric Association.

I am responsible for whatever inaccuracies or limitations the work contains.

As ever, my wife Dottie patiently made room for me to work and spend time away from her, even during our vacations. Her support and encouragement never wavered.

NONVERBAL
LEARNING
DISABILITIES

Introduction

The knowledge acquired about brain function in the past two decades has greatly enhanced our understanding of some childhood disorders. The role of nature has taken its rightful place alongside that of nurture in our view of development and psychopathology. Among the children who have benefited from this perspective are those with learning disorders. There is little remaining controversy that disorders such as attention-deficit/hyperactivity disorders (ADHD), executive dysfunctions, and nonverbal learning disabilities are the result of brain-based impairments rather than acquired disorders resulting from deficiencies in the nurture the child received from caregivers. The environment may either enhance or mitigate the constraints that nurture imposes on a child's development.

Clinical Definition of NLD

Learning disabilities are neurobehavioral disorders that affect children or adults of (at least) average intelligence. These conditions are present at birth and arise from brain dysfunctions whose etiology is often unknown; they are not the result of trauma or neurological abnormalities, such as brain lesions or strokes. Over 6.4 million children between the ages of 3 and 21 were served under the Individuals with Disabilities Education Act in the school year 2001–02. Learning disabilities are conditions that affect one or more of a broad range of academic, cognitive, social, or vocational functions. Often the disabilities manifest as a discrepancy between a child's potential and his or her school performance. The severity of the deficits is highly variable; some children have deficits in a single area, whereas others have them in several areas.

Until recently there was no unanimity among experts about the number of subtypes of learning disabilities (Coplin & Morgan, 1988; Morrison & Siegel, 1991). A consensus exists, however, that it is possible to make a simple demarcation between two broad subtypes: *verbal learning disabilities* and *nonverbal learning disabilities*. Verbal learning disabilities include the dyslexias, auditory processing difficulties, and other disorders that affect the reception, expression, and processing of verbal and written language. Nonverbal learning disabilities include the disorders in which deficits occur in the processing of nonlinguistic information and impairments in social–emotional functioning (see Drummond, Ahmad, & Rourke, 2005).

The following is a preliminary clinical definition of a nonverbal learning disability. As the work progresses this definition will be refined and elaborated (see Chapter 7 for a more detailed definition).

> A nonverbal learning disability (NLD) is a developmental brain-based disorder that impairs a child's capacity to perceive, express, and understand nonverbal (nonlinguistic) signs. The disorder is generally expressed as a pattern of impaired functioning in the nonverbal domains, with higher functioning in the verbal domain. The neuropsychological deficits associated with this disorder constrain children's capacity to function in the academic, social, emotional, or vocational domain and lead to a heterogeneous set of neurobehavioral symptoms. The brain dysfunctions affect children's behaviors, their social interactions, their feelings about themselves and others, and their emerging personality patterns—all of which may manifest as symptomatic behaviors.

The Social Features of NLD

Between 38 and 75% of children with learning disabilities have social–emotional problems serious enough to require intervention (Bryan, Burstein, Ergul, 2004; Bauminger, Edelsztein, Morash, 2005; Tur-Kaspa & Bryan, 1994). According to Elksnin and Elksnin (2004), one-third of children who have a learning disability (LD) also have an NLD—or what some call a *social–emotional learning disability* (SELD). These children, in addition to neurocognitive deficits and a pattern of underachievement in some academic subjects, have self-esteem problems, social information-processing difficulties, and social-behavioral problems (O'Connor & Pianta, 1999). Rourke (1989a) reviewed and summarized the literature from 1980 to the time of publication of his work and concluded that no single personality pattern or psychopathological outcome is common to all children with learning disabilities—although he did state that children with NLD have a tendency "to develop an internalized form of socio-emotional disturbance" (pp. 85–86). In her review of the literature on the social–emotional functioning of children with NLD, Little (1993) found "some support for the hypothesis that individuals with nonverbal learning disabilities may be at greater risk than other individuals with LD for both

internalized and externalized emotional, behavioral or social problems"
(p. 662).

In this book I examine the effects that an NLD has on the social and
emotional development of the child. The social problems of children with
a NLD are dissimilar, in important ways, from those of children who have
behavioral or psychiatric problems. The children with NLD demonstrate
general social ineptness; they lack the social skills necessary to negotiate
interpersonal relationships. Although they display an interest in socializ-
ing with other children, when they have the opportunity to do so, they are
unsuccessful in sustaining social contact. Generally, they do not function
well in peer groups and have no close friendships, even though they verbalize a desire for such friendships. Their social communication is odd,
and they may come across as tactless or rude. They often do not make eye
contact during conversations, or their eye contact is fixed and unnatural.
They do not display appropriate facial expressions and appear unable to
read others' facial expressions. Their speech lacks prosody, making it difficult to detect the emotional undertones of their communications. Furthermore, they may become overly anxious in novel situations and find it
difficult to make transitions from one situation to another. At the emotional level, they have problems managing their feelings. They seem unable to regulate or modulate their affective states. As we will see, in
contrast, children with Asperger have many of the features of NLD but
also have autistic features that children with NLD do not have.

Here I focus on the social features of children with NLD for several reasons. First, psychotherapists have given insufficient attention to the relationship between children's neuropsychological deficits and the social
behaviors that they display. In part, this lacuna is the product of a historical emphasis by psychotherapists on factors related to nurture. Consequently, these children's problems are often misdiagnosed; indeed, some
therapists even give psychodynamic explanations for their neuropsychological difficulties. Although some children benefit from psychotherapy
under those conditions, the fact remains that the therapy does not address
their central problem. In this work, I attempt to redress this imbalance.

Second, as a heterogeneous disorder, NLD is expressed in different
forms and consequently confounds diagnostic categorization. Some neurologists and neuropsychologists regard the disorder as a single syndrome,
others as two different disorders that are conflated (i.e., NLD and SELD).
Still others regard the children as having impairments in social cognition
that would place them within the autistic spectrum, closely related to Asperger's Disorder. The controversy centers on the relationship between the
children's neuropsychological deficits and their social behaviors. Later on I
maintain that one of the features that distinguishes children with NLD

from those with Asperger's Disorder is that the problem in social cognition and the capacity for intimacy are more severe and disabling in the latter group than they are in the former.

The neurological and neuropsychological literatures often focus exclusively on the relationship between the hypothesized brain dysfunction and the overt behavior. That model appears to me to have significant explanatory limitations when applied to children with NLD. It is true that in some neurological conditions, such as those that result from brain insults, and in some serious psychiatric disorders, such as autism and schizophrenia, a direct correlation exists between the disorders and the patients' behaviors. This conclusion does not seem to apply to children with NLD.

My background as a child therapist with a psychodynamic orientation led me to wonder about other factors that might contribute to the behaviors. Although the etiology of NLD remains unidentified, factors in several domains are known to contribute to the individual differences we see in these children's social behaviors; these domains include biological, contextual, and developmental factors. Neuropsychological strengths and weaknesses are obviously major factors in the ultimate configuration of the child's social behaviors, although they do not exclusively determine that outcome. Bruner stated: "The biological substrate, the so-called universals of human nature, is not a cause of action, but, at most, a constraint upon it or a condition for it. . . . [B]iologically imposed limits on human functioning are also challenges to cultural intervention" (1990, p. 21). Temperamental factors also play a role in shaping the child's behavior (Chess & Thomas, 1977; Teglasi, Cohn & Meshbesher, 2004).

Furthermore, the brain's plasticity can lead to compensations that permit some areas of the brain to take over functions that impaired areas cannot perform. Whereas brain function affects the way children display these differences, environmental factors may affect brain development (Gilger, Whipple, & Spitz, 2001; Kandel, 1999; Leckman & Lombroso, 1998). Some genes provide the blueprint for the brain's organization, whereas the expression of other genes is contingent upon environmental triggers. Environmental factors such as diet, illnesses, toxins, and physical or psychological trauma also can trigger the expression of genes that will modify or aggravate the severity of the deficit and, in turn, modify the behavior the child displays.

The diagnostic controversies surrounding entities such as Asperger's Disorder, and Pervasive Developmental Disorders (PDD) and, at times, unfamiliarity with NLD have made it difficult for psychotherapists to distinguish clearly between neuropsychological, social, and psychodynamic factors in their assessment of children with NLD. The lack of clarity makes it difficult to plan for the child's treatment and to make appropriate interventions with caregivers and others in the child's environment. The confounding diagnostic factors can alert clinicians to the dysfunctional areas in these children that require greater attention.

My third source of motivation in the writing of this book was caregivers, teachers, and others involved with these children, who often misunderstand the reasons for the children's behaviors. Because they are often unaware that the child has a learning disability, they misattribute the child's behavior to willfulness, defiance, oppositionality, inattentiveness, laziness, or other pejorative sources. Professionals attach labels to the behavior such as "behavior disorder," "oppositional defiant disorder," "conduct disorder," or give them other inappropriate designations. Each of these labels misses the mark, and when applied to a child, it accentuates rather than alleviates the child's problems.

Assumptions and Conceptual Framework

A major assumption in this work is that, as a developmental disorder, NLD imposes certain constraints on the direction of a child's development. Some of these constraints are cognitive, some are social and emotional, and some are intrapersonal. An individual's phenotype is the composite of the total characteristics the person displays that results from the interaction between the genotype and the environment. From a subjective perspective we may refer to the phenotype as the person's sense of self. In the case of children with NLD, the manner in which a particular phenotype is expressed depends on several factors: (1) the severity of the deficits, (2) the point at which a specific deficit or impairment impedes a set of functions during development, (3) the responses of the child to his or her disorder, and (4) the responses to the child of caregivers and others in the context in which the child is raised.

The heterogeneity of the phenotypes is due to the multiplicity of factors that contribute to the final common path that development takes. We may conceive of the phenotype as the product of multiple streams of factors that have fed into it. Those streams arose out of tributaries that themselves arose from a watershed of factors present at birth. The three domains or tributaries that I consider significant for the development of the child with NLD are those related to the *neurobehavioral manifestations*, the *factors related to social and emotional functioning*, and the *intrapersonal factors*. Each of these domains has subcomponents that feed into the developmental stream and that may enhance or constrain the subcomponents of the other domains.

As a psychodynamically oriented child therapist who has treated many such patients, I have been interested in integrating aspects of the large body of knowledge gathered by psychoanalysis on children's development with a neurobehaviorally informed perspective. This effort centers on the determinants of social behaviors and emotional disturbances. The study of children with NLD presents an opportunity to approach the task of integrating these theories.

Each discipline, the neurobehavioral, the social, and the psychodynamic, grasps only part of the picture. To gain a full understanding of the whole child requires that we integrate the knowledge we possess from all three disciplines into a conceptual framework that can explain the social behaviors associated with the syndrome. In other words, rather than seeing the behaviors as simply the product of brain dysfunctions, we need to interpose between brain function and the behaviors a set of psychological processes that contribute to the manifest behaviors. The understanding we gain of children's development can complement our knowledge and shed light on some of the heterogeneity of the symptoms they present. For professionals in the health sciences, it is essential to understand what makes it possible for some people to relate to others normatively, whereas others are incapable of the most elemental acts of relatedness.

To be successful, our quest for integration requires a strategy that will guide us in this task. This strategy must allow us not to lose sight of the whole person as we focus on one aspect of functioning, to the (temporary) neglect of others. Even as we deconstruct the person, we must remain aware of the topography of the entire domain in which we are conducting our explorations.

NONLINEAR DYNAMIC SYSTEMS

The methodology of the emerging discipline of nonlinear dynamics (Gleick, 1987) is best suited to deal with the interrelationship among all the factors (discussed above) that contribute to children's behaviors. In simple terms, nonlinear equations present an alternative to the view that events are related to each other in simple linear cause-and-effect relationships. Instead of seeing causal relationships as "A" leading to the effects "B," nonlinear equations explore what happens when the cause "A" is reinserted each time into the series of the effects "B." We then get an effect "AB," which itself is again affected by the initial cause "A" to become "AAB," and so on. What emerges is *chaos*. However, *chaos* is a misleading term to describe the sequence of events, for this chaos is not the same as randomness. Chaos, as described in nonlinear dynamics theory, is a highly structured nonlinear sequence that produces a set of events that retain a constant orderly pattern (Barton, 1994; Galatzer-Levy, 1995). What is distinctive about this pattern is that it reproduces itself at the macro level as well as the micro, leading to the familiar images that are called *fractals*. These patterns are the product of an operator that guides the process, called an *attractor*, which shapes the sequence and gives it an orderly appearance (S. R. Palombo, 1999).

Gleick (1987) referred to the possibility of viewing human development as guided by nonlinear relationships. As clinicians, we have always discerned this complexity but had no way to grasp how that complexity operated. According to traditional psychoanalytic theory, children are the products of their parents' personality and of the maturational forces that are at play during their development. As they mature, children may identify with aspects of one or the other of their parents. Freud proposed that libidinal forces shape each phase of the developmental progression, giving a distinctive stamp to the child's personality. The environment's effect is to vary the course that leads to the mature personality. Arrests at, or regressions to, different phases modify the configuration of those personality traits. The question raised by chaos theory is whether the classical view of cause-and-effect relationships is too simplistic to do justice to the great complexity of these events. Those classical explanations ignore the fact that at each phase a set of causes, as attractors, reenter the process to affect its course. The chaos we see in the variety of personalities that populate our world is due to the nonlinear course of human development. There is not only great diversity but there is also a sense of order in the existing patterns that we recognize as universally present. Unfortunately, given the present state of our science, we are not in a position to apply this powerful tool to our investigations. We can only keep in mind that any simple linear causal explanation is at best naive and at worst inaccurate (Palombo, 2000a).

The Three Domains and Their Perspectives

To avoid the pitfalls of simple linear explanations, I weave together three major domains of knowledge—the neurobehavioral, the social, and the intrapersonal—that complement each other and provide a more comprehensive account than currently exists of the social–emotional problems of children with NLD. Each of these domains has its own particular methodological perspective. (1) In the *neurobehavioral perspective*, the locus of the observer is external to the subject of the observations; that is, the observer takes an objective, descriptive, neutral stance in relation to the phenomena. (2) In the *social perspective*, the locus is within the interaction between the people that are the subjects of our observations; that is, the

observer makes his or her observations from the midst of what is occurring. (3) In the *intrapersonal perspective*, the locus is from within the experience of the person who is the subject of our observations; that is, the
observer empathically enters into the subjective experience of the person
and attempts to understand the meaning the person attaches to his or her
experiences.

THE NEUROBEHAVIORAL DOMAIN

In Part I, I address the issues related to the neurobehavioral perspective.
This perspective provides a phenomenological description of the child's
NLD symptoms and discusses the neurobehavioral theories that attempt
to explain the social impairments associated with the syndrome. Within
the neurobehavioral paradigm, the limitations or deficits in cognitive capacities and the neurological variations in endowment *cause* the learning
disabilities: "Explanatory constructs within this paradigm involve reference to the degree of intactness and organization of various systems in the
brain that are purportedly involved in specific kinds of intellectual performance. . . . [S]ince these systems are often assigned to specific locations
in the brain deficient performance on intellectual tasks is frequently explained in terms of damage or malfunctioning of certain areas of the
brain" (Torgesen, 1986, p. 401). The theories infer that the children's
social–emotional problems stem either directly from those neuropsychological deficits or from the children's reactions to the deficits.

Some neurologists and neuropsychologists hypothesize (Rourke 1989a;
Voeller, 1986) that the etiology of the NLD syndrome reflects an underlying right hemisphere dysfunction. These theories propose that although
the primary deficit is in the domain of visual–spatial processing, other
neurocognitive domains may also be affected. Specific social–emotional
difficulties result from the children's processing deficits in these domains.
Critics of this theory (Denckla, 1991; Pennington, 1991) maintain that
children's visual–spatial problems are dissociable from their social–
emotional problems. They suggest that two disorders have been conflated:
(1) those of NLD, as a right hemisphere disorder that manifests as deficiencies in academic performance in math and handwriting, and (2) those
of social cognition.

Part I concludes with the hypothesis that three different domains may
be involved in the social impairments of children with NLD: (1) the domain of nonlinguistic perceptual processing, (2) the domain of attention
and executive function, and (3) the domain of social cognition. Each domain is associated with different social impairments. The heterogeneity

evident in the social–emotional functioning of children with NLD reflects, in part, the existence of subtypes of NLD, each of which is associated with different social behaviors. This discussion permits us to define the core deficits of NLD that are associated with the social impairments the children display.

THE DOMAIN OF SOCIAL COGNITION

Part II addresses the social perspective via what some have called a "two-person psychology." This perspective contrasts with the viewpoint used in the neurobehavioral perspective, which is that of a "one-person psychology" in which individuals are not contextualized but examined as isolated systems whose functioning is independent of others.

For many years the theories of Vygotsky and Piaget dominated the domain of developmental social cognition (Hala, 1997). Their competing theories specified the developmental trajectories of children's cognitive development. However, they did not address directly children's emotional development. Those theories implied that the mental processes involved in the domains of cognitive and affective development were separate and distinctive. Social psychologists have moved away from that position, asserting that affect and cognition are closely entwined. In addition, research into the neurobiology of social cognition is beginning to enhance our understanding of the mental processes that undergird sociality (Adolphs, 2001, 2003, 2003b). A final difficulty of these cognitive theories is that they do not address the area of intention and motivation, which is imbued with emotional contents and an essential component to a comprehensive understanding of social behaviors.

The social perspective enlarges upon one of the major domains of dysfunctions in children with NLD by focusing on children's social context and the relational aspects of the children's interactions with others. Using the concept of social cognition as the organizing construct, I examine three domains of functioning in which impairments may occur; (1) reciprocal social relationships, (2) social communication, and (3) affect processing. Although this approach does not include consideration of the motivational aspects of behavior, it does enlarge our view of the factors that contribute to the behaviors of children with NLD.

In the discussion of the domain of reciprocal social interaction, I focus on theory of mind as the central feature that may be impaired in these children. Impairments in this domain set constraints on the children's capacity to develop appropriate relationships with others. The domain of language is central to all social communication. All social interactions occur within a context that imbues those interactions with communicative acts, both verbal and nonverbal. Through language, we engage in a form of communication that I call "mindsharing." We convey our feelings and thoughts to others who attempt to grasp not just what we say, but also what we intend to convey. Although verbal language is an area of strength for children with NLD, they suffer from significant deficits in the domain of nonverbal communication. However, they also suffer from deficits in the domain of verbal language that have not received the attention they deserve.

Although many theories of NLD refer to the children's emotional problems, they do so in the context of their discussion of the children's social behaviors. I discuss the receptive, expressive, and processing problems these children experience in this domain from the perspective of affective neuroscience. In addition, Greenspan's contributions enrich our understanding of the way in which failures in the integration of affects may derail a child's development. This section concludes with a definition of the social features associated with the four subtypes of NLD.

THE INTRAPERSONAL PERSPECTIVE

In the intrapersonal perspective, which comprises Part III, the locus of the observer is an imaginary point within the child's mind. The observer directs his or her efforts at understanding the child's experience, his or her motives, and the meanings he or she has attached to experience. Empathy permits us to understand and apprehend the contents of another person's mind, leading to an understanding of how a person feels, thinks, and perceives reality. It allows the observer to resonate affectively with the internal state of the person being observed through the vicarious association with the other's experiences. This perspective assumes that the observer, because of the common human bond that exists between all human beings, can decipher the psychic reality of others and the special meanings they attach to their experiences.

The intrapersonal perspective introduces the concept of mindsharing as central in understanding the development of the sense of self. I define the concept of mindsharing as a form of intersubjectivity in which, through mutual interaction with a caregiver, the child learns how to enter into the experience of another person, how to be regulated by another's activities, and can understand another's intention. The focus in this section is on the child's subjective experience, which includes the relational issues of the mother–infant interaction and the attachment process.

Theories of attachment contribute to our understanding of the child's internalization of regulatory functions through the interactions that occur between the child and the mother. Using self psychology as my psychodynamic paradigm, I review the state of the child's sense of self, specifically examining the effects of neuropsychological deficits on the development of a sense of self-cohesion and the coherence of the child's self-narrative. Self-narratives reflect the integration of personal and shared meanings each individual derives from his order experience. The child weaves meanings together into a coherent whole.

I conclude with a view of the sense of self that integrates the neurobehavioral, social, and intrapersonal perspectives and leads to an exploration of the disorders of the self that may emerge and the specific forms they may take. With the enhanced understanding that the examination of these issues provides, I then discuss the types of emotional disorders of the self that emerge concomitantly with the neurobehavioral symptoms in children with NLD and touch on the issue of comorbidity. The addition of disorders of the self to the definition of the social features of NLD provides a more comprehensive definition. Finally, because impairments in social cognition are involved in both NLD and Asperger's disorder, the relationship between the two disorders is clarified.

SUMMARY

The accompanying figure (see Figure I.1) summarizes the three domains and their components. (1) The neurobehavioral domain is comprised of

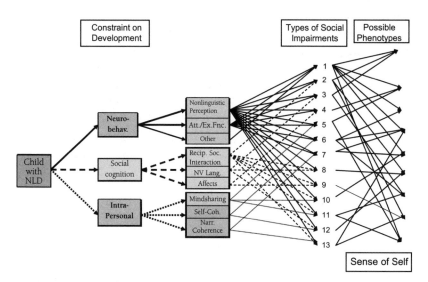

Figure I.1. Possible NLD phenotypes.
Schema for the generation of possible phenotypes that may result from the constraints that neurobehavioral factors, in combination with social-cognitive and/or intrapersonal factors, impose on development. Each phenotype represents aspects of a person's sense of self that display particular social features.

nonlinguistic perception, attention and executive function, and other neurological dysfunctions. (2) The domain of social cognition is comprised of reciprocal social interaction, social communication, and affects. (3) The intrapersonal domain is comprised of mindsharing, self-cohesion, and narrative coherence. I hypothesize that each component sets constraints on the development of the child with NLD, contributing to the problems the child presents. In turn, the interaction among these components contributes, in nonlinear fashion, to the ultimate phenotype or sense of self.

For example, the presence or absence of one of the factors within the intrapersonal domain, such as the sense of self-cohesion, which is partly related to the type of relationship the child forms to its caregiver, we note that will set constraints on the earliest responses of caregivers to the child. The child, in turn, will respond in his or her own unique way. Those constraints will determine the nature of the child's attachment to his or her caregivers. The attachment, whether secure, anxious, or disorganized, may then take a life of its own, determining critical aspects of the kind of relationship the child will have with others.

At a different stage during maturation, the child will enter a social world of peers and other adults beyond the family orbit. At that point different constraints emerge on the possible types of relationships that child can form. As he or she carries over the patterns of interactions shaped by the earlier bond with his or her caregivers, success in establishing reciprocal social interactions with others will be limited by the constraints these patterns impose on those relationships.

As the meanings the child draws from his or her experiences are filtered through this endowment, the resulting constraints of neurobehavioral deficits impose a further level of complexity on her development (Palombo, 2001a). Because he or she is unaware of the nature of these deficits, the child will seek to explain to him- or herself the reasons for the disruptions in his or her relationships to others. The child will construct explanations to integrate into his or her self-narrative, that is, the story the child constructs about his or her life experiences. Some of these explanations will become themes in this self-narrative that will shape the child's expectations of how others might respond to him or her.

At a different level of abstraction, we can look upon the child's sense of self as the center around which personality traits begin to emerge. The sense of self incorporates the totality of the child's experiences—the multiple factors that contributed to the child's neuropsychological, social, and intrapersonal development. Finally, it is important to avoid thinking that psychopathology is the inevitable outcome of these factors because the child's assets can enhance areas of functioning and compensate for some deficits. A child's resilience, the protective factors that may be at play, as well as a capacity to compensate for deficits may immunize the child from the development of a disorder of the self.

Psychoanalysis and Neuroscience

In recent years, numerous efforts have been underway to bring together the disciplines of psychoanalysis and the neurosciences, as evidenced by the publication of a new journal titled Neuro-Psychoanalysis (see Cooper, 1985; Douglas, 2000; Gilkerson, 2001; Kandel, 1998, 1999; Olds, 1994; Olds & Cooper, 1997; Rass, 2002; Reiser, 1984; Rothstein & Benjamin, 1988; Rothstein, Eisenstadt & Glenn, 1999; Schore, 1997; Shapiro & Applegate, 2000; Solms, 1998; Solms & Turnball, 2002; Watt, 2000; Westen, 1998). In this work, I propose to highlight the interface between the two theories and to indicate the areas of possible overlap as applied to NLD as a neurobehavioral developmental disorder. A psychodynamic perspective would bring greater understanding of these children's social behaviors and emotional problems.

In the domain of social and emotional functioning, psychoanalysts Greenspan (1979, 1997; Greenspan & Shanker, 2004) and Basch (1974) have attempted to integrate Piaget's developmental cognitive theory with traditional psychoanalytic theory. Over the years Greenspan has offered a paradigm that applies psychoanalytic ego psychology to neurologically or genetically based deficits, particularly for children with autistic spectrum disorders (Greenspan, 1988, 1989a, 1989b). Although making extended use of Piaget's concepts, Greenspan regarded Piaget's theory as incomplete because it considers affects to be secondary to cognition. In his most recent contribution, Greenspan and his colleague Shanker (2004) noted that affects antedate cognition from an evolutionary perspective. They present the possibility that all mental development, including the development of social relationships, emerges from the capacity to communicate affectively. They propose an "affect diathesis hypothesis" that assumes that emotions and cognition are closely entwined, and that psychopathology results from the failure to integrate sensations with meaningful behavior.

Psychotherapy of Children with NLD

In Part IV, I address the issues of treatment and working with the children's caregivers. Before instituting any treatment plan, it is essential that the clinician have a clear diagnosis in hand, made through psychoeducational and/or neuropsychological testing. Although it is possible to arrive at a clinical diagnosis from neurological or behavioral observations, these alone do not establish a definitive diagnosis. In addition, it is most helpful for therapists to have a clear idea of the child's specific strengths and deficits, which such testing can provide.

The success of any treatment of children with NLD is dependent on the establishment of a sound alliance with the parents. The parents are entitled to the best explanation available of their child's problem. Close attention should be given to collaborative efforts with school personnel and others who are in a position to help the child. Here I discuss the value of interventions other than individual psychotherapy in working with parents.

NLD, as a brain-based learning disorder, is being increasingly identified in the population of school-age children. It is a poorly understood disorder that is often confused with Asperger's Disorder. The strategy I offer to explain this disorder is meant to account for its complexity. By approaching the children's symptoms from three different perspective, the neurobehavioral, the social, and the intrapersonal, it becomes possible to gain a broader understanding of the underlying causes of the symptoms and to devise appropriate interventions for their treatment.

Part I

THE SYNDROME

A NEUROBEHAVIORAL PERSPECTIVE

1

Clinical Presentation

Mr. and Mrs. Z called me[1] about their 5½-year-old son upon recommendation from their pediatrician. They were struggling to help Jason go about the most basic aspects of day-to-day life without tension or conflict. The pediatrician saw the struggles as more than typically developmental; indeed Jason often displayed argumentative or resistant behaviors in his office during examinations. The pediatrician thought that additional guidance might be helpful for them because they felt little sense of efficacy in parenting their son.

Jason was easily frustrated with even the most routine expectations of family life. Mrs. Z reported that "things are very rough in the morning." Brushing teeth or coming to the table for breakfast involved major battles. "Mornings are the worst, but he'll fight me about anything big or small. We try not to get into all the yelling, as happened in our own families, but we do, and it's embarrassing to say, it's distressing, there is too much yelling even about the simplest things." Mr. Z agreed, adding, "Some days we have tantrums several times a day; usually we have at least one tantrum every day. There are a lot of kids on our block, but he has hurt or offended most of them. We have to apologize for his behavior—what do they think of us? It's not good." Jason wants to be friends with these kids, but something bad always happens.

---

[1] The therapist in this case was Joshua Mark.

Jason attends a religious day school and is in kindergarten. The parents reported that his teachers complain that he is easily frustrated. He often resorts to hitting other children and teachers. The staff has a difficult time predicting when outbursts will occur. One staff member commented: "He can be wonderful, but the slightest thing can set him off." Jason also struggles with cooperative play activities and transitions.

His mother reported that "he's kind of a perfectionist in a way; he'll keep doing something again and again until it's how he wants it, but he is usually not happy with what he has made." She added, with tears in her eyes, "He doesn't seem happy or even content very much at all."

Early History

Mrs. Z. had a problem free pregnancy and delivery. There was some difficulty with breastfeeding, and Jason was shifted to formula in the first month, after which feeding progressed smoothly. However, he was "colicky, fussy, and irritable" the first 4 months. He did respond to cuddling and being held, and his motor development was typical. Mrs. Z reported that "he was very verbal, even before age 1, and before he actually developed language, he would chatter away. He didn't have a vocabulary, but that didn't stop him." Toilet training was difficult because of constipation problems.

Jason's early play was described as more solitary than interactive. From his first social contacts he had difficulty playing cooperatively with other children because he would dominate the situation or become destructive or aggressive. His parents always worried that he might lash out at a playmate or that he might say something rude and hurtful to a child. They felt burdened by the need to supervise his play with other children 100% of the time. There were instances when Jason played more successfully with playmates, but only when he was involved with a much older or a much younger child. He has never had a long-lasting friend or buddy. When alone, he would play with Lego blocks for hours. If others tried to join in Jason's play, he resisted, and eventually they gave up. His parents do not remember his engaging in symbolic or imaginative play such as making up stories and acting them out.

Jason experienced a myriad of problems at the private religious preschool that he attended. Jason had problems following directions, even when routines were clearly established. He "couldn't keep his hands to himself or sit still." Transitions from one activity to the next were a challenge and would all too frequently end up in a "meltdown." Mrs. Z cried when she reported, "Jason was just not liked by the other kids, and no one wanted to sit next to him. It is sad. I was always waiting to get a call saying that he had to be sent home or would be kicked out of the school. His status there was always hanging by a thread."

Diagnostic Interviews:
Sessions One through Three

Jason came to see me after being told by his mother and father that I "was a friendly person who helps people with their feelings."

There were no separation tensions as Jason walked briskly into my office, bouncing on his toes with each step. He looked back once at his parents and then immediately had a series of specific questions for me. "What is your address? What is your full name? What do the letters on your briefcase mean?" Very focused on these pieces of information, there was no "warm-up" or sense of tentativeness as Jason asked for paper to start drawing. He wanted to draw the interior of my office, which he promptly began to do with my felt-tip pens. He became frustrated because some pens were dry, and the ink did not flow out evenly. "What is this? These don't work!" I began to sort through the pens and pick out the ones that worked, but I am not sure he noticed me. He was working intently now, pressing very hard on the paper, attempting to draw my desk, doorway, etc. He grimaced and groaned as he drew, complaining aloud that it didn't look right. He put down the pen and looked up at the ceiling with a frustrated look. I commented that I could tell he was drawing everything on and near the desk, and "that you're really good at noticing everything you see over there."

"It's not turning out right!" he complained. I tried to offer my encouragement, but he only exhaled loudly and then went back to work. He was upset because the brown pen was too dry to use, and he wanted to draw the door in brown. He smiled at me when I found another brown pen. I felt some reciprocal connection with Jason for the first time. He went back to work in an intense manner.

I tried to ask him some general questions. He told me about his school, giving the address and name, then adding that "all the teachers are mean." Yes, he had friends there, and he gave me their names. I wondered aloud if I was bothering him with my questions, because he did not look up and he retained a serious expression on his face. Jason just grunted, which left me wondering. I explained that I wanted to get to know him and wanted to help him feel comfortable as he got to know me. He then looked up and told me in a terse way "I hate dinnertime, because I always get yelled at, and I love Nintendo, okay?" We ended the appointment on a more peaceful tone when Jason finished his drawing and proudly showed it to me.

I noticed the casual way in which Jason left his mother for our second session, not looking back and almost rushing into the room. This time Jason explored my small office by walking around and looking at the many toys and objects. He perused all the "kid stuff," the couch, the desk, and then commented, "This is like a house with everything smushed into one room. Do you live here?" I felt again a glimmer of connection with Jason as he expressed his curiosity about me. He wanted to know my exact home address and was frustrated when I would only disclose that "we live in the same town." He settled for receiving the exact address of my office and went on to make a drawing of the office door with the address above it. He was unhappy with his work and began to crumble up the paper. I tried to engage him about his unhappiness with the drawing, then to praise his efforts, but he grabbed the paper and made it into a tight ball, with both elbows parallel and vibrating with exertion. He then threw the balled-up paper as hard as possible, complaining that it looked like a "baby's drawing."

Exploring the room again, Jason found a nerf ball. He threw it against the wall as hard as he could, then looked at me and laughed. I wondered aloud if he was still frustrated with the drawing. He made no response at all. I commented, "I'm glad that was a nerf ball, because otherwise I might have a hole in my wall." "But this IS a nerf ball" Jason countered, as if I was an idiot for thinking otherwise. He threw the ball at me full force, and it bounced off my body. I acted as if it knocked me to the floor and tossed it softly back to Jason. He caught it, and I commented, "Nice catch!" Without a smile, he threw it back, again quite hard, and I was again unable to catch it. I threw it back gently to Jason. He caught it and whipped it over my head. I moved as far back as I could in the small office, commenting, "these fast balls are hard for me catch, can you slow it down a little, Jason?" He rolled his eyes and groaned, "C'mon!" For the remaining minutes I tried to engage him in a simple game of catch but was unsuccessful, as he repeated this pattern. I wondered aloud if he might be upset or mad, because he was continuing to whip the ball at me with all his might. He answered, "Well, I can't help it if you can't catch!", again rolling his eyes. Jason had some difficulty leaving the office when our time was up; he continued to throw the ball around the office.

The third session began with Jason walking in quietly with his head down. He looked up for a moment to respond to my greeting. I tried to engage him verbally, asking him how he was doing and encouraging some verbal report about school or home. I wondered what his own "story" was regarding the difficulties he was experiencing. He told me that he wanted to make a picture again and that he would rather not talk while working. He noticed that I had bought a new batch of colored pens and told me that was "good, because you really needed them, your other ones were all dried up and worthless." I told him that I was sorry about that, and I hoped these would work well, because he was the first to use them.

Jason's further questions focused on where I had purchased the pens. He asked me many questions about what the drugstore looked like, etc. I could see he was frustrated with me again, because every landmark or street name I offered was confusing for him and not helpful. He worked on a drawing of his school's front door but was only unhappy with it. "It's just not right; it really doesn't look like that!" I told him that I liked the doors and could imagine that *this is where he walked into his school. "How would you know?" he asked. "You already said that you've never been there." He was able to point out which door he entered each morning, and he told me some details about who held the door open, etc. He showed me the address on the door and the name of the school. He pointed out the red brick walls and the certain type of windows. I commented on each point and praised his attention to the detail of things.*

Jason ended by shaking my hand as he once again asked, "How come you won't tell me where you live?" I answered, "Well, that's kind of private, and we'll only be meeting here at this office." I repeated the office street address. He seemed satisfied with that answer, although I was not sure. Nevertheless, he was bouncing on his toes as he walked down the hall to his mother in the waiting room. No longer looking at me, he shouted out a goodbye to me by name, with his back to me, as he disappeared down the hall.

The Clinician's Impressions

I felt challenged to understand Jason's inner world. I struggled to make sense of what he was doing and how he was relating to me, if indeed he was relating to me. He displayed little of the anxiety that securely attached young children often display when meeting a new adult in a novel situation. He left his mother quite matter-of-factly, and once in my room, seemed to relate more to my office than to me, immediately focusing on the details of its contents. I felt that I had to intrude to begin relating to him and was hesitant to do so in the diagnostic interview.

I noticed the intensity with which he did almost everything. There was a driven quality to his drawing activities, his questioning of me, and his ball throwing. However, it seemed that he was his own harshest critic. I saw much of his frustration and his feelings of failure. I felt that he was intensely unhappy with his artwork. The driven and perseverative quality of his work was worrisome and noteworthy. He seemed stuck and easily derailed by his perfectionism. In his play with the ball, there was little sense of reciprocity or nonverbal dialogue. He seemed unable to comprehend that my being unable to catch the ball was due to the way he was throwing it. There was no evidence that he received the nonverbal feedback I gave him, and indeed he argued with me about my verbal feedback. Although he seemed to be getting something out of the experience of throwing the ball, there were none of the simple exchanges and the reciprocity inherent in a "game of catch."

I also noted the absence of any symbolic or imaginative play. He disregarded the puppets, figures, playhouse, and similar toys that many other 5- to 6-year-olds might explore. I struggled to soothe him, wondering if I was indeed connecting with at all. However, with persistence I picked up a sense that despite all my failures, I was beginning to form a relationship. It was a modest beginning.

I discussed my observations and the beginnings of my clinical formulation with Jason's parents. I told them that perhaps in therapy I could begin to help Jason build better relationships with other people. I expressed the hope that I could try to help him tune into the "other" (me) to receive useful social information. He had many strong feelings that I would try to understand. In turn, I would attempt to help Jason understand what he was feeling. I referred them for a neuropsychological assessment of Jason and recommended that we plan for weekly individual therapy for him and regular separate parent sessions.

Author's Discussion

Jason presents with a mixture of symptoms that is not readily explainable. His parents describe a child who is uncooperative, negative, and even oppositional. When his parents set expectations for him that he cannot meet, Jason quickly reaches the level of his tolerance for frustration and has a meltdown. For reasons that are not clear, it is difficult for him to conform to the simple demands of day-to-day living. It is also as difficult for him to relate to others as it is to conform to his parents' expectations. In the social context he channels his frustration by becoming assaultive.

The clinician's observations add another dimension to the symptom picture. The clinician wondered about a possible attachment disorder because of the lack of overt emotion shown by Jason. However, such a diagnosis does not explain many of the other behaviors, such as Jason's dissatisfaction with his drawings, which he judges to be like a "baby's drawing." His peculiar form of playing catch is also noteworthy, as are his preoccupations with the configuration of the office furniture and with the location of the clinician's home, which he guesses to be the office.

On the surface, these behaviors are not consistent with any common psychodynamic formulation. Some of the social features that he presents may indicate an attachment disorder. We might also postulate a developmental arrest that would explain some of the infantile behaviors. Alternatively, we might hypothesize a disorder of the self, such as that seen in children who require constant stimulation. Some might claim that Jason has a personality disorder, that he is oppositional/defiant, citing his nonconformity as evidence. However, as I pointed out in the Introduction, such labels, when attached to children such as Jason, indicate a misunderstanding of the nature of the disorder.

From a psychodynamic perspective, Jason's self-criticism would indicate an unconscious awareness of the nature of his dysfunctions. His criticism of the clinician's dysfunctional pens would support such a view, because the pens would symbolize what is dysfunctional about himself. His aggressive ball-playing style would be a metaphor for his difficulties in relating to others. From Jason's perspective, something goes wrong whenever he attempts to interact with others, but he is unsure why. He would like to blame the other person, but he is also aware that he is contributing to the disrupted dialogue.

In the absence of clear diagnostic markers of a disorder that stems purely from psychodynamic factors, we could turn to the social conditions that might be responsible for Jason's symptoms. A family therapist might suggest that the behavior is symptomatic of the family's own turmoil. Jason was "chosen" by the family system to reflect overtly the unconscious tensions between the parents or the family system's failure to cope with some of its dysfunctional dynamics. Such explanations, although plausible, do not explain many of his other behaviors, such as his difficulties with drawing.

A different diagnostic claim might be made from the perspective of his social dysfunctions: that his problems lie in the realm of social cognition. It is clear that he misreads social situations and has little understanding of others' intentions. He has difficulties with the regulation of his own affective states. From a cognitive perspective, although his language development may be advanced for his age, his concrete responses to the clinician's attempt at humor and his efforts at dealing more abstractly with questions that he asks indicate communication deficits. The absence of a capacity for imaginative play may suggest that he falls within the autistic spectrum and may be diagnosed as having Asperger's disorder. However, the level of his relatedness seems to preclude such a conclusion.

Finally, we turn to intrapersonal causes of his behaviors that are due to factors related to his endowment. Here we are handicapped by the absence of neuropsychological testing that would delineate the nature of his deficits. A clinician experienced in the diagnosis of children with LD would quickly point to the evidence of a visual–spatial problem, and Jason's inability to draw would suggest a visual–motor deficit. His peculiar form of playing catch also would indicate that he has problems with visual–spatial relationships. His preoccupation with the clinician's living space, the office, his home—all would point in the same direction. We might speculate that Jason is aware of his impairments and is deeply troubled by them; hence his desire to communicate these impairments as best he can to the diagnostician.

I would suggest that all of these diagnoses may be accurate; the factors mentioned in the three positions discussed above might all play a part in Jason's symptom configuration. The psychodynamic, the social, and the neuropsychological factors give shape to the end product that we see in the clinical setting. The child's sense of self is the product of all the elements that contributed to its formation. As I stated earlier, the multiple streams that feed into each factor arise from tributaries that themselves arose from the large watershed of the child's potential at birth. We may be able to identify specific conditions in the watershed that fed into a particular tributary, but ultimately it may be very difficult to point to the particular content that gave rise to a given stream that is responsible for a specific behavior.

2

Neurobehavioral Profile of NLD

In this chapter I present a profile of the developmental path some children with NLD follow. This profile provides a broad overview of the factors that contribute to a particular phenotype. As I refine our understanding of the disorder, I will enlarge and refine the definition that I provided in the Introduction. For the present, clinicians who are unfamiliar with NLD or who receive detailed and complex neuropsychological reports may find this overview to be useful.

Several qualifications must be kept in mind in appraising this profile. First, because of the heterogeneity of the disorder, no single child will display all the features of the disorder. Second, the extent of the deficits, their severity, the child's age at assessment, and other factors contribute to the expression of a given phenotype. Third, the balance between strength and deficits may either enhance or diminish the severity of the symptoms. Compensations or strengths may mask some symptoms, whereas their absence will make the child look more dysfunctional than other affected children. Fourth, seldom do children suffer from the presence of a single developmental disorder. Coexisting conditions, whether neuropsychological or psychiatric, compound the clinical picture and, at times, confound the diagnostician. Finally, psychodynamic factors add their contribution to the mix of neuropsychological, temperamental, and social factors. Yet, in spite of the complexity of the combinations of these factors, clear-cut patterns emerge that make the clinical presentation distinctive and diagnostic of the condition. This inclusive profile of the possible deficits from which a child may suffer leaves out the catalogue of the child's possible strengths, although these are critical for any planned intervention.

Presenting Problems

The following provides a summary of the way in which parents generally report on the developmental histories, academic problems, reasons for referral, and presenting problems of children with NLD.

BIRTH AND DEVELOPMENTAL MILESTONES

Children with NLD are generally the product of a full-term pregnancy with no serious prenatal problems or labor and delivery complications. In some instances mothers reported that their children were overly active and irritable infants or had a "naturally intense" and demanding temperament, as well as a history of basic behavioral dysregulation. More often, parents describe these children as having been an "extremely cuddly" and easy-to-care-for infant who nursed often.

Caregivers often report that as infants their children were physically inactive, failed to engage in exploratory play, and did not respond as expected; they could not use toddler toys or enjoy coloring or drawing and were unable to assemble puzzles (Johnson, 1987a). When they started to walk, the visual–spatial–motor problems emerged. They appeared clumsy and uncoordinated; caregivers had to watch them closely because they bumped into furniture, were unsteady on their feet, broke toys, and endangered themselves. Slow to learn from their caregivers' limits and instructions, these children appeared unable to understand causal relationships; their caregivers had to intervene and correct them constantly. In turn, they responded with frustration and anger. Many caregivers report that by the age of 2 the temper tantrums were much more intense than those that normally occur at this age. Furthermore, self-help skills do not develop comparably to those of other children the same age. Caregivers note that their children were slow to learn to feed and dress themselves and did not master tasks such as hand washing or grooming when expected; they had to be helped and reminded to complete these tasks well into latency, whereas other children already performed these tasks independently.

By the age of 3, these children go through an initial stage when their speech is difficult to understand because of articulation problems; then these problems dissipate, and their verbal skills emerge as an area of strength. They then become quite adept at verbal communication. Caregivers who become overreliant on the verbal channel to relate to their children reinforce their verbal competencies; making less use of nonverbal modes of communication. In preschool, the children have difficulties interacting with other children in groups; they do not seem to know how to play with others. They cling to their caregivers and find it difficult to separate. If this strategy is unsuccessful, then they isolate themselves.

By the time children with NLD reach kindergarten or first grade, other problems become evident. They appear to be quite bright and to have excellent verbal abilities, but their behavior does not match the expectations for a child this bright and verbal. They have major problems in the area of peer relationships and are unable to form friendships or associate with other children even for brief periods without an eruption ensuing.

Caregivers notice that these children are different from their other children. Nevertheless, they are hard put to pinpoint the nature of this difference. They find themselves frustrated in their efforts to understand their children; they seem unable to decode their children's cues and find them to be socially unresponsive; they feel forced into a position of constantly having to correct, limit, or punish their children; they are puzzled when the children respond with fury at what they experience as unfair treatment. Family activities are controlled by the child with NLD. Caregivers often feel guilty and blame themselves for what they believe to be their failure to parent properly. This frustration may initiate a cycle in which caregivers feel rejected by their children and, in turn, distance themselves emotionally from them. Some caregivers are intuitively able to read their children's messages but soon find that they are the only ones who can communicate effectively with their children. If no intuitive understanding occurs, then the difficulties are compounded by the children's increasing demands on caregivers, who are increasingly unable to cope.

Some caregivers unwittingly contribute to the confusion because of their own personality difficulties, some themselves have NLD. The household then appears like that of a family in which each member speaks a different language. Although a measure of communication occurs, there are large areas that are fraught with misunderstandings. The level of frustration, the anger resulting from constant injury, the lack of gratification in having such a difficult child—all contribute to the ensuing chaos. By the age of 7 or 8 these children manifest the full-fledged syndrome, and it is often at this point that they are referred for assessment.

ACADEMIC PROBLEMS

Academically, the children start out in pre-school having difficulty decoding letters and words, but once they discover the rules they become good readers. As they progress to higher grades, their comprehension of more complex materials does not match their decoding skills. The children's writing is often quite illegible. Their small motor problems and their visual-spatial difficulties make this task particularly difficult. Arithmetic difficulties emerge once teachers introduce simple computation.

Doug, a second grader, could read and focus for approximately 20 minutes; however, when he was asked to tell what he had just read, he was generally unable to do so. He tended to acquire details more than derive inferences and main points. He was described as having difficulty categorizing information, developing and using mnemonics for the retention of information, and sequencing. It was not clear whether he comprehended to the degree that he could decode. His reading comprehension dropped as he moved to higher grades. Complex material became much harder to grasp.

Doug's writing capability was low average to below average compared to classmates. A specific disability in written expression was identified, based on weaknesses in legibility of written output, visual–motor integration, and spatial organization. He tended to write only briefly and factually, with insufficient elaboration or enumeration of supportive ideas.

Doug experienced specific difficulties and excessive anxiety around engaging in quantitative reasoning and mathematical operations. He had difficulty learning abstract concepts. He encountered difficulty developing and implementing strategies in mathematical problems that required multiple steps, and more broadly, in any multistep problem that required hypothesis testing and logic.

PRIOR EVALUATIONS AND INTERVENTIONS

Children with NLD often arrive for an initial assessment after being previously evaluated by a variety of professionals and having received a variety of diagnoses and interventions. They may have undergone speech and language evaluations, psychoeducational testing, occupational therapy assessment, or a neuropsychological evaluation. At times, a psychiatric evaluation has resulted in a prescription for stimulant medication for suspected ADHD, or medication to deal with anxiety or depressed mood. The children may have been in peer group counseling in the school setting for their behavior problems. The family may have been in family therapy or attended a support group for parents of children with behavioral problems.

REASON FOR REFERRAL AND PRESENTING PROBLEM

Children with NLD are generally referred around the age of 9 or 10 because of academic underachievement, behavioral problems, or social isolation. Boys are often referred because of behavioral problems, whereas girls are referred because of their social isolation. Clinically, both boys and girls often present with clinical signs of severe anxiety, depression, attentional problems, obsessional preoccupations, and self-esteem problems. They perform poorly in some academic areas, but not in all.

These children demonstrate either average or above-average verbal language skills. They have good syntax, although their pragmatics leaves something to be desired. They have problems with prosody; they tend to speak in a monotone or with a "sing-song" voice. At an early age, they may have reversed pronouns, but their usage usually clears up with maturation. They have good memories and manifest rote memory verbalization that makes them look much smarter than they actually are. Their concepts lack preciseness; their problem with concept formation limits their capacity to reason, analyze, and synthesize materials. Although they appear linguistically sophisticated, there is a shallowness to the content of their expressions. They may use a vocabulary that seems advanced for their age, but the communications are not always well connected, and the content appears superficial.

In school, children with NLD are also reported as having problems with attention, exploratory behavior, dealing with novel materials, and adjusting to new situations. In interactions with others, they have difficulties reading between the lines, making inferences, and understanding the double meaning of expressions. When giving a narrative account of an event, they grasp one aspect of the total picture and miss the broader gestalt. Consequently, when they are asked to report on an event, they give an account that appears disconnected and devoid of feeling. It is very difficult to reconstruct what happened from their reports. Finally, they do not conform to expected behavior, giving the impression that they are oppositional or disrespectful.

Neuropsychological Profile

Among the findings of a neuropsychological assessment are some of the following[1]:

IQ MEASURES/INTELLIGENCE

On the Wechsler Intelligence Scale for Children–Third Edition (WISC-III) the verbal IQ (VIQ) scores of children with NLD are generally one or more standard deviations (15 points) above their performance IQ (PIQ).

---

[1] I discuss speech and language and social–emotional problems at greater length in Part II.

Such a discrepancy indicates that these children have a problem. Furthermore, there is wide scatter in some of the subscores on the verbal and performance tests. Table 2.1 lists the results of a WISC-III administered to Jim, a child age 10 years, 5 months.

In this example, one of the significant scores in determining Jim's problems is not simply the 27-point differential between his VIQ and his PIQ, but rather the 28-point differential between the Verbal Comprehension

Table 2.1 Results of a WISC-III

Verbal Tests Scaled Score		Performance Tests Scaled Score	
Information	19	Picture Completion	10
Similarities	13	Picture Arrangement	8
Arithmetic	9	Block Design	11
Vocabulary	13	Object Assembly	9
Comprehension	13	Coding	9
Digit Span	14	Symbol Search	10
VIQ 121	PIQ 94	Full scale IQ (FSIQ) 108	
	Verbal Comprehension	125	
	Perceptual Organization	97	
	Freedom from distractibility	109	
	Processing Speed	93	

Note. VIQ = verbal IQ; PIQ = performance IQ; FSIQ = full-scale IQ.

and the Perceptual Organization. The Verbal Comprehension score excludes the arithmetic score, thus removing a confounding factor in determining his comprehension abilities. A common misconception is that the differential between the VIQ and PIQ score, with the PIQ lower than the VIQ, is indicative of NLD; this is not the case. Some children may have average scores in both subtests and yet have NLD, although wide scatter may exist in the subtest scores.

MOTOR FUNCTIONS

Children with NLD usually manifest some type of motor difficulties. Clumsiness, delayed motor reaction time, slowness in the acquisition and execution of skills, significant differences between right- and left-sided function, avoidance of midline crossing, decreased motor control, and poor handwriting are some of the specific difficulties observed. Additional difficulties involve motor planning, a function that allows the individual to discern internally the possibility for movement or manipulation of objects/tools (e.g., using scissors, riding a bicycle).

Julie's early developmental history revealed that she was delayed in achieving many of her early motor milestones. She learned to crawl and stand late, and she walked at approximately 18 months of age. She was relatively slower than her peers in acquiring some gross-motor skills (e.g., dressing herself, riding a tricycle) and fine-motor skills (e.g., using scissors, crayons, buttons, zippers, tying shoelaces). Her mother reported that Julie's motor difficulties led her to be a "messy" eater. Her performance in gym class was not always well regulated, due to both motor and attentional difficulties. There were deficits in Julie's fine-motor coordination, visual–motor skills, and motor planning. At age 9 she still does not ride a bicycle and has a somewhat "clumsy and odd running gait." Across her development, she has shown little interest in constructional activities such as putting together jigsaw puzzles and building with blocks. Her handwriting is practically illegible.

Kevin also was generally clumsy in his day-to-day activities. He spilled his milk when trying to reach for it; he could not throw or kick a ball; his capacity for motor planning was impaired (e.g., he had great difficulty learning how to approach riding a bicycle, i.e., which leg to raise to get on the bicycle). Tasks such as tying his shoes, identifying which shoe went on which foot, and buttoning his shirt were not mastered until he was 8 years old. His judgment of directions and distances was poor, as was his ability to read maps.

VISUAL PROCESSING

Visual processing is a major area of weakness in children with NLD. They score lower in all tasks in a battery of tests requiring visual–spatial working memory and visual imagery. For example, they have difficulties recognizing people's faces, particularly those with whom they have little familiarity (Cornoldi, Rigoni, Tressoldi, & Vio, 1999).

The neuropsychologist expressed concerns regarding David's visual–spatial weaknesses. He found that problems existed in the areas of visual–spatial organization and processing, visual–motor integration, visual sequencing, and tactile processing. David, who is in first grade, did not enjoy constructional tasks, such as those that involve putting together puzzles or blocks, solving mazes, or drawing. He had problems completing complex psychomotor tasks that require cross-modal integration of visual perception and motor output, such as putting together puzzles.

ATTENTION

Children with NLD display several behaviors suggestive of attentional problems, such as reduced attention/concentration, impetuous behaviors, visual and auditory distractibility, and motoric restlessness. Although their inattentiveness may be due, in part, to the limitation in processing visual–spatial information and nonverbal information, it may also be caused by ADHD, often a coexisting condition (Voeller, 1986).

Fidgetiness
Mike, a second grader, displayed a high level of fidgetiness, silliness, and activity. He consistently had difficulty sitting still for activities, stories, or the completion of tasks, unless he was very interested.

Distractibility
He was highly distractible, inattentive, and restless in class. He easily became distracted while working at his seat and periodically got out of his seat, often to talk with friends.

Impulsivity
He always rushed through everything, wanting to finish quickly. He generally resisted completing his homework without his mother's help and insistence. He discontinued tasks impulsively and was easily distracted by the numerous stimuli in school. He also called out responses, disrupting the class.

Inattentiveness
He showed fluctuations in attending to, and persisting with his work, despite high intellect. He displayed reduced motivation, concentration, impetuous behaviors, visual and auditory distractibility, and motoric restlessness. He tended to require the repetition of directions, and he needed frequent reminders to "listen carefully."

EXECUTIVE FUNCTIONS

Executive functions include those cognitive abilities necessary for complex goal-directed behavior and adaptation to a range of environmental changes and demands. These functions include the ability to plan and anticipate outcomes (cognitive flexibility) and to direct attentional resources to meet the demands of nonroutine events that require self-monitoring and self-awareness for appropriate behavior. Children with NLD often have problems in executive function. They have difficulties with organization and planning, time perception, fluid reasoning, cause-and-effect reasoning, novel situations, and problem solving (Denckla, 1994; Torgesen, 1994).

Organizational Problems
Mike, age 11, was not self-directed or motivated. He encountered difficulty ac-cumulating and arranging papers into the proper folders to take home or bring back to class. He usually misplaced or lost essential school items (e.g., writing utensils) in addition to keeping a messy work area. He was slow to initiate tasks, and once started, left them unfinished, because he was sidetracked. His ability to remember homework materials, assignments, and to hand them in fluctuated. His parents noted that he "fell apart" near the end of the last academic year, at which time he lost assignments and appeared quite disorganized. His mother also noted that Mike has trouble cleaning his room, although she reported that he is much better at cleaning it when she helps to break the task down into smaller parts. Mike also was reported to procrastinate and to have trouble an-ticipating how much time tasks would take to complete when planning projects.

Fluid Reasoning and Problem Solving
Ben, age 11, had great difficulty maintaining a consistent problem-solving ap-proach throughout a task. He tended to lose track of the goal and showed signif-icantly better reasoning when the task involved verbal information alone than when social and pragmatic problem solving was required. His oppositional and intellectualizing behaviors often precluded his engagement of problem-solving behaviors. He was never able to negotiate with peers during play. If he broke a rule, he insisted that he was right and that everyone else was wrong. His rigidity would disrupt the play to the point where others refused to be with him.

Problems with Transitions
In preschool, between the ages of 3 and 5 years, 6 months, Andy's teachers re-ported that their primary concern was that he was observed to experience some difficulty in making transitions in the classroom, managing his behavior when making a transition from one task to another. He became easily frustrated, dis-inhibited, anxious, oppositional, aggressive, or disruptive during transitions. He got upset with changes in routine; he accommodated best when given a warning of a change in routine.

Problems with Novel Situations
Matt, a third grader, had difficulty applying his academic skills to new situa-tions, he could not accommodate or adapt to contextual aspects of novel or un-predictable situations. He responded to novel situations with distress or anxiety and became oppositional or aggressive when faced with new tasks. He was also reported to overreact to situations, apparently in response to the anxiety aroused

by any type of novelty. This anxiety, at times, converted into angry outbursts. Matt seemed to perform best when given preparation about what to anticipate in such situations.

MEMORY

Memory is discussed in terms of the following categories: working memory; declarative memory, which consists of semantic memory and episodic memory; and nondeclarative memory (Baddeley, 1988; Schacter, 1996; Schacter & Scarry, 2000; Squire & Kandel, 1999; Torgesen, 1996).

The term *working memory* refers to the short-term memory buffer that retains immediate/recent auditory inputs and/or visual images. It also refers to the information we hold before us when working on a task. In children with NLD the visual processing aspect of their working memory is often impaired.

Ethan, a 12-year-old, generally an excellent student, was failing biology, to his teacher's and parents' puzzlement. The teacher reported that Ethan had failed several tests in which he was required to reproduce images that were discussed in class and found in his textbooks. He complained that he could not do the assignment because he was "terrible in art." In fact, he could not recall a diagram and reproduce it even right after he had seen it.

Semantic memory refers to retention of facts; it is our dictionary memory. It is an area of strength in children with NLD, whose rote memory is generally excellent.

Greg took pride in his ability to remember all the presidents of the United States, the names of their wives and children, the dates and places of their birth, as well as the dates of their terms in office. He also knew the names of every country's capital, even though he could not consistently locate the country on a map.

Episodic memory refers to memory of personal experiences (in contrast to the knowledge of facts previously learned). Children with NLD are restricted in episodic memory, probably because of their inability to process nonverbal information. Their difficulties in providing a coherent narrative of episodes to which they were exposed reflect the weaknesses in this area.

Matt, age 8, repeatedly came home from school complaining about the way his peers treated him. When asked to report on what had happened, he seldom could give an adequate rendition. He would repeat that the kids had been mean, that they had made fun of him. Even when closely questioned, he could not pro-vide the context for these occurences.

Nondeclarative memory (also termed *implicit memory*) is the storehouse for nonconscious memories. It includes associative learning (i.e., the recall of conditioned responses), reflexive behaviors, and procedural memory. Procedural memory involves the development of habits and routine pro-cedures that we undertake without thinking, such as brushing teeth, driv-ing a car, swimming, riding a bike. There is no indication or evidence that this memory function is restricted in children with NLD, although their difficulties with organization may stem partly from weaknesses in their procedural memory.

Social–Emotional Profile

The functioning of children with NLD in social situation is often problem-atic. Grasping the subtle nuances of a social situation is difficult. They in-teract quite well with adults, but not as well with peers. This may be because adults are more predictable in their responses, and the children often do not engage them verbally. However, these children are unable to decode the social cues involved in "reading" other people's body language, facial expression, and vocal intonations. Often, they are inept in social sit-uations. Their eye contact (gaze) seems unnatural; they seldom make solid eye contact, and they lack a sense of humor. They do not know when they are being teased, because they interpret colloquialisms or metaphorical expressions concretely.

They seem to lack basic social skills. Sometimes, they are thought to be rude, although they are not consciously being disrespectful. They may be overly familiar with strangers and ask personal questions too quickly; they will start conversations with strangers as though they were old friends. They do not respect the privacy that we generally assume as needed. They share personal facts too quickly, giving intimate details to strangers. Be-cause they do not understand the physical aspects of social boundaries (i.e., personal space) and they have a poor sense of body in space, they do not respect the usual, culturally determined parameters of physical close-ness versus distance in conversation. With peers, their play is disruptive; they appear unable to negotiate social interchanges with other kids.

The area of emotional communication is problematic for children with NLD. In the receptive area, they appear unable to decode prosodic or vo-cal intonations. They are unable to decode the emotional messages con-veyed by people's faces, and they are unable to read bodily gestures. In the expressive area, they do not use vocal intonations; either they speak in a flat monotone or with a "sing-song" voice. It is difficult to read their mood from their facial expression; it is hard to tell whether they are really happy or unhappy. They do not use body gestures when speaking; they appear wooden and constricted. Finally, in the area of processing, they may have problems in decoding affective states, responding to emotionally laden situations with anxiety, withdrawal, or sadness. They have problems in modulating or regulating certain affects, lose control often, and have temper tantrums when frustrated. They respond to most feelings with a generalized excitement that is unfocused and lacking in content. They appear to have no compassion or empathy for others.

Psychiatric Symptomatology

Comorbidity with other diagnoses is often present in children with NLD. They generally suffer from high levels of anxiety and severe self-esteem problems; depression, obsessive–compulsive symptoms, and attentional problems that lead to a diagnosis of ADHD are commonly comorbid. In contrast to children with Asperger's syndrome, they appear to crave social contact and to be capable of relating to others. They try to reach out to other people; however, their attempts are inept, and others misinterpret their overtures. Withdrawal is reactive rather than primary in children with NLD. At a young age, their frustration with the confusion they experience in social situations often leads them to feel emotionally overwhelmed and fragmented. In younger children this frustration lends itself to motor output such as hand flapping, jumping up and down excitedly, or extreme temper tantrums. They are then mistaken for children who suffer from Asperger's syndrome or mild autism.

Conclusion

Parents and professionals often find it difficult to understand the nature of the problems exhibited by children with NLD. Nevertheless, the children's distress is evident. The negative responses they tend to evoke from others, who are put off by their dysynchronous responses, compound their distress. My clinical definition of the disorder highlighted the children's impaired capacity to perceive, express, and understand nonverbal (nonlinguistic) signs. These impairments challenge the children's capacity to function adequately in academic and social environments and produce difficulties in their capacity to integrate their experiences. Of particular concern are problems that emerge in the domain of emotional functioning—not only the high anxiety and frequent meltdowns but also the

seeming disconnection and isolation from others. Unless we can understand the neuropsychological deficits underlying these manifest behaviors,
the problems in social cognition, and the psychodynamics, we will remain
in the dark as to what instigates the social behaviors. I address these issues
in the chapters that follow.

3

Neurobehavioral Theories of the Social Features of NLD

As we set about trying to understand the social and emotional problems of children with NLD, I begin with an exploration of the contributions made by neurologists and neuropsychologists to our understanding of the disorder. Their contributions provide an important component to the total picture, a descriptive perspective that is a slice out of the child's functioning at the moment of the diagnostic encounter. This perspective does not dwell on the historic, developmental, and contextual factors that contribute to the child's functioning. To obtain a full picture, the perspective will have to be supplemented by the contextual factors contributed by the environment as well as the psychodynamic factors that operate from within the child.

As we consider definitions of NLD, it is useful to keep in mind Pennington's (1991) suggestion that we make the following distinctions in how a particular disorder manifests. Each disorder has:

1. A *primary core* set of symptoms that are specific, universal, and persistent;
2. A set of *correlated manifestations*, in which the etiologies of the primary symptoms are accompanied by symptoms that reflect deficits from different brain regions;

3. A set of *secondary consequences* or *concomitant symptoms* that usually accompanies a primary symptom; and,

4. Finally, it may have a set of symptom manifestations that are *artifactual*—that is, the set of symptoms may appear to accompany primary symptoms with some regularity but are unrelated to the disorder.

Such a framework provides useful distinctions in our attempts to understand the sources of the social–emotional difficulties experienced by children with NLD. It enables us to ask questions such as, Are the social–emotional behavioral manifestations associated with this disorder's "primary core symptoms"? Or are they "correlated manifestations," "secondary consequences," or purely "artifactual" and unrelated to the core deficits?

History of the NLD Concept

Johnson and Myklebust (1967) coined the term *nonverbal learning disability* to identify a residual group of children that they uncovered through their research. These were children who did not have verbal language problems but did have a variety of symptoms that interfered with their school functioning. At first, Johnson and Myklebust used the term "disorders of social imperception" to describe these children's problems. They gave as an example "a child who fails to learn the meaning of the actions of others, so he cannot grasp the game 'cowboy'; he cannot pretend and anticipate, as to do his playmates. He fails to learn the implications of other's actions e.g., gestures, facial expressions, and caresses, as well as other manifestations of attitude. He is unable to understand the relevance of time, space, size, direction and various aspects of person and self-perception. This child has a deficiency in social perception" (p. 272). They classified information as *nonsocial/nonverbal, social/nonverbal,* and *verbal* and concluded that "Nonverbal disabilities fall at the level of perception and imagery and therefore constitute a more fundamental distortion of total experience" (p. 273). Myklebust (1975) defined the problems as *social imperceptions*: that is, "a child's . . . lack of ability to understand his social environment, *especially* in terms of his own behavior" (p. 86). He concluded that these children have difficulty understanding the meanings of the social cues that others display (see Figure 3.1).

The concept did not enjoy immediate popularity and was not included in any of the major definitions of learning disabilities. Following a series of important studies of the disorder, Rourke (1989a) proposed in 1989 a

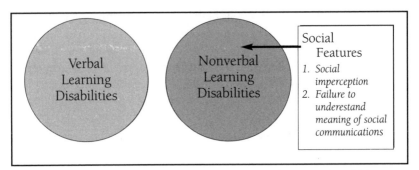

Figure 3.1 Social Features of NLD According to Johnson and Myklebust.
Johnson & Myklebust labeled the group of children who did not have verbal learning disabilities children with nonverbal learning disabilities. They concluded that the children with nonverbal learning disabilities had problems of social imperception. They failed to understand nonverbal social communications.

model that contributed significantly to the literature and to our understanding of NLD. Johnson (1987a) clarified that the children's receptive problems interfered with learning patterns and therefore led to expressive problems. She related the children's social problems to their misinterpretation of the meaning of nonverbal signs, which led to their inappropriate responses.

Left unclear was the issue of whether this form of "social agnosia" (Badian, 1986, 1992) is due to the misreading of social cues because of visual–spatial deficits or because of deficits that prevent the translation of nonverbal signs into meaningful content—that is, deficits that prevent the comprehension of nonverbal signs. We can draw an analogy between language problems such as dyslexia (analogous to visual–spatial deficits) and reading comprehension problems (analogous to nonverbal comprehension problems). In dyslexia the problems lie in the failure to associate the written symbol with its unique sound, whereas reading comprehension problems, which make it difficult to understand the meaning of what is being read, may lie at the level of semantic and conceptual processing. The latter problem can occur in the absence of dyslexia. A child may have language-processing difficulties but still be a fluent reader.

We encounter an analogous situation in NLD. As we will see, the initial hypothesis regarding NLD suggested that some children have visual–spatial problems that interfere with their ability to *decode* social cues. In this view, their comprehension of the meanings of the social cues is unimpaired, because it would be derived from sources other than visual–spatial processing. Thus faulty decoding is seen as responsible for some of their social problems. I designate this group of children as the group that has *problems of social imperception.*

Some children may have intact visual–spatial processing abilities but have varying degrees of difficulties in processing tasks involving social cues, that is, tasks that require the *comprehension* of social communications. If their difficulties in the comprehension of social communications were in the mild to moderate range, then the children would be diagnosed with NLD. If, on the other hand, they have the visual–spatial deficits common to children with NLD but their comprehension difficulties are in the severe range, then those children, as we will see later, would be diagnosed with Asperger's disorder.

The insight we gain from the discussion so far is that it is useful to differentiate two groups of children with NLD: One group has difficulties in the *reception* of social information, and the other has difficulties in the *comprehension* of that type of information.

DURING THE YEARS FOLLOWING THE INITIAL IDENTIFICATION of the disorders, contributors to the literature gave a variety of labels to this population. The labels applicable to the samples studied were partly arbitrary, although the hypotheses they investigated remained the same. The major hypothesis these investigators pursued was that a right hemisphere dysfunction produced the symptoms displayed by children with NLD.

Each investigator selected different samples of children or adults for study. Given the state of technology at that time, researchers did not always specify the type and specific location of the brain lesion, or the extent of the trauma to other regions of the brain. Many of these investigators selected subjects who had suffered strokes or manifested frank signs of neurological impairment. Although there appeared to be much overlap of symptoms within those groups much uncertainty remains as to the validity of comparisons between these studies. Investigators applied labels to different cohorts they studied. These labels include the following:

> Disorders of social imperception (Johnson & Myklebust, 1967)
> Left Hemisyndrome (Denckla, 1978)
> Nonverbal learning disability (Rourke, 1989a, Johnson, 1987a)
> Social–emotional learning disability (Denckla, 1983; Voeller, 1986)
> Right parietal lobe syndrome/developmental learning disability of the right hemisphere (Weintraub & Mesulam, 1982)
> Right hemisphere deficit syndrome (Voeller, 1986)
> Right hemisphere syndrome (Semrud-Clikeman & Hynd, 1990)

Disorders of spatial cognition (Pennington, 1991)
Social emotional processing disorder (Manoach, Sandson, & Weintraub, 1995)
Developmental right hemisphere syndrome (DRHS); (Gross-Tsur, Shaley, Manor & Amir, 1995)

There is no consensus among researchers as to whether each of these labels applied to distinct populations of children and adults or whether some of the subjects suffered from the same syndrome but were labeled differently by different researchers. The term *nonverbal learning disability* complicates the picture by the ambiguity inherent in the label. It appears to denote features the syndrome does not include, that is, the absence of a verbal learning disability, rather than denoting the primary features the syndrome *does* possess, which is the presence of a deficit in the capacity to process nonverbal signs. A more accurate label for the disorder would be *nonverbal processing disorder* or, more accurate still, *nonlinguistic processing disorder*. However, widespread usage of the term *nonverbal learning disability* makes it necessary to retain it rather than compounding the difficulties of nomenclature by adding yet another term.

NLD: A Right Hemisphere Disorder

The dominant neurological and neuropsychological theories of NLD of the 1980s and 1990s hypothesized that NLD stem from right hemisphere dysfunctions. The first set of theories suggested that an association exists between right hemisphere dysfunctions and the social symptoms of children diagnosed with NLD. Some considered the relationship between the neurocognitive deficits and the social features to be nonspecific; others maintained that the neurocognitive dysfunctions cause the social symptoms; still others insisted that the cognitive and social problems are dissociable from each other.

A major limitation of the explanations given by these theories of the neurobiological underpinnings of the social features of NLD is that most of the studies relied on patients with brain lesions. Although these studies have been useful in narrowing the range of possible dysfunctional systems and identifying those that remain intact, they have limited applicability to developmental disorders such as NLD. Developmental disorders follow a different ontogenetic path than that taken by intact brains that have suffered trauma: Developmental disorders seldom affect discreet brain regions but are diffuse, affecting a broad band of systems. In the absence of current research using the newer technologies, such as functional magnetic resonance imaging (fMRI), we are left to organize our discussion based on what is available.

Before proceeding to a discussion of these theories, however, a brief review of right hemisphere function is in order (see Rogers, 2003).

CEREBRAL LATERALIZATION

The concept of cerebral hemispheric *lateralization* "refers to the relative specialization of one cerebral hemisphere for the processing of the particular task" (Hynd & Hooper, 1992, pp. 20–26). This concept is different from the concept of cerebral *localization* that was popular some years ago. Historically, our understanding of brain function emerged out of studies such as those of Broca (in 1861) and Wernicke (in 1876) who hypothesized that specific areas of the cerebrum are responsible for specific functions (see Gazzaniga, Ivry, & Mangun, 2002). Although localization theories were much in vogue in past decades, they failed to provide an accurate depiction of brain processes. Brain functions are now considered to be widely distributed. Luria (1973), taking issue with localization theories, proposed three functional, interacting units as organizing brain activity: the unit for regulating arousal, waking, and mental states; the unit for receiving, analyzing, and storing information; and the unit for programming, regulation, and verification of activities. Luria led the way to conceptualizing brain function in holistic terms rather than as a set of isolated systems that have little impact on one another.

In thinking about the problems of children with NLD it is important to remember that, although many of their symptoms appear to be the products of right hemisphere dysfunctions, this need not mean that the left hemisphere and subcortical regions make no contribution to their problems. Kolb and Whishaw reminded us that "laterality is relative, not absolute, because both hemispheres play a role in nearly every behavior; thus, although the left hemisphere is especially important for the production of language, the right hemisphere also has some language capabilities" (2001, p. 180).

HEMISPHERIC SPECIALIZATION

There is now ample evidence that cerebral lateralization exists and appears early in infancy. Pally describes the ontogeny of hemispheric specialization. Ontogenetically, the right hemisphere matures earlier than the left hemisphere (Nass, Petersen, & Koch et al., 1989; Pally, 1998), and it is only with the beginning of language acquisition that a shift occurs to the left hemisphere as it becomes dominant for most children. This information has led to the conclusion that disruptions in perinatal and postnatal neurological development may impair right hemisphere functions more significantly than left hemisphere functions. Geschwind and Galaburda, referring to asymmetries of structure in both hemispheres, emphasize that "although genetic factors are important we . . . lay stress on several factors that, in the course of development, both prenatal and postnatal, modify the direction and extent of these structural differences" (1985, p. 428; see also Springer & Deutsch, 1989). In addition, the brains of male children mature at a slower rate than those of female children, a fact that may account for the greater frequency of learning disorders in boys than in girls.

It is important to keep in mind that the left hemisphere controls the functions of the right side of the body, whereas the right hemisphere controls the left side of the body.[1] Bundles of fibers connect the two hemispheres; among the largest bundle is the corpus callosum. These fibers permit each hemisphere to communicate with the other. In some genetic disorders, where development of these fibers is either absent or incomplete, the affected children present with symptoms that are similar to those of children with NLD.

With regard to cerebral hemispheric specialization, the left hemisphere has greater facility for utilizing information previously learned. It is more specialized in processing verbal language (a representational system that is shared by the cultural context in which the child is raised), the verbal manipulation of numbers, and logical and analytic thinking. In right-handers the left hemisphere is more specialized for skilled or fine-motor movements (Mesulam, 2000, p. 80).

There are many ways of categorizing the functions performed by the right hemisphere. Some prefer to organize them by cortical areas: frontal, parietal, temporal, and occipital. This approach has some validity, but it introduces the danger of localizing the functions too specifically. I have chosen Mesulam's framework as the simplest and most applicable to the dysfunctions associated with NLD and because with it, it is possible to specify the social features that co-occur with each set of functions. Mesulam (2000, p. 81) noted that the right hemisphere has numerous behavioral specializations that can be divided into at least four categories: (1) complex and nonlinguistic perceptual tasks, (2) paralinguistic aspects of communication, (3) spatial distribution of attention, and (4) emotion perception. The functions that can be subsumed under each realm are too numerous to enumerate. I limit myself to those that we encounter most

---

[1] For our purposes, it is not necessary to consider the complexities introduced by left-handedness or vision, which has complex representations that register in both hemispheres.

often in children with NLD. The following material modifies and expands Mesulam's categories.

Complex and Nonlinguistic Perceptual Tasks

Complex and nonlinguistic perceptual tasks include *auditory* abilities to recognize pitch and melody; the ability for *visual discrimination*, such as the ability to recognize faces, identify complex geometric shapes; the *visual–spatial* abilities for depth perception, spatial location, mental rotation, line orientation, visual perspective taking; and the ability to perform *visual–motor* tasks, such as tracing mazes and block design. Also involved are *memory* for complex spatial relationships and *time* perception. Many of these abilities are essential to successful social communication. The social impairments associated with deficits in these functions would be similar to the "social imperceptions" identified earlier.

Paralinguistic[2] Aspects of Communication

Communicative competence involves the ability to decode, process, and give expression to nonlinguistic social signs. *Decoding* is the ability to read those signs, such as reading others' facial expressions and vocal intonation; *encoding* is the ability to form mental representations of those signs and store them in memory. *Processing* involves understanding what the signs communicate within the context in which they occur. Finally, the *expression* of a sign involves its retrieval from memory and its production through some motor output. All of these abilities are critical to the nonverbal comprehension, expression, and processing of social communication. Their impairment leads to the kind of disruptions in social dialogue that we encounter in children with NLD. In addition, as Mesulam noted, "Right hemisphere lesions, especially those that involve the superior temporal gyrus, promote excessive language output and the use of unnecessarily complicated technical vocabulary" (2000, p. 86). The verbosity that we encounter in children with NLD is only partly related to the reinforcement they get for their verbal abilities; it may also be related to the dysfunction of their right hemisphere. (Many of these issues are addressed in Part II.)

Spatial Distribution of Attention

A common phenomenon observed in patients who have suffered from a right hemisphere lesion (e.g., a stroke) is the "neglect" they manifest of the

---

[2] Different authors define *paralanguage* differently. In this context, the term refers to the broad range of nonlinguistic signs used in communication, such as facial expressions, gestures, and body language.

left side of their body. For reasons that are not entirely clear, they appear unconcerned about, or even deny, the fact that the left side of their body is no longer functional. The absence of tactile signals from the left side seems to impair their awareness of their condition. The implications of this phenomenon are unclear for children with NLD. It may be that this deficit produces their lack of concern about personal space (i.e., their unawareness of body boundaries) and their inability to appreciate the proper physical distance to maintain when speaking to others. Pally (1998) suggested that body image is associated with a right hemisphere function, a fact that would partially explain some of these problems. Because we have few data regarding the body image of children with NLD, the relevance of this phenomena to their social problems requires further exploration.

Emotion Perception
The right hemisphere is specialized for the processing of the *perception* of affect states. It is also responsible for the coordination of many aspects of emotional expression and experience. "It is involved in the ability to *express* emotional tone through speech prosody, facial expression, or gesture and also the ability to *identify* the nature of the emotion expressed through prosody and facial expression" (Mesulam, 2000, p. 84). Furthermore, the frontal cortical and subcortical regions contribute to emotional experience and expression (Davidson, 2003a, 2003b, 2003c). Each hemisphere introduces an emotional valence to our experience. The left frontal cortex adds a positive valence, whereas the right frontal supplies a negative valence. Each region exerts an inhibitory effect on the other so that a balance exists between the two. Damage to the right hemisphere disrupts that balance and leads to a seeming indifference to adversity (Springer & Deutsch, 1989, p. 209). The right hemisphere is better equipped than the left to recognize and process a wide range of nonverbal cues, including the expressions of emotion in vocal intonations and gestures. Furthermore, the right hemisphere processes and modulates affects that are involved in the development of social skills (Semrud-Clikeman & Hynd, 1990). I discuss these issues as part of social cognition in Chapter 6.

WE CAN NOW DRAW A PARALLEL BETWEEN DISORDERS OF verbal language and impairments in nonverbal communication, although as with any analogy, the parallel may break down if pushed too far. The categories mentioned above represent the functions that subserve the nonverbal domain. Deficits in the specialization for decoding of complex nonlinguistic perceptual information would be equivalent to dyslexia, in which the deficit interferes with the ability to associate the visual sign with a lexicon of stored images. The child with an NLD that is impaired by this deficit is unable to "recall" what the nonverbal sign stands for or, alternatively, associates the sign with an unconventional image. The failure in decoding occurs because of the impairment in the capacity to process nonlinguistic perceptual information that includes visual–spatial perception. I borrowed Johnson and Myklebust's (1967) term to designate this process as "social imperception." It is a critical aspect of the deficits from which children with NLD suffer. Impairments in receptive capacities might also lead to expressive problems. A child who is unable to decode nonverbal signs may manifest confusion in the selection of a sign to use to express him- or herself. This confusion does not necessarily mean that the child does not have the ability to understand the meaning of the sign, had he or she decoded it properly, nor that he or she would not know its proper usage.

The two other categories, the paralinguistic aspects of communication and affect perception, involve processing the meaning of the sign and its associated emotional valence. These processes involve the comprehension of the communication, that is, its salience; they also involve the pragmatic aspect of social interchanges—that is, communicative competence. Social cognition is the domain that processes these areas.

MESULAM'S (2000) CATEGORIES OR FUNCTIONS ARE HELPFUL in identifying the social sequelae of impairments in those functions and may permit us to answer questions such as "How do deficits in each of these functions affect a child's capacity to relate to others or to how the child feels about him- or herself?" "What are the relationships between specific impairments and the child's social problems?" As we continue to explore these theories, we will find that some theories of NLD associate specific behavioral manifes-

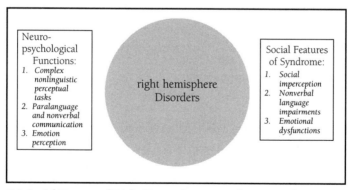

Figure 3.2 Social Feature of Right Hemisphere Disorders According to Mesulam.
Following Mesulam (2000), we note that (1) complex nonlinguistic perception, (2) paralanguage and nonverbal communication, and (3) emotion perception are right hemisphere functions. right hemisphere disorders may lead to social imperception, impairments in nonverbal language, and impairments in emotional communication.

tations with specific dysfunctions, whereas others disassociate the deficits from the social problems (see Figure 3.2).

Contributions from Neurology

During the 1980s and 1990s several investigators conducted studies of children and adults with a variety of right hemisphere brain lesions. Many of those studies concluded that the sample of patients studied manifested distinctive patterns of symptoms that led to conjectures about the existence of a syndrome. The behavioral symptoms associated with this syndrome appeared to be similar to those of children with NLD. The plethora of labels to which I alluded earlier is a result of those studies. A common denominator in all the studies was the finding of social problems associated with right hemisphere dysfunctions.

Weintraub and Mesulam (1982) published the first study of a sample of patients with long histories of emotional and relational problems as well as difficulties with speech prosody, poor perception of social cues, and poor social skills. All patients in the sample revealed neurological and neuropsychological signs consistent with a right hemisphere dysfunction. They concluded that "damage to the right hemisphere suffered early in life, or inherited, may lead to chronic emotional difficulties, the disturbance of relational skills, and poor visuospatial ability" (p. 463) and hypothesized that "there is a syndrome of early right hemisphere dysfunction that may be genetically determined and that is associated with introversion, poor social perception, chronic emotional difficulties, inability to display affect, and impairment in visuospatial representation" (Weintraub & Mesulam, 1982, p. 468). In neuropsychological terms, we would identify such a syndrome as a nonverbal learning disability.

Voeller (1986) described a sample of 15 children "with behavioral disturbances, a characteristic neuropsychological profile, and neurological findings consistent with right hemisphere damage or dysfunction" (p. 1004). She found that almost all the children had attention-deficit disorder, difficulty in interpreting social cues, difficulty in expressing their feelings, and a low level of awareness of other people's feelings. Voeller's study adds to our understanding of the children's social problems with the finding that the attentional problems may make their own contribution to the children's social difficulties. This finding suggests that these problems are not always exclusively the result of a right hemisphere dysfunction. Gross-Tsur, Shaley, Manor, and Amir (1995) replicated the finding of attention deficit/hyperactivity disorder (ADHD) in all the children in their study and, based on the characteristics of 20 children, described a developmental right hemisphere syndrome (DRHS), which they considered to be a nonverbal learning disability. Thirteen of the children had "soft" neurological signs on the left side of the body, and all the children were diagnosed as having ADHD. Marked slowness of performance and severe handwriting problems were found in almost three-fourths of the children.

Finally, Semrud-Clikeman and Hynd (1990, 1991) presented a comprehensive review of the NLD subtypes that were current at the time of publication. Focusing on the effects of the children's arithmetic problems and social–emotional deficits, they concluded that further research would be necessary to clarify the nature of the disorder (see also Carey, Barakat, Foley, Gyato, & Phyllips, 2001).

From this brief review of the neurological literature, we may conclude that if a right hemisphere syndrome exists, it would encompass a range of social dysfunctions. First are the "social imperceptions" that interfere with the decoding of social signs. Second are the impairments in the comprehension of those signs that are mediated by processes of social cognition and that include difficulties in affect processing. We must now add a third array of impairments: the deficits in attention, executive function, and sensory and motor dysfunctions that are not necessarily part of the right hemisphere dysfunctions but are associated with social impairments. I return to a discussion of this component later in this chapter.

We may now modify the clinical definition of NLD I gave in the Introduction to the following working definition:

> NLD is a disorder in which the primary core deficit resides in the capacity to process nonlinguistic perceptual information. I identify two subtypes: (1) deficits that impair the ability to decode social cues, and (2) deficits that impair the ability to decode social cues and, deficits that in addition produce mild to moderately severe problems in the comprehension of social communications (i.e., in understanding the meanings of social cues). The social–emotional problems of children with NLD are concomitant manifestations that may be causally related to the neuropsychological deficits or secondary consequences of them.

Rourke's Neuropsychological Contributions

Rourke (1985, 1989a, 1993; Rourke & Fuerst, 1991), a leading advocate for the development of subtypes of learning disabilities, was among the first to conduct extensive studies of children with NLD. Beginning in the late 1960s, he undertook a set of studies that differentiated learning disorders into subtypes. He selected a sample of children with learning disabilities who were deficient in at least one school subject, had full-scale WISC

IQ scores that were within the normal range, and were free of primary emotional disturbances. Based on the discrepancy between their verbal and performance IQs, he divided the children into three groups. The first group (R-S-A, for performance deficits in reading, spelling, and arithmetic) had verbal IQ (VIQ) scores that were at least 10 points higher than performance IQ (PIQ) scores. The second group's (R-S, for performance deficits in reading and spelling) VIQs and PIQs were within 4 points of each other. The third group's (A, for performance deficits in arithmetic) PIQs were at least 10 point lower than the VIQs. Rourke hypothesized that these discrepancies reflected the relative strengths and weakness in the abilities that the left (VIQ) and right (PIQ) hemispheres subserve. He noted that the patterns of neuropsychological deficits and social–emotional problems of the children in group A were virtually identical to children with NLD. He emphasized that although the children shared a common set of features, not every child within a group had all the de-scribed features (Rourke, 1989a). In addition, he stressed that, from a de-velopmental perspective, children display different levels of impairment at different ages. The symptoms become more clearly delineated as the dis-order emerges with the child's maturation.

Three aspects of Rourke's contribution are significant for our discussion of the social impairments of children with NLD: (1) the neuropsychologi-cal and academic assets and deficits associated with the NLD subtype learning disability, (2) the social–emotional disturbances associated with NLD, and (3) his white-matter hypothesis.

NEUROPSYCHOLOGICAL AND ACADEMIC ASSETS AND DEFICITS OF NLD

Because the focus in this work is on the social–emotional features of NLD, I briefly highlight Rourke's findings on the children's neuropsychological and academic assets and deficits before discussing his views on their social–emotional problems.

In several publications Rourke describes a hierarchy of cascading assets and deficits, which he categorizes as primary, secondary, tertiary, verbal, academic, and socioemotional/adaptive. Each asset or deficit contributes to the child's functional abilities or disabilities and compounds the effects of those in the next lower category (Rourke, 1989a, 1993, 1995a, 1995b, 2000; Rourke & Tsatsanis, 1996). He described primary assets in auditory perception, simple motor tasks, and rote functions; secondary assets in auditory and verbal attention; tertiary assets in auditory and verbal mem-ory; verbal assets in some of the basic skills involved in academic tasks, such as the retention of rote materials and spoken and written productions. The children tend to have good verbal memories, well-developed language skills at the receptive and expressive levels, and they tend to do well in academic subjects involving reading, writing, and spelling.

The children were also found to have significant deficits in other categories. They demonstrated primary weaknesses in tactile perception, which is involved in tasks such as keyboarding, recognizing by feel, with eyes closed, the value of a coin, or identifying objects such as a pencil, an eraser, a ruler. Deficits in their visual perception affected their discrimination and recognition of visual details (e.g., facial features and other nonverbal cues). The children also evidenced primary deficits in dealing with novel materials. Secondary deficits were reported in the areas of tactile and visual attention, which are used in tasks such as copying and writing. Difficulties with exploratory behaviors and in making transitions from one situation to another were noted. Furthermore, tertiary deficits, involving underdeveloped abilities in concept formation, nonverbal problem solving, and hypothesis testing, were detected. These are skills required in the negotiation of challenging new tasks and social relationships. Finally, although verbal language is the preferred mode of communication for these children, they have pragmatic language problems that create difficulties that make them appear superficial and concrete when conversing with others. In the academic sphere, they have problems comprehending complex written materials and the mechanics of arithmetic and science.

It is worthwhile to consider Rourke's explanation of why the children have problems with arithmetic, because this explanation is relevant to his understanding of the children's social–emotional difficulties.

SOCIAL–EMOTIONAL DISTURBANCES

Rourke (1993) listed several types of problems in mechanical arithmetic that account for errors made by these children in the social–emotional domain, stating:

> When a . . . qualitative analysis of the *psychosocial* behavior of children with NLD is carried out, we find that the neuropsychological assets and deficits that appear to lie at the root of their social adaptation deficiencies are virtually identical to those that have a negative impact on their performance in mechanical arithmetic. In short, the maladaptive social behaviors of children with NLD is seen as stemming from the same neuropsychological deficits as their problems in arithmetic calculation (e.g., those in visual–perceptual–organization, psychomotor, and concept-formation skills, and difficulties in dealing with novel problem-solving situations). (Rourke, 1993, p. 221)

He noted that the children showed marked impairments in the social–emotional domain of functioning. They have great difficulty adapting to novel situations. They rely on ready-made, learned responses, irrespective of their applicability to the situation and context in which they find themselves. Their social perception and judgment are impaired. As they get older, they tend to withdraw from social situations and isolate themselves. At the emotional level they display symptoms of anxiety, depression, and other "internalizing" forms of disorders (Rourke, 1989a, pp. 81–86). Rourke's theory proposes that the children's social behaviors are the product of their primary neuropsychological deficits. As he forcefully states in the quote above, there are specific parallel between their errors in mechanical arithmetic and their social impairments although these are not the exclusive sources of the children's social-emotional problems. Other sources include the primary, secondary, and tertiary deficits in tactile perception and attention, concept formation and problem solving, as well as the problems with prosody, and pragmatic language.

- *Errors in spatial organization*. In arithmetic, these include errors misaligning numbers in columns and problems with directionality. As applied to social situations, the children typically have difficulties orienting themselves in space, which may result in poor judgment regarding personal space as well as other situations that involve making judgments about spatial relationships. For example, a child may inadvertently bump into other children while standing in line, may touch another child inappropriately, or may stand too close while speaking with others.
- *Errors in visual detail*. These would include errors in reading the mathematical sign or the placement of the decimal point in a problem. In social situations, such errors are reminiscent of the "social imperceptions" to which I referred earlier. For example, a child may not notice a teacher's nonverbal gesture directing him or her be quiet or wait his or her turn.
- *Procedural errors*. In the case of arithmetic, these errors include missing or adding a step in the process of solving a problem or applying a learned rule from one procedure to a dissimilar procedure. Similar errors are present in the social context. For example, a child complained that her teacher was not being polite because the teacher did not always begin her requests to work with "Please"!
- *Failure to shift psychological set*. Children sometimes fail to shift set and instead inappropriately apply a practiced procedure they learned in other contexts to the new operation. In social situations,

children may fail to take into account the shift in context in attempting to deal with a social interaction. For example, a child may engage a stranger in conversation, asking personal questions without realizing that such conduct is inappropriate.

- *Memory problems.* In some cases, these children demonstrated a failure to access a rule that they knew applied to a particular situation. The errors associated with this dysfunction may be due to working memory problems. In social situations these errors may be the result of the inability to reevoke the visual image that is associated with the social context, leading the child to provide an inept response. For example, when confronted with a group of two or more children, the child may not be able to keep visual track of all the relevant, simultaneous interaction. The overload in working memory, as well as the visual deficits, would lead to inappropriate responses.
- *Errors in judgment and reasoning.* Children may attempt mathematical problems that are too difficult, not realizing that they do not have the abilities necessary to be successful, or they may generate responses that appear reasonable to them, but are incorrect. In social situations, they may attempt to deal with situations or questions that are beyond their capabilities, or they may fail to generate reasonable plans of action. Such errors appear to reflect deficits in executive function in which children are required to keep in mind the goal toward which they are striving, in order to implement a plan that would lead to the achievement of the goal. Such an activity would include inhibiting irrelevant responses, monitoring progress, and taking corrective actions when necessary. For example, a high school sophomore who had difficulty with his lunchroom situation, because he had no one with whom to sit, tried at first to sit with the popular children. Feeling clearly rejected but not wanting to sit by himself and wishing to be accepted, he devised a plan by which he would demonstrate how knowledgeable he was about the presidential candidates. He manipulated the conversation to a discussion of one of the more obscure candidates, then was completely surprised that his peers discounted and ridiculed his comments. He found himself on the defensive but refused to yield ground. Unable to modify his failed strategy, he went on a campaign to convince everyone of his position. The disastrous result was further rejection and more ridicule, yet he still failed to understand why his strategy had not worked.

In searching for the relationship between learning disabilities and social–emotional disturbances, Rourke generated three hypotheses. The first hypothesis stated that social–emotional disturbances cause learning disabilities. Rourke dismissed this hypothesis, which is still current in some psychodynamic circles. Although it may be true that social and emotional conditions may create circumstances that interfere with the ability to learn, such learning difficulties cannot be equated with brain-based learning disabilities. The second hypothesis he put forward was that all subtypes of learning disabilities cause social–emotional problems. The data do not support this hypothesis because of the high variability of learning disabilities. Some learning disabilities are not associated with any social–emotional difficulties, whereas others clearly produce such difficulties. He concluded that the personality characteristics of children with LDs are heterogeneous and that there is no unique type of LD personality. What remained to be determined was the exact relationship between the two. Rourke proposed a third hypothesis that "specific patterns of central processing abilities and deficits cause specific manifestations (subtypes) of learning disabilities and specific forms of socioemotional disturbances"

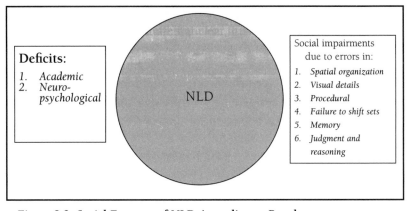

Figure 3.3 Social Features of NLD According to Rourke.
Rourke maintains that the children's neuropsychological deficits and their poor academic performance cause the social-emotional problems of children with NLD.

(Rourke & Fuerst, 1991, p. 69) such is the case with children with NLD (see also Rourke, 1993; see Figure 3.3).

Rourke believes that the primary visual–spatial–organizational output deficits—that is, the difficulties in visual–spatial–organization (e.g., identification and recognition of faces), the nonverbal problem-solving deficits, the visual memory problems, and the problems in judgment and reasoning—*cause* the children's social–emotional, and adaptive difficulties, much as they cause the arithmetic problems (Rourke & Fuerst, 1994, p. 409). With regard to the social–emotional problems of these children, Rourke concludes that the pattern of central processing abilities and deficits (i.e., the nonverbal learning disabilities) increases the risk for psychopathology. The significant deficits in social perception, social judgment, and social interaction skills, together with the marked tendency toward social withdrawal and isolation as age increases, place these children at risk for the development of social–emotional disturbance, especially "internalized" forms of psychopathology (Harnadek & Rourke, 1993, p. 145). In the early years of my practice, we used to distinguish between internalizing and externalizing forms of psychopathology in terms of "children who *feel* troubled" and "children who *make* trouble." Hoffman provides a more accurate distinction[3]:

> At the internalizing end of the spectrum, we include children with the large variety of emotional disorders with dysphoric affects (anxieties, depression, bipolar disorders, grief, post-traumatic stress disorders, obsessive–compulsive states, eating disorders, gender dysphoria, and psychosomatic states). In these states one would observe self-recriminations, overt guilt and/or shame. At the externalizing end of the spectrum, we include children and adolescents who manifest the following symptomatic constellations reflective of disruptive disorders: Attention deficit hyperactivity disorder, oppositional defiant disorder, conduct disorder, other impulsive states. In these states, one would tend to observe a lack of "insight" into personal responsibility.

In earlier publications, Rourke and Young (1989b) associated the children's serious internalizing psychopathology with suicidal risk. In a paper titled "Childhood Learning Disability That Predisposes Those Affected to Adolescent and Adult Depression and Suicide," Rourke and his colleagues (Rourke, 1989a; Young, & Leenaars) gave the impression that this risk was not uncommon. Fletcher (1989), in discussing this paper, cautioned against making this extreme association. Interestingly, in later publications Rourke does not mention this risk factor. Instead, he cited a serious risk for the development of a "psychosocial disturbance" (Rourke, 1989b) or "internalized psychopathology" (Pelletier, Ahmad, & Rourke, 2001). The psychopathology becomes much more evident with increasing age. My clinical experience leads me to believe that the connection between NLD and suicidality is artifactual rather than a consequence of the NLD.

[3] Personal communication, Leon Hoffman, April 4, 2004. Leon Hoffman, M.D., is the director of the Pacella Parent Child Center of the New York Psychoanalytic Institute and Society.

ROURKE'S WHITE MATTER HYPOTHESIS

Rourke proposed the "white matter model" (Rourke, 1989a, 1995b; Tsatsanis & Rourke, 1995; Fuerst & Rourke, 1995) to explain the neurobiological processes that undergird the symptoms of NLD. The brain's white matter, as opposed to the gray matter that covers the cerebral cortex, is composed of myelinated fibers, protein sheaths that appear white and that cover the neuronal axons. There are three sets of white matter bundles: the *commissural fibers*, of which the corpus callosum (which connects the right and left hemispheres) is the largest; the *association fibers*, which interconnect cortical regions within the same hemisphere; and the *projection fibers*, which connect the subcortical region, including the brainstem and the spinal cord, to the cortical regions. According to Rourke, when damage, dysfunction, or underdevelopment compromises the integrity of those fibers, the conditions are set for the development of NLD. Two conditions must be satisfied: (1) *damage* to white matter, and (2) the occurrence of the damage in the *right hemisphere*. In brief, damage to right hemisphere white matter causes the kinds of processing difficulties and deficits associated with NLD. Given that the right hemisphere contains more white matter than gray matter, as compared to the left hemisphere, and that in infancy the right hemisphere is dominant, the right hemisphere processing abilities are more likely to be affected than those of the left when adverse conditions occur. Whites matter underdevelopment, damage, or dysfunction therefore leads to both structural and functional reorganization of the brain.

Rourke (1982) relied heavily on Goldberg and Costa's (1981) framework of brain function for his model, even though he states that their framework is "based primarily upon data gathered and *speculations* [italics added] derived from investigations of human adults" (Rourke, 1989a, p. 111). According to Goldberg and Costa, the right hemisphere tends to approach every task as a novel stimulus. They state, "the right hemisphere has a greater ability to perform intermodal integration and to process novel stimuli; the left hemisphere is more capable of unimodal and motor processing as well as the storage of compact codes" (p. 144). In other words, the left hemisphere is more specialized for processing and integrating information from specific areas. It analyzes and classifies information into existing schemas, whereas the right hemisphere processes new information and constructs schemas that are then shared with the left hemisphere (Semrud-Clikeman & Hynd, 1991). The right hemisphere is better equipped to process nonverbal languages, which are structured differently from the linear sequential verbal mode of communication mediated by the left hemisphere.

Based on this framework, Rourke concluded that his group A children (the NLD group) "exhibit patterns of neuropsychological abilities and deficits that are strongly suggestive of relatively dysfunctional right hemisphere systems" (Rourke, 1989a, p. 75). His explanation for the problems of these children with concept formation, problem solving, and hypothesis testing is worth mentioning. He uses Piaget's developmental psychology for part of his explanation, contending that because exploratory behavior is inhibited during the sensorimotor phase of development, these children do not acquire the sensorimotor schemas that eventually form the basis of higher-order language. When the children acquire language, they apply verbal labels to objects without the necessary foundations in experience. Consequently, their ability to process and synthesize knowledge is shallow or impaired.

Finally, in support of his hypothesis, Rourke extends his model to several neurological diseases, disorders, and dysfunctions that appear to exhibit a similar phenotype to NLD. It is beyond the purview of this book to present or evaluate these conjectures. Rourke's white matter hypothesis departs somewhat from the hypothesis of a right hemisphere dysfunction in that it suggests a much broader basis for the children's deficits. However, the white matter hypothesis encompasses the explanations given by the right hemisphere hypothesis.

COMMENTARY ON ROURKE'S CONTRIBUTION

Rourke made a signal contribution in furthering the identification of subtypes of learning disabilities. He moved the discipline away from the simplistic thinking that did not sufficiently distinguish among subtypes, and he insisted that the discrepancy between VIQ and PIQ is *not* a reliable diagnostic indicator for NLD, as was previously believed.

Rourke makes a strong case for NLD as a primarily right hemisphere disorder. His impressive list of publications and his work in exploring the applicability of his white matter model to other neurodevelopmental disorders makes it difficult to challenge his hypotheses. Nevertheless, two questions deserve consideration. First, the test data on which he based his conclusions have been superseded by more refined tests that generate different data sets—a fact that he concedes in a later publication (Pelletier et al., 2001). He defends his position on the grounds that his studies cover a period of over 20 years; hence the inevitable evolution in instruments used to test the children. Absent from his data are tests for executive function problems (Denchla, 1991; Pennington, 1991), for ADHD, for memory problems other than visual memory, and for the role of affect in the disorder. However, it is not my intention to question the validity of

Rourke's findings. My interest lies in the association he makes between specific neuropsychological deficits and the social and emotional functioning of children with NLD.

The second question addresses the relationship he attempts to establish between the children's neuropsychological deficits and their social–emotional problems. Although he refers to a "socio*emotional*" (italics added) problems, he pays scant attention to the emotional dimensions of the children's functioning, except for prosody. The emotion component, which is central to relationships and serves as an indicator of motivation in human thoughts and behaviors, is highly consequential for the types of social behaviors displayed by children with NLD.

It is important to note that Rourke considers the categories in which errors occur in arithmetic as paradigmatic of these children's social problems. There is little doubt that a relationship exists between the children's visual–perceptual problems and their decoding of social cues. It is not clear, however, that a direct causal relationship exists between the two; after all, it is possible to have visual perceptual problems but no social impairments. However, many of Rourke's findings on the social–emotional functioning of children with NLD are consistent with the functions of two realms of right hemisphere function as categorized by Mesulam (2000): the complex and nonlinguistic perceptual functions, and the paralinguistic aspects of communication and nonverbal communication. In that sense, his position lends support to the view that either their visual–spatial deficits or their impairment in the processing of social information produces the children's social–emotional difficulties.

Although Rourke's catalogue includes deficits other than the visual-spatial neuropsychological deficits, such as attentional and organizational deficits, he does not consider the relationship between these deficits and the children's social problems, nor does he discuss the limitation that their processing of emotional information introduces into their relationships with others.

The Dissociability of Visual–Spatial Processing and Social Cognition

The next theory that we consider is that of Pennington, a neuropsychologist whose position represents an important departure from the position of the researchers discussed above. In contrast to Rourke, Pennington contends that the right hemisphere problems of children with NLD emerge as symptoms in academic tasks such as arithmetic and handwriting and reflect deficits in *spatial cognition*, whereas the social problems of these children represent deficits in the domain of *social cognition*, which involves the limbic and orbital frontal regions in addition to the affected right hemisphere systems. Pennington argues that it is "conceptually clearer to consider deficits in math and handwriting separately from deficits in social cognition. There are children who present with math/handwriting deficits but no deficits in social cognition," and vice versa (Pennington, 1991, p. 111). This view is consistent with the clinical impression that only a subset of children with visual–spatial problems has social impairments.

The domain of spatial cognition includes the following functions: "object localization and identification, short- and long-term visual or spatial memory, deployment of attention to extrapersonal space, mental rotations and displacements, spatial imagery, and spatial construction (e.g., drawing or building)" (Pennington, 1991, p. 9). Pennington places problems in social cognition within the autistic spectrum, which includes Asperger's disorder. Children with social cognition problems present with difficulties in making social contact and understanding social contexts. Pennington follows Stern's (1985) developmental theory that suggests that social cognitive processes are aspects of intersubjective development, which culminates in the emergence of a theory of mind around age 4. Children with autism suffer from deficits in both the capacity for intersubjectivity and theory of mind, which raises the question of the status of both these functions in children with NLD. Pennington does not address this issue. I try to answer the question of the relationship between NLD and Asperger's disorder in Chapter 11. As we will see, children with Aspergers' Disorder have symptoms such as echolalia, stereotypies, deficits in symbolic play, and more serious pragmatic language problems, than children with NLD.

More generally, Pennington considers NLD to be a right hemisphere dysfunction that manifests as handwriting and math problems in academic activities. He believes it to be misleading to localize both social and cognitive processes in the right hemisphere; multiple brain systems subserve some of these functions. For example, the limbic system and portions of the frontal lobe subserve emotional and social cognitive processes (Pennington, 1991, p. 12). Rourke's hypothesis that a *causal* relationship exists between white matter dysfunctions and both arithmetic abilities and social problems establishes a necessary connection between the two; Pennington contends that the social problems may be only secondary consequences of the primary deficit. As we have seen, nonlinguistic perceptual deficits may exist in the absence of social problems; no necessary causal connection need exist between the two (see Figure 3.4).

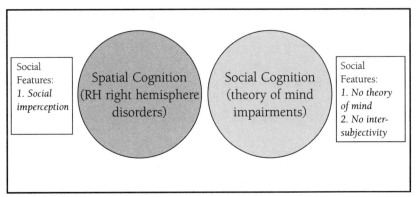

Figure 3.4 Dissociability of Social Features of Spatial Cognition &
Social Cognition According to Pennington.

Pennington (1991) contends that spatial cognition, which is subserved by right hemisphere
functions, is dissociable from social cognition, which is subserved by limbic, frontal orbital, as
well as some right hemisphere functions. Spatial cognition produces social imperceptions, whereas
deficits in social cognition produce impairments in theory of mind and limited capacity for
intersubjectivity.

Other Neuropsychological Deficits

The status of attentional problems in NLD is also problematic. As we have
seen, studies refer to the presence of attentional problems, although frequently the *Diagnostic and Statistical Manual of Mental Disorders*—Fourth
Edition (American Psychiatric Association, 1994) classification was not
used in the diagnosis of the condition. Further, many children are referred
for evaluation because ADD or ADHD is suspected. In some cases a diagnosis is established and medication prescribed. However, no data exist as
to the frequency of a verified diagnosis or the effectiveness of medication
in children with NLD. It is arguable that ADHD is a comorbid condition
in some cases. However, given the frequency with which some ADHD
symptoms co-occur, I would suggest that we tentatively include the presence of some of the ADHD symptoms as possible correlated symptoms.

A somewhat similar status must be assigned to problems in executive
function (Barkley, 1996; Denckla, 1996; Ellenberg, 1999; Goldberg, 2001;
Pennington, Bennetto, McAleer, & Roberts, 1996). Clinically, we observe
that a significant number of children with NLD have organizational difficulties. Because no criteria equivalent to those of the DSM-IV exist at this
time for the diagnosis of this disorder, it is unclear as to whether we may
say that this is a comorbid condition or a correlated set of symptoms. The
possible relationship between attentional problems and difficulties in
executive function remains to be established. Filley (2005) suggested that
the relationship may lie in white-matter dysfunction, which would affect
both attention and executive function. Children with both types of problems have social impairments that are distinct from the social impercep-

tions of children with nonlinguistic perceptual deficits. These distinct social impairments constitute an added layer to the neurobehavioral problems of the children when the two conditions coexist. The early neurological studies frequently found that their subjects had attentional problems.

From a clinical perspective, it is difficult to ignore the contribution that the presence of attentional problems makes to the social difficulties of children with NLD (see Palombo, 2001, Ch. 8). A similar set of findings attests to the organizational problems in many of these children. The presence of an executive function disorder can compound adjustment problems within the family, at school, and with peers (see Palombo, 2001a, Ch. 9). Finally, least studied by neurologists but deserving attention are the children's sensory and motor problems, which Rourke emphasizes. These problems appear to be quite prevalent among these children, although the type of dysfunctions and frequency of occurrence remain unexplored.

Neuropsychological deficits seldom exist as discreet impairments that affect only specific areas of functioning. It is, therefore, important to consider the possibility that many children with NLD have concomitant deficits in other brain regions than those that produce the NLD. These deficits have correlated social features that compound the child's social functioning. I suggest that we consider these deficits in our assessment of children with NLD and make room for them in our definition of the disorder.

We may now add a third subtype to our current working definition of NLD:

> Children who have deficits that impair their ability to decode social cues and, in addition, have attentional/executive function or other neuropsychological deficits that interfere with their social functioning.

Critique of the Theory of Right Hemisphere Dysfunction

Denckla (1991) suggested that historically a parallel was drawn between dyslexia as a left hemisphere disorder and NLD as a right hemisphere disorder. The finding that social problems are associated with NLD seems to make intuitive sense but also raises questions. Denckla also questioned the hypothesis that right hemisphere dysfunctions cause the social impairments of children with NLD. There are problems inherent in any explanation based on strict lateralization of function and greater danger in localizing NLD to the right hemisphere. She suggested that NLD may result from inadequate contributions of modules within the left hemisphere that are not linguistic; the left hemisphere performs many visual tasks, she notes, such as those that are featural, detailed, and connected sequentially (p. 718). She is less critical of Rourke's (1995b) white-matter hypothesis because it leaves open the opportunity for confirmation or falsification through further research. However, she prefers to approach the discussion of NLD by examining three sets of competencies that are involved in math and social skills: (1) the attentional/executive function component, (2) the linguistic/sequential information-processing component, and, (3) the visual–perceptual/simultaneous information-processing component. This approach permits the expansion of possible explanations to include some left hemisphere functions. Denckla concluded her discussion by stating that much research remains to be done and that "it is possible that . . . nonverbal disabilities are indeed rare and, unless associated with SELD [social–emotional learning disabilities], executive dysfunction, or deficient attentional processes, NVLD [nonverbal learning disabilities] need not cause clinical or educational complaints" (p. 723). In her published work, although she is clearly supportive of the proposal for the creation of a new diagnostic category called SELD, she does not pursue the suggestion or elaborate on what such an entity might look like.

THE EARLY INVESTIGATORS HOPED TO FIND A SIMPLE correlation between right hemisphere dysfunctions and a particular set of symptoms that would identify NLD. That hope did not materialize. Researchers have used many labels to identify groups of patients with symptoms similar to more that Johnson and Myklebust (1967) and Rourke (1989a) called NLD. Their goal was to establish a causal relationship between the deficits and the academic, neuropsychological, and social–emotional problems was not achieved. As Denckla and Pennington correctly point out, there are a number of problems with the linear thinking embedded in the hypothesis of a causal relationship between the neuropsychological deficits and the children's social—emotional problems. The argument that spatial cognition and social cognition are dissociable opens the possibility that the social problems may have a different etiology from the neuropsychological problems or that some of them may be secondary consequences that are unrelated to the primary deficits.

Pennington and Denckla conclude that although there may be a right hemisphere disorder that affects spatial cognition, the etiology of disorders in social cognition are unrelated to a right hemisphere disorder. Except for noting their existence, they do not discuss the social features associated with the right hemisphere functions noted by Rourke, such as problems in dealing with novelty, concept formation, hypothesis testing, and others that may impair a child's social function. Nor do they directly address the issue of a possible relationship between visual–spatial deficits and some types of social problems.

Conclusion

The story of NLD began with Johnson and Myklebust's (1967) findings on a group of children who did not fit into their schema of language-based learning disabilities. Their work, paralleling the work on dyslexia, led to the hypothesis that the children's symptoms were a manifestation of a right hemisphere dysfunction. They suggested that the social problems resulted from "imperception" of social cues, leading the children to fail to understand the meaning of the signs.

From a neurological perspective, lesion-based studies pointed to the similarities between the social problems of children with NLD and those with right hemisphere dysfunctions. Mesulam (2000) summarized the major functions of the right hemisphere as the mediation of (1) complex nonlinguistic perceptual tasks, (2) the spatial distribution of attention, (3) the paralinguistic aspects of verbal and nonverbal communication, and (4) the perception of emotional states. Because little is known about the spatial distribution of attention in children with NLD, I excluded that set of functions from consideration. A modified form of this categorization continues to inform the discussion in this work. A limitation of this categorization of right hemisphere function is that it does not permit the inclusion of two areas of dysfunction that appear in our data: problems in *attention* and *executive function*. These two functions are obviously not fully lateralized and consequently present problems when we try to assign aspects of those functions to one hemisphere, to the exclusion of the other.

Rourke (1989a) broadened the right hemisphere hypothesis and the scope of inquiry when he hypothesized that the pattern of assets and deficits manifested by these children is due to an underlying dysfunction in white matter that emerges developmentally in the right hemisphere but has consequences for left hemisphere development. He proposed that those brain-based dysfunctions caused problems in social–emotional competencies that are identical to those in arithmetic skills. Those symptoms appear to occur along a spectrum, with no clearly demarcated boundaries. Rourke explains this phenomenon as due to the neurodevelopmental and maturational phases of childhood; different levels of symptom differentiation are associated with different ages.

It is now possible to postulate that the social impairments of children with NLD stem from several sources. Their visual–perceptual processing deficits are clearly established; I refer to these as nonlinguistic perceptual deficits, following Mesulam's (2000) terminology. These difficulties at times also coexist with mild to moderately severe problems in the comprehension of social communications. The attentional and executive function deficits as well as deficits in other neuropsychological functions comprise a separate set of factors that impairs the child's social functioning. All these factors constitute a set of constraints to the typical development of a child with an NLD. The constraints shape the formation of the child's developing sense of self, the symptoms that will emerge, and the type of psychopathology that will ensue.

Denckla's critique of the right hemisphere hypothesis and Pennington's (1991) proposal that spatial cognition is dissociable from social cognition raise questions as to the validity of the right hemisphere hypothesis to explain the social impairments found in children with NLD. Whereas, there is agreement that spatial cognition is lateralized to the right hemisphere, as we will see, there is little evidence for the lateralization of social cognition to that hemisphere. This critique also opens for exploration the arena of the impairments in social cognition that produces difficulties in the comprehension of social signs as well as in the processing of affect states. I undertake an exploration of this arena in Part II.

Part II

THE INTERPLAY
WITH THE CONTEXT

A SOCIAL PERSPECTIVE

4

Impaired Social Functioning

Multiple domains of knowledge intersect in the study of children with NLD. Among these are the domain of neuropsychological functioning, which I examined in Part I; the domain of social relationships, with which I deal in this part; and the domain of subjective experience, which I address in Part III.

The domain of social relationships, as contrasted with the domain of neuropsychological functions, requires that we shift our focus from the descriptive to the social perspective. In Chapter 3, it was possible to talk about neuropsychological deficits as decontextualized limitations, seemingly isolated symptoms reflective of underlying brain dysfunctions. Social behaviors contextualize these functions, placing them within the interchanges that occur with other people. As social beings, we cannot exist without others; our lives can have no meaning without others. Our endowment, in part, not only shapes our sense of self, but is also shaped by our responses to others and others' responses to us. We are all situated in contexts that contribute to how we develop, who we are, and what we become. The communities in which we are raised, in part, define the meanings of our experiences.

Caregivers convey to each child a view of the world, a shared vision of the reality to which the child is exposed. And, just as the context lends an imprint to the child's experiences, the child, in turn, interprets those experiences, through the lens of his or her neuropsychological strengths and weaknesses. The child is neither a *tabula rasa* upon whom experiences are inscribed nor entirely the creator of the reality to which he or she is exposed. Each contributes its share to the child's final vision. To understand fully the influences of context on the developing child, we must avoid the extremes of both social constructivism and naive realism. The child's reality is neither totally constructed by the context, nor is it unalloyed by what the child contributes to it. Whereas the context contributes a worldview through a set of beliefs or biases and prejudices, the child brings to his or her world an interpretation that shapes the resulting vision of reality.

Numerous hypotheses have been offered to explain the presence of social—emotional problems in children with learning disabilities (Elksnin & Elksnin, 2004). From a social perspective, these impairments may include deficits in reciprocal social interaction with others, social communication, and affect processing. When we discuss reciprocal social interactions we address the type of relationship a person has with another. Social communication deals with the medium through which relationships are conducted. Whereas affect processing adds the dimension of feelings that pervade all social intercourse. From a developmental perspective, factors such as temperamental traits, the quality of the child's attachment, and the personality traits that result from patterns of interaction with significant caregivers, contribute to the final path (i.e., the course that leads to the phenotype or sense of self) the child takes and the overt behaviors that the child displays. Comorbid psychiatric disorders may also confound any symptoms that the child presents.

Social Cognition and NLD

Social cognitive theory is the discipline that attempts to understand the relationship between social development and cognitive development. Social cognition is "the ability to construct representations of the relations between oneself and others, and to use those representations flexibly to guide social behavior" (Pinkham, Penn, Perkins, & Lieberman, 2003, p. 816). Bryan (1990) stated: "Social cognition attempts to understand the linkages between social development and cognitive development, and between social behavior and social cognition. It involves perspective taking, moral development, social problem solving, self-efficacy, and communicative competence" (p. 285).

The field of social cognition is distributed among several disciplines, including social psychology, developmental psychology, animal and primate studies, and the emerging field of cognitive neuroscience. Each of these gives primacy to particular domains of social functioning. From social psychology has emerged an interest in affects and motivation that was previously absent in those studies (Kunda, 2000). Piaget and Vygotsky dominated the field of developmental psychology for many years (Hala, 1997). With recent development in attachment theory, and the place of affects in development, which they did not address, their contributions are less influential. Among psychoanalysts, Greenspan (1979; 1989a) attempted to integrate Piaget's cognitive psychology and ego psychology. I discuss his contribution in chapter 6. In the fields of anthropology and ethology, studies of nonhuman primates have focused on language acquisition, imitation, and even empathy. Lastly, cognitive neuroscience has explored the neurobiological underpinnings of social behaviors (Gazzaniga, Ivry, & Magnun, 2002).

Theories of social cognition provide a framework within which to examine the social and emotional functioning of children with NLD. Using this framework, I discuss impairments in the domains of (1) *social functioning*, which allows us to look at the children's reciprocal social interaction, (2) *social communication*, which permit the exploration of the use of verbal and nonverbal language as the source of some of the children's social difficulties, and (3) *emotional functioning*, which provides insight into the children's capacity for *affect perception and processing*. The choice of these domains is based on the extensive literature on autism and Asperger's disorder, and in part follows Wing's (1988) suggestion of a triad of impairments that characterize the disturbances of children within the autistic spectrum. The triad includes impairments in social interaction, communication, and imagination (Wing, 1991, p. 118). I have substituted emotional functioning for imagination in part because discussing the capacity for fantasy and imagination, although clinically relevant, is elusive, and also because I consider emotional functioning to be pivotal to understanding human motivation. In this chapter I begin with a discussion of the children's reciprocal social interactions as reflective of their level of social functioning. A description of the development of theory of mind, which is a critical component to social competence, follows that discussion. First let us look at the data.

Clinical Presentation: The Social Profile

The following profile describes some of the major areas of social difficulties experienced by children with NLD in greater detail than the descriptions given in Chapter 2.

Some children appear out of step with those around them; they lack the ease and fluidity in social discourse that we associate with social competence. At times, they make people anxious or uncomfortable, and they appear to have little awareness of the impact they have on others. Some children appear to be *socially disconnected*; they are out of touch with what goes on around them. In a group, they respond by withdrawing into silence, or, if they attempt to engage others, their comments reflect little understanding of the subtleties of the groups interactions.

His junior kindergarten teacher noted that Jason tended to withdraw from peer interactions. In senior kindergarten he continued to experience significant difficulty interacting with the other children in his class. He avoided social engagement, had difficulty initiating and maintaining conversations, was unresponsive to others when spoken to, made comments unrelated to the topic of conversation, and did not grasp the impact of his behavior on others—all of which resulted in his rejection and subsequent isolation of himself, preferring to be alone. He did not engage in the creation of games, the acting out of stories, or fantasy play. His teacher noted that during a play, he spoke as if he were "talking to a wall" rather than to a person. She described his verbal expressions as declarative rather than reciprocal. For example, he frequently attempts to play with his younger sister; however, this "play" usually involves Jason stating directions or giving commands rather than engaging her in dialogue and interpersonal negotiations. He appears to be unaware of the other child's feelings or experience. His mother noted that he tends to be a social loner, preferring to sit and watch group activities rather than participate in them.

Some children appear to be *socially clumsy* or inept at making social contact. Their efforts to initiate conversation are either overly conventional or superficial, leading people to have little interest in interacting with them.

Sam, at age 9½, is socially awkward, inappropriate, and maladroit. He applies learned rules of behavior mechanically, asks overly personal questions, or makes inappropriate or irrelevant comments that make others uncomfortable. He does not pick up or use the norms of social interactions that others use, and he interprets social situations idiosyncratically or in an overly personalized way. At times, he is offensive, intrusive, or hurtful in his comments or behaviors, without awareness of the impact he is having on others.

Sometimes these children's odd behavior is attributed to *social immaturity* by people who may believe that the children were not raised to conform to the norms of children their age or were overindulged by their caregivers.

Doug, a third grader, relies on socially immature ways of problem solving. He will tattle on other children instead of working out conflicts with them. He needs more frequent reassurance than other children his age, seeks approval constantly, is clingy and dependent, frequently needs affection, and requires structure typical of children younger than he. His second-grade teacher was concerned about his sucking his thumb and picking his nose in class. At times he still engages in parallel play and needs to be guided to show more interactive play. He prefers not to be alone at home and, instead, stays near his parents. Additionally, he sleeps in their bed frequently, stating that it is not fair that they get to sleep together but that he has to sleep alone. He does appear to enjoy interacting with younger children, a tendency that the teacher attributes to his social immaturity.

Some children *behave inappropriately*, leading others to think that they do not realize that their behavior is socially unacceptable. They embarrass those around them or alienate peers by violating implicit rules of conduct.

Dan, age 10, asks inappropriate questions of other children in a clear attempt to obtain information that others might pick up intuitively. He has difficulty in perspective taking, which he displays by making bragging comments to peers without apparent awareness of their reactions. He also engages in behaviors that serve to distract and irritate his classroom peers, such as making noises that tend to escalate when his classmates complain. Dan does not easily discern social rules simply by being in social situations, and he is therefore at risk of making comments or displaying behaviors that seem irrelevant or unrelated, at best, or inappropriate, at worst, which results in other children teasing or embarrassing him. His mother indicated concern that Dan tends to commit "social blunders," for example, dancing without inhibition at a sports event in a manner that most children his age would feel embarrassed to do in public. For a child his age, Dan does not accurately judge the appropriateness of a given behavior and does not adapt his behavior based on the cues from his peers. His father states: "It is as if he doesn't know how to be a kid." He may laugh too long or too loudly at a joke. Sometimes even his friends become frustrated with him, the good news is that most of the children in his classroom are used to, and tolerant of, his idiosyncrasies. He cries often, especially in school, and does not cope well when he loses or when he feels that others are teasing him.

Parents often complain that their child's behavior is *socially dysfunctional*. The child may be *argumentative*, making it difficult for the family to function in daily tasks. Every request is met with opposition; every attempt at getting the child to conform to the simplest expectation is met with resistance. Some children can be so *socially disruptive* that families find themselves in constant chaos as they respond to crises that require a great deal of time and attention. Caregivers must deal with frequent meltdowns that appear to be triggered by simple requests; they are often baffled by the unpredictable nature of the child's eruptions.

Charlie, a second grader, is extremely bright but displays disruptive behavior with some aggressiveness. He exhibited severe tantrums from the time he was 18 months until he was 3 years old. After feeling bewildered or disappointed, he would be overtaken by frustration and lash out physically. Charlie's behavioral difficulties (i.e., aggressive outbursts with other children, tantrums, and overall irritability) prompted his placement in a self-contained classroom for children with behavioral and learning difficulties (BD/LD) during his second-grade year.

Charlie's explosions tend to occur when he is interacting with peers or at school. Typically, he yells and cries, occasionally throwing things. During one of these episodes, he had to be carried out of the classroom by the school maintenance person. In a recent event, which took place on the summer camp bus, he became physically aggressive with another child, who had reportedly taken a special rock from him. Charlie became very upset and apparently had to be restrained by the bus driver. His teacher reported that he engages her in power struggles and projects blame for his own acts onto others.

Children with NLD have great difficulty establishing *peer relationships* and *friendships*, although they yearn for both. Some children may find a child who is willing to accept them and is not troubled by their outlandish behaviors. However, many of these children, although wishing desperately to a have a friend, unwittingly alienate other children by their behaviors.

During kindergarten, Laura began to recognize that other children with whom she wanted to play did not consistently want to play with her. Her mother reported that this was the first time that Laura began to experience feeling rejected and isolated from her peers, as a result of her aggressive and impulsive behaviors. Laura, who is now in fourth grade, has a history of difficulty with initiating and maintaining peer relationships, and she does not understand what is expected of her in peer-related social situations. This lack of understanding interferes with her ability to interact appropriately with her peers, and her inappropriate behaviors elicit negative responses. She tends to interrupt others quite frequently and tends to exhibit demanding behavior in her interactions with others. Laura frequently becomes "silly" when she is interacting with others, and this silliness rapidly escalates to a level that feels "out of control" to those around her. She also tends to appear uncomfortable if she is not "in complete control" of a game or conversation with her peers. She often misinterprets the intent of other children, as they attempt to interact playfully with her, as ag-

gressive or threatening. In addition, she engages in behaviors that distract and irritate her classroom peers, such as making noises that tend to escalate when her classmates complain. Engaging competitively with the boys, Laura is often unable to negotiate typical peer conflicts without resorting to physical aggression. She wants to "play by her own rules" and does not appear to be able to interact in a reciprocal manner with peers. Instead, her interactions tend to end rapidly in a conflict between her and the other child or children. She appears to be unaware of others' feelings or experiences and is not able to engage in an appropriate way without an adult present to mediate the interactions. Laura has no close friendships, has difficulty forming and keeping any positive peer relationships, is bossy, aggressive, and defensive, relies on rules in her interactions with others, relates better one-to-one than in groups of peers, and has trouble fitting in with groups of children.

Perhaps the cruelest aspect of the lives of children with NLD is the way in which other children *reject* and *tease* them. They often appear to be easy targets for ridicule and are unable to protect themselves from bullies. They do not seem to have the resources to respond to or develop alliances with others who might come to their rescue.

Jeff, now in second grade, was teased so badly by other students that the teachers were unable to manage the situation. He has been the target of peer ridicule from an early age; this ridicule played a central role in his removal from his original first-grade class. He continues to experience some ridicule and ostracism by his peers and reports that other children bully him. When he is teased and scapegoated, he gets unfairly blamed for things, which prompts him to further provocative remarks and actions. It is likely that some children pick on Jeff simply because they perceived him as different. His older brother provokes him repeatedly and intensely, and Jeff becomes tearful and furious when discussing this situation. He feels humiliation and frustration.

In summary, these children's social interactions are fraught with difficulties. Often, their inability to process social cues dates back to their earlier years and compounds their difficulties as social demands increase and their lack of experience adds to their ineptness and clumsiness.

Reciprocal Social Interaction

Reciprocal social interactions require social competence and social skills. Social competence is analogous to literacy: children who are literate are fluent in reading and writing; children who are socially competent are fluent in the elements of social discourse and have the social skills necessary to relate effectively. The domain of social skills encompasses communicative competence, which includes nonverbal communication skills and pragmatic language verbal skills. These skills are discrete proficiencies that permit a person to be successful in interactions with others. Social competence also involves the ability to (1) initiate a conversation; (2) follow conventional scripts during discourse; (3) empathize with others; (4) match others' social skills to the demands of particular situations; (5) conceptualize alternative scenarios; (6) anticipate possible developments; and (7) use cause-and-effect reasoning.

To possess social skills presumes that the person is competent in verbal and nonverbal expression, capable of accurately assessing the intentions behind the other person's message, and has the executive know-how to select and enact an appropriate response. The basic hypothesis is that nonverbal behavior represents a social skill that socially competent people use in their everyday interactions. People who are most effective in their social interactions are successful at decoding the nonverbal behavior of others and also are able to express previously encoded nonverbal information in a manner that others can understand. Those who are socially deficient might be said to suffer from a lack of nonverbal encoding and decoding skills (Feldman, Philoppot, & Custrini, 1991). Children with NLD are impaired in this domain of behavior.

Theory of Mind

The term *theory of mind* refers to the ability of typically developing children to attribute mental states, such as desires, beliefs, and intentions, to themselves and others as a way of making sense of and predicting the behavior of others (Tager-Flusberg & Baron-Cohen, 1993). The ability entails understanding that other people's behaviors are intentional or purposive, that a desire either to express their state of mind or to communicate with others motivates them. A pathological deficit in theory of mind abilities is believed to underlie autism. Autistic children have no difficulty understanding causal sequences, or even social routines and interactions, but they show significant impairment when asked to understand intentional tasks. Investigators who study autism consider this construct critical to understanding that disorder. (Baron-Cohen, 1997; Baron-Cohen, Tager-Flusberg & Cohen, 1993; Frith, 1989a, 1989b; Happe, 1993; Tager-Flusberg & Baron-Cohen, 1993).

Developing a theory of mind is central to social competence. The central question for us revolves around whether some of the features we encounter in the social presentation of children with NLD are due to the underdevelopment of, or deficits in, their theory of mind. A developed theory of mind creates the foundation for social competence. With that foundation firmly in place, a child may then be able to acquire the fundamentals of appropriate social discourse and the concomitant social skills. Social skills are similar to the pragmatic aspect of language. For successful discourse to occur, social skills must be grounded in the comprehension of how people interact and in the intentions behind their overt communications.

The false-belief test is a task devised to determine whether a child has achieved the capacity for a theory of mind. The examiner conducts the test with the child in the presence of an observer. First the examiner asks the child to guess how the observer would respond to a "game." In the presence of the child and the observer, the examiner places an object, such as a candy bar, in one of two identical covered boxes. The examiner then asks the observer to leave the room, whereupon he or she removes the candy bar from one box and places it in the other. The observer is then asked to return to the room, and the child is asked to guess which of the two boxes the observer would think contains the candy bar. A child who has a developed theory of mind will comprehend that the observer does not know of the deception and will correctly state that he or she thinks the observer will think it is still in the original box. Children who do not have a theory of mind will maintain that the observer will believe that it is in the box into which it was transferred.

The development of a theory of mind occurs through a set of developmental stages or phases (for a more detailed description of these phases, see Chapter 7; see Baron-Cohen, 1993; Baron-Cohen & Tager-Flusberg, 1993). In the first phase infants are able to attend to others as separate entities and can differentiate personal-human causation from physical-mechanical causation. In the second phase babies are able to understand that others can gaze at, try to reach for, and emotionally react to real-world objects and actions. This phase of development provides evidence that the infant understands that others have the subjective capacity to perceive, want, and emotionally experience objects. In the third phase, 2-year-olds understand that others have *desires* for things, but they do not yet understand that others can have beliefs. A child can have a simple desire, such as the wish to have another child's toy, but need not have the ability to infer that the other child has beliefs. A belief, in this context, is a mental state that a person possesses that is private, that is, it is inaccessible to others (e.g., a child may believe "mom is mad at me," but has no way of knowing whether that is the case (Tomasello, 1999; Wellman, 1993).

Three-year-olds struggle with the notion that others have *false belief*, but have little trouble with understanding *false* or *unfulfilled desires* (e.g.,

"Jack says he wants my truck"; they also understand that "Jack doesn't really want it—he just doesn't want *me* to have it!") but they do not realize that "Jack is planning to take my truck when I am not looking." By the age of 4 they have developed the capacity for mental attribution; that is, they are able to understand that others have desires, beliefs, and intentions/motives that guide their actions. These capacities allow the child to make *first-order representations*: the ability to form a mental representation of the state of another person's mind (e.g., "Mommy is mad").

Two related capacities that co-occur at the time the child develops a theory of mind are the capacities for *deception* and *pretense*—that is, the ability to engage in imaginative play. Research indicates that children with autism suffer from a deficit in both these capacities. (Baron-Cohen, 1993; 1997; Sodian & Frith, 1993). Understanding deception involves understanding that I can have a thought that you cannot access. The capacity to deceive or to know that someone is lying is an interesting case of a theory of mind. To lie entails knowing that the other person cannot know what you know. It is indicative of your assurance that the other person cannot know what is in your mind. Consequently, lying involves knowing that you have a mind that is private and cannot be "read" by others.

Pretend play involves knowing that something imaginary can stand for something that might be real. It provides evidence of the child's capacity to segregate the contents of his or her mind from external reality. The fact that a child can share imaginary scenarios with other children, knowing that they also share the same belief in the imaginary scenario as she does and that the discourse is not about reality, is indicative of the capacity for a theory of mind. For Pennington (1991) the representations made possible by first-order representations link the child's development of theory of mind to symbolic play. Now the child can decouple primary, veridical representations from their object referents so that the representations can be used in pretense (e.g., a wooden block becomes a car). A first-order representation can take the form of "I think she is thinking about my toy." The presence of this capacity indicates that the child has a theory of mind. The capacity for *second-order representations* a higher order of cognition, does not appear to develop until the age of 7. It takes the form of "I think she thinks he is thinking of taking my toy!"

Children with autism do not understand how physical objects differ from thoughts about objects. Given a list of words that refer to mental states, such as *think, know, imagine*, they are unable to distinguish these from words with concrete pictorial referents; for example, they cannot see that there is a difference between saying "he believes in Santa Claus" and saying "he has a new GameBoy." Although they can understand simple causes of emotion, they have difficulty understanding more complex causes of emotion (e.g., they can understand "he is sad because he lost his blanky" but cannot understand "she is disappointed because she did not get a part in the school play" (Baron-Cohen & Swettenham, 1997). Not all children with autism fail the false-belief test, 20–30% pass the test, although they are unable to explain their observations in terms of mental states. Those who pass have a minimum verbal mental age of 5 years, 6 months and a minimum chronological age of 11 years, 6 months (Leslie & Roth 1993). Baron-Cohen introduced the term "mindblindness" to characterize the absence of a theory of mind in children with autism (Baron-Cohen, 1997).

One other cognitive deficit emerges as important: Children with autism fail tests of executive function. There seems little doubt that there is an executive dysfunction in autism. However, it is likely that the theory of mind capacity is not reducible to executive function and that the latter co-occurs with theory of mind deficits because they probably share the same frontal regions of the brain (Baron-Cohen & Swettenham, 1997). Frith and Frith (2001) stated, "Poor performance on mentalizing tasks [such as false-belief tasks] is not simply a consequence of executive function problems" (p. 153).

CHILDREN WITH NLD

In the absence of data from the administration of such tests as the false-belief task to children with NLD, we must rely on our clinical data to infer whether they are capable of succeeding in such tasks; that is, that they have the capacity for a theory of mind. The data cited above indicate that children with NLD (1) have difficulties with reciprocal interchanges, (2) are socially immature, (3) behave inappropriately, (4) are argumentative and socially disruptive, (5) have difficulty maintaining friendships, and (6) are often rejected by their peers. It is significant that, in general, these children have a desire for friends and relationships with others—behaviors that do not suggest difficulties with theory of mind functioning. However, children with NLD do lack social competence, social skills, and seem unable to comprehend and follow the rules for appropriate social conduct. Yet they are capable of deception and imaginative play. In fact, much of the conflict between these children and their caregivers centers on the children not revealing to their parents that they have homework or that they failed to turn in their work. Often, a desire to avoid punishment or the caregiver's disapproval motivates these deceptions.

In regard to understanding that others have beliefs and intentions, the clinical data suggest that they do not have much difficulty with this type of cognition. For example, a 14-year-old girl, who was diagnosed with an

NLD but refused to accept the diagnosis, insisted that her mother needed to believe that she had the disorder because her mother felt guilty that she had not done a good job raising her. The mother could excuse her conduct by claiming that the girl had this illness, when, in fact, the child insisted that it was her mother who had the disorder. The girl was accurate in her observation that her mother did indeed appear to have an NLD.

A question arises as to why these children, who are often teased and taunted mercilessly, appear incapable of defending themselves against those assaults. At the simplest level of analysis, teasing involves identifying a vulnerability in another and using the knowledge of that vulnerability to hurt or embarrass the person. Socially competent children have no difficulty parrying such attacks either by dismissing them as idiotic or by counterattacking the perpetrators. One hypothesis as to why children with NLD appear helpless to defend themselves is that they are unable to read the intention of the perpetrator; they take literally what others say about them and consequently can find no response to the attack. This hypothesis suggests a theory of mind deficit that does not allow them to process the intentions of perpetrator. However, a different explanation is available that does not necessitate this conclusion.

Don, age 11, complained bitterly to his therapist that kids continually teased him. When asked what they said, he reported that they accused him of being cruel and sadistic to his beloved cat. They said he enjoyed hurting his pet or that he had set fire to his cat's tail, none of which was true. His response was to protest loudly that he was not that kind of person and would never do such things to his pet. However, his reaction only inflamed the other kids, inciting them to escalate their teasing. Don's responses were to no avail in stopping the teasing. In this instance, what appears as a deficit in a theory of mind may be secondary to the child's concrete interpretation of the verbal exchanges. Don could not get beyond the literal meaning of what his peers said; he could not see through their remarks to discern their motives. Once these motives were pointed out to him, he was able to take what the other kids said as a "joke" and respond with his own brand of humor. The problem lay with his pragmatic language skills rather than with the absence of a theory of mind. Children with NLD do have the capacity for second-order mental representation but may not have the pragmatic language skills to understand what is being asked of them. Some of the research on the neurobiology of theory of mind cited below lends support to this interpretation of the children's responses.

Regarding pretend or imaginative play, the anecdotal clinical data indicate that children with NLD are quite capable of dealing with metarepresentations of reality. A 10-year-old boy with whom I worked in psychotherapy reported having multiple imaginary companions with whom he played a rather poignant game. They were part of an "intelligence agency" whose task was to decode the messages from enemy sources. All messages received had to be vetted either through him or one of his companions. After engaging in this game with him for some weeks, it became evident that he was so fearful of misunderstanding other people's communications that he used his imaginary companions as a strategy to make sure he understood what others were saying. As I recognized with him the role of his NLD in the social difficulties he was having, he became less reliant on that strategy and more focused on obtaining clues as to what others were communicating.

Regarding the relationship between executive function deficits and the lack of a theory of mind: Because there are no firmly established relationships between the two functions, we cannot conclude that children with NLD who have executive function difficulties also have deficits in their theory of mind. The latter is dissociable from the former.

NEUROBIOLOGY OF THEORY OF MIND

Recent studies provide evidence that brain systems subserve the functions that a theory of mind performs. One study concludes: "[A] language-based Theory of Mind task activated distributed brain regions that are important for representing mental states of the self and others, retrieving memory of personal experiences, and coordinating and monitoring the overall performance of the task. The activations in the medial frontal cortex replicate findings in previous Theory of Mind studies" (Calarge, Andreason, & O'Leary 2003, p. 1954). Frith and Frith (2001) discussed the ability to "mentalize," which they consider to be a component of social intelligence that underlies theory of mind functioning. Mentalizing requires the capacity to develop representations of actions, understanding the goals implicit in those actions, and the intentions behind them. Specific brain systems—the medial prefrontal cortex and the posterior superior temporal sulcus—subserve this capacity.

The investigators in a study by Siegel and colleagues (Siegal, Carrington, & Radel 1996) compared a sample of adults with right hemisphere damage with patients who had left hemisphere damage on a theory of mind task and found that those with right hemisphere damage performed more poorly on the false-belief test than those with left hemisphere damage. However, when the investigators provided a verbal explanation that clarified what they were asking, almost all the subjects with right hemisphere damage gave the correct response. In their discussion of the results, the investigators speculated that the reason for the initial failure of subjects with right hemisphere damage was their problem with pragmatic language, also a right hemisphere function. Once those language difficulties were bypassed, they were able to give the correct responses. A second confounding element concerned the test, which, by its very nature, involves visual–spatial processing—a function affected by right hemisphere damage. The investigators, however, felt that, had that been a factor, the subjects would not have been able to give the correct response after receiving the verbal explanation.

The significance of this study for children with NLD is that it touches on the issue of the role of language and visual–spatial processing in their social difficulties. The findings suggest that not passing the false-belief test would not necessarily indicate an absence of theory of mind abilities. In addition, the findings suggest that if they could compensate for their difficulties with "verbal mediation" (a technique used with children with NLD to help them compensate for their deficits in nonlinguistic perception)—that is, through the translation of the visual–spatial tasks into verbal language—then they would have no difficulty understanding that others have intentions and beliefs and would be able to negotiate social situations that were once difficult. On the negative side, even when they succeed in translating verbally the situations they confront, they may still not know which rules apply to which situations, and consequently may not perform as well as expected in life situations.

In a more recent study, Siegal and a colleague (Siegal & Varley, 2002) attempted to answer some of the questions raised by the first study and found that grammatical language problems and executive function difficulties are dissociable from the deficits in theory of mind functioning. Whereas widely distributed neural systems support the functions that undergird theory of mind tasks, the core components that are compromised are in the amygdala. They stated: "The integrity of the circuitry of the amygdala system is a necessary, but not sufficient, condition to Theory of Mind, which requires support from co-opted systems for its emergence" (p. 468). The coopted systems include the language and the executive function systems. Furthermore, they conclude that an essential element in the development of a theory of mind is the scaffolding that occurs developmentally through conversations with significant others. These conversations perform a critical function in the emergence of a theory of mind.

How do these findings apply to the difficulties experienced by children with NLD? Given the children's verbal abilities and the fact that adults typically engage these children in conversation early on, it would appear that such conversations might facilitate the emergence of theory of mind abilities. A more likely candidate for the social deficit, in addition to the language problems, would be the dysfunction in the amygdala, which manifests in the children's difficulties in affect processing.

Finally, in support of this position, Brothers and King (1992) suggested that theory of mind abilities involve more than pure "cold" cognitive processing. The representation of another's mind includes a value that the agent attaches to the person whose intentions are being "read." That is to say, we have feelings about the person to whom we attribute intentions; we do not simply evaluate those intentions cognitively. The false-belief task does not include this complex component and consequently may be excluding an important comfounding factor in the assessment of the presence or absence of theory of mind abilities.

Conclusion

The data indicate that children with NLD have mild to moderately severe difficulties in reciprocal social interactions. However, their difficulties do not rise to the level of severity of children with Asperger's disorder or high-functioning autism; neither do they approach the level of severity of children with severe psychiatric disorders, such as schizophrenia or borderline personality disorders. For the most part, these children appear to retreat into isolation as a result of the responses they receive from others. This withdrawal behavior leads me to believe that, at some level, they are aware of the extent of their social dysfunction but feel unable to correct or remediate their behaviors.

The specific causes of these social dysfunctions are probably multiple. In part, the social dysfunctions are due to a history of social imperception; in part, they may be due to the progressive lack of experience, and as they get older, an increased demand for more sophisticated responses to the situations they encounter. In part, they may be due to brain-based difficulties in processing nonverbal and paralinguistic aspects of communication.

We encounter several problems in our attempt to apply what we have learned about theory of mind abilities to these children's social dysfunctions. First, the absence of data as to whether the children would pass the false-belief test leaves us to speculate only as to whether a deficit in theory of mind functioning is a contributing factor. It is my impression that if a sample of these children failed the test, the result would be due to other causes than the absence of a theory of mind. The children's difficulties with pragmatic language may have interfered with their understanding of the questions they were asked. Their abilities to use deception and imaginative play support the proposition that have the capacity for theory of mind functioning.

Second, *theory of mind* is a cognitive construct that does not provide for a sufficient appreciation of the role of affects in human interchanges. Affects and emotions color every aspect of those interchanges, providing the fuel that propels actions and motives. Neglecting the motives behind the attribution of others' beliefs or intentions diminishes our understanding of the meaning and content of the actions being investigated. Although Brothers (1989) proposes a view of theory of mind functioning that includes affective functioning, no other research has followed her suggestion.

Another facet of this issue is related to the manner in which we apprehend or intuit others' internal states. Some would argue that we do not process those motives or meanings on a purely cognitively level; rather, we arrive at an understanding of others' internal states through the use of empathy. Empathy is defined as vicarious introspection (Kohut, 1959); it is a tool with which we apprehend the thoughts, beliefs, desires, and feelings of others. Clearly, the capacity for theory of mind functioning is closely related to the capacity for empathy. A child who has no theory of mind abilities would have difficulty feeling empathy for another's internal state. The converse may not necessarily be true, however. That is, someone who has difficulty being empathic with others may have theory of mind abilities but be incapable of apprehending others' emotional states. These observations have critical importance for our understanding of children with NLD and for the types of interventions we use in treatment or remediation of their deficits.

Third, by its very nature, the false-belief test leads to a result that is categorical rather than dimensional; that is, it leads to a conclusion that the child either has or does not have a theory of mind, precluding the possibility that there may be gradations in the extent to which we can understand others' intentions and beliefs. It is possible to have a partial or incomplete understanding of another's motives; it is also possible to be deceived by people who conceal their intentions. Some people are more credulous and unsophisticated than others; a person who appears believable may "take them in" more easily. We also tend to endow people in authority with qualities that make them believable. Such phenomena are not as indicative of deficiencies in people's theory of mind abilities as they are of the emotional need people have to place their trust in those on whom they depend. By subtracting those factors from an assessment of theory of mind functioning, we diminish its value as a construct and concretize its presence or absence. In Chapter 8, I suggest that the broader construct of "mindsharing" can overcome these deficiencies.

Lastly, current research into the neurobiology of theory of mind abilities raises question as to the correctness of the hypothesis that right hemisphere functions are exclusively implicated in the processing of the false-belief task. The results of some studies point to a set of widely distributed systems, including the amygdala, as involved in the processing of elements of that task.

5

Impaired Social Communication

As we turn to the domain of social communication from the domain of reciprocal social interaction, we enter a world where communicative competence is essential for successful social intercourse. This world is not only verbal but nonverbal and emotional as well. Because nonverbal communication is essential to successful social discourse, gaining a clear understanding of what we mean when we speak of nonverbal communication provides a direction through the specific areas of difficulty experienced by children with NLD.

Social communication deals with the medium (i.e., verbal and nonverbal language) through which relationships are conducted, whereas reciprocal social interactions deal with the way in which people relate to one another (i.e., feel attached to, intimate with, or disconnected from, others). Through language, whether verbal or nonverbal, we engage in what I call a form of "mindsharing" (discussed at length in Chapter 8). Mindsharing is the ability to "be with" another through verbal and nonverbal communication. Much as we share in others' emotional experiences through empathy, we enter into another's world through language. Theory-of-mind abilities involve a form of mindsharing, through which people are able to understand each other.

All experience is encoded directly into a sign system, a language, from which it is inseparable. We see, hear, smell, taste, feel, and through each of these senses, we translate our experiences into signs that have meanings for us. We use signs to give expression to our feelings, thoughts, fantasies, and dreams. Volosinov states: "There is no such thing as experience outside of embodiment in signs" (as quoted in Innis, 1985, p. 52).

Among many of the obstacles that can interfere with the establishment of meaningful relationships and social discourse with others are the failures in social communication. Children with NLD are particularly at risk of not achieving the former because of difficulties in the latter domain. We have seen that decoding nonverbal communication as a language system is particularly challenging to children with NLD. Three levels of analysis are involved in this discussion of social communication. 1) The receptive level in which decoding social signs is critical to understanding discourse. 2) The level of the comprehension of the meaning of those signs, which is even more critical for successful interactions to occur. And, 3) the expressive level in which the person draws from past experience to communicate with others. The reception and processing of social signs are intertwined with one another and at times inseparable from one another. They can only be discussed separately to clarify their roles in any given set of interactions. The difficulties involved in discussing the expressive level is that it is clinically challenging to tease out the source of the problems in expression and identify whether they are due to poor decoding or to impaired processing of social cues. I beg reader's indulgence if at times two or more of these levels are conflated in my discussion.

As we will see in Chapter 6, all human discourse is also embedded in the affective states of the interlocutors. In fact, most nonverbal communications convey affective messages through channels that are different from those that verbal language utilizes. Emotions are therefore central to our understanding of the social problems that children with NLD encounter in attempting to engage in dialogue with others. As Mesulam (2000) pointed out, the right hemisphere subserves both nonverbal communication and emotion perception. It becomes evident that any theory of NLD that does not take into consideration this aspect of pragmatic language will be incomplete (see Levin, 1991).

Clinical Presentation: NLD and Nonverbal Signs

For those children with NLD who are unable to process nonlinguistic perceptual information, such as visual–perceptual or visual–spatial information, the domain of nonverbal communication is like a foreign language. In fact, it is more like having dyslexia (Badian, 1986) in that the deficits lie in the inability to combine visual stimuli with visual percepts. Because the most common iconic and indexical signs require visual processing, the children's impairment interferes with their ability to decode those signs and understand their meanings. Their difficulties lie at the receptive level of decoding social signs. (See Noth [1990, pp. 387–420] for an informative discussion of nonverbal communication.)

As stated earlier, the relationship between the children's receptive and expressive problems in the domain of nonverbal signs is unclear. It may be that their failure to read adequately such signs interferes with their ability to make use of the signs expressively. It may also be that different factors are at work that produce their expressive difficulties.

RECEPTIVE LEVEL

At the receptive level, decoding gestures, gaze, facial expressions, body language and proximics requires visual or visual–spatial processing. One set of errors the children make occurs at the morphemic level of decoding; that is, they are unable to read the specific sign (e.g., gesture, vocal intonation). Decoding messages at the morphemic level is essential to the perception of social nuances. Missing those nuances can lead to difficulty.

Alex, who is 10½ years old, is a poor interpreter of social situations. He has difficulty reading social nuances and does not understand what is expected of him in peer-related social situations. These difficulties interfere with his ability to interact appropriately with his peers. He has trouble integrating important aspects of situations, or he focuses on details that are less relevant, thereby missing the main point. Because he tends to overgeneralize or misapply rules derived from dissimilar situations, his interpretations are either inaccurate or overpersonalized. His reaction to being teased by others is to respond in a hostile or defensive manner. His parents reported several incidents in which he was teased by other children and/or adults. Even when engaged in an affectionate manner in such interchanges, his response is typically to feel hurt and angry.

Of all the means through which people communicate nonverbally, facial signals are probably the most extensively studied. Tomkin's (1962, 1963) work on the relationship between facial expression and the eight categorical affects is well known. As we will see, Ekman (2001) and Izard (1991, 1997) undertook cross-cultural studies to determine the extent to which emotional expression was determined by nature or by culture. They determined that although there are physiological determinants to emotional expression through facial features, these are capable of extensive modification by cultural display rules. In addition, Noth (1990) noted that "the permanent features of the face contain essential indices for the identification of a person; they are an index of a person's identity. They

also indicate age, sex, or ethnic or family origin. They are popularly believed to correlate with a person's character" (p. 402).

At the expressive level, the problems of children with NLD are compounded by the fact that their visual deficits interfere with the basic capacity to imitate acceptable social behaviors. Here, too, the children often
maintain a blank facial expression, which makes it difficult for others to
read what they are trying to convey. At times, this absence of expression is
misinterpreted as disinterest or boredom. Because conventions for social
interactions are culturally determined and no formal instruction is given
as to their proper usage, children must pick up these conventions through
their nonverbal interactions with their caregivers. Not only is the avenue
of imitation not open to children with NLD, but they fail to be formally
initiated into such sign usage. Their difficulties become evident in the
pragmatic area when dialoguing with others.

*Henry, an 8½-year-old, has both receptive and expressive problems. In addition
to his not being able to read others' facial expressions, his facial expressions are
limited, strained, grimaced, muted, neutral, or flat; they do not reflect his emotional experience, are insufficiently communicative, do not convey underlying
emotions (or may even suggest contrary emotions than those felt), are not well-
modulated, and come across as awkward, stilted, exaggerated, or out of proportion to the situation.*

Gestures

Gestures are bodily communications accomplished through moving the
hands, arms, or head. They often accompany speech as a means of displaying emotions or for emphasis. Children with NLD appear stiff and constricted in the use of their hands and body for communicative purposes.

*Josh, a fifth grader, uses few bodily or hand gestures. When he does use them,
they may be muted or neutral or do not match his verbal output; for example,
he nods head to indicate "yes" but says "no." His gestures are insufficiently communicative and show little emotion; or, if they do show emotion, they seem awkward or stilted, exaggerated or out of proportion to the situation.*

Gaze

Gaze is the eye-to-eye contact we make during discourse or in relating to
one another. Developmentally, we regard the infant's gaze into its mother's
eyes to be one of the precious moments of motherhood. Although there are

cultural differences regarding the appropriateness of maintaining eye contact, in Western societies we tend to consider it normative to monitor the person with whom we are speaking through periodic eye contact. One of the characteristics of the expression of shame is the aversion of eye contact; on the other hand, a piercing gaze is regarded as rude or hostile. Typically, children with NLD seem to avoid making eye contact, giving the frustrating impression that they are not paying attention to those who are addressing them. If asked directly what they heard, however, they can repeat every word. Some were taught to look at people with whom they are conversing; the result is that they will do so, but their gaze is piercing or unnatural.

Fred, age 11, generally averts his gaze and makes insufficient use of eye contact or does not accommodate to others' eye contact in conversation. His eye contact is fleeting, fluctuating, variable, minimal, inconsistent, or gaze-like.

Prosody
Prosody refers to the intonation used while speaking; some people refer to it as *paralanguage*. It includes the major ways in which emotions are expressed in language: via pitch, speed, rhythm, pauses, emphasis, and loudness. It serves functions such as providing emphasis in making a point. Children with NLD often speak with little inflection or in a flat monotone. At times they speak so softly that they can barely be heard, or too loudly, unaware of the changes in their tone of voice.

At 8 years of age, Ray's tone of voice is soft, flat, and not well modulated; it lacks prosody or fluidity. Sometimes, however, his prosody is exaggerated or overdramatized, either too loud or too soft, "sing-songy" in quality. Often, his prosody does not express his feelings but comes across as awkward, stilted, exaggerated, or out of proportion to the situation.

Tactile Communication
Tactile communication involves any kind of body contact, ranging from affectionate embraces to physical assaults or injuries. Touch serves both protective and reproductive functions and can substitute for absent visual or auditory communication. The display rules for touch vary widely from culture to culture, from highly permissive to extremely formal. Children with NLD often seem unaware of what is appropriate or inappropriate in the area of physical contact. They will touch peers whom they barely know as intimately as they touch their caregivers.

While standing in line between classes, Paul, a 9-year-old, jostled and pushed his classmates and intrusively tried to look into their lunch bags, unaware of his own behavior. At times, he would ask for a hug from his teachers or try to sit on his social worker's lap. When angered by his peers' teasing, he became physically assaultive, going so far as to bite one of his classmates.

Proximics

Proximics refers to the permissible distance between people in day-to-day contact. This acceptable distance varies in different cultures. Rules of territoriality dictate the boundaries of each person, and specific meanings attach to the violation of these rules. From a psychological point of view, a person's boundary defines the outer limits of a person's sense of self. The expression "in your face" often describes the interactions of children with NLD. They might stand 3 inches away from another child while talking to him or her. If the other child moves back or tries to distance him- or herself, the child with NLD will continue to maintain the inappropriate closeness.

Peter, a third grader, frequently leans up against other children, appearing to be unaware or unappreciative of interpersonal boundaries, and is often experienced by others as intrusive. His teachers report that he does not keep sufficient "social space" between himself and others.

Chronimics

Chronimics refers to a culture's attitudes regarding objective time (as contrasted with subjective time). In psychotherapy, time is a defining characteristic of the process; beginning and ending on time are inviolable rules. Meanings are attached to the violation of these rules, whether it is that lateness means resistance or that refusal to leave at the end of the session means that the patient has difficulties with separation. Awareness of time is multiply determined, and children with NLD seem to have little of it. They seldom wear watches, and even if they do, they pay little attention to them. Caregivers find themselves constantly having to remind the child to hurry up or stop dawdling.

Jack, age 11½, never seemed to feel any sense of urgency to get to where he was supposed to be. In the mornings his mothers had to repeatedly remind him to get ready to catch the school bus. Nevertheless, he would frequently miss the bus and have to be driven, arriving late to his classes. He appeared distracted and seemed to dawdle. During test or quizzes, he was always surprised when time was called for him to turn in his papers, and he was always the last one to get to the bus after school.

Social Skills and Social Cues

At a broader level children with NLD have difficulties with the pragmatic aspects of nonverbal communication. They seem unfamiliar with the protocols that accompany social interactions; that is, they lack social skills. These difficulties may be due less to their deficits in decoding social cues and more to their failure to understand their meanings.

Randy, a 16-year-old young man who was accompanied by his mother for the first session, greeted me when I opened the door with his head down and loudly and urgently asked, "Where's the bathroom? Where's the bathroom?" With this, he barged into the office looking for the bathroom, obviously totally disoriented and oblivious to the inappropriateness of his behavior.

Some children have difficulty understanding nonverbal social cues. They do not respond to gestures (e.g., a "shushing" request that they be quiet) or monitor other people's gaze to pick up subtle indicators of intent. When people turn away from them, they cannot decode the meaning of the signal.

Beckie, a second grader, does not understand nonverbal cues. For example, she does not know when to end comments as others signal that it is time to move on. She either does not understand or misinterprets social contexts and consequently experiences the world as puzzling, surprising, or antagonistic. She does not know how to go about getting the information necessary to read and anticipate occurrences in the world; for example, she appears not to notice that other children are annoyed with her and may not like her. She is puzzled as to why her behavior is perceived as disturbing to others. In conversations, she persists in talking about her own interests, not noticing that others are no longer interested. She is poor at deriving social rules, and when he does derive a rule, she encounters difficulty translating the information into her own actions. For example, her mother instructed her to say "Hello, Mrs. Smith" when their neighbor came over. Beckie would repeatedly greet the neighbor even if she had seen her an hour earlier.

Humor

A common clinical observation is that children with NLD do not understand humor, in particular, jokes, sarcasm, irony, or puns. It is difficult to comment on this phenomenon, other than to make note of it, for two reasons. First, we have few data on the specific nature of the children's difficulties. Second, the psychology of humor is a large and complex discipline where little consensus exists among investigators as to the underlying psychodynamics that operate in people's responses to humor. We may speculate that the children's limited capacity to understand humor is due to (1) their inability to appreciate linguistic subtleties; or (2) their problems with theory of mind perceptions (see Leslie, 1987) and mind-sharing, which interfere with their understanding; or (3) their inability to read the facial expressions that often accompany jokes, which interferes with their ability to decode the communication. At this moment, I feel that we are in the dark about what operates and we must await further research.

The Semiotics of Nonverbal Communication

The categories in which human nonverbal activities occur are numerous. To name a few categories we find:

> *In the performing arts*—music, theater, ballet, opera, puppet shows
> *In the visual arts*—graphic arts, painting, sculpture
> *In academic disciplines*—mathematical notation, chemical formula
> *In public displays*—dress codes, liturgical order, political protocol
> *In interpersonal communication*—gestures, gaze, vocal intonation
> *In forms of entertainment*—play, sports, card games
> *In psychopathology*—the symptoms that patients display to indicate their distress.

There is no doubt that children's nonverbal learning disabilities constrain their appreciation of many of these activities, the study of which remains to be investigated. In this work, I restrict my discussion specifically to the sign system that people use to communicate with one another in the social context. I refer to this sign system as "communicative acts."

DEFINITION OF COMMUNICATIVE ACTS

In any communicative dialogue, there is a speaker (addresser) and a listener (addressee). Presumably, the speaker has a message he or she wishes to convey to the listener. This message generally involves a meaningful communication that may, or may not be verbally encoded; it is conveyed in some kind of a *code*, however, such as spoken words, numbers or musical notations, and it is conveyed through a *channel* of communication that can be oral, visual, electronic, or other. Finally, for a message to be interpreted correctly, the listener must decode the message taking into account the *context* in which it is conveyed (Jakobson, 1985). In this discussion of nonverbal communication, we will focus on the *channel* and the *code* through which people communicate.

The Channel

Verbal communication occurs through two channels (oral and visual) and uses two types of codes (spoken words and written expression). Nonverbal communication, however, occurs through an array of four or more channels: the oral, visual, tactile, and kinesic.[1] Other channels that are more difficult to classify also may be involved, such as the olfactory and gustatory sensory modalities. Facial expression, gestures, posture, and gaze involve the visual channel. We look at people's facial expressions, we track their gaze, whether they are making eye contact or not, we take note of their gestures and posture as significant in their emphasis of a point or in reflecting their general mood. Another variable that involves the visual channel is proximity; proximics, as noted, is the study of the acceptable physical distance between people within a given social context. The auditory channel processes prosody; some people's voices are highly inflected whereas those of others are relatively uninflected. Actors have exceptional capacity in conveying through their voices the feelings associated with the text. A final area that involves neither the visual nor the auditory channels is that of chronimics. Chronimics is also the study of social time, it involves not only such things as the pauses we make in conversations, turn taking, but also that elements of our culture with which we are much preoccupied, such as being on time, keeping schedules, celebrating anniversaries or birthdays, and the like.

The Code (Signs and Sign Systems)

Semioticians regard languages as composed of meaningful signs (a code) that may be either verbal or nonverbal. Verbal language is encoded within a sign system that is different from the sign system used in nonverbal communication. The "word sounds"—for example, "book"—are the morphemes that we use in speaking. These are created by each culture (Saussure, 1985) and reflect the basic concepts a culture uses in denoting primary aspects of the world and ideas. Messages are encoded in a set of signs to which we assign meanings. Semioticians use a threefold system of classification for all signs: iconic, indexical, and symbolic (Buchler, 1939; Peirce, 1940, 1958, 1991). *Iconic signs* are nonverbal signs such as maps,

---

[1] The term *kinesic* is used in semiotics to denote any form of bodily action that has communicative value.

diagrams, and pictures, in which a one-to-one correspondence exists between the sign and what it represents. *Indexical signs* point to something beyond themselves; they establish joint attention with the sign(er) and point to the object—for example, a flag, a footprint, a gesture, a cry. Bruner (1990) suggested the term *enactive* to refer to indexical signs such as the sensorimotor activity through which people pantomime a message. (Charades that do not use signs to spell words involve enactive signs.) Finally, *symbolic signs* are those that bear no relationship to the objects for which they stand. Generally, verbal signs fall into this category. Any of these types of signs can be nonverbal, but only indexical and symbolic signs can be verbal. Iconic signs can be translated into verbal language but lose much in the translation. As the saying goes, a picture is worth a thousand words. In this categorization, semioticians do not privilege verbal over nonverbal signs, nor do they place them within a hierarchy that sets one set of signs at a higher developmental level than the other.

As with verbal language, nonverbal communications occur through a set of signs that stand for concepts that have meanings to the participants in the dialogue. Unlike verbal language, these signs are frequently iconic or indexical; they are signs that directly resemble or point to that for which they stand. A facial expression that represents how we feel is an example of a nonverbal iconic sign. Gestures are often indexical signs that point to what they represent. As Winnicott (1953) brought to our attention, the earliest dialogue between caregiver and infant occurs through gestures.

PREVERBAL AND NONVERBAL COMMUNICATION

A distinction must be made between preverbal and nonverbal modes of communication. All preverbal communication is nonverbal, but not all nonverbal communication is preverbal. The failure to make this distinction leads to the mistaken belief that nonverbal modes of communication are less mature than verbal modes. All interchanges between caregiver and infant occur both preverbally and nonverbally until the infant acquires verbal language. Preverbal experiences are encoded nonverbally and stored in memory as either iconic or indexical signs. Even after the acquisition of verbal language, these nonverbal signs continue to exist within a nonverbal language system; they do not need to be translated into verbal signs in order to retain their meaning. Prior to the acquisition of language, children use gestures to communicate in two ways: When they point to an object, they are declaring that the object is present; when they reach toward an object that is out of their reach, they are requesting that object. As children acquire language, they integrate these nonverbal modes smoothly into their communicative styles, apparently acquiring much of the content of the nonverbal style through identification with, or imitation of, caregivers.

The acquisition of nonverbal signs as a form of communication follows its own path that parallels verbal language and becomes entwined with the latter once the child acquires verbal language. Whether nonverbal communication constitutes a formal language in the same sense that verbal discourse does is open to controversy. Some linguists maintain that because nonverbal signs are accompaniments to the more privileged mode of verbal communication and are absent in written language, they cannot be given the status of a separate language system. The question revolves around what constitutes a language.[2] If we consider that languages are composed of signs that are organized into a system governed by a set of rules, then we would note that in contrast to verbal language, which has well-defined component parts, nonverbal signs are not organized in the same way. Verbal language, as a system of signs (i.e., a code), is generally comprised of four components: (1) a *lexicon*, which constitutes the vocabulary of the language; (2) a *syntax*, which refers to the set of rules that specify how words should be combined to produce meaningful phrases and sentences; (3) *semantics*, which refers to how the meaning of a word or sentence is related to objects or events in the world; (4) *pragmatics*, which deals with the rules that tell us how to use language effectively in conversational discourse. In contrast, nonverbal communications are not organized in a similar manner, although parallels exist.

CONTRAST BETWEEN NONVERBAL AND VERBAL SIGNS

A number of elements differentiate nonverbal signs from verbal ones. First, *there is no lexicon or standard dictionary of nonverbal signs* to which one can refer for an explanation of the meaning of nonverbal signs. Even within a particular culture, the conventions for nonverbal expression are much looser and more dependent upon context than are the conventions for verbal language. Furthermore, unlike verbal signs, *nonverbal signs cannot be broken into components, such as phonemes or morphemes, as are verbal signs.* There is no equivalent unit of meaningful expression to the morpheme of verbal language; there is no alphabet, no set of vowels and consonants. Gestures, vocal intonations, and body postures are not broken into units that we can string together into meaningful words or sentences.

---

[2] American Sign Language, which is generally considered a full-fledged language, is a special case of nonverbal communication that deserves separate discussion.

Yet we take these nonverbal expressions so much for granted that it is only when we come across their inappropriate or dramatic usage that we notice their significance and the specificity of the messages they convey when used conventionally. In spite of the fact that we provide no formal instruction in the use of nonverbal signs in our society, we expect children to know what these signs generally mean; there is a consensus among the community of users as to the meanings we attribute to signs.

Second, *nonverbal signs have no general syntax or grammar* that guides the sequence in which expressions must be ordered for meaningful communication to occur. Verbal communication takes place in linear fashion; the words in a sentence occur sequentially. Nonverbal communication, in contrast, is processed simultaneously. The entire gestalt of the speaker's message is taken in at one time. The meaning of the message is extracted in its entirety from the total impression the speaker conveys within the context in which the communication occurs. Nonverbal signs are often used to accompany and enhance verbal expression, although occasionally these may be used without verbal expressions. Although there are no grammar books on the usage of nonverbal signs, it is possible to argue that there are rules that guide their usage. These are implicit display rules that each cultural context dictates. At times, these rules dictate the sequence in which we should use nonverbal signs, as when we smile in return to another person's smile or as in the performance of religious rituals where the order in which a ritual is performed is of paramount importance. More commonly, the context dictates the display rules, and these rules indicate what we consider to be dignified, coarse, insulting, or deferential. A grammar of manners rigidly dictates what is appropriate to the situation. Diplomatic protocol is an example of a grammar of nonverbal conduct that requires specific meanings to attach to each interaction. Similarly, there is a tacit protocol for the conduct of psychotherapy, whereby clinicians attach unconscious meanings to some nonverbal interchanges.

We are far from having a consensus as to the semantics *that attach to specific communications.* The ambiguities inherent in many nonverbal signs leave much room for personal interpretation. The issue of semantics is embroiled in the latitude people have in reading meanings into nonverbal communications. As clinicians we read meanings into the presence or absence of eye contact from a patient; we interpret lateness; we notice body language, dress, and adornment as indicative of the presence or absence of depression. Yet these meanings are not necessarily the meanings that the broader community would read into those nonverbal signs. Each community or subculture has its own conventions that indicate the common meanings attached to specific displays of nonverbal signs.

The pragmatic aspect of nonverbal communications is highly individualized. Linguists generally refer to pragmatics as the rules that guide conversational discourse within a given context. Good usage leads to successful communication between interlocutors. Poor pragmatics may indicate a lack of manners or an ignorance of the rules. In the verbal domain, we teach children the rules of turn taking in conversations, of suppressing irrelevancies, and of contextualizing their remarks so that we understand the situation they are discussing. Similarly, in the nonverbal domain, although we do not teach our children in any formal sense how to gesture or how to use proper prosody in their speech, we do say "Look at me when I'm speaking to you!" and "Sit up straight, stop slouching in your chair!" "That dress is too provocative, you can't wear it to this party!" Caregivers give these instructions informally, often as admonitions rather than as part of an instructional program. In this domain children learn these rules informally rather than in a formal academic program.

Finally, an important attribute of nonverbal communication is that much of it occurs out of awareness, that is, nonconsciously. At times, gestures can convey information or feelings in more powerful ways than words. In such instances, the content expressed is clearly conscious. Some people consciously learn to modulate their voices or to accentuate their verbalizations with gestures; most people take these accompaniments of verbal language for granted. In general, people are unaware of the messages they convey with their posture, the expression of their eyes, or their sense of personal space boundaries.

We may conclude that the definition of what constitutes a language specifically covers verbal languages. Applying that definition to nonverbal signs rules out nonverbal signs as a language system. Nevertheless, the domain of nonverbal communication includes signs that have common currency in every culture and have significant communicative value. Nonverbal signs represent a code through which communication occurs, much as other codes we use to communicate.

This discussion of nonverbal communication opens an avenue for understanding some of the sources of communication difficulties experienced by children with NLD. It may be possible to identify whether their impairments occur at the iconic, indexical, or symbolic level of processing. Because the iconic and indexical levels often utilize the visual channel, it is possible to detect deficits in nonlinguistic perceptual processing by identifying any lacunae in their perception of such signs. On the other hand, difficulties at the symbolic level entail higher orders of processing and involve the comprehension of the meaning of the sign. This differentiation in levels of processing may provide confirmation for the distinction that I am proposing between the decoding of signs and their interpretation.

In spite of its label, the domain of nonverbal communication as a language system has not received the attention it deserves in the literature on NLD. The study of this domain may provide insights into several aspects of the disorder. At the level of the children's symptoms, such research may allow us to distinguish the aspects that are related to deficits in processing nonlinguistic perceptual stimuli from those that are related to the absence of formal education, from those that are tied to cultural display rules, and from those that are due to failures in understanding the meaning of the signs. At the interpersonal level, further study of this domain may shed light on the factors that interfere with the emergence of communicative competence in children with NLD. We need answers to questions such as, How do the children's difficulties in their receptive and expressive capacities in this domain affect their social relationships? What measures can we use to identify and quantify the specific dysfunctions? Finally, at the level of etiology, we need to reevaluate the fact that we attribute the processing of nonverbal information to the right hemisphere, yet clearly the left hemisphere must also subserve aspects of the processing of this type of information—which is, after all, a system of signs.

CULTURE AND NONVERBAL COMMUNICATION

In assessing whether a child has an NLD, it is important to consider cultural factors in relation to the content of the child's nonverbal communication as well as the display rules that are conventional for his or her culture. To the extent that a sign is given expression through a modality that is more iconic or indexical, its cross-cultural interpretation is likely to be the same. To the extent that it is emblematic or symbolic, its interpretation will differ cross-culturally. For example, facial expressions appear to be interpreted as indexical referents to the same affect states universally, whereas body posture has different meanings in different cultures. The custom of bowing as a sign of respect for a higher authority, however, seems to be widespread across many cultures. Kneeling, however, has different meanings in different cultures, whether it occurs in a political context, as kneeling before a queen, or in a religious context before an altar. Vocal intonation, gestures, gaze, tactile communication, proximics, and chronimics all appear to be more culture bound than the others. They are more arbitrarily determined, much as are the phonemes used in word sounds.

Each culture makes choices from a limited repertoire of possible signs. These choices vary from group to group. We can draw the following analogy between verbal and nonverbal forms of communication. In verbal languages, cultures choose sounds from the total range of human sounds that vocal cords can produce. Some sounds overlap those used in other cultures, whereas others are distinct and not recognizable by people from other cultures. Similarly, humans are endowed with the capacity for a range of behaviors that becomes incorporated into modes of nonverbal communication. Cultures have display rules that dictate what is permissible or impermissible to display in public and in private. Here again, the choices a culture makes differ from those another culture may make. There may be overlapping or different meanings assigned to similar behaviors.

Much of nonverbal communication also deals with the expression of emotion, and the repertoire of emotions is initially developmentally restricted and universally the same. As the child matures, he or she acquires a set of display rules that is characteristic of the culture in which the child is raised, so that by maturity the displays appear to be quite dissimilar from that of other culture. However, the underlying vocabulary of emotions remains constant across cultures. During a comprehensive assessment of a child with NLD, clinicians must guard against neglecting the cultural component in the child's presentation. For example, a child from a Japanese family was referred to me because of a suspected diagnosis of NLD. It was not surprising to discover that what the referring source saw as a lack of affective facial expression, stiff body posture, and fixed gaze, was behavior the child had been instructed to display in the presence of people outside his intimate family circle. Within the family, he displayed none of those traits.

Dyssemia

Nowicki and his associates (Nowicki & Duke, 1992) coined the term *dyssemia* to identify the difficulties that some people have in the use of "nonverbal signs and signals" (p. 11). They describe the characteristics of children who are dyssemic in terms that are similar to those describing the social problems of children with NLD. Among the characteristics of dyssemic children, they list (1) difficulties in reading nonverbal or social signs; (2) difficulties in recognizing the contingencies between their behaviors and the consequences of those behaviors; (3) persevering in actions or activities even when they lead to punishment or rejection; (4) difficulties understanding the rules and sequences of games; (5) feeling sad, bewildered, lonely, confused, and anxious; (6) being rejected by peers, and (7) being described by parents, teachers, or peers as tactless, insensitive, different from others, lacking in social maturity.

In contrast to NLD, which is a brain-based disorder, the causes of dyssemia may be neurological, emotional, or due to the absence of opportunities to learn appropriate ways of decoding and responding to nonverbal messages. Nowicki and Duke constructed the Diagnostic Analysis of Nonverbal Accuracy (DANVA) test "to measure the individual differences in the accurate sending and receiving of nonverbal social information" (1994, p. 9). The DANVA (the second edition), which is designed for adults and children, is a test of receptive abilities for four emotions: happy, sad, angry, and fearful. It measures the ability to decode the paralinguistic features of posture and gestures, and the capacity to identify the four emotions in verbal expressions. This test is used widely and has been normed for several age groups.

The authors also have written helpful guides for parents and teachers who are interested in educating children in the use of nonverbal signs, and they have devised a remediation program that they have implemented in some public schools (see Appendix 2).

Verbal Language Problems and NLD

The speech and language problems of children with NLD deserve special consideration, given that verbal language is an area of strength, whereas nonverbal communication is an area of weakness (cf. Rourke & Tsatsanis, 1996 for an informative discussion; see also Beeman & Chiarello, 1998a). Speech and language pathologists distinguish speech from language. Speech involves the capacity to articulate feelings and thoughts and to coordinate motor functions to give expression to one's thoughts. In contrast, language refers to the sign system discussed above.

Some children with NLD experience difficulties learning to talk primarily because of the delays in their motor development. Although they often overcome their early articulation problems, some have residual impairment that make their speech difficult to understand.

Alex's early speech milestones were reportedly somewhat delayed, specifically in speech enunciation. He was somewhat delayed in speaking his first words, which he did at approximately 18 months. He had a history of difficulty expressing himself verbally, did not readily relate feelings or describe events to his parents after school, and had difficulty articulating clearly enough for strangers to understand him. As a consequence, he received speech therapy between the ages of 3 and 5 years. Now in fourth grade, he continues to have trouble in his articulation of certain phonemes and displays disinhibited verbalization with imprecise articulation and attention jumping from one activity to the next.

HIGHER-ORDER VERBAL LANGUAGE IN NLD

Rourke and Tsatsanis (1996) noted that the focus on the domain of non-verbal communication in children with NLD has led to a failure to appreciate the full extent of their deficits in linguistic skills. We have noted the children's strengths in word decoding, auditory perception, attention, and verbal memory. Additional strengths are found in verbal attention, memory, reception, and repetition. They have solid capacities in verbal storage, verbal association, and output. Their intact decoding skills, well-developed vocabularies, and excellent memories for facts often lead listeners to gloss over the deficits in higher-order language processing, such as the difficulties in metaphoric and pragmatic language usage. The children often are unable to understand humor and struggle with finding the logical interrelationships among events, problem solving, and fluid reasoning (discussed in detail in Chapter 2). Although they can recall facts and repeat verbatim prose segments, the content of their communication appears superficial and conveys little about themselves.

Cory, a fifth grader, has good syntax and pragmatics but has problems with prosody. He tends to speak in a monotone or "sing-song" voice. He has a good memory and manifests rote memory verbalizations that make him look much smarter than he is actually. His concepts lack preciseness, although they appear sophisticated. His vocabulary seems advanced for his age, but the communications are not always well connected, and the content appears superficial.

In summary, although the verbal language of children with NLD appears advanced or even sophisticated, closer scrutiny of the content reveals limitations in their capacity to process abstract and complex material.

Mark's problems with concept formation limit his capacity to reason, analyze, and synthesize materials. Although in fifth grade, he cannot organize a narrative to pick out the main points from supporting details, the relevant from irrelevant. When he gives a narrative account of an event, he grasps one aspect of the total picture and misses the broader gestalt. Consequently, when asked to report on an event, he gives an account that appears disconnected and devoid of feeling. It is very difficult to reconstruct what happened from his reports.

From the point of view of pragmatics—that is, everyday language usage—children with NLD lack an appreciation of the rules of social discourse. When they learn a strategy through which to communicate with others, they cannot judge when it is appropriate to make such a response.

They cannot apply rules of social discourse correctly because they are unable to process when a specific rule applies and when it does not. They do not use, prosody, contextual markers, or indicators of relevance/salience of the material they are discussing to facilitate their communications. They therefore come across as tangential, repetitive, and monotonous. The lack of prosody makes it difficult to draw any indication of the emotional dimension of their experience. When relating the details of an event, they give piecemeal accounts of the event, leaving out important details that would allow the listener to reconstruct what happened. It appears as though they suffer from a deficit in episodic memory. In addition, their problems with visual sequential processing may not allow them to organize the details of the events into a whole; it may be that they cannot retrieve what has not been stored.

LANGUAGE PROBLEMS AND THE RIGHT HEMISPHERE

Loveland and colleagues (Loveland, Fletcher, & Bailey, 1990) conducted a study in which children were shown videotaped scenarios in verbal and nonverbal formats and then asked to describe verbally or enact with puppets the events depicted in the stories. The children in the sample, chosen because they had arithmetic problems, were compared to control groups. The children had more difficulty with nonverbal aspects of the story tasks. When responding to the observation of nonverbal events, they omitted more information from their observation of enacted events and reversed the role of the actors they had watched. However, they made no more errors than controls in response to the verbal presentation in which they were asked to describe or to enact the events. These data led the investigators to support the hypothesis that these types of social communication problems vary with the type of learning disability.

Two studies (Beeman & Chiarello, 1998b; Brownell & Martino, 1998) have documented deficits that patients with right hemisphere damage display in understanding the main points of stories, fables, and even scenes represented in drawings and paintings. These patients have more difficulty when they must abstract from individual pieces to apprehend how the pieces fit together. This deficit is called the "gist comprehension impairment." The studies also indicated that these patients have problems reading people's emotions from their facial expressions and speech prosody. They also have difficulty with social cognitive tasks, including understanding the internal states and feelings of others—that is, theory of mind. Finally, patients with right hemisphere damage have trouble formulating differences in social context about the behaviors of others; they favor external over internal explanations for the motives of others behaviors

(Brownell & Martino, 1998). For example, after reading a story about a clerk in a law firm who misplaced a file, they were asked why the clerk had done that. The subjects favored a response that attributed the misfiling to the office being messy.

The verbal language problems of children with NLD exemplify the involvement of both left and right hemispheres in their symptoms. Although verbal language is generally considered a left hemisphere function, the right hemisphere makes its own contribution (see Beeman & Chiarello, 1998a). "The most important point is that right hemisphere processing is engaged for all components of language comprehension, and this right hemisphere processing appears to be qualitatively different from left hemisphere processing" (Beeman & Chiarello, 1998b, pp. 381–382).

Studies of patients with right hemisphere lesions indicate that they have problems with prosody, higher-order abstraction, understanding humor, and pragmatic language (Plante, Boliek, Mahendra, Story, & Glaspey, 2001). Brownell and Martino (1998) found that "substantial evidence confirms that patients with RHD [right hemisphere damage] exhibit inference deficits that affect discourse performance and, more generally, interpretation of their social world" (p. 324). Their subjects made faulty inferences in the comprehension of the main point of a narrative, in situations involving affect states, and in understanding other's people through theory of mind. As the studies summarized below demonstrate, it is not too difficult to find similarities between the verbal language problems of these patients and the problems with communicative competence experienced by children with NLD. These studies lend support to the hypothesis that the children's difficulties are not simply due to inadequate decoding capacities, but also to their impaired interpretations of the interactions to which they were exposed.

Prosody
Evidence exists to support the association between right hemisphere dysfunction and problems with prosody (Ross, 1981, 2000). In a study of 10 right-handed patients with focal lesions of the right hemisphere and disorders of affective language, Ross (1981) found that "the disorders of affective language seem to be classifiable in the same manner as the aphasias. Thus, the term 'aprosodia,' preceded by specific modifiers such as motor, global, transcortical, sensory, etc., seems appropriate when classifying the various disorders of affective language that occur following right hemisphere damage" (p. 561). Starkstein and associates (Starkstein, Federoff, Price, Seiguaric, & Robinson, 1994), in a study of patients with acute stroke lesions, found that those with difficulties in the comprehension of emotional prosody showed a higher frequency of right hemi-

sphere lesions. Heilman (2002) noted that the left hemisphere is important for recognizing rhythms and the right for recognizing melody and timbre, whereas the right hemisphere is dominant for understanding emotional prosody. Right hemisphere damage interferes with emotional intonation/expression. The left hemisphere can also comprehend emotional prosody; however, the right hemisphere is dominant.

Semantics and Pragmatics

In a study of adults with right hemisphere lesions, Shields (1991) reported copious and inappropriate speech—symptoms that resemble those of children with semantic—pragmatic language disorders. He notes that the hyperlexia found in some children reflects an underlying problem in the integration of semantic information with knowledge of the world (see also Bishop, 1989).

As mentioned earlier, Rourke and Tsatsanis (1996) suggested a possible explanation, based on the developmental perspective of Piaget, for the lack of synthesis in verbal expression in children with NLD. They hypothesized that during the sensorimotor period of development, children acquire schemas of their experiences based on their interactions with the world. Because these early interactions are primarily preverbal, the right hemisphere mediates them. Deficits in right hemisphere function lead to deficiencies in the formation of the schemas. In turn, because the schemas form the foundation on which verbal language is based, the words associated with the schemas lack the understructure that would tie them to the world of experience. The result is a verbal language system that is only loosely associated with the common experiences that others have of the world.

Benowitz and colleagues (Benowitz, Moya, & Kevin, 1990) document similar problems in subjects with right hemisphere impairments. They note that in addition to the well-documented problems in processing visual–spatial information, the subjects had severe impairments in higher-order language abilities, including the understanding and recall of narrative material. They conclude "The results of this study demonstrate that damage to the right cerebral hemisphere causes impairments in certain language-based abilities that are as pervasive and as severe in magnitude as the more commonly recognized visuospatial deficits" (p. 239). Furthermore, right hemisphere damage results in "striking impairments in certain higher order language abilities, including the understanding and recall of narrative material" (p. 240).

Martin and McDonald (2003) summarized some of the pragmatic language difficulties of patients with right hemisphere damage. The speech of these patients may be tangential and socially inappropriate. Patients tend to misinterpret, or ignore, the intentions of others conveyed in discourse. They are less able to use the information provided about the mood of an individual to interpret whether a conversational remark has a sarcastic or joking content. They have difficulty understanding the main point of conversations and stories and have difficulty using the theme of the story to aid comprehension. They are often concrete and literal in their use of comprehension of language and are often reluctant to revise the initial interpretation of language even in the light of new contradictory information. They have particular difficulty with the comprehension of language tasks that require a flexible interpretation, such as metaphor and irony, narrative humor, or short-story jokes, and demonstrate deficits in inference-making abilities. Paralinguistic deficits accentuate these problems by producing impairments in speech prosody as well as difficulty reading emotion in facial expression. They have difficulty reading social-emotional cues and using these cues to further their communication. The overlap between many of these difficulties and those of children with NLD is apparent.

These researchers further consider the issue of whether pragmatic language disorders in patients with right hemisphere damage are related to (1) problems in "central coherence"—that is, failure of the central system whose job it is to integrate sources of information; (2) failure in "social inferencing"—that is, attempting to explain or predict the thoughts, intentions, and behaviors of others, which includes theory of mind abilities; and or (3) executive dysfunction—that is, problems in concept formation, abstract and inferential thinking, dealing with novel situations, and motivated and adaptive behaviors. They conclude that although each of these areas addresses a specific level of processing, the heterogeneity of the types of right hemisphere damage confounds the issue of the origins of the difficulties.

The evidence suggests that such deficits as those related to prosody and semantic and pragmatic processing support the hypothesis that right-hemisphere dysfunctions contribute to children with NLD's language processing problems and to their difficulties in interpreting the meanings of communicative acts. Although, as Martin and McDonald (2003) indicated, the heterogeneity of the subjects' right hemisphere damage is a confounding factor. Furthermore, the earlier studies were all lesion-based studies, which do not provide definitive evidence for the hypothesis. In spite of these limitations, the indications are that some of the problems with extracting the gist of a communication, contextualizing the contents of what a person is communicating, and, in particular, determining the salience of what to reveal or not to reveal appear to be related to right hemisphere dysfunctions. Relevance theory may shed additional light on this issue.

Relevance Theory and Theory of Mind

The relationship between language, language acquisition, and theory of mind abilities is complex. In studies comparing linguistic expression of children with autism and those with Down's syndrome, Tager-Flusberg (1996) found a bidirectional relationship between language acquisition and theory of mind abilities: The failure to understand that others are intentional beings appears to delay language acquisition, and cognitive delays in the functions associated with language acquisition interfere with the development of theory of mind abilities.

Relevance theory offers us further insight into the relationship between language and theory of mind abilities. Ramos noted that "the general objective of RT [relevance theory] is 'to identify underlying mechanisms, rooted in human psychology, which explain how humans communicate with one another' " (1998, p. 317). Relevance theory assumes that each event has an implicit context in which it occurs. That context may need to be made explicit, depending on the listener to whom the communication is addressed and the circumstances under which it is made (Bezuidenhout & Sroda, 1998). Relevance theory presents a framework with which we can determine whether communications are purely *ostensive* or *ostensively-inferential* (Happe, 1991). Statements are *ostensive* when they are used literally and when words are used instrumentally. Statements are *ostensively-inferential* when they require that the listener interpret the speaker's intention in making the statement. Descriptive statements that refer to first-order representations are ostensive in the sense that the semantic meaning of the statement lies in the point to which the statement refers. For example, "John took my toy!" is a declarative statement about an action the speaker wants to convey. On the other hand, the statement "You are acting like a couch potato!" requires further decoding for the listener to extract its meaning. First it requires a context, which may be implicitly understood. Second, it requires inferences to be made—"Mom thinks I am acting like a couch potato!" And "Mom disapproves of my acting this way!", and it requires decoding of the term *couch potato* as a metaphor for being inactive, lethargic, lazy, and probably negligent of duties that await attention.

Using this type of linguistic analysis, relevance theory suggests that it is possible to determine whether a person has, or does not have, a theory of mind. Theory of mind abilities are necessary for a person to decode the message as an ostensively-inferential communication. The message would include the context, a second-order representation of the speaker's intent, and an understanding of metaphorical or figurative language. Furthermore, the person who could decode the message would also be able to convey these linguistic elements expressively, in order to communicate successfully with another person.

Researchers (Baron-Cohen, 1997; Baron-Cohen, Tager-Flusberg et al., 1993; Frith, 1989a; 1989b; Sodian & Frith, 1993) have found that children with autism who fail the false-belief task do not meet these criteria in receptive or expressive communication; in short, they are unable to use relevance theory (Happe, 1991, 1993). The question for us is whether we can apply this type of analysis to children with NLD to determine whether they have theory of mind abilities. The clinical data do not give a definitive answer to this question. First, there is the fact that children with NLD are poor at reporting their experiences in a coherent manner, which could be interpreted as evidence that they lack the capacity for making ostensively-inferential statements. However, there may be other explanations for this phenomenon that would lead to the conclusion that they do have theory of mind abilities. For example, their visual–spatial deficits may interfere with an accurate or complete encoding of the events to which they are exposed; thus an incoherent report of an event would be due to impaired encoding. However, if that were so, the children ought to be able to acknowledge the incompleteness of their account or express confusion as to what occurred. Because they do not always do so, we remain uncertain about what interferes with their communicative competence. A different explanation may be that a right hemisphere deficit interferes with their ability to perceive the entire gestalt, and that incomplete perception, in turn, interferes with their ability to produce a coherent account. This explanation is more plausible, although it does presume a right hemisphere deficit. Nevertheless, this account would suggest that the problem is not necessarily related to the absence of theory of mind abilities.

Second, children with NLD have a poor understanding of humor, which may also be interpreted as due to an inadequate theory of relevance. They certainly have difficulties with sarcasm and irony. It may be that these forms of humor require more mature modes of cognition than the children possess; nevertheless, the concrete and instrumental use of language may be the source of their difficulties. I have wondered about the fact that I have not encountered any adolescents with NLD who can write poetry, as adolescence sometimes do. Might this absence of poetic expression be related to the difficulties they have in the use of figurative or metaphorical language?

Third, quite frequently (though not always), children with NLD fail to contextualize their comments. They appear to begin talking in the middle of the conversation. At times, they do not identify the people whose names they mention. (e.g., "Bob grabbed my toy and ran away with it"— no mention is made of who is Bob; is he a classmate, neighbor, a sibling or other relative?). Often, it takes a while to get oriented to the place and time of the occurrences they report. They appear to assume that the listener knows the people they know or has been to the places they have been. Is this evidence of the absence of theory of mind abilities? Or is it simply evidence of the difficulties they have with the pragmatic use of language (Leinonen & Kerbel, 1999)? The question remains an open one. What is clear is that relevance theory may provide an avenue for further exploration of this issue with children with NLD.

Conclusion

In nonverbal communication, as in verbal communication, we use a set of signs for the expression, reception and processing of information. We give expression to our nonverbal messages through a variety of channels: visual, auditory, and kinesic. Similarly, we receive nonverbal messages through visual, auditory, kinesic, and other channels. Our processing of these nonverbal messages occurs through a set of meanings we assign to these nonverbal signs.

Nonverbal communication begins with the earliest preverbal exchanges between infant and caregivers. This form of communication then extends into the rest of the lifespan, becoming closely entwined with verbal communication. We noted a number of differences between verbal and nonverbal communication. Unlike verbal communication, nonverbal communication has no standard lexicon or dictionary, and the vocabulary of gesture, vocal intonations, and postures is limited in range and richness. In addition, there is no universal syntax that guides the sequence in which the expressions are communicated and no formal pragmatic rules that dictate its proper usage in discourse. Furthermore, cultural factors often dictate the display rules that indirectly govern nonverbal communication.

There is agreement that all nonverbal expressions carry emotional messages. Whether it be through gaze, vocal intonation, gesture, or interpersonal proximity, each conveys a message about our feelings and is read by others as a message about how we feel. In this respect facial expressions are a privileged modality and more valued than nonverbal modes of communication (interestingly, facial expressions have the same associated meanings across cultures).

Nonverbal communications often involve iconic or indexical signs, but they may also be symbolic signs that have a communicative function. The problems of children with NLD in processing visual stimuli lead to difficulties in decoding iconic and indexical signs. This fact may lend support to the view that at the core of their difficulties is the issue of social imperception. The impact of deficits in this modality of social perception is pivotal to the social problems experienced by children with NLD. Those deficits have a significant bearing upon the quality and nature of any social relationship.

Aside from their problems with prosody, the children also have verbal language problems that appear to be unrelated to their visual–spatial deficits. These problems seem to find expression in two areas of functioning. First, there are the pragmatic language problems, which manifest as an overuse of the verbal channel and as difficulties in making correct inferences about what is being communicated. In this regard, relevance theory may provide an avenue through which to enlarge our understanding of the children's pragmatic language problems by specifying the ways in which language usage may indicate an understanding that others have intention (Leinonen & Kerbel, 1999). Further studies may clarify whether the language usage of children with NLD can indicate whether they have theory of mind abilities. Second, these children manifest difficulties in extracting the gist or main point of a story that they either heard or read; they tend to draw literal or concrete meanings, missing the salience of the speaker's intentions.

Consistent with Mesulam's (2000) categorization of right hemisphere functions and with Denckla's (1991) category of simultaneous processing of information, there are indications that children with NLD suffer from a generalized right hemisphere dysfunction in both nonverbal communication and verbal language. These dysfunctions produce a variety of social problems that appear to be unrelated to those that result from the visual–perceptual deficits. This conclusion would support the view that visual–perceptual functions are dissociable from those of social cognition. This perspective does not preclude the involvement of other brain regions in the processing of verbal and nonverbal forms of communication.

6

Impaired Emotional Functioning

Affective communication is the third domain that I examine to evaluate the social functioning of children with NLD. The task of dealing with the topic of affects is both daunting and unavoidable. It is daunting because of the difficulties we encounter in addressing the issues surrounding this domain—issues such as (1) the problems of differentiating between the terms *affects, emotions,* and *feelings*; (2) the choice of a theoretical framework within which to frame the discussion; and (3) the explication of the neurobiological underpinnings of affects. It is unavoidable because affects are a primary vehicle for nonverbal communication, which is, as we have seen, a problematic area of functioning for children with NLD.

Although the term *social–emotional dysfunction* is used freely by investigators of NLD, few of those investigators have ventured into the realm of affects per se. The discussions always combine the social aspects of the children's difficulties with their emotional adjustments (Pennington, 1991; Rourke, 1991; Semrud-Clikeman & Hynd, 1990). Yet children with NLD have serious challenges from the receptive, expressive, and processing dimensions when it comes to dealing with affects. This chapter addresses two central questions: How do the core deficits of children with NLD impair their emotional functioning? How do the deficits in the reception, expression, and processing of emotional communication affect their social interactions?

Theories of emotion abound; we hear of Darwinian theory, the

James–Lang theory, cognitive theories, social constructivist theories, and cognitive neuroscience theories (Cornelius, 1996). The cognitive neuroscience perspective informs the discussion in this chapter (Davidson, 1993; Panksepp, 2001; Solms & Turnbull, 2002). During the past decade, neuroscientists have turned their attention to the study of affects, and their efforts have contributed significantly to our understanding of their importance in human communication. Some of these investigators have written books that are accessible to the public; such are the contributions of Damasio (1994, 2003), LeDoux (1996, 2002), and Gazzaniga (1988). In addition, a large body of technical literature may be found in a simple search of any library's data base.

In contrast to these new emerging theories, psychoanalytically informed theories of affect have been available for over a century. Beginning with Freud (1916/1960), who emphasized the significance of affects as motivators of human behavior, to current theories that detail the central role of affects in mother–infant interaction and attachment, all psychodynamic theories regard affects as critical to an understanding of human personality and relationships. Furthermore, from a psychodynamic perspective, social links emerge from a person's sense of self and the formative experiences that occurred during development. Those interactions, in conjunction with the motives associated with the affective experience, organize the sense of self and relationships to others across the lifespan. Greenspan's contribution, which I review at the close of this chapter lies squarely in this tradition.

As I stated earlier, the literature on NLD generally has examined the problems in reception and expression of emotion in these children from a social perspective; the communicative function of emotions is the nearly exclusive focus of this work (Voeller, 1991, 1994, 1995, 1997). There is little discussion of the larger issues of the children's dispositional states and their difficulties with self-regulation. Dissociation of the contributions of cognition and emotion in the reception and expression of emotion introduces a further problem. Because an understanding of the broader functions served by emotions in human behavior is essential to an informed view of child development, I find it necessary to address the broader domain. My discussion of this important domain, however, must rely on inferences made from existing theories and speculations that extrapolate to children with NLD from the findings of other populations. In what follows, I discuss the clinical manifestations of affective communication problems in children with NLD. To gain a deeper understanding of the complex roots of the children's dysfunction in affective processing, it is necessary to turn to the contributions of researchers in the field of affective neuroscience.

Before proceeding, a brief definition of the terms I use is in order. There is no consensus on definitions of these terms; I suggest the following usage: *Affects* are states of physiological arousal characterized by alteration of feeling tone and physiological changes. *Emotion* is the mental representation and external behavioral manifestation of affects. Emotions may be appraised cognitively, linked to thoughts, and expressed behaviorally. The subjective experiences associated with affects/emotions are *feelings*; these are responses to internal or external stimuli that have a positive or negative valence and that have meaning to the person having the experience.

The Universal Language of Emotions

In Darwin's evolutionary perspective, the biological responses associated with the emotions were incidental residues of habits formed by the selection process. The communicative function of emotions was secondary to those biological responses. The capacity for emotional communication was *selected* because of its function as preparation for action. Human emotions are now considered to have an adaptive role both because they serve a communicative function, as warning signals to self and others, and because they provide motives for thoughts and behaviors. In their communicative functions, emotions serve as signs of others' intentions; as dispositional responses they serve as signals of our inner states. They are like a sensory modality that is outwardly and inwardly directed to pick up stimuli from either source.

We are preadapted to respond to others' expression of emotion, and our emotions trigger responses in others. As we know, emotions are the primary medium of communication between infants and caregivers; they act as powerful motives to sustain the bond between both partners in the dyad. Many aspects of the expression of emotion are nonverbal. There are four aspects of the processing of emotional information that are relevant to this discussion: the *expression of emotion*, the *reception of emotion*, the *dispositional states* associated with emotions, and the capacity for the *regulation of emotion*.

We *express* and display emotions through nonverbal signs, primarily indexical and iconic signs such as facial expressions, vocal intonations, gestures, and other. *Receptively*, we may identify others' emotions from their facial expressions or other forms of nonverbal communications. We can also understand how another person feels through empathy, attunement, or resonance with his or her inner state. A theory of mind ability is required for the successful interpretation of the meaning of another person's communication (Harris & Saarni, 1989).

Dispositional or feeling states serve to inform us of our moods, anxieties, and self-states. Feelings provide the capacity to evaluate the state of our well-being and to organize and integrate our experiences. Finally, *affect regulation* reflects the ability to cope with over- or understimulation; it involves processes that amplify, attenuate, or maintain the level of emotional arousal. When successful, this capacity leads to the reestablishment of baseline state levels of responsivity. Failures in this capacity lead to emotional flooding, uncontrolled outburst, or apathy. Tomkins states that we strive for conditions in which: "(1) positive affect should be maximized; (2) negative affect should be minimized; (3) affect inhibition should be minimized; (4) power to maximize positive affect, to minimize negative affect, [and] to minimize affect inhibition should be maximized" (1981, p. 328). He adds that affects (i.e., emotions) serve to amplify and magnify some of our experiences, thus assuring that they are retained in memory and enhance our learning from those experiences.

An additional dimension to consider is the relationship of emotions to verbal language. Although this topic might be seen as belonging in the discussions of the previous chapter, I include it here to underscore the importance of the relationship. I revisit the topic of prosody from the perspective of the contribution of emotions to it and discuss the *lexical aspect* of verbal language, which includes the emotional content of verbal communications.

NLD and Affects, Emotions, and Feelings

The difficulties that children with NLD have with the reception and expression of emotion, in conjunction with their social problems, are well documented. For methodological reasons, there are far fewer studies of children's capacities for the expression of emotion than for the reception of emotions.

RECEPTION OF EMOTIONAL COMMUNICATIONS

There is no doubt that visual–perceptual and visual–spatial functions are involved in the reception of emotional information, and that some of the difficulties of children with NLD may be associated with the impairments in those functions. Dimitrovsky, Spector, Levy-Schiff, & Valek (1998) studied the ability to identify facial expressions of happiness, sadness, anger, surprise, fear, and disgust in nondisabled children and in children with LD ages 9–12. They reported: "Overall, the nondisabled group had better interpretive ability than the three learning disabled groups and the VD [verbal disabled] group had better abilities than the NVD [nonverbal disabled] and BD [both verbal and nonverbal] groups" (p. 286). In a study of children diagnosed with an NLD, Petti and her colleagues (Petti, Voelker, Shore, & Hayman-Abello, 2003) used the DANVA to support the hypothesis that these children have problems in the perception of emotions. They found that compared to a group of children with verbal learning disabilities, these children were less accurate in their interpretation of the emotional expressions of adult faces.

The children's inability to read others' feelings has often led to the misconception that they lack empathy—that is, the capacity to understand and appreciate how another person feels. On further examination, however, it is clear that these children are not insensitive to others. In discussions with them, they demonstrate the capacity to understand others' feelings; where they fail is in the correct interpretation of what transpired. Their misreading of others leads to responses that are considered insensitive and therefore unempathic.

Kevin, age 10½, has difficulty reading other people's emotional expressions and identifying or recognizing feelings in others; he has difficulty identifying others' emotional communications through facial expressions, gestures, vocal intonations, or others nonverbal social cues. Often, he seems unaware of other's emotions and cannot understand and interpret others' feelings or the conventional meanings that feelings have for others. He recognizes feelings in others only if they are expressed with intensity, and he has similar difficulties identifying feelings in himself.

THE EXPRESSION OF EMOTIONS

One of the more frustrating experiences of caregivers in their interactions with some of these children is that it is difficult to know how the children feel. Because they often give little indication of their feeling states through their facial expressions, caregiver cannot reliably know what is going on within the child. If they guess at the child's feeling, they find themselves in an argument with the child, who claims not to feel that way at all. The child ends up feeling misunderstood and further isolated. Yet the children expect to be understood in spite of their expressive difficulties.

Studies indicate that the right hemisphere plays an important role in processing the emotions associated with facial expression. According to Heilman, "Patients with discrete brain injuries suggest that the right hemisphere is normally important for comprehending and expressing facial emotions. . . . While it is clear that the right hemisphere plays a dominant role in both the comprehension and expression of nonverbal emotional signals, the brain mechanisms underlying these functions are more difficult to ascertain" (2002, 65).

Cory, a fourth grader, appears unable to display feeling states; his expressions do not always seem to reflect his emotional experience; he does not display his feelings through eye contact or facial or gestural expressions; his facial or gestural expressions appear to convey contrary emotions to those felt. He seldom discusses his own feelings, and he seems not to pick up on emotional cues from other children.

DISPOSITIONAL STATES

Our data indicate that the difficulties experienced by children with NLD in managing their emotions occur in three areas: (1) their feelings about themselves, (2) their feeling state (i.e., the way they feel episodically on a day-to-day basis), and (3) the way they regulate or modulate affect states. Here we are discussing the children's subjective states rather than their social interactions—although, clearly, these subjective states have a large impact on what occurs in their interactions with others. Much as is the case with people who have alexithymia, who do not appear to experience or express their emotions, children with NLD appear not to understand the language of emotion. Although they are capable of experiencing intense anger or frustration, they seem unable to get in touch with the more modulated set of feelings.

Feelings about Self
Various authors define self-esteem differently. In this work, I propose a technical definition based on self psychology: Self-esteem is the ability (1) to feel valued and worthwhile, (2) to appreciate that others have value and are owed a measure of respect, and (3) to feel a sense of kinship with others who belong to the same community (Palombo, 1987, 1995, 2001a). When a child lacks self-esteem, he or she may feel worthless, self-critical, and disrespected by, or alienated from, peers and others. Clinical data support the view that many children with NLD have negative feelings about themselves that are the product of low self-esteem. Some respond defensively, believing themselves to be special or superior to others, demeaning or denigrating others. Some appear oblivious to these issues, displaying a curious lack of awareness of their status, and apparently taking no ownership of their condition.

Jack, who is 11 years old, is self-critical, perfectionistic, and expresses a lack of self-confidence. He appears to feel inadequate, has low self-esteem, and feels unworthy or undeserving. Jack's parents believe that he views himself as being different from other children, although they are not clear whether or not he perceives this difference negatively. He exhibits a poor self-image, particularly due to a lack of peer acceptance at school and inadequate social skills. Despite attempting to appear confident, his self-esteem is fragile.

Oversensitivity and overreactivity to criticism is understandable in this population and are related to their narcissistic vulnerabilities. The fragile state of their sense of self leads them to be injured easily and to fall apart under the stresses that come with perceived failure. The lack of success in social relationships reinforces a view of themselves as weird or undesirable, leading them to feel marginalized and rejected.

Andy, who is 8 years old, becomes tearful easily. He feels neglected or rejected, vulnerable or helpless, and often self-conscious. He is easily hurt by minor critical comments; he interprets others' responses as victimizing or scapegoating; and he blames himself even though he is not responsible for what occurred.

Feeling States

The anxiety of children with NLD, which is generally pervasive, deserves special consideration. One view, held by some clinicians, is that the anxiety is systemic in the sense that it is part of the disorder; no studies exist to support this hypothesis. Another view is that the anxiety is in response to the multiple injuries the child has suffered over the years at the hands of others who have not responded adequately to his or her needs (Palombo, 1995, 2001a). Such a view is plausible when we consider that the child has suffered failure after failure in social interactions and often has been teased or bullied mercilessly. It is therefore no surprise that children with NLD develop an aversive response to social contact. The anxiety leads to an aversion to painful situations, which turns into a chronic state of avoidance as the child practically becomes phobic about social interactions. To my mind, this explanation is partially valid but falls short of being satisfactory. It seems to me there is more to be said about it. I extend the discussion of this issue in the section on affective neuroscience.

Ten-year-old Emily often appears worried (e.g., her face is flushed and her eyes are wide open), uncomfortable, and fidgety. Wary of the situations in which she finds herself, she manifests signs of nervousness, appears distraught, is fearful, and complains of stomachaches. She expresses worries about bad things happening to people she cares about (e.g., family members, in particular). She is overly concerned about her performance of tasks and is hesitant for fear of failure. She "furrows her brows and frowns a lot," exhibits much frustration and anxiety, despite wishing to appear confident. Between the ages of 5 and 6, Emily frequently engaged in nail biting, and she still grinds her teeth while sleeping. Her parents are concerned that she worries excessively about flying and about insects. Ac-

cording to her mother, Emily has always been highly emotional, an excessive worrier who cries easily when upset. She experienced difficulty separating from her parents at the beginning of her first school year (age 3) and worried about being away from home. This separation anxiety has resurfaced again during school overnight trips. In addition, she experiences assorted other fears, such as fear of sleeping in her own bedroom at night in case a car crashes into it.

The constant frustrations to which children with NLD are exposed lead them to feel helpless and enraged. They often direct their anger at care-givers who are blamed by the child for their own difficulties. Siblings and other also become targets for displaced anger.

Matt's parents experience him as increasingly argumentative, demanding, and angry. They continue to be concerned about his low frustration tolerance and inattentiveness, despite the fact that he is almost 12 years old. His teacher con-siders his angry behavior toward adults to be at times, "outrageous." In a recent report, it was noted that Matt became extremely angry and agitated with his teachers, threatening them with what were considered to be graphic descriptions of annihilation. After feeling bewildered for a period of time, disappointment and frustration would overtake him and he would lash out physically. His mother describes Matt as being "volatile" with "bursts of frustration." There also seems to be excessive sibling conflict, in which Matt is very confrontational with his younger brother. Matt frequently demonstrates frustration and anger in re-sponse to difficult tasks, and he does not persist at these tasks to completion.

Many children with NLD vacillate between exited hyperactivity and low-keyed sadness. They give the impression of suffering from a low-grade depression that pervades their lives. They appear joyless and can find little pleasure in most activities. They report feeling bored and search-ing for something exiting to do to dull the pain of their sadness.

Affect Regulation
The issue of affect regulation is pivotal to our understanding of the way in which children with NLD deal with their emotions (Blair, 2002). Affect regulation involves the ability to modulate states of physiological arousal. These children have much greater difficulty displaying the milder forms of emotional expression than the more extreme forms. Their expression of feelings such as sadness, anger, or even happiness is overly intense and appears inappropriate to the context. The children seem to have little restraint over their feelings. They can be explosive in the expression of their anger, they can have "meltdowns" that are equal to a 2-year-old's tantrums. In short, they lack the modulation that we expect in a child that

age. When a child has a meltdown, caregivers often interpret the child's responses as directed at them or, at best, as requiring a response from them. The child, however, does not intend to inflict his or her condition on those around him or her; the child is merely manifesting what he or she cannot help but feel. As stresses mount, the child becomes overburdened and soon reaches a breaking point.

Jason, who is in third grade, has difficulty modulating his affective states, which are labile. His expressions of affect are overly intense, poorly controlled, disinhibited, dramatic, and exaggerated. His moods fluctuate; if suppressed, intense and poorly regulated displays of emotions or meltdowns soon emerge.

Frank often feels overwhelmed. He is easily overstimulated, experiencing the world as too complicated to decipher and understand. He becomes easily confused or disorganized in his thinking when confronted with difficult situations; at such times, he has difficulty integrating ideas or stimuli.

Prosody
Several studies implicate a right hemisphere dysfunction as underlying the absence of prosody in affected patients. Ross and Mesulam (1979) and Ross (1981) suggested that patients with right hemisphere dysfunction are unable to express emotions through prosody or spontaneous gesture (aprosodic–agestural syndrome). Their subjects disclosed that they felt emotions subjectively but could not convey them. Heilman (2002) stated: "The left hemisphere is important for recognizing rhythms and the right for recognizing melody and timbre. Because melody and timbre recognition is mediated by the right hemisphere, I had begun to think that the right hemisphere might also be important for understanding not what is said but how it is said" (p. 56). These studies lend further support to the hypothesis that some of the problems of children with NLD are due a generalized right hemisphere dysfunction.

LEXICAL ASPECTS OF LANGUAGE

Lexical refers to the verbal dimension of an emotional message. The right–hemisphere has some capacity for language processing at both the single-word and discourse levels. The right hemisphere contains a vocabulary of nonverbal emotional signals (facial expressions, prosody, and gestures). We refer to this vocabulary as the nonverbal affective lexicon (Bowers, Bauer, & Heilman, 1993). Patients with right hemisphere damage have linguistic deficiencies and difficulties with complex or abstract language (Borod, Bloom, & Haywood, 1998). Borod and Madigan (2000) referred to the emotional dimension of verbal communications as a *lexical aspect*. Although the right hemisphere has a nonverbal emotional vocabulary, verbal language—a left hemisphere function—can incorporate the emotional dimensions that are part of the right hemisphere. That is, verbal dialogue activates both left and right hemispheres.

The significance of this finding for us lies in the further finding that patients with right hemisphere damage treat "emotion words" differently from normal controls. They appear more impaired in the identification and discrimination of words that are emotionally laden. Such patients also use less appropriate language to communicate feelings and are less accurate than controls in the report of emotionally laden stories. Finally, their autobiographical reports lack specificity and emotionality (Happe, 1991).

If a link exists between right hemisphere dysfunctions and the deficits of children with NLD, then we may conclude that the children's problems with processing emotions extend to their verbal outputs as well, not just the lack of prosody in their speech. The absence of feelings in their verbal communications compounds their social difficulties.

The Contributions of Affective Neuroscience

The suggestion that difficulties in emotional expression stem from right hemisphere dysfunction only partially takes into account the possible explanations for the children's problems in affect processing. As a clinician working with patients who manifest great difficulties with the expression of emotion, the problems appeared to me to be of a more generalized nature. I have wondered about the differences that exist in people's capacities for affect arousal. Some people, who do not have an NLD, present with highly labile and histrionic emotional states, whereas others appear to contain and constrain the expression of their emotions. These differences may be only partially the result of social or cultural display rules. Some of these patients clearly suffer from emotional inhibitions that reflect their psychodynamics. There appear to be multiple contributing factors to what may be called "the common pathway" followed to the end result.

Two major theories of affective neuroscience are those of Panksepp and Davidson. Although there are differences between the two theories, each sheds light on the problems of our children—although any conclusions I draw can only be consider speculative. I begin with Panksepp's contribution, focusing on its relevance to children with NLD (Panksepp, 2001; cf. Solms & Turnbull, 2002).

PANKSEPP'S CONTRIBUTION

According to Panksepp there are four basic emotion-command systems: seeking, rage, fear, and panic. The *seeking system* is a reward system associated with the terms *curiosity, interest*, and *expectancy*. On the perceptual side, this system generates the feeling that something "good" will happen as a result of activating the seeking behavior. On the motor side, it promotes exploratory behavior. The seeking system is intimately associated with the memory system, which provides the representations of objects that enable the organism to learn from experience. The lust subsystem is part of the seeking system that is associated with gratification—that is, with consummation of the appetites that activate the seeking system. The mechanisms of this system are subject to the influences of higher cognitive functions that can modulate, modify, and inhibit them. As we have seen, most children with nonlinguistic perceptual processing difficulties have problems with exploratory behavior; in some of the children these are compounded by motor problems. We may conjecture that the effects of the problems in this emotion-command system on the children's emotional disposition is that they withdraw from situations and are less likely to express curiosity and interest in their surroundings. They are disappointed in their expectation that "something good" will happen, because their forays into the world are seldom rewarded but rather experienced as punishing. The failures of those attempts appear to ensure a punishing outcome.

States of frustration activate the *rage system* when goal-directed actions are thwarted. Feelings of anger/rage (the perceptual aspect of this system) release stereotypical motor programs associated with "fight" responses. The word *irritability* describes the effects of this system when tonically activated at a low level (Solms & Turnbull, 2002, p. 125). The rage system of children with NLD is clearly activated with high frequency. Because they experience frustrations in most of their social encounters, their expressions of rage seem to follow a clear pattern. Their inappropriate behavioral outbursts are a consequence of chronic irritability, which escalates to the point of necessitating a physical discharge of their rage.

Once again, the question must be raised as to what fails to develop in these children to cause their inability to regulate their emotions. There are two parts to the answer to this question. The first is that the disorder itself includes a deficit in the ability to inhibit affective responses. This inhibitory deficit may be related to their attentional problems. Some of the children, but not all, have components of this condition but not the full disorder. The second part of the answer to the question is that a developmental failure occurred in the internalization of an important set of regulatory functions. Once more, the evidence points to the possibility of an attachment disorder, and a secure attachment, as we will see, is critical to the development of affect regulation. The nature of the child's deficits actively interferes with a critical developmental process; both nature and nurture conspire to produce the patient's difficulties.

The fear system activates fear-anxiety. On the perceptual side, the experiences are associated with feelings of extreme anxiety or terror in the child with an NLD; on the motor side, they stimulate the person to run away and try to hide. Mild stimulation leads to a "freeze" response. Transitions and situations with novelty present the child with stimuli that are experienced as unfamiliar and consequently potentially threatening. The sense of danger in those situations may very well elicit fear anxieties that can assume "paranoid" proportions i.e., the danger is projected to sources outside the person rather than being experienced as emanating from within the person.

The panic system (or separation/distress system) is associated not only with panic/anxiety (depression), but also with feelings of loss and sorrow. It is intimately connected with the quality of social bonding and the process of parenting. The care subsystem is a subsystem of the panic system that is associated with the mother/infant bond. It develops within the child and is the social–emotional system that influences the mother's behavior no less than the child's. When the early relationship to caregivers is disrupted or when a bond is not effected, the panic system may be activated in children with NLD. The disruption may occur because of the failure in the nonverbal dialogue between infant and caregiver, and the failure in attachment may be related to interferences that the visual–spatial impairments create in the process of bonding.

The hypothesis I propose is that some aspects of the children's anxiety, which may have its origins at the beginnings of social interactions, in part, stem from an insecure or anxious attachment to the primary caregivers. The panic system is activated by what the child experiences as premature separation from the caregiver. The anxiety associated with this activation reflects the feelings of loss, sorrow, and fear at the rupture created in the social bond with the parent. This hypothesis requires that we examine more closely what occurs during early infancy in the relation between these children and their caregivers, which I undertake in Chapter 8.

DAVIDSON'S CONTRIBUTION

Davidson (1993, 1994, 2000, 2003a, 2003b, 2003c, 2003d) makes a significant contribution to our understanding of the problems children with NLD experience in processing affective states. He begins by challenging the notion that affects and cognition are separate systems of information processing. He contends that because both systems are widely distributed and overlap in many areas, they cannot be separated. We can draw an analogy of the relationship between affects and thoughts to the relationship between objects and their colors. In the same way that there cannot be colorless objects, so there can be no thoughts without affective colorations. According to Davidson, the prefrontal cortical regions are involved in sustaining the quality of the emotions that a person experiences. He identified two categories of emotions that are activated in those regions: *approach-related emotions* and *withdrawal-related ones*. Approach behavior is associated with a reward system, whereas withdrawal behavior is associated with a punishing system.

Davidson contends that the left hemisphere mediates positive emotions, and the right hemisphere mediates negative emotions. When both hemispheres are intact, they balance each other. Damage to either hemisphere, however, disrupts this balance. The higher the pattern of activity in the left prefrontal cortex, the more positive the person feels. People in whom higher activation occurs are more responsive to approach behavior and are more likely to experience positive mood states; they might be called the "optimists." Conversely, people whose higher pattern of activity is located in the right prefrontal cortex tend to feel generally anxious and fearful; these individuals are more prone to enact withdrawal behavior and are more likely to be avoidant and temperamentally "pessimistic." Damage to the left hemisphere produces the "catastrophic reaction" common to stroke patients. Damage to the right causes the disavowal of the injury and its effects, most noticeable in the "neglect" of the dysfunctional left side (Springer & Deutsch, 1989). Heileman (2002) stated that "patients with left hemisphere damage are often said to be anxious, while those with right hemisphere damage can be either indifferent or inappropriately happy" (p. 79). Damage to the left prefrontal region is associated with higher activation of the amygdala and with feelings of sadness and depression; patients who suffer such damage lose interest in their environment, experience little pleasure in activities, and have difficulty initiating activities. The effects of damage to one hemisphere on the functioning of the other hemisphere's ability to perceive and process emotions remains to be studied.

Davidson proposes that people have "affective styles" that guide their dispositional states. Every person has a normative emotional disposition that characterizes his or her day-to-day activities. Davidson identifies several factors that characterize a person's affective style or profile. Among those factors are (1) the *threshold levels* at which the person responds to a stimulus that elicits emotion, (2) the *intensity of the response*, and

(3) the *time to reestablish the normative* (baseline) *level* of functioning. The profile of these characteristics indicates the person's competence or impairment in the capacity to regulate and modulate affect states (Davidson, 2000).

Davidson's contributions are richly evocative in their application to children with NLD. To the extent that right hemisphere dysfunction characterizes the brain functioning of these children, we might speculate that what motivates their patterns of withdrawal is not just others' responses to them, but also the low activation levels of their right prefrontal cortices. Their early avoidance of exploratory play, their impairments in reading nonverbal cues, the negative responses they elicit from others—all seem to conspire to patterns of withdrawal from their environments. Those patterns reinforce their feelings of loneliness and overall demoralization. The attendant anxiety would certainly be an accompaniment to the brain dysfunction and would fit into the same system dysfunction.

The children's problems in self-regulation would be explained as fitting their affective style. The profile of their patterns of responsiveness to stimuli would indicate a low threshold for frustration, an intense reaction that manifests in rage and meltdowns, and difficulties in returning to baseline states. This profile certainly characterizes many behaviors of children with NLD.

Greenspan's Contribution

Beginning in 1979, with the publication of his first book, *Intelligence and Adaptation* (Greenspan, 1979), Greenspan, independently from Davidson, took the position that affects and cognition are inextricably linked from birth. In that work, Greenspan attempted to integrate Piaget's cognitive psychology, which Piaget called genetic epistemology, with psychoanalytic theory. He proposed that Piaget's view that affects and cognition develop in parallel is incomplete or incorrect.

Building on that work and on a method for the treatment of children with disorders that fall within the autistic spectrum, Greenspan arrived at a six-stage developmental schema that describes the emotional, intellectual, and social growth of the child. His premise, which he and coauthor Shanker elaborate in their latest book, is that emotions serve to create and organize many of the mind's most important functions. As the title of this book, *The First Idea* (Greenspan & Shanker, 2004), indicates:

> The first idea is . . . the emergence of the capacity to invest a free-standing image with emotional meaning to make it into a meaningful multisensory, affective image (i.e., an idea or image). . . . Symbols

come about by separating a perception, which is the ability to form an image, from it action. The child achieves this state by co-regulated, emotional interactions with other human beings. Ongoing co-regulated emotional interactions provide emerging and later symbols with meaning throughout the course of life. (p. 37)

Greenspan's major assumption is that every experience that an infant registers is "double coded"; that is, it is laid down as a perception with an accompanying affect. Affects permeate all experience, forming the matrix within which development occurs. Early affect signaling is responsible for the development of mind, that is, of cognition, speech, memory, and the higher forms of intelligence. Although Greenspan acknowledges the existence of constitutional variations that affect our experiences of the world, he also insists that culture plays a major role in the transmission of specific behavior patterns. His six stages of development (Greenspan & Schanke, 2004) represent elaborations of these assumptions (Greenspan, 1997). Greenspan (1997) elaborated these 6 stages into 16 stages that cover the entire life cycle. I do not discuss these because they go beyond the parameters of this work.

- *Stage 1 extends from birth onward*: Initially the child is aware only of sensations that are linked to emotions. The child has only a beginning awareness of the physical and emotional world around him or her, from which he or she forms a set of sensory affective patterns.
- *Stage 2 extends from 2 to 4 months of age*: A growing feeling of engagement and intimacy begins as the infant perceives adults signaling their feelings. The child is not yet fully intentional, that is, cannot respond to the meaning of those signals.
- *Stage 3 extends from 4 to 8 months of age*: The infant participates in a preverbal gestural dialogue and begins to realize that he or she can elicit responses from others. Two-way intentional emotional communication begins to occur.
- *Stage 4 extends from 9 to 18 months*: More complex forms of pre-symbolic communication take place. The infant can distinguish facial expressions and discriminate basic emotions. A presymbolic self emerges as "islands" of intentionality coalesce into patterns of behavior.
- *Stage 5 extends from 18 months on*: The infant acquires verbal language, which permits the use of words in conjunction with actions.
- *Stage 6 extends from 2½ years on*: The child learns to build bridges among symbols. This stage makes possible the differentiation among feelings and emotions that shape the child's intentions.

Within this developmental schema, Greenspan · suggests that psychopathology manifests when the linkages between experiences and feelings fail to occur. This linkage failure can take place during any stage; however, the earlier the occurrence, the greater the psychopathology. Autism is symptomatic of a breakdown that occurs during stage 1. The goal of therapy is to reestablish the missing links between the child's experiences and their concomitant emotional valences. Greenspan has developed a rich repertoire of techniques through which this reestablishment may be accomplished. In a chart review of 200 children, Greenspan and Wieder (1997) found that, with appropriate intervention, a significant number of children developed the capacity for empathy, affective reciprocity, creative thinking, and healthy peer relationships.

A major clinical implication of Greenspan's theory of development for our understanding of children with NLD is the need to focus attention on the children's emotional development. The key to the impairments in their social relationships is found in the broken linkages between their experiences and their affective states. When applied to these children, his intervention techniques may yield results that were not obtained by other modes of intervention.

Conclusion

Given the significance of affects and emotions in human communication, it is unfortunate that little research has been conducted on these aspects of the problems of children with NLD. The children display impairments in emotional functioning in the receptive, the expressive, and regulatory areas. These impairments interfere with social communication and contribute to their problems in social interactions. It becomes clear that any discussion of the social features of children with NLD that excludes consideration of their emotional states will be incomplete.

As Mesulam (2000) pointed out, the right hemisphere is specialized for the perception of affect states and the coordination of affect expression and experience. This fact lends further support to the hypothesis that right hemisphere dysfunctions may be responsible for some NLDs. However, there are other important factors that contribute to the children's multiple impairments. I suggest that (1) dysfunction in their seeking system leads to the inhibition of exploratory behavior. (2) Their rage system is chronically activated by the constant frustrations they meet in day-to-day life. Furthermore, (3) the dysfunction in their fear system may contribute to an avoidance of novelty, and (4) the dysfunction in their panic system may interfere with the mother/infant relationship, giving rise to an attachment disorder.

Based on Davidson's (2003a, 2003b, 2003c) theory of emotion, we may speculate about the contribution of right hemisphere dysfunction to the affective styles of children with NLD; that is, their low threshold levels, the intensity of their responses, and the time it takes them to reestablish a normative level of functioning.

Greenspan and Wieder (2000) suggested an approach to the treatment of children with NLD that no one has applied so far. Given the success that Greenspan (Greenspan & Wieder, 1997) has experienced, especially with higher-functioning children within the autistic spectrum, it behooves us to experiment with this approach and develop data to substantiate its effectiveness.

7

The Social Features of NLD Subtypes

It is now time to pause to review where matters stand in relation to the status of the social–emotional problems of children with NLD. My strategy has been to approach our understanding of the children's problems from three perspectives: neurobiological, social, and intrapersonal. Part I reviewed the neurobiological perspective, which included an overview of the neurological and the neuropsychological theories of NLD. The prior chapters of this part reviewed the relevant aspects of social cognition theory. In Part III, we consider the intrapersonal perspective that will add another layer of complexity to our view of the children's social emotional problems.

I suggested that a useful approach to making diagnostic differentiations was to begin by distinguishing between two sets of processes. The first set involves the simple decoding of nonverbal perceptual information; the second set involves the interpretation of the meaning of that information. The review of the contributions of neurologists and neuropsychologists indicates that these investigators of NLD appear to have taken as their model the work of Broca, who found an association between the aphasias and left hemisphere brain dysfunctions. By investigating populations of patients with right hemisphere dysfunction, the early investigators discovered similarities in those patients' symptoms and the symptoms of children identified as having an NLD. Rourke (1989) expanded on that work and proposed his white matter hypothesis to explain the dysfunctional brain systems that undergird the disorder. His theory lends support to the hypothesis of a right hemisphere dysfunction. Furthermore, Mesulam's (2000) categorization of right hemisphere functions lent support to the differentiation between the two sets of processes made earlier. His category of complex and nonlinguistic perceptual functions encompasses most of the functions that others refer to as visual–spatial processing deficits, and his conceptualization of the paralinguistic aspects of nonverbal communication and emotional perception parallel the distinction between decoding and understanding.

I concluded that it is possible to integrate the various theories into a consensus position by specifying the domains that investigators regard as impaired in children with NLD. Three major domains suggest themselves: (1) the *domain of complex and nonlinguistic perceptual function*, which includes Denckla's (1991) visual–perceptual/sequential information-processing functions and some of Rourke's (1989) visual–spatial organizational processing functions (there is broad consensus that this domain forms part of the core symptoms of NLD); (2) Denckla's (1991) *domain of attentional/executive functions*, which is an area that is insufficiently considered, although Voeller (1986, 1991), Rourke (1986), and other researchers (1996) find evidence for it; and (3) the domain of *social cognition*, which Pennington (1991) regarded as dissociable from the domain of spatial cognition, and which includes Mesulam's (2000) right hemisphere functions of paralinguistic communication and affect perception. It is notable that the deficits in these domains often coexist with higher functioning in other domains, such as the verbal domain.

I suggested that a defining feature of NLD is the coexistence of nonlinguistic perceptual deficits and the social impairments that are associated with those deficits. I called these impairments *social imperceptions*. These conditions—the presence of nonlinguistic perceptual deficits and social imperception—constitute the necessary conditions for a diagnosis of an NLD. An unanswered question remains as to why some children with nonlingistic perceptual deficits develop social difficulties whereas others do not develop them. Further research is required to answer this question. Those who develop the social problems may also suffer from subtle deficits in social cognition that remain to be uncovered. Such evidence would open the door to the view that problems in social cognition are primary, whereas the nonlinguistic perceptual deficits are coexisting conditions. We would then be in a position to posit a broad category of social learning disabilities with several subtypes. In any case, the neuropsychological perspective documents the developmental constraints imposed by the deficits in nonlinguistic perception, the attention and executive dysfunctions, and the associated social impairments. Children with those deficits and impairments face challenges in their efforts to function in academic, social, and day-to-day life activities.

Following Denckla (1991) and Pennington (1991), I accepted the hypothesis of the dissociation of visual–spatial cognition and social cognition. The domain of social cognition then became pivotal in understanding some of the children's social–emotional dysfunctions. This focus led to the exploration of social cognition as one of the major domains that contributes to the core impairments in children's social–emotional functioning. I chose three sets of functions that are commonly associated with social cognition to evaluate the extent to which these might contribute to the children's impairment. In the last three chapters, I examined each of those domains: that of reciprocal social relationships, that of the children's language impairments, and the domain of emotional function. My conclusion is that (1) children with NLD have mild to moderately severe impairments in the domain of reciprocal social interactions, but probably have the capacity for theory of mind functioning; (2) their difficulties with nonverbal communication contribute to their relationship problems, and although their language problems extend to verbal language as well, the latter are not sufficient to lead to major impairments in social relationships; and (3) the impairments in emotional functioning, although moderately signifi-

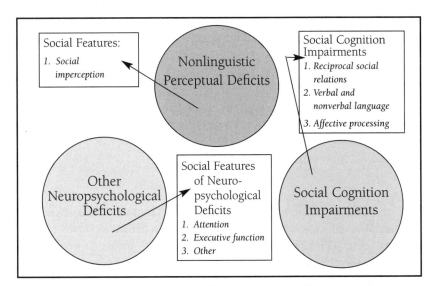

Figure 7.1 The Social Features of the Components of NLD Subtypes.
Impaired domains in children with NLD and their associated social features. Children who demonstrate an inability to process complex and nonlinguistic perceptual information have concomitant social problems characterized as social imperceptions. Those with neuropsychological deficits in the areas of *attention* and *executive function* have, in addition, social problems characteristic of children with those deficits. Those with *impairments in social cognition* manifest problems in reciprocal social interactions, social communication, and emotional functioning.

cant, were not sufficiently disabling as to preclude the capacity for intimate social relationships. The last two domains are dissociable from the first and from each other, although it is a question as to whether they should be considered as part of the core symptoms of NLD, as correlated manifestations, or as comorbid conditions (see Figure 7.1).

Each domain contributes a different set of possible behavioral problems. (1) The impairments in complex and nonlinguistic perception produce symptoms that I labeled *social imperception*. Rourke (1993) documented similar problems in his analysis of the children's errors in mechanical arithmetic. (2) The social problems associated with attentional and executive function deficits are secondary consequences rather than correlated manifestation of the deficits. They are therefore more varied and less predictable than those of the first domain. Finally, (3) deficits in social cognition may impair reciprocal social relationships, social communication, and emotional functioning. Each of these domains contributes to the constraints on the child's development and determines the specific expression of the phenotype as well as the child's sense of self.

Patterns of Social Impairments in Four NLD Subtypes

It is now possible to hypothesize four subtypes and their patterns of social impairments, as they are associated with deficits in the three domains of nonlinguistic perception, attention and executive function, and social function.

Definition: NLD is a developmental neurobehavioral disorder characterized by a primary core deficit in the processing of nonlinguistic perceptual information. The deficit produces receptive problems in the decoding of such information and may also result in expressive problems. The diagnosis is warranted if, and only if, this deficit produces concomitant social impairments.

NLD Subtype I

The first subtype, *NLD subtype I*, includes those children who demonstrate an inability to process complex and nonlinguistic perceptual tasks as their primary core neuropsychological deficits. Only children with these deficits who also develop concomitant social problems are included in this subtype and given a diagnosis of NLD (see Figure 7.2).

These children have problems in the following areas:

1. *Neuropsychological deficits.* Perceptual deficits occur in *some* of the following areas:

    a. *Auditory* abilities (e.g., recognizing pitch and melody);

    b. *Visual discrimination* abilities (e.g., recognizing faces, identifying complex geometric shapes);

    c. *Visual–spatial* abilities (e.g., depth perception, spatial location, mental rotation, line orientation, visual perspective taking);

    d. The ability to perform *visual-motor* tasks (e.g., tracing mazes, block design);

    e. *Memory* for complex spatial relationships;

    f. *Time* perception.

2. *Social impairments.* The social imperceptions interfere with social communication and manifest in some of the following difficulties:

    a. *Nonverbal communication*

        i. Auditory perception: Has receptive and expressive problems with prosody; may misread a loud tone of voice or not inflect own voice to convey intended emotion.

        ii. Visual discrimination: Has problems in the use and interpretation of gestures, gaze, facial expression, and body language; may not notice a teacher's nonverbal gesture to stop talking or wait his or her turn.

        iii. Visual–spatial processing: Has poor judgment of proximics, i.e., social space; has difficulties orienting self in space, which may result in problems with judgments about personal space as well as other situations that involve making judgments about spatial relationships; may inadvertently bump into other children while standing in line, may touch another child inappropriately, or may stand too close while speaking with others.

        iv. Visual–motor functions: Has problems playing games that involved fine motor control.

    b. *Reciprocal social interaction*: Has difficulty reading social cues and responds inappropriately to such communications; appears socially disconnected, socially clumsy, or immature; has few friends and does not socialize appropriately when he is with them.

Ron, age 9 years, 8 months, has been evaluated repeatedly and has a long history of identified problems. He has had articulation and speech problems, fine-motor problems, and at times he becomes perseverative.

Ron is in fourth grade, where he is doing reasonably well academically. His social adjustment is the source of concern. His teacher reports that in groups he has trouble connecting with peers, does not appear to realize how he comes across to others, does not know when to talk and when to listen. He seems to miss the big picture by focusing only on tangents. Characteristically, when at-

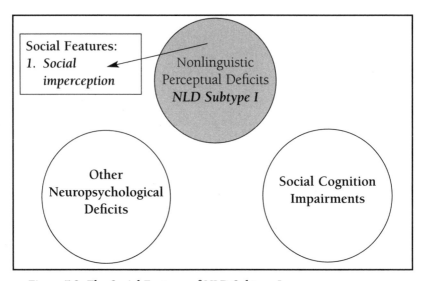

Figure 7.2. The Social Features of NLD Subtype I.
NLD Subtype I: includes those children with nonlinguistic perceptual deficits. Only children with these deficits who also develop concomitant social problems are included in this subtype and given a diagnosis of NLD

tempts are made to correct him, he stubbornly holds to his view and will not let go. If his father interrupts him to explain something, Ron continues talking and does not acknowledge that he is being addressed. As an example, his father was helping him with a Pine Wood Derby project, and Ron insisted on painting the car backward. When his father tried to point out the error to him, Ron stubbornly insisted that he was correct and would have none of it. His father had to back away and let Ron proceed in his own fashion.

His parents report that in spite of all these problems, Ron has a stunning lack of insight into his behavior. He does not seem to worry about others' perceptions of him. He copes well on his own, enjoys computers, takes karate, and participates in Cub Scouts. The fact that he has no friends does not appear to trouble him. His parents see this oblivion as a positive, and do not wish to interfere with it at the risk of "cracking his shell." He may come to a different realization about his problems later on.

Another trait that characterizes Ron is the fact that he likes to stay up late at night. The other night, his father found him walking around in his room at 10:45 P.M. This behavior does not appear to be related to the stimulant medications he is taking for his ADHD, because the pattern existed prior to his being on medication. If left on his own he will get to sleep by 11 P.M. and get up by 10 A.M.

The parents also reported that Ron manifests considerable anxiety. While sitting quietly, he will pick up Kleenex and pick it apart. The blanket in his room has been shredded from his fidgeting with it. Ron is also not a good historian; he has trouble reporting incidents that have occurred, seems to miss the important details, and cannot report on the sequence of events.

NLD Subtype II

The second subtype, *NLD subtype II*, includes children who meet the criteria for inclusion in NLD subtype I *and* have neuropsychological deficits in the areas of *attention* and *executive function* (see Figure 7.3).

1. *Neuropsychological deficits.* These children have deficits in some of the following areas:
   a. *Attention*: problems with inattention, impulsivity, or hyperactivity, but does not necessarily meet criteria for a diagnosis of ADHD. If the child qualifies for a diagnosis of ADHD, then we may consider the ADHD to be a comorbid condition.
   b. *Executive function*: Difficulties in the initiation, conception, and implementation of a plan; inability to manage time, organize resources, self-monitor and self-regulate to translate a plan into productive activity that ensures its completion; and impairments in psychomotor function, fluid reasoning, and dealing with novelty.
   c. *Psychomotor or other neuropsychological functions.*
2. *Social impairments.* These children have problems in some of the following areas:
   a. *Attention and impulse control.* Appears inattentive in social contexts, leading interlocutors to believe that the child is not listening and does not care about what is being said; social and familial relationships may be impaired because of the child's impulsivity, disruptiveness, bossiness, or oppositional behaviors.
   b. *Executive function.* Caregivers and teachers become increasingly impatient with the child's disorganization as well as the reasons for the underachievement. The child makes procedural errors in the process of solving a social problem or applying a learned rule from one situation to a dissimilar situation; fails to shift psychological set in different contexts in attempting to deal with a social interaction, and inappropriately applies a practiced procedure to the new operation; exhibits memory problems that may be related to working memory problems (in particular, visual memory) and possibly the result of an inability to reevoke the visual image associated with the social situation and the context, leading to an inept response.

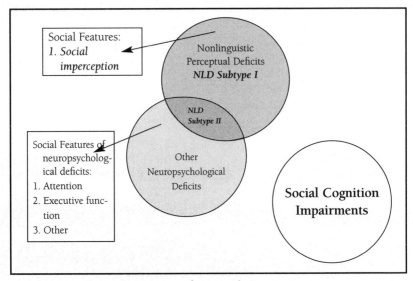

Figure 7.3. The Social Features of NLD Subtype II.

NLD Subtype II: includes children who demonstrate an inability to process complex and nonlinguistic perceptual tasks as their primary core neuropsychological deficit, have concomitant social problems *and* have neuropsychological deficits in the areas of *attention* and/or *executive function*.

Jordan is a 12-year, 9-month-old adolescent who just completed the seventh grade. He is an intellectually gifted youngster whose history of attentional, behavioral, and social difficulties (dating back to preschool) has interfered with his peer relations, general social–emotional adjustment, and, at times, his schoolwork.

Jordan's mother described him as having been a very active toddler who would engage in serious tantrums. He learned the alphabet by 18 months; by age 3, he was climbing and jumping off the jungle gym, unafraid of the risks. As a student in grade school, his teachers said he always rushed through his work, made careless mistakes, and was poorly organized. They also said he needed to show more control and not speak out so often in class.

In early school years, Jordan often had difficulty completing tasks independently and appeared to lose interest midtask, often requiring one-on-one supervision. He often misplaced or lost essential school items (e.g., writing utensils) in addition to keeping a messy work area. He often needed reminders to listen to instructions carefully and exhibited much frustration and anxiety; despite attempting to appear confident, his self-esteem was seemingly quite fragile. In fifth grade his teacher asked his parents to empty his desk into a garbage bag because it was so messy and unorganized. His lockers and desks were unorganized and messy throughout his years at school.

From grade school through high school, his mother would joke that she was going to tie him to his desk. When he went to his room to study, he would stay 10 minutes, at most, and she would next find him watching TV or teasing his brother. He seldom brought home his assignments, would procrastinate getting to work on them, and would forget to take them back to school even if he completed them. Jordan's mother constantly had to prod and nag him to do his schoolwork.

He had very poor time management skills. In the mornings, after waking him up, his mother frequently found him lying in bed 15–20 minutes later. It was a daily battle to get him out of the house and to school on time. His bedroom and bathroom were cluttered with papers, clothes, and books, and he never followed through with his chores. It seemed as if he were not listening; some tasks would take 3 days of nagging and reminding before he completed them.

Jordan has difficulty getting along with peers. He was reported to be aggressive with his peers, although not intentionally hurtful. He appears to have great difficulty adjusting his behavior to fit differing social situations; this difficulty impedes peer relationships and transitions between daily routines and tasks. Despite his demonstrated academic abilities, Jordan's motivational, organizational, and attentional difficulties appear to be preventing optimal learning and classroom performance.

Socially, Jordan's interactions continue to involve awkward (e.g., brief eye contact, overly familiar interpersonal style) and aggressive overtures (e.g., poking, bumping, hitting) that are reportedly meant "in fun" but are not interpreted benignly by recipients. His ability to judge facial expressions, gestures, and share feelings with others is poor and adds to his social difficulty, because he is unable to utilize subtle, nonverbal feedback regarding his inappropriate attempts at social intercourse. Furthermore, Jordan abandons effort to communicate when words don't come easily and his mother states that he can present as "extremely sarcastic and pessimistic, which comes across as rude and inconsiderate."

Jordan shows particular difficulty understanding the complexity of people's feelings and the need to moderate behavior in relation to each context. Jordan becomes overwhelmed when facing strong or complex emotional situations, notably negatives ones. In response, he experiences feelings of anxiety, depressed mood, and anger and demonstrates overreliance on his intellect to preserve a positive self-perception and to (hopefully) impress others. This coping style assists Jordan in avoiding complex and uncomfortable emotions and interpersonal relationships but causes further disconnectedness for him.

Jordan wants to make contact through relationships but is extremely cautious, even hypervigilant, because of his sensitivity to loss and rejection. Indeed, he often feels immobilized, partly due to feeling discouraged and demoralized. He needs more time than most people need to become comfortable with an individual and a setting in order to interact effectively and develop useful perceptions of the social interchange. He seems to hold simplified or immature perceptions of people and relationships (in strong contrast to what would be ex-

pected from his serious, mature, and intellectualized demeanor). Jordan tends to relate to one or two aspects of an individual. At times, he relates instrumentally rather than developing an integrated understanding of the multiple facets, both positive and negative, of individuals. Jordan's low sense of self-worth at times prompts him to project a negative, unitary reaction onto other people, anticipating their judgment of him and anger at him; he may act in a way to either pre-empt these feelings, avoid the situation, or indeed elicit these feelings in order to maintain a sense of control.

At some level, Jordan is aware of his social derailments and relative isolation. His social life has been tilted more strongly to interaction with adults than children, and his hypersensitivity to remarks from authority figures have left him self-critical—at times, painfully so. As a consequence he attempt to suppress his feelings, which are often negative; although his attempts provide immediate if temporary relief, they leave him with insufficiently informed and integrated understandings of life's complexities. The data indicate that Jordan is currently depressed, though he may not be aware of this condition because he suppresses negative feelings so strenuously.

NLD Subtype III

The third subtype, *NLD subtype III*, includes children who meet the criteria for NLD subtype I *and* have *social cognition impairments* that manifest in reciprocal social interactions, social communication, and emotional functioning (see Figure 7.4). These children have social impairments in the following areas:

1. *Reciprocal social interactions.* The children lack social skills, are socially clumsy, appear socially disconnected when with others, and are immature or inappropriate. At times their behavior may be socially dysfunctional as they become argumentative, disruptive, or disrespectful. There are not successful in maintaining peer relationships, have no close friendships, and are rejected, teased, or bullied by peers. In addition, they may have diminished capacity for theory of mind. They are not always aware of the fact that others have beliefs, desires, and intentions and consequently appear to disregard others' thoughts and feelings. Their capacity for pretense (i.e., imaginative play) and deception is also diminished.

2. *Social communication difficulties.* In addition to the difficulties in nonverbal communication (i.e., in the use of gestures, vocal intonations, gaze, and do not notice these in others) associated with NLD subtype I, these children have some verbal language problems. In particular, they have difficulties with the *pragmatic aspects of verbal*

communication. They may not have an appreciation of social rules or may misapply rules they have acquired. They also do not contextualize their communication sufficiently for the listener to grasp fully what they are trying to convey. They are also not sufficiently selective in what to communicate and what to leave out, so that the salience of their communication is lost; that is, they have problems with relevance theory.

3. *Emotional functioning difficulties.* These children have difficulties in the reception, expression, and processing of affective modes of communication. Their self-esteem is damaged by the frustration that results from failure to complete tasks that appear simple to others, and their lack of success in social relationships. They suffer from chronic anxiety and have difficulties in self-regulation.

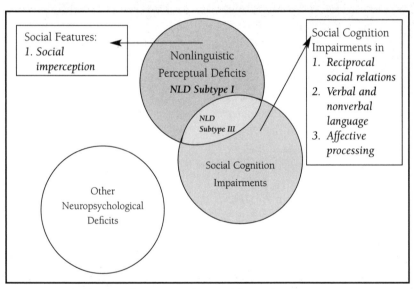

Figure 7.4. The Social Features of NLD Subtype III.
NLD Subtype III: includes children who demonstrate an inability to process complex and nonlinguistic perceptual tasks as their primary core neuropsychological deficits, have concomitant social problems *and* have *social cognition impairments* that manifest in reciprocal social interactions, social communication, and emotional functioning.

Jonathan is 10 years, 6 months old and has a history of throwing temper tantrums, including crying, yelling, throwing items, and periodically striking people, since the age of 3 (he was also a fussy infant). In general, Jonathan holds on to ideas rigidly and, in particular, tends to display rigid adherence to rules; when others violate these rules, Jonathan becomes enraged. Difficulties regulating his emotional display and his insufficiently developed social skills impede the development of friendships.

Jonathan's explosions tend to occur in the school setting or during interactions with peers. During one of these episodes, Jonathan had to be carried out of the classroom by the school maintenance person. His tantrums are usually precipitated by feeling that other children are not listening to him or that they have broken a rule. Jonathan adheres rigidly and literally to instructions from authority figures and has difficulty gleaning meaning from the intent of the rule and generalizing rules across situations. According to Jonathan's mother, he sometimes feels that other children are violating rules when they are not. He then becomes very angry when he tries to tell the children that they have broken a rule, and they respond by ignoring him. Jonathan's temper tantrums occur approximately two times per week at school. Furthermore, he does not have sufficiently developed social skills to initiate and develop friendships. He tends to gravitate toward younger children. The combination of soft voice, speech misarticulations, and gentle demeanor makes him a target for teasing.

Jonathan has a tendency to become emotionally overwhelmed during emotionally charged interpersonal situations. When this occurs, he either becomes aggressive or withdraws from the situation in an attempt to regulate his feelings. His inability to modulate his emotional reactivity may lead to feelings of helplessness and social isolation.

Jonathan's mother is concerned about her son's rigid and self-righteous behavior with other children. She realizes he misperceives the intentions and behavior of his peers and that these misperceptions interfere with his ability to engage in normal peer relations.

During our session, he had difficulty making appropriate eye contact at nodal points in the conversation and instead displayed a wandering gaze. He also blinked his eyes frequently. He showed little emotional responsivity to social cues and jokes but smiled and acted pleased with his performance on various assessment devices. When he responds to humor, his response is usually the kind of humor a 6-year-old child would appreciate but that most 10-year-olds would find childish and demeaning.

Jonathan does not always perceive and interpret situations in the manner that most others would. His perceptions are accurate at times, but he focuses on details of situations that are less centrally relevant than others. At other times, when there are many facets to a situation, he may develop an idiosyncratic interpretation of the factors leading up to the situation and the meaning of the situation. His ideas about such situations are unusual at times, and his comments in peer social situations may seem unrelated to the conversation. He can become easily confused, has a difficult time integrating ideas to develop a synthesized meaning, and when he is overwhelmed, may show a daydreaming, wide-eyed, or blank gaze, as if he were in a daze.

Jonathan cannot easily read facial or vocal emotional expressions, except for the most obvious of smiles. Therefore, he cannot make inferences about, or derive meaning from, people's emotional reactions and motivations. He does not discuss his own feelings, which may suggest that he encounters difficulty identifying them. Not surprisingly, he does not ask about others' feelings, because this communicational language is not obvious to him. He shows a full range of facial and vocal expressions, but his voice is too loud at times, with an unusual intonation, and his gestures, when present, seem awkward and stilted. He shows a high degree of depressive mood, anxiety, and fearfulness. However, the referents of these feelings may be relatively trivial in the context of most people's experience, and he might not develop these emotional reactions to situations that would prompt such reactions in other people. His marked difficulty reading other people's emotional expressions leads him to understand poorly the impact of his behavior on others and consequently to not show interpersonal feelings such as guilt and empathy, which are predicated on a knowledge of others' feelings in relationship to self. Furthermore, Jonathan shows dramatic emotional lability, fluctuating between a quiet, gentle demeanor and an extremely agitated one that is often an overreaction to a minor situation or results from his misinterpretation of a situation. Jonathan's distress at these times has led to destruction of objects, aggressive behavior toward other children, and even self-injurious behavior. Jonathan is indeed quite self-critical and self-blaming. However, as mentioned, he does not understand the impact of his behavior on other children, so he does not have an objective sense of his strengths, weaknesses, and contributions to interpersonal impasses or conflicts. His emotional agitation and self-blame have grown so strong at times that he has threatened to kill himself.

He shows less social greeting than do most children his age and weak skills in initiating interactions. He shares toys and items with people only selectively or when strongly urged. He misinterprets the good-natured aspects of teasing and overemphasizes the critical, verbal aspects. Furthermore, he shows little tolerance for interpersonal frustration. Feeling rejected by peers, he has sought either younger children or adults with whom to interact. He tends to distrust others, expecting rejection, and at times even anticipating that others intend him harm. His behavior may be annoying and even provocative, though usually unintentionally. Jonathan does not always understand the role that he has played in interpersonal conflicts and tends to externalize blame and responsibility onto others. He is a poor loser at games and often overfocuses on perceived transgressions of rules shown by other children. With adults, Jonathan needs continual reassurance, and tends to display a dependent, clingy, interpersonal demeanor.

Jonathan shows an inability to read emotional communication in any modality except for the most obvious communication. He is relatively unable to derive meaning and inference from the ways in which the emotional aspects of communication color the literal, verbal communication. As such, he is immature in developing dyadic emotions such as guilt, shame, and empathy, and has difficulty with perspective taking. His eye contact is inconsistent and he does not always *accommodate the other person's interest in a conversation. Without such basic abilities, Jonathan is relatively unable to orchestrate the reciprocal nature of interpersonal peer relationships. He has a hard time initiating interactions, and because he does not anticipate the interests, needs, and feelings of the other person, he does not progress in his relationships to the degree of intimacy expected by his age. His organizational and emotional comprehension difficulties lead him to misinterpret social situations, particularly ones that involve conflict, and he is therefore unable to deal with interpersonally and emotionally laden situations. It is no wonder that he has a history of emotional meltdowns and tantrums. His only way of learning and understanding social–emotional situations is by following explicitly learned rules, to which he adheres too concretely.*

Because Jonathan is relatively unable to read others' emotions, he does not have an understanding of the impact of his behavior on others. As such, he does not track his contribution to interpersonal conflicts. Nevertheless, he understands at some level that most of his interpersonal relationships are not rewarding or even functional, and his self-esteem suffers as a result. He blames others for the pieces of the conflict that he understands—for example, the transgressions against individual rules—but privately feels that he has failed. Because he does not understand the contributions of his behavior to the failings, he does not take responsibility for these aspects. These factors, in addition to his difficulty reading, predicting, and accommodating himself to situations, result in a base-

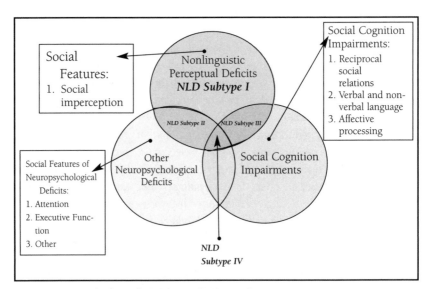

Figure 7.5. The Social Features of NLD Subtype IV.
NLD Subtype IV: includes children who demonstrate an inability to process complex and nonlinguistic perceptual tasks as their primary core neuropsychological deficits, have concomitant social problems, have neuropsychological deficits in the areas of *attention* and *executive function, and* have *social cognition impairments* that manifest in reciprocal social interactions, social communication, and emotional functioning.

line of depressive and anxious mood. His internalized feelings, poor social skills, and difficulty reading complex social situations leave him relatively isolated.

NLD Subtype IV

Finally, *NLD subtype IV* includes children who meet the criteria for NLD subtype II *and* have the same *social cognition impairments* as those described in subtype III (see Figure 7.5).

Janice is a 15-year, 6-month-old high school sophomore in special education. Her behavior has deteriorated since entry into adolescence. She has become rebellious, spends a lot of time lying on her bed listening to CDs, and picks friends who are into drugs (although her mother believes that Janice is not on drugs). She was caught drinking in school once, but that appears to have been an isolated incident. Last spring she ran away from home after she was forbidden to associate with a friend; she was found at the home of another friend.

In the emotional domain Janice does not appear to exhibit much emotional depth; last November she was thought to be depressed and placed on Prozac. She has low self-esteem, often talks about suicide, and has cut herself on one occasion. She has had a chronic sleep problem but seems to need little sleep. From a social perspective she has poor social skills and has been disruptive in some classes and truant from many others. At times, she has hostile relations with some teachers, administration officials, and other students. At a cognitive level, she obsesses on topics, dwelling on things for an inordinate period of time. She does not understand directions. This year she passed only the courses in the self-contained classes.

Janice exhibited social problems from early on. For example, when asked to line up with other children, she did not conform but would keep going to the back of the line. She would initially resist going to birthday parties, but appeared all right once there. She never seemed to be curious about anything and almost never asked any questions. She liked solitary activities, especially reading. She read voraciously, insisting on reading book series in sequence. She read the entire series of Sweet Valley High—150 books—and was able to remember the entire contents in order. However, according to her mother, she never seemed to understand people's intentions or motives. For example, she would ask her mother, "Why are you smiling at me?" She could react with appropriate empathy to situations that were magnified and obvious, but not to subtle situations. She was minimally involved in Brownies, and then only because her mother was the troop leader. If her mother tapped her affectionately and gently on the leg, she would ask, "Why are you hitting me?" If a child accidentally bumped into her seat, she would react as though it were done intentionally. She also was a picky eater until she reached adolescence.

Last year was Janice's first year in high school, and she seemed more determined to figure out relationships with other children. She appeared to wish to find a group to which she could belong. She seemed to gravitate to kids who are losers and who act outrageously. She imitates their flamboyant style, some of whom have dyed hair and piercings in various body parts. This year she has associated with kids from broken homes who are on drugs. She got drunk one day in school; she walks in and out of class whenever she feels like it, sometimes entering an ongoing class to speak to a friend; and she feels free to walk into the teachers' lounge to get a soda from their machine. It seems as though she wishes to identify herself as rebellious, to present an image of "If you screw with me, I'll get you!" Last spring, she went to a school where a friend was taking a class. Since she was not a student there, she was asked to leave. She did, then returned, and finally the police were called. It took considerable effort on the part of the child's mother to explain to the police that Janice was disturbed and should not be taken to detention. Other inappropriate behaviors include tackling a child and beating him up because he said something to her. If she is upset with another child, at the very least she will stare at him or her to induce discomfort.

On returning from a trip to California, she was found to have a bag of marijuana and was grounded by her parents. When she was forbidden to associate with a friend, Janice ran away from home—although it was evident that this was not a serious attempt at running away since the mother of the friend to whose house she went called Janice's mother. Two months ago at school she was found cutting herself with the blade of a safety razor. Her parents found out that a friend was cutting herself, and Janice appeared to be imitating her. There has been no recurrence of the cutting behavior. When she and mother were in a bookstore, she decided that she wanted to buy the autobiography of Courtney Love, her pop star idol. When her mother forbade her from doing that, she threatened to steal the book but did not. Then in the car she refused to put on her seat belt and threatened to jump out of the car on the expressway. When they got home, she went into a kitchen drawer and took out a knife, threatening to kill herself. Her mother took the knife away with no difficulty.

Organization is a tremendous problem for Janice. She tends to lose assignments and seems unable to pull all the pieces together to complete major assignments. Her teacher reports that Janice does not pay attention fully in class activities, whether in the whole-group or small-group format. When confronted with her behavior, Janice usually denies it. She often turns in tasks with less than 10% of the answers completed. During cooperative group work, other students complain that Janice does not contribute. On field trips parent leaders have noted that she did not pay attention to the docent. In class she often fiddles with papers and other things in her desk and does not make eye contact with the speaker. At times she talks with other students and at other times seems to stare into space. Overall, Janice's difficulties with organization and integration seem to be significantly affecting her learning, information processing, and social functioning. She has much trouble putting together numerous, disparate pieces of information into a meaningful coherent whole. She seems able to manage only small portions of information at a time. Consequently, she does not fully understand what is happening, whether it is learning a lesson at school or watching a television show at home.

Janice's approach to memory/learning tasks indicates that she seems to get overwhelmed by too much information and will anchor herself by understanding or memorizing some specific details, but lose the overall gestalt of the task. Her current problems, such as losing assignments because there is too much for her to keep track of, or not understanding academic subjects that require putting together complex ideas, suggest that Janice has no effective organizing and integrating strategies. She performs better on tasks that are broken down into more manageable pieces of information, so that she can integrate and internalize the overall structure, piece by piece. She needs specific help with developing strategies, such as categorizing pieces of information, clustering like items, and the use of mnemonic cues to help her organize and remember to do her assignments.

Because Janice does not readily integrate different kinds of information or appreciate the gestalt of interpersonal situations, she has difficulties with understanding the meaning of social experiences. Being able to take into account a person's intonation, content of speech, facial and body gestures, as well as the overall context of an interpersonal interaction requires putting many different kinds of information together. This is hard for Janice. She also struggles with accessing her own feelings and expressing herself emotionally. Janice would benefit from social situations that are more structured.

Staff members in the student center have found Janice to be extremely difficult to assist. If someone offers help, she refuses it. She comes to the student center at her scheduled time but with no materials. When sent back to her locker for work, she most often returns without any material. She will not sit in a seat to work. She frequently makes inappropriate comments to staff when they speak to her. For example, when asked to find a place to sit, her reply was, "Don't give me the teacher stare, they don't work on me." Another time her teacher asked her to find a place to sit, whereupon she stacked four chairs, sat down, and then scooted them around the room. Her reply was, "You didn't say I had to stay in one place." Many times when the student center staff have been busy with other students, she has walked out. On one occasion, a staff member told her very firmly to take a seat and she replied, "Since you asked me so nicely, I will sit down." Within moments, however, she was on the move again. She continually talks to students when tests are in progress and many times has kicked or hit other students.

When she is speaking to people, she looks at them only infrequently. If she does make eye contact while speaking, she does not maintain it. Janice has a difficult time with peer relationships. She alienates herself from her peers by her physically in appropriate behavior and her verbally inappropriate comments that turn students away. For example, at one time during the year Janice had a problem of staring at students in her classes. Her teachers addressed this situation and eventually it subsided.

Conclusion

Which of these three domains should be regarded as constituting the *primary core set of symptoms* for the disorder, and which are *correlated manifestations* or *comorbid conditions* unrelated to the primary core symptoms?

I would suggest that *deficits in the domain of complex and nonlinguistic perception, and their associated social impairments, constitute the primary core symptoms.* I want to underscore that I have labeled the domain as deficits in *complex and nonlinguistic perception* in accordance with Mesulam's (2000) designation, because the domain includes more than the processing of spatial or visual–spatial information. Both the neuropsychological deficits and the social impairments are *necessary conditions* for the diagnosis of an NLD. Those children who have nonlinguistic perceptual deficits but do not have social difficulties would not receive the diagnosis of NLD.

The inclusion of this domain is in keeping with the hypothesis that some functions associated with the right hemisphere are impaired in children with NLD. There appears to be considerable evidence to support this hypothesis, even though some of the symptoms reflect deficits in functions that are more widely distributed and that may involve other brain systems. Further investigation of Rourke's (1995) white-matter hypothesis may shed light on the nature of these dysfunctions.

As to the neurobiological underpinnings of NLD, the evidence is inconclusive. Much of the support for the hypothesis of a right hemisphere dysfunction comes from lesion-based studies that predate the advances made in the past decade in our understanding of brain function. More recent studies implicate dysfunctions in the right hemisphere that resonate with the symptoms of our children. None of the studies followed up on Rourke's white-matter hypothesis, so the status of that hypothesis remains unknown. We are left with the uncertainty that one or both hypotheses may be correct or, at best, incomplete. The fact that all recent evidence about brain function points to the wide distribution of all processes means that we are far from the goal of formulating a hypothesis that takes into account the data as well as current thinking.

We may now be able to begin to explain the heterogeneity of this disorder and the variety of phenotypes that are expressed developmentally. However, this is not the end of the story, as we have yet to consider the contribution to the children's social behaviors of the third perspective— the intrapersonal perspective—which imposes its own constraints on children's development.

Part III

THE SENSE OF SELF

AN INTRAPERSONAL PERSPECTIVE

8

Mindsharing, Aloneness, and Attachment

The neuropsychological and social perspectives discussed in the preceding chapters provide an incomplete account of the state of the whole child, unless they are supplemented by the intrapersonal perspective that deals with children's subjective experience. An integration of all three perspectives can occur through the articulation of a developmental viewpoint that specifies the way in which children's mental processes organize their experiences into a coherent whole. These processes are embedded within the sense of self and give rise to enduring personality traits that give individuals a clear, recognizable, and unique identity.

To discuss neuropsychological functions detached from the rest of the person is to discuss disembodied elements that provide an incomplete understanding of the motives that drive behaviors. Considering a person simply as a social entity also limits our understanding to the interactions that occur between people, giving little sense of the person's inner life. The intrapersonal perspective contextualizes the neuropsychological and the social within the person's sense of self and permits us to speak of *mindsharing*, a form of intersubjectivity through which we enlarge our sense of self to encompass the social milieu as well as those to whom we feel attached. More broadly, we feel connected to others within our community by our shared language, values, and beliefs. We are at one with those for whom we care, whether they be blood relatives or others who are members of our community. Their connection to us lies in the bond we share with them. A threat to that bond or to our values and beliefs touches us as deeply as any personal injury. The boundaries of our minds are located far beyond those of our physical being. They extend to the outer limits of the environment in which we live and define what we hold dear.

Psychodynamic theories have traditionally emphasized the role of care-givers in shaping the children's behavior, placing less stress on neurobio-logical contributions and the function of emotions in determining motivation. Caregivers are critically significant on several levels: (1) They provide the emotional sustenance that nurtures the infant and leads to a feeling of being valued; (2) they engage the child in patterns of interaction that provide templates for the child's emerging personality; and (3) they attach meanings to the child's experiences that eventually form the core of the child's view of the world.

By focusing on the *psychological functions* that caregivers perform for children during development, this perspective allows us to enter into chil-dren's experience, their selfobject needs, and the mindsharing aspects of their relationships. Human beings are incomplete without the mindshar-ing functions that others provide in the psychological domain. Selfobject functions as well as adjunctive functions are necessary for children to sur-vive psychologically. The deficits in nonlinguistic perception and the im-pairments in social communication of children with NLD interfere with caregivers' performance of those functions. The psychological deficits that ensue have consequences for the children's sense of self-cohesion and for their construal of a coherent self-narrative; a disorder of the self may be the result.

Understanding children's motives involves understanding the patterns that organize their experiences. Because all social interactions and com-munications are suffused with emotions, these patterns incorporate not only children's experiences but also the affect states (i.e., emotions) elicited during their occurrence. As we will see in the next chapter, these patterns turn into themes that organize children's self-narrative and their view of the world.

The main question in Part III is, "How does the interplay among the child's neuropsychological deficits, the impairments in the capacity for so-cial communication, and the responses to and by those in their context affect the development of the sense of self in a child with an NLD?" To answer this question requires that we describe the development of the sense of self as the psychological structure that integrates the various com-ponents of children's experiences. The absence of a developmental theory in self psychology has led to the neglect or even disregard of attachment theory as providing explanations for some of the phenomena we observe. (Schore [2002] has attempted such an integration.) In preparation for my discussion of the development of the sense of self in the next chapter, I summarize some of the findings of attachment theory, focusing on the relevance of those findings for our children.

The central organizing theory of Part III is that of self psychology. The construct of mindsharing brings together several components of the theory. This construct permits the inclusion of some of the concepts of attachment theory into a framework that describes the development of the sense of self (Schore, 2002). With this framework as a foundation, I define the construct of mindsharing and describe its ontogeny for children with NLD. I then discuss the applicability of some of the findings of attachment theory to the children.

I found it necessary to coin the term mindsharing for several reasons, among them are the following: (1) The limitations of the concept of theory of mind, which I pointed out at the conclusion of Chapter 4, led me to feel that a term is required that includes an understanding of how others feel in addition to an understanding that others have beliefs, desires, and intentions. Furthermore, in contrast to the theory of mind, which suggests that these abilities are either present or absence, we require a concept that permits us to think of the presence of gradations in those abilities. The concept of mindsharing permits such gradations. (2) As clinicians we are aware of the importance of the capacity for a connection with others as the foundation for a relationship. The concept generally used to refer to this capacity is intimacy. The capacity for intimacy and for caring and feeling affection toward others is central to the development of a relationship. Mindsharing, in its metaphorical sense, presumes that to feel intimacy we must be able to be with another (Stern 1983) and to feel close without fear of engulfment. (3) Through the experience of empathy we are able to understand how another person feels as well as share in that person's experience. Empathy requires that we become part of that person while maintaining our own boundaries. The point of contact is a meeting of minds that is illustrative of the experience of mindsharing. In what follows I elaborate on these and other points and include a discussion of the ontogeny of mindsharing.

Mindsharing

Stern (1983) approaches the issue of intersubjectivity from the perspective of the need to conceptualize experiences of "being with" another. (See Teicholz [2001] for an instructive discussion of intersubjectivity.) As an example of intersubjectivity, he discusses the mother–infant interchanges in which the infant experiences a sense of separateness and a sense of agency. He described three types of "being with": (1) *self–other complementing*, in which each partner complements the other's actions or psychological states; (2) *mental state sharing and tuning*, in which there is some sense of isomorphism and commonality, particularly in experiencing emotional states; and (3) *state transforming*, in which the activities of the caregiver can physically sooth and comfort a distressed infant. Stern notes that "state sharing by its very nature creates subjective intimacy" (p. 77). To "be with" a person is to be available to him or her as someone with whom to share meaningful emotional experiences—which, in turn, raises the hope that unsatisfied longings for emotional responses will be acknowledged and gratified.

It is possible to translate what I refer to as *mindsharing* as a form of "being with another" that includes Stern's three components of subjective experience. Stern's "self–other complementing" is akin to what I describe as the complementary functions that others perform (Palombo, 2001a). Complementary functions are forms of mindsharing in that others in the child's context provide psychological functions that the child does not posses. Such complementarities help the child maintain a sense of self-cohesion. Among these complementary functions are the selfobject and adjunctive functions that significant others provide. *Selfobject functions* include the provision of approval, admiration, regulation of affect states, and creation of a sense of belonging to a community of like-minded others. *Adjunctive functions* are part of the psychological supports the child needs in order to survive; these include reminding a child of tasks to be performed, organizing a child's schedule, and helping the child anticipate new situations. Mindsharing is an important motivational system that provides the impetus to maintain and build upon the attachment the child forms with a caregiver. It is significant that most mindsharing functions occur nonverbally, in the form of activities that seem not to require verbal expression as part of the interchanges that occur between people such as empathizing with another, comforting another by holding or hugging them, following their gaze when they look at something.

Empathy is a type of mindsharing in that it represents a form of what Stern (1983) called "mental state sharing and tuning" (p. 50). The human capacity for empathy differentiates us from our evolutionary and biological ancestors. We alone of all biological organisms can feel and perceive ourselves in others. Empathy is the act through which we apprehend the contents of another person's mind—a process that leads to an understanding of how the other feels, thinks, perceives reality, and gives meaning to his or her perceptions. By empathically reflecting upon another person's experience, we can understand that person's perception of the events that impinged upon him or her and the manner in which these affect him or her. By reflecting on our own experiences, we are able to vicariously feel and comprehend how another person feels and experiences events.

Language is another type of mental state sharing because it arises out of the shared experiences with caregivers, who provide sounds that label the concepts the child forms. Words then become a vehicle for intersubjectivity; a new way of "being with" is created. Language requires a form of mindsharing for comprehension to occur. In this respect, mindsharing is the subjective obverse of theory of mind functioning. Theory of mind is a construct that describes a cognitive function. Mindsharing brings the focus to the processes involved in the exercise of that function while maintaining an intersubjective viewpoint that includes affect states.

THE WORK OF WINNICOTT

Winnicott (1953) described yet another type of mental state sharing. He was impressed by the use that some children make of a blanket or teddy bear, which he called "transitional objects." He found it curious that children cling to these inanimate objects for comfort and security and become painfully distraught and unable to function without them. What seemed curious to Winnicott was the fact that children seemed to respond to a separation from these objects with the intensity associated with a separation from Mother herself. He proposed that the child must attribute to the objects some of the qualities that had been experienced in the relationship with the mother. As Mother became less accessible to the child, the child found a devise by which he or she could carry a symbol of her with him or her. The child's anxiety could be alleviated by transferring onto a concrete object the attributes and functions of the mother. Thus the child experiences the functions of the transitional object as part of him- or herself. Through the transitional object, the child experiences the function that Mother provides. The transitional object mediates the mindsharing function.

Winnicott (1953) made one of his most creative contributions by adding that in adulthood the intermediate area, the area of the illusory between reality and fantasy, is transformed and finds expression through the arts. The derivatives of these experiences of transitional objects permit us to enjoy the merger into a play, an opera, a novel. We let ourselves be carried away by the emotions evoked, as though the events to which we were being exposed were real. These domains of nonverbal experience extend the boundaries of mind to encompass creative endeavors, which represent forms of mindsharing.

THE MINDSHARING SPECTRUM

We can look upon the spectrum of autistic disorders as ranging from mindblindness (Baron-Cohen, 1997) to various degrees of mindsharing. Children with NLD do not fit into the autistic spectrum; they suffer from deficits in the capacity for mindsharing in a specific domain of mental state sharing. The domain affected is delimited to nonverbal and affective communication; even then, the deficits are not as pervasive as those of children with Asperger's disorder. The concept of mindsharing encompasses much more than the experiences that denote the presence or absence of theory of mind abilities. At one extreme end of the mindsharing spectrum are people with profound retardation or advanced Alzheimer's disease who lack all capacity for mindsharing; at the other end of the spectrum are those unusual individuals who have an exquisite capacity to understand human beings with minimal clues from others. At the pathological end of the spectrum are those who are symbiotically attached to others with the related loss of a sense of agency and a sense of self.

The constructs of selfobject functions, through which soothing, comforting, and admiration, and that of adjunctive psychological, through which it is possible to remediate neuropsychological deficits, come closest to Stern's mental state transforming, (Stern, 1983). The therapeutic function of interpretation through which the therapist explains to the child how his or her mind works is also a related construct.

We will return to Stern's third component of "being with" (i.e., "state transforming") in our discussion of the treatment of children with NLD. A major therapeutic goal is that of bringing about a change in the child's "internal milieu"—that is, in the way the child feels about him- or herself, experiences the world, and relates to others.

In summary, I am suggesting that the concept of mindsharing encompasses several constructs that others have used in depicting mental functions and in identifying the process through which changes occur in our mental states or those of others. Constructs that attempt to depict others' mental functions include Stern's concept of "mental state sharing," Winnicott's concept of "transitional object," the concept of empathy, and the concept of theory of mind.

With these considerations, I can now turn to a description of the development of the mindsharing function, discussing its specific relevance to our understanding of children with NLD.

THE ONTOGENY OF MINDSHARING IN CHILDREN
WITH NLD

According to Pally (2001), vision as well as nonverbal and emotional modes of communication play a critical role in the dialogue between mother and infant during the first 9–12 months after birth. She stated:

> From the moment of birth, the mother and infant engage in distinct patterns of nonverbal interaction, involving olfactory, tactile, auditory, visual, and motor systems. As verbal capacities develop, what has been learned nonverbally is integrated with linguistic systems. Nonverbal systems that begin in infancy also continue their own lines of development into more mature forms of nonverbal relatedness between adults. (p. 76)

In these interchanges we can find the emergence of the capacity for mindsharing that lays the foundation for the development of theory of mind abilities. Between birth and 10 months, infants communicate through crying. By 5 days after birth, they cry on hearing other infants cry (Brothers, 1989; Franco, 1997; Harding, 1982), and they imitate facial expressions within 3–5 days. They manifest a preference for Mother's face, and soon after, monitor all caregivers' faces. Turn taking and dialoguing in proto-pragmatic communication occur as early as the first feeding experiences, and they interact in dyadic face-to-face routines. The smiling response emerges at around 8–10 weeks. By 6 months, infants demonstrate that they can use and understand gestures, such as pointing and showing. They have the capacity to follow another person's gaze at 10–12 months, and they understand teasing (e.g., tickling as play, peek-a-boo games, pretending to give something and quickly taking it away). These developmental markers are indicative of infants' emerging capacity to "be with" the caregivers—to share their experiences and to have share in their experiences—in other words, the embryonic emergence of the capacity for mindsharing.

The child with nonlinguistic perceptual deficits may have difficulties engaging the caregiver in such a dialogue. If the child cannot process the gestalt of the mother's face to read her expression, then this child may be at risk of not being able to form a secure attachment to his or her caregivers (much like the blind children in Fraiberg's studies [Fraiberg, 1971; Fraiberg, Siegel, & Gibson, 1966]), unless other modalities are available through which the child can compensate. Similarly, if the child is impaired in the ability to communicate nonverbally, then he or she may not be able to decode the prosody in the caregiver's vocalizations. In addition, the child may experience the tactile contact with the caregiver as disruptive rather than comforting because of his or her sensory, motor, or vestibular overresponsivity. Because of the limitations their deficits impose on the development of the mindsharing function these children would be at risk of developing of an attachment disorder.

If the mother experiences her child as unresponsive to her, then she would have to surmount her own anxiety and guilt for a secure attachment to occur. In such situations, some caregivers attribute the miscommunication to their failure to correctly signal or respond to the child. After several tries, they may begin to attribute motives to the child for not responding appropriately. With increasing frustration, caregivers may decide that the child is willfully disregarding their injunctions and punish the child for perceived misbehavior. Alternatively, some caregivers feel rejected by the infant and deal with the injury by detaching themselves from the child. A further disruption in the process of mindsharing then occurs.

According to Stern (1985), the domain of the subjective self emerges between 7 and 15 months, at which point the infant realizes that others have minds. Intersubjectivity may be said to begin at this age, although some (e.g. Trevarthan, 2003) speak of a primary intersubjectivity that begins much earlier. The development of the capacity for "joint attention," between the ages of 11 and 18 months, provides further evidence of mindsharing. Infants are able to follow someone else's gaze and the gestures that point to an object. The infant's gesture represents the earliest form of communication, according to Winnicott (1971). By the age of 1 year, children understand "social referencing"—that is, they are capable of monitoring a caregiver's gaze and facial expression to "read" whether the caregiver approves or disapproves of what the child is about to do. They will then act upon those perceptions. They seem to "read" what is in the other person's mind. By 15–18 months, toddlers pass the mirror self-recognition task; that is, they can recognize themselves in a mirror. It is at this point that they begin to consolidate their sense of agency. Once more, nonlinguistic perceptual deficits may impede the ability to monitor mother's gaze or facial expression to detect whether she is signaling approval or disapproval, in turn, impeding the development of mindsharing abilities.

Infants arrive in the world having evolved the capacity to respond to the expression of emotions in others. Although their initial cries and gestures do not necessarilly have semantic meaning, caregivers interpret those as meaningful. Crying elicits comforting responses, and the infant's smile evokes tender feelings. During these months, a significant part of the process centers on the interchanges through which caregivers and infants mutually regulate affective intensities (Beebe, 1986; Beebe & Lach-

Poppies in October

Even the sun-clouds this morning cannot manage such skirts.
Nor the woman in the ambulance
Whose red heart blooms through her coat so astoundingly --

A gift, a love gift
Utterly unasked for
By a sky

Palely and flamily
Igniting its carbon monoxides, by eyes
Dulled to a halt under bowlers.

O my God, what am I
That these late mouths should cry open
In a forest of frost, in a dawn of cornflowers.

Sylvia Plath

mann, 1988, 1998). Caregivers attempt to regulate and modulate the infant's affect states through monitoring and responding accordingly. In turn, caregivers modulate their own affects in an effort to match and regulate those of the infant. Through empathy, caregivers attune themselves to the infant's inner experiences. According to Schore (2001), the right hemisphere mediates the contents of these interchanges, leading to the child's internalization of the capacity for self-regulation. The infant eventually internalizes some of these functions as autonomous homeostatic processes; other functions may continue to be regulated by external factors.

For the child with an NLD, who may already have deficits in the capacity for affect regulation, the absence of the reinforcement of those functions because of the disrupted relations with the caregiver can intensify the effects of the deficits. The frequent meltdowns that we commonly encounter in these children have their origins not only in the neuropsychological deficits but also in the disruptions of the caregiver—infant relationship. These disruptions may provide evidence for some of the differences that we see in the symptoms, their heterogeneity may be the product of nature *and* nurture, rather than simply reflecting the variability in the neuropsychological deficits.

By the age of 2, toddlers begin to acquire mental representations, indicating an emerging ability to symbolize objects and events. Symbols are the foundation on which verbal language builds; symbol usage indicates that the child has begun to engage a communal currency through which to communicate. Some children with autism, whose development appears to be arrested around this period, may acquire language but are delayed or cut short in their further development of mindsharing.

By the age of 30 months, children can identify gender. By age 3, they understand the difference between the idea of an object and the object itself; that is, they understand the difference between mental entities and real objects, and between a "dream" and "reality." Three-year-olds firmly divide the mental and physical worlds and distinguish appropriately between real and mental entities. In addition, they understand the subjectivity of thoughts and emotions (Wellman, 1993).

As noted, anecdotal data indicate that children with NLD are capable of understanding that other children have beliefs and desires. The social problems that occur for children with NLD at this age (during the third year) appear to be due to their inability to process the multiple elements of a situation. For example, John, who has an NLD, may respond inappropriately to Jane, who gestures toward John, asking for his toy. John responds by assaulting Jane, having misread her gesture as an attack. The evidence would indicate that John can form a mental representation of Jane's desire for the object but would have difficulty, at this age, conceiving that Jane is making a request for the toy, even though she knew that he did not wish to share the toy with her. That is, he could not understand that she did not understand what was in his mind. This deficit in mind-sharing becomes evident as the children demonstrate many ways in which they misinterpret others' desires and intentions.

Between the ages of 36 and 48 months, children grasp the concept of causality; that is, they comprehend that people have beliefs and desires (cause) that guide their actions (effect)—for example; mother's desire that the child go to sleep will cause her to put him in bed. Beyond understanding cause-and-effect relationships in the world of objects, they understand that people can be responsible for causing injury, distress, or comfort. By 3½ or 4 years old, children are capable of perspective taking; that is they understand that others may have a different perspective from their own. The developmental steps outlined so far shape the ontogeny of mindsharing and are precursors to the development of theory of mind abilities.

By the age of 4 years, children have developed the capacity for mental attribution; that is, they have the ability to understand that others have desires, beliefs, and intentions/motives that guide their actions. Mental attributions entail having the capacity for first-order representations—representations of the state of another person's mind (a "metarepresentation"). As such, it is evidence of the capacity for mindsharing. The capacity for symbolic/imaginative play is an indicator of the capacity for theory of mind functioning and of a higher-order capacity for mindsharing.

Children with NLD are definitely capable of various degrees of mindsharing. They understand that others have desires and beliefs—an indicator of theory of mind abilities. However, they clearly have limitations in this capacity that interfere with their communicative competence. They may misread others' intentions, for example, due to mindsharing deficits. Other deficits may also interfere with the perception of others' intentions. The children's expressed desire to be with others and the observation that they isolate themselves from social contact permits us to elaborate on and clarify the role of the mindsharing difficulties associated with these behaviors. For this elaboration and clarification, I turn to a discussion of the concepts of *aloneness* and *loneliness*.

Aloneness and Loneliness

In a 2004 publication, Stern returned to the topic of intersubjectivity by discussing the experience of "the present moment" during the therapeutic process. For Stern, intersubjectivity is an innate, primary system of motivation that is essential for the survival of our species; as a motivational system, it is as fundamental as attachment. Intersubjectivity promotes the formation of social groups, enhances group functioning, and facilitates group cohesion by giving rise to a moral sense. The regulation of intersubjective closeness and distance occurs through the balance in our need to read others' intentions and feelings while maintaining our sense of self-cohesion. Too great a distance leads to cosmic loneliness; too great a closeness leads to the disappearance of the self. Distance gives rise to intersubjective anxiety; yet we need others through whose eyes we can find ourselves (Stern, 2004).

The concept of aloneness defines the experience of feeling isolated and perhaps detached from others. There are times when we wish to be alone, to be with our thoughts and feelings. These experiences do not necessarily reflect an inability to be with others, but simply the desire to be apart, perhaps for restorative purposes. There are children who feel alone, however, because they are incapable of being with others. Although solitary, they do not seem to be distressed by their isolation. Children with Asperger's disorder or autism appear not to feel the need for contact with others. Their isolation appears to be the result of the absence of a capacity to feel any connection with others. Such children may find themselves in a crowd of people and feel content in their aloneness.

Loneliness is a different experience from aloneness in that it implies discontent with the solitary state. The desire for human contact is fundamental to our sense of well-being. A report of loneliness suggests that the child desires or even longs for companionship. A feeling of sadness colors the experience of loneliness, as often happens to children with NLD. These children's psychological requirements are different from those of children with Asperger's disorder or autism. They experience their isolation as a painful deprivation of social contact, and their hunger for social contact leads them to devise strategies to get others involved with them. The fact that these strategies often misfire is due to their deficits rather than to their lack of desire.

It is possible for a child to be alone and not feel lonely if he or she can imagine being with what Stern (1985) called an "evoked companion." An evoked companion is like an imaginary playmate that young children create to keep them company. Such an evoked companion may mitigate the effect of the child's loneliness. However, the act of imagining an evoked companion presumes that the child has had sufficient positive experiences from which to draw when the need arises; it also presumes that the child has the capacity for mindsharing. Further evidence that children with NLD have the capacity for mindsharing comes from their ability to have imaginary companions (see case example in Chapter 4).

The distinction between aloneness and loneliness revolves around the capacity for mindsharing. Without that capacity the child is, perforce, alone and isolated. He or she does not feel a sense of loneliness, sadness, or distress about his or her isolation. The relationship between aloneness, loneliness, and the capacity for attachment is also interesting to explore. It is possible for a child to have a secure attachment but not have the capacity for mindsharing. Children with Asperger's disorder and autism demonstrate such attachments even though they do not have the capacity for theory of mind functioning. The person to whom they have the attachment fulfills emotional needs, and when not present, they experience as something missing. Once restored, the distress dissipates. For further clarity on this issue, I discuss attachment theory. First, a clinical example of a child with an NLD, who suffered from an oppressive sense of loneliness, may help concretize the distinction between the two concepts. The following is a composite example drawn from my clinical experience with some of these children. These are the experiences of an 8-years-old boy with an NLD, whom I will call Mark:

From the earliest days that he can remember, Mark had no reason to doubt that his perceptions correctly reflected of the world around him. Yet experiences did not always validate his perceptions. Physical objects did not respond in a predictable manner, and he found himself bumping into things he thought he was avoiding. He spilled his milk trying to reach for it, misjudged heights when jumping from steps, could not hold his crayons to draw, and could not put puzzles together. These failures led him to distrust himself in situations that involved manual dexterity or physical agility.

His confusion was compounded by the criticism he received from caregivers. He found it hard to understand why they were being so hard on him. In addition, children avoided or stigmatized him, and he always felt unfairly treated. In response, he often fought back, protesting that they were picking on him. Eventually he found himself in so much trouble that it seemed easier to withdraw into solitary play or watching television.

As he got older, the world became a place where satisfactions were difficult to obtain. The world was unrewarding, unpredictable, and unintelligible. He tried to memorize rules that would explain how people were supposed to behave, but then was mystified as to when they applied and when they did not. Yet part of him very much longed for contact with others. He occasionally made forays to befriend someone, hoping for different responses from those he had received in the past. For a while, things would go smoothly, but then, unexplainably, relationships would fall apart, and he would be thrown into his former isolation once again.

Given this unpredictability, he felt that he must exercise great caution in negotiating situations. His anxieties escalated. Soon he became fearful of many situations and unfamiliar places. He could not organize his perceptual world to be sure of where he was or how to find his way back from where he came. Since he could never quite get his bearings and could not follow directions, he started refusing to go to neighbors' homes or stay overnight at friends' homes. Even going upstairs in his home to get ready to go to bed became fraught with pitfalls. He also developed night fears, fears of going down to the basement or of going to rooms on different floors of the house. He began to require someone to accompany him to bed and to stay with him until he fell asleep. He insisted that his parents not leave him with babysitters, fearing that they would get into serious accidents or die. He would then be bereft of their help.

Mark's parents became increasingly impatient with these fears, which they did not understand. In response, they began to force him into the very dangers he wished to avoid. He developed a terrible sense of uncertainty regarding the responses he was likely to receive from them. He feared he would be punished or criticized. The only defense left was to fight back or to withdraw from all activity. As he withdrew, he became more passive and unmotivated, losing interest or curiosity in any activities. Television or video games became the focus of his life. The world of fantasy was more inviting than reality. If he fought back because he felt that his life depended on opposing the tasks imposed on him, he was punished. His parents could not understand how endangered he felt. He resorted to violent tantrums or assaultive behavior to make his point. These drastic actions only provoked more severe counterresponses.

His school performance was below his own expectations, bringing disappointment to himself and his parents. Although initially he was convinced that he was smarter than many of the kids in his class, he felt that he never had a chance to demonstrate his capabilities. With time and failure, he concluded that he was "dumb," incapable of doing the work or of succeeding in school. Feeling threatened, he became school-avoidant and sought to escape a setting that represented a world filled with painful and unmanageable situations.

At times one of the parents, usually his mother, provided some solace. She was able to make things comprehensible for him. She verbally translated situations so that they no longer appeared as unintelligible or dangerous. It then became imperative that she be his constant companion. Without her intercessions, chaos ensued; only she could restore the good feelings necessary to regain a sense of security.

Things were not as bad in familiar situations as when he was exposed to new settings or routines. New settings evoked a feeling of estrangement and disorientation. It was like entering a Halloween haunted house. He could not gain a footing; he never felt sure about where he was or the significance of what surrounded him. He tried to pick up clues through other than visual means to guide him, but these efforts were not enough. Consequently, powerful anxieties were stirred up and the wish to escape from them overwhelmed him.

Experiences with people and situations often made no logical sense to him.

His attempts to process occurrences were defeated by his inability to find connections between discrete happenings. In social situations, causal relationships between how people felt and acted eluded him. He experienced adults and peers alike as unreasonable, as acting entirely arbitrarily. On occasion, he found adults to be more receptive to listening to him than were his peers. He therefore got into the habit of approaching adults he met with the expectation that he could befriend them. He experienced no stranger anxiety; to the contrary, the conversations with adults willing to listen were very gratifying.

Mark only understood the world of feelings intellectually because people talked about feelings. To him, feelings constituted a foreign language; only when they reached a threshold of intensity that led to an eruption could he experience a particular feeling. Most often, the feeling was one of rage, frustration, or terror. Otherwise, he lived in a gray world, lacking the affective colors associated with modulated emotional states.

Attachment in Children with NLD

The significance of attachment theory for our understanding of the social impairments experienced by children with NLD is twofold: (1) it helps clarify the type of attachment the child forms with his or her caregiver, and (2) it helps us understand the contribution that failures in the developmental dialogue between child and caregivers make to the nature of the child's attachment. We know that several factors may contribute to the type of attachment that emerges. Among them are those that environmental factors produce, such as serious illnesses, traumatic separations, parent neglect, or abuse; equally significant are the child's neuropsychological strengths and weaknesses and temperamental factors (see Amini, et al., 1996).

Assuming that caregivers bring average to optimal skills to the task of parenting, we can ask whether the deficits of children with NLD will affect the type of attachment they form with their caregiver. The developmental data suggest that their nonlinguistic perceptual deficits, the impairments in nonverbal communication, and their difficulties in processing affects place children with NLD at risk for attachment disorders. These deficits constrain the development of the child's capacity for mindsharing, which, in turn, interferes with the formation of an intersubjective connection with a caregiver.

In psychoanalysis, the development of a positive bond between the child and caregiver, called object relationship, is considered central to the child's mental health. Conversely, deficits in that capacity are indicative of psychopathology. The neuroses, borderline conditions, and psychosis indicate the presence of a disruption in object relationship.

Freud (1916) explained the process through which we form object relationship as due the libidinal investment of others. This investment is brought about by the functions, particularly the nurturing functions, which caregivers provide to their child. Other theories, such as object relations theory, explain the process as resulting from the internalization of patterns of relationship to which the child is exposed during the early years. Stern (2004) stated that attachment is a motivational system that provides the impetus for the formation of relationships. Attachment theories explain the bond as the product of preprogrammed responses between the dyad (see Diamond & Blatt, 1994).

BOWLBY'S THEORY

The dominant theory of attachment is Bowlby's theory (Fonagy, 2001; Holmes, 1996; Schore, 2002, 2003a, 2003b). Bowlby (1969, 1973) proposed an ethological theory that was influenced by Konrad Lorenz's work on the imprinting of baby geese to their mothers. Bowlby maintained that the infant is preprogrammed to seek proximity to a caregiver in order to find a secure base that is reliable, can protect the infant from environmental intrusions, and can provide the necessary sustenance. The infant's cries, smiles, and other movements and vocalizations evoke responses that bring the dyad together.

Bowlby (1969, 1973) went beyond this formulation to elaborate a developmental theory influenced by cognitive psychology and classical and operant conditioning. This theory proposed that as a result of the repeated interactions with the caregiver, the infant develops a set of sensorimotor schema that permit him or her to achieve a homeostatic balance. These schemas reflect the actual interaction between infant and caregiver and later shape the relationships the child will have with others. As they become internalized as forms of regulatory mechanisms, these schemas are eventually structured as mental concepts or representations—what Bowlby called "internal working models." Following the internalization of these working models, the child is less reliant on the environment for regulation and is able to self-regulate (Bretherton, Ridgeway, & Cassidi, 1990).

Disruptions in the relationship between infant and caregiver, caused by separations or loss of connection, lead to well-defined patterns of responses that begin with *protest* and are followed by *despair*, and finally withdrawal and *detachment* from the surroundings. These responses are behavioral manifestation of social dysfunctions. Ainsworth (see Sroufe, 1995, pp. 182–185) devised an experimental task, based on these behavioral manifestations, to measure the type of attachment between infants, ages 18–24 months, and their caregivers. This task, called the "Strange

Situation," involves placing the parent and infant in an experimental room. A stranger is the introduced into the situation, and the parent leaves the room for a brief period. The parent returns and leaves again with the stranger. The stranger reenters the room, and soon after, the parent joins the infant and stranger.

The infant's behavior with the stranger and responses to the reunions with the parent permit an examiner to classify the type of attachment demonstrated into one of three categories: (1) a *secure attachment*, in which the infant seeks proximity to the mother and is welcoming of her return; (2) an *avoidant attachment*, in which the infant avoids and excludes the mother from interacting with him or her; and (3) an *anxious/ambivalent* attachment, in which the infant approaches or avoids the mother in an angry or hostile manner. A fourth category was later added, *disorganized attachment*, in which the child appears hypervigilant and demonstrates mixed or conflicting responses (Sroufe, 1995).

Schore (1994, 2001, 2003a, 2003b) built on Bowlby's (1969, 1973) theory by adding a neurobiological dimension to the attachment process. For Schore, attachment theory is a regulatory theory. The processes of attachment begin with the infant's gaze into the caregiver's emotionally expressive face. The caregiver attunes him- or herself to the infant's state to regulate the infant's arousal level. Schore considers the orbitofrontal region of the cortex to be the seat of emotional regulation. Its maturation depends on emotion-laden interactions between infant and caregiver. Because the right hemisphere is dominant in the early months, and nonverbal channels of communication are the primary modes through which interchanges occur, the cortical and subcortical systems of that region mediate the regulatory functions that the infant internalizes.

As we have seen, the interchanges between infant and caregiver occur through the nonverbal channel. At first, infants use smell, taste, and touch to interact with the caregiver. Soon after birth, the visual channel develops sufficiently that the infant is capable of directing his or her gaze at the caregiver. That channel becomes central to the affective exchanges that occur within the dyad. Synchrony develops in the dyad as each partner resonates with the other's inner states. The neurobiological goal of attachment behavior becomes the regulation of the infant's state. When functional, this process provides the foundation for a secure attachment. Through this process, the infant internalizes patterns that are consolidated into functions that form the core of an internal working model (see Beebe, 1986; Beebe & Lachmann, 1986, 1988a, 1988b)

ANIMAL RESEARCH

Kraemer's work with nonhuman primates provides insights into the specific processes that are involved in the interaction between the dyad. He (Kraemer, 1992, 1995) finds that Bowlby's (1969; 1973) theory does not sufficiently explain the biological mechanisms that undergird the attachment process. Kraemer rejects Bowlby's notion that infants seek proximity with a secure base through which to form an attachment. His research, in the same laboratory in which Harlow made his major findings, leads him to conclude that infants choose or reject an object based on the stimulus characteristics of the object. For example, monkeys will attach themselves to terry-cloth–covered surrogates in preference to wire-mesh surrogates that provide nourishment. Infants, he contends, are preprogrammed to process specific multimodal sensations such as warmth, taste, and smell. They respond with fixed behaviors and, in particular, physiological patterns. These patterns act as regulatory mechanisms that organize brain function. Hofer who called them "hidden regulators" studied the specific stimuli in detail.

Finally, Hofer (1984, 1990, 1995a, 1995b, 1996, 2003) studied the effects of separation in rats and their pups and discovered that a number of separate stimuli operates during the contact that the pups have with their mother rats. Among these are warmth, the effects of smell, and the specific taste of mother's milk. The mother's responses to her pups regulate the pups' internal state, their heart rates, and their sleep–wake cycle. When a separation from their mothers occurs, each of the modalities produces different physiological changes in the pups. Although it is possible to substitute for one or more of these stimuli by artificial means, none of the substitutes is as effective in returning the lost homeostasis as a return to the mother. Even then, some of the disruptions continue to operate at the physiological level. Hofer concludes that a symbiosis exists between the pup and its mother such that the mutual regulation, synchrony, and reciprocity that exist in the dyad are unique. Hofer describes these early interactions as having the characteristics of a symbiosis between infant and caregiver, and he ties his findings to Mahler (1968, 1975), who proposed an early "symbiotic phase" between infant and mother between the ages of 2 and 4 months.

ATTACHMENT THEORY UNDERSCORES THE SIGNIFICANCE OF neuropsychological deficits on the possible disruption of the relationship between infant and caregiver. Deficits in nonlinguistic perceptual functions may bring forth responses from caregivers that compound the infant's developmental difficulties. In particular, because the deficits interfere with nonverbal communication between the child and caregiver, failures in communication are more likely to affect the process through which a secure attachment develops. When the needed affective communication fails to take place, a disconnection occurs within the dyad such that the infant experiences a loss of synchrony between his or her state and that of the caregiver. For example, the infant may experience the mother as withdrawing from him or her—a deprivation that interferes with the infant's experience of the caregiver as a secure base. The regulatory functions the caregiver provides are no longer available to the child, who is flooded by negative affect states. Other disruptions in the child's physiological state may also occur. Attachment disorders may follow when some or all of these processes fail.

We lack the data to support the hypothesis that children with NLD may indeed suffer from attachment disorders and that some of their social impairments are, in part, the result of these disorders. We can make a case for the hypothesis that some of their problems in the modulation of affect states are the result of a failure to internalize regulatory mechanisms because of insecure, ambivalent, or disorganized attachment. It would be difficult to distinguish whether the deficits in such mechanisms are due to the type of attachment or are related to the deficits associated with the disorder. In any case, there is no doubt that the type of attachment affects brain development; consequently, the sources of the deficits may be indistinguishable.

Conclusion

The concept of mindsharing and the findings from attachment theory research contribute additional dimensions to our understanding of the development of the sense of self in children with NLD and their social–emotional problems. Because mindsharing functions occur primarily on nonverbal levels, the children's deficits in nonlinguistic perceptual processing may interfere in major ways with these functions. The symptoms these children display are not only the product of social imperception or the secondary consequences of their neuropsychological deficits or even their impaired social cognition. At the intrapersonal level, each of these has its impact on the child's sense of self. By connecting some of the sequelae of these processes with impediments in the development of mindsharing and attachment, we arrive at a higher level of complexity. Each of these adds yet another layer to the behavioral picture. As this discussion progresses, the definitions given in Chapter 7 are amplified by the addition of the disorders of the self. Included are (1) the challenges that children with NLD face in the development of mindsharing abilities,

(2) the nature of their attachment, and (3) any disorder of the self that either or both of these factors these might produce.

By focusing on the significance to children of their investment in others and the development of a capacity to share in the internal world of others and have others share in their internal world, our understanding of salience of such experiences is broadened. Yet infants and children are not passive recipients of those experiences. They not only actively participate in them but they also process and integrate their meanings in their own unique ways. As we will see in the next chapter, the child's sense of self serves to integrate all those experiences into a coherent whole. The drive to maintain a sense of self-cohesion and to arrive at a coherent self-narrative is focal to the unique way in which each child brings together his or her neuropsychological assets and deficits and to his or her experiences.

9

Self-Cohesion and
Narrative Coherence

Self psychologists regard the self as the psychological structure that under-girds the totality of a person's experiences, both conscious and uncon-scious. It represents the subjective dimension of the person's psychic organization. The cohesive self is an enduring and stable psychological structure through which a person experiences a sense of intactness, in-tegrity, and vitality. Once firmly established, it embodies the person's val-ues and worldview and provides a stable foundation for the integration of experiences (Kohut, 1971; Palombo, 2001a; Wolf, 1988).

The development of the self may be viewed as a set of phase-specific ex-periences that reflect the intersection of the child's neuropsychological strengths and weaknesses, the responses of the community to him, or her, and his or her responses to the community's expectations. Each child brings to the world a set of competencies that include the capacity to feel, think, learn, and act; the capacity to generate and interpret signs; the capacity for self-awareness, self-criticism, self-control, and selfinterpretation; and the capacity for attachment to others. Furthermore, people are capable of a sense of privacy, of being in error, of having motives of which they may be unconscious. These competencies represent each person's endowment and result in the accrual of learned habits, as well as defenses, compensa-tory structures, and aggregated functions. These functions may find expres-sion in beliefs, desires, feelings, or actions.

Development is also the process by which a child gradually constructs an evolving self-narrative within a stable mindsharing context that includes others. This self-narrative represents an ongoing series of changes that reflect the increasingly complex levels of organization of a maturing individual. Two primary motives that engage a person's sense of self are the desire for *self-cohesion* and the desire to maintain the *coherence of the self-narrative*.

Self-Cohesion

The concept of *self-cohesion* is used descriptively to characterize a state of self-consolidation (Stolorow, Brandchaft, & Atwood, 1987, p. 90). Most infants are endowed with a capacity for a *cohesive sense of self* (Kohut, 1978). Some, however, do not have this capacity because of serious deficits; these infants may go on to develop schizophrenia, autism, or other severe psychiatric disorders. Severe trauma or other forms of environmental toxins (e.g., smoke and pesticides) can undermine a child's sense of cohesion. Self-cohesion is not a static state but a dynamic one that represents the organizing capacities that are always in play to synthesize and integrate self-experiences. Across the life cycle, the sense of cohesion is maintained as a result of the success a person experiences in integrating new experiences with old ones, reworking old experiences and reinterpreting them in the light of new ones, and maintaining a secure attachment to those who provide selfobject functions. Maintaining self-cohesion does not involve striving for a stable homoeostatic or nirvana-like state. Rather, it is a dynamic, active process of continual movement from stabilization to destabilization to restabilization.

An NLD may disrupt the development of self-cohesion in several ways. The children's responses to their learning disorder may disrupt their sense of self-cohesion, or the learning disorder itself may interfere with the capacity. The movement from destabilization to restabilization is complicated by neuropsychological strengths and deficits. Depending on the nature and severity of the deficits and the responses to those deficits, the swings between stability and instability may be much greater than in children without those deficits.

SELFOBJECT FUNCTIONS AS A FORM OF
MINDSHARING

Viewed from the perspective of the child's subjective experience, the context provides two types of mindsharing functions that are essential for the development of a sense of cohesion: *selfobject functions* and *adjunctive func-*

tions. These functions may act as protective factors that prevent a child with an NLD from developing a disorder of the self; conversely, the absence of these functions may place the child at risk for the development of a disorder of the self (Anthony, 1987; Cohler, 1987).

In self psychology the concept of *selfobject* has been useful in delineating the ways in which others provide psychological functions necessary for a person to maintain a sense of self-cohesion (Kohut, 1991). Emotions permeate the selfobject functions that caregivers provide for their children. By definition, selfobject functions always carry a positive emotional valence. Most often, these functions operate silently and outside the person's awareness. Even though another person may provide them, the receiver experiences them as within and part of the sense of self. In other words, the human context becomes a part of the person's sense of self in a form of mindsharing. Eventually, some selfobject functions are internalized and the capacity to maintain internal harmony is developed, although we can never totally dispense with the need for selfobject functions. Three common selfobject functions are those of *idealizing, mirroring,* and *alter ego.*

Idealizing Selfobject Function

Caregivers of children must function as psychological protectors and as providers of emotional support. Caregivers are responsible for seeing to it that children feel safe from external dangers. For children to experience such feelings of safety, they must have faith that the caregivers are sufficiently powerful. In addition, caregivers must direct their efforts at modulating and regulating children's affect states so that they do not become overstimulated or overwhelmed. The provision of these selfobject functions can result in the internalization of self-control, self-discipline, and self-regulation.

The idealizing selfobject function is critical for children with NLD. As we have seen, during development, caregivers provide a milieu within which they mutually regulate their own and infants' internal states. Infants then internalize those regulatory functions. When we speak of the idealizing function, we are referring to the subjective counterpart of this process. From the intrapersonal perspective, children experience caregivers as "powerful others" who can modulate their internal states and who, by providing comfort, can mitigate the effects of stressful factors. Given the vulnerabilities and deficits in self-regulatory abilities of children with NLD, they may experience caregivers as failing to provide this critical function, and they may begin to form a view of caregivers as uncaring or neglectful of their needs. The stage is set for a "de-idealization" of caregivers—that is, perceiving them as incompetent in the performance of their parenting tasks. As these children mature, the de-idealization may be transformed into disrespect for, and hostility toward, the caregivers.

Mirroring Selfobject Functions

For self-esteem to develop, children must experience their caregivers as cherishing and affirming their uniqueness and specialness, as treating them as the center of the caregivers' universe. When parents mirror their children's worth, by expressing and demonstrating their delight and joy, the children experience a sense of worth, positive self-regard, dignity, and self-respect.

The many factors that interfere with the dialogue between children with NLD and their caregivers may set the stage for an attachment disorder or a disorder of the self. Attachment disorders are characterized by feelings of anxiety and panic at the thought of losing the connection to the caregiver. Disorders of the self are a broader category of disturbances that range from loss of self-esteem to the loss of self-cohesion. Attachment disorders invariably produce disorders of the self, but not all disorders of the self are caused by attachment disorders. The disrupted relationship, whether caused by an attachment disorder or a disorder of the self, evokes negative feelings that make it difficult for caregivers to feel truly admiring or even loving of their children, much to their distress. Often, these children are not easy to parent; they are a source of constant worry and perhaps guilt. Caregivers feel constrained to correct the children and criticize them for not conforming to their expectations. It is difficult for caregivers to provide the kind of unqualified mirroring that is required at this early developmental stage. Children may then internalize these ambiguous (at best) responses and rather than feeling admirable, may begin to feel deficient in some mysterious fashion. They may begin to doubt their value. Vulnerabilities in self-esteem emerge as they struggle to understand why they do not feel as cared for as their siblings or their peers.

Alter-Ego Selfobject Functions

The experience of a common bond with others that ties all human beings together and that leads to feelings of kinship with others is critical to the healthy development of all children, but particularly to children with NLD. These experiences lead to the development of alter-ego selfobject functions. Once internalized these functions permit the children to feel intact, and healthy. The functions provide a sense of well-being and wholesomeness without which we can feel dehumanized.

As devastating as are the deficits in the other selfobject functions, the feelings of being different and of being excluded from peer groups, deficits in alter-ego selfobject functions lead to greater despair. Children with

NLD realize that they are different at an early age, although they have no clue as to what makes for that difference. As a result, they feel helpless in their efforts to be accepted by others; injured by rejection, they retreat into isolation. As we have seen, this isolation is not self-imposed at first, because they desire contact with others, but after repeated rejections, they see no other way to protect themselves. In their isolation, they begin to brood and to feel enraged. Eventually, they feel so alienated and dehumanized that they lapse into despair.

ADJUNCTIVE FUNCTIONS

There is another group of phenomena that appears to operate in a manner similar to selfobject functions in that it serves to complement the sense of self, but must be conceptualized differently. I designate this group as adjunctive functions, which also are forms of mindsharing.

Although all selfobject functions complement the sense of self, not all complementary functions are selfobject functions. Caregivers may perform adjunctive functions that carry positive, negative, or neutral emotional valences. Some examples may help clarify this distinction. Children—especially those with NLD—often need to be reminded to perform a task or to prepare themselves for school in the morning. Sometimes directions must be repeated to them, either because they were inattentive or because they misheard the caregiver's tone of voice. In performing these functions caregivers are providing adjunctive cognitive functions for the children, they are complementing an area of deficit, but are not necessarily providing selfobject functions.

Children with NLD tend to draw from caregivers adjunctive functions to complement their immature or deficient psyches, functions that are not usually identified as part of the parenting process. Sometimes it is impossible to identify specific delays or deficits early in infancy. Parents are then in the dark as to what that the child requires. Some caregivers respond intuitively; through their empathic capacities, they may be able to fill in the child's neuropsychological deficits. In fact, these parents, if they have other children, recognize the differences in the child and feel they must respond as they do or cause the child serious distress. When parents either cannot or do not complement the child's deficits, the child suffers. The reason for the child's distress is seldom clearly evident early on. Parents often feel much puzzlement and guilt, because they assume that they are the cause of the problem.

CHILD COMPENSATIONS

Compensatory functions are not mindsharing functions, but they are important to consider as strategies children with NLD use to achieve desired goals without the mediating intervention of another person or tool. The compensatory strategies children develop are limited only by their creativity. Some children develop strategies other than those of verbal mediation. Some learn to structure their environment to minimize their reliance on areas of weakness. Others, with help, learn to anticipate and avoid encounters with situations that would expose their weaknesses. When a child is capable of using such compensatory strategies, the negative impact of the disability is attenuated, as are the psychological problems.

Clearly, not all children compensate for deficits in their development; some do so very well whereas others do not. For reasons that are not clear, some children do not acquire compensatory functions. These children may learn to rely on others to complement their deficient functioning, or they may fail to be effective in dealing with life tasks (Miller, 1991, 1992). The capacity to use adjunctive functions and the reasons why some children do not or cannot use them are not well understood.

Compensatory functions do not help children "outgrow" deficits, but they do help them get around the problems created by the deficits by strengthening areas of weakness or using areas of strength to attain the desired goals. At times, some children take a perspective that involves denial or acceptance that permits them to function quite adequately. They may depreciate or devalue what is difficult and therefore neutralize the negative effects of their deficits. Some transform the meanings of the deficits, making them into a badge to be displayed, joked about, or used as a source of pride. In all of these cases, the children turn to other areas of competence to obtain satisfaction. Compensation results in a greater sense of narrative coherence, a stronger sense of self-cohesion, and less vulnerability to others' estimation of them.

To summarize, we can distinguish two types of mindsharing: those that address the children's emotional needs, and those that deal with their neuropsychological needs. Selfobject functions address children's emotional needs and are necessary for a sense of self-cohesion. Providers of these functions are not interchangeable, because each person who performs these functions assumes a special value to children that makes the relationship distinctive. These selfobject functions are critical to the mental health of children with NLD. The second type of mindsharing functions are those that complement the child's cognitive and emotional deficits. Caregivers may extend a child's cognitive capacities by operating in the "zone of proximal development" (Vygotsky, 1986, p. 187) or providing scaffolding that permits them to accomplish tasks that they could not accomplish without assistance. Finally, compensatory functions used by children attempt to fill in deficits in their sense of self but do not require the intervention of others.

Self-Narratives

Children's *self-narratives* provide a window into their subjective experiences (Brandell, 1984; Brandell, 2000; Bruner, 1984, 1987, 2002; Hanley, 1996; Klitzing, 2000). Self-narratives reveal (1) the *meanings* children construe from their experiences; (2) how others in their context *confer meanings* on those experiences; and (3) how the children *organize those meanings* into thematic units within the narrative to create a coherent story. Events are encoded in implicit and explicit forms of memory. Preverbal and nonverbal experiences tend to be processed by implicit memory, which registers the event and the accompanying affects. Early experiences with caregivers are inscribed as nonverbal scripts of generalized rules that guide future conduct. Scripts contain within them both the affective valence and those elements of the event that are experienced as salient at the time of their occurrence. For example, a common experience of children with NLD is that they feel ineffective in working in groups. A child may then assume that the reason for that ineffectiveness is that others do not like him. That reason may then become a script or theme in the child's self-narrative that taints his view of relationships and dictates how he anticipates others to respond to him. Scrips become themes in the self-narrative that become organizers of experience and relationships in the sense that they become part of a "belief system" that is used to predict what will occur and formulate the responses to those occurrences (Palombo, 1994, 2001a; see also Nelson & Gruendel, 1986; Tomkins, 1979, 1987)

The neuropsychological strengths and weaknesses children bring to the process, in combination with the community or context in which they are raised, determine their interpretations of their own experiences. As children integrate and synthesize these meanings, their self-narratives acquire structures and contents that provide central motives for their behavior. A central structure of a self-narrative is the script or theme that organizes the elements of the narrative. These themes emerge from children's earliest experiences, which are encoded with the affect states that are present at that moment. Narrative themes, with their powerful emotional contents, become motives that guide children's actions.

As children are exposed to new experiences, the themes or motifs within their narratives are reworked into the emerging narrative. New meanings can merge with old experiences, which may be seen in a new light. Continuity in the self-narrative exists as these meanings are integrated into a whole, providing children with a sense of their history. The progression may include a return to old themes as well as a suspension of ways of interpreting the past and present. Novel ways of understanding meanings are thus created. A rhythmic and characteristic set of patterns emerges for every individual.

Children with NLD are challenged in their efforts to create a coherent self-narrative. The fact that their handicap is not concretely recognizable or visible means that they cannot easily conceptualize what is wrong inside them or why things go wrong in their lives. They are often left to their own devices in trying to explain to themselves the causes of their distress. The extent to which they fail to integrate the meanings of their deficits into their self-narratives determines the impact that the lack of coherence will have on their sense of self and whether they will develop a disorder of the self (Palombo, 1991, 1993, 1994, 2001a).

When given verbal expression, self-narratives become autobiographical statements that reveal children to themselves and to others. In the clinical setting such autobiographical statements may be viewed much as a dream that includes both conscious and unconscious content. The manifest content is but the tip of an iceberg; the latent content remains beneath the surface. As further details of the life story are revealed, more of the unconscious content emerges. Gaps, distortions, and self-serving statements all point to dimensions that, once explored, offer areas for greater understanding of the child.

Autobiographical statements present one component of the self-narrative; another component includes nonverbal contents enacted in the interactions with others (Hanley, 1996). Stern (2004) considered a "present moment" to contain the essential elements of a lived story. He stated, "From a clinical perspective the present moment reveals a 'world in a grain of sand' " (p. 138). A lived story is a narrative about a set of experiences. This narrative has a form and content. The form specifies the protagonists, the time period, and the location in which the action occurred. It also has a plot that provides a line of dramatic tension. This plot stipulates the motives or intentions that drive the action and the affects that color the content. Sharing a present moment draws us into the web of that person's entire sense of being. It ensnares us into his or her subjective experience as it comes into being. When a child with NLD relates an incident in which a teacher unfairly punished him, saying that everyone else was doing what he was doing, we have a fragment of a narrative that encapsulates many of the child's problems, his deficits, and the central theme of his self-narrative, although what may have occurred is that as an outsider to the group, he is often manipulated by other students into being blamed for their acting out. We note his deficits in his failure to specify in which class the occurrence had taken place, what else was occurring, what he was doing, and how the teacher responded. The central theme of his self-narrative is that he feels constantly victimized by others, feels helpless to defend himself, and that no one care about him. Within the grain of sand (see Stern, 2004) that this vignette represents is contained the child's entire story.

A self-narrative organizes personal and shared meanings into a coherent whole that defines the sense of self. To the extent that children organize their self-narratives around personal meanings only, their capacity for mindsharing will be limited. Only when the meanings of experiences are shared so that others can understand what those meant to the children can there be a greater sense of mindsharing (see Astington, 1990). Personal and shared meanings create *a sense of history* that provides a sense of continuity to one's experiences. It is important to emphasize that "coherence of the self-narrative" does not refer to a logical coherence of accounts; rather it refers to the sense individuals derive from their own experiences through whatever criteria they apply. Because self-narratives integrate *personal* and *shared* meanings drawn from experience, what appears as coherent to children who create these self-narratives may seem completely incoherent to adults. Gazzaniga explained this meaning of coherence:

> Our interpretive mind is always attributing a cause to felt states of mind, and we now know that these interpretations are frequently irrelevant to the true underlying causes of a felt state. Our mind's explanations become more relevant only as we come to believe our own theories about the cause of a state like anxiety. The fact appears to be that some people are genetically disposed to an anxious response while others are not. Those who are anxious search for a theory to explain their anxiety and commonly seize on the number of decisions they make a day as a likely source of their state of mind. . . . Yet as the anxious person comes to believe his own theory, he begins to change his life pattern in ways that can easily be imagined. (1988, p. 98)

By focusing on the self-narratives of children with NLD, we can obtain an intimate understanding of the ways in which they experience the events in their lives, organize them into scripts or episodes, and store them for later retrieval. The circumstances in which an event occurs, the feelings stirred up by it, the state of mind of the child at the time of the occurrence, and the child's particular configuration of neuropsychological strengths and weakness are all part of the encoding of these episodes into scripts that are stored in memory. Some of these episodes acquire much greater significance than others. Indeed, they become themes or motifs that organize children's perceptions and shape their responses to people and events in their life. Such themes become the underlying plot that structures children's self-narratives and shapes how they act and whom they are perceived to be.

Central Coherence

Frith (1989a, 1989b) proposed the construct of "central coherence" to explain some puzzling aspects of the behaviors of children with autism. She noted that although they appear to be capable of doing well on tasks such as block design, they are incapable of noticing the broader gestalt of a social context. Their visual perceptual capacities are sufficiently intact to permit them to successfully perform the former task but not in the latter one. She defined central coherence as related to the drive to integrate information into context, gestalt, and meaning. In order to explain the phenomenon in children with autism, she differentiated between *local coherence* and *global coherence*. Children with autism have the capacity for local coherence but not global coherence. They are therefore said to have weak central coherence.

This construct has relevance for us on two scores: (1) its relationship to the concept of narrative coherence, and (2) its applicability to the self-narratives of children with NLD. The capacity for central coherence is a necessary condition for the creation of a coherent self-narrative. Without that capacity, children can only give a disjointed and fragmented account of their history, as is the case of the histories given by children with Asperger's disorder and autism. It should be kept in mind that narrative coherence is not an absolute requirement for mental health. If that were the case, most of us would fail that criterion. There is a difference between having gaps in one's self-narrative and having an incoherent self-narrative or no capacity whatsoever to generate a self-narrative. The latter is the case for children with autism.

Children with NLD have the capacity to generate self-narratives, but not necessarily ones that are entirely coherent. The question, then, is whether their failure is related to an impairment in central coherence or whether they have intact central coherence but cannot generate a coherent self-narrative for other reasons. I would lean in the direction of the position that they do possess central coherence but have gaps in the information they acquire and fail to integrate the nature of their disability. In other words, their impairment in the acquisition of nonlinguistic perceptual information or nonverbal information would lead to the incomplete encoding of the elements of the situations to which they are exposed. Their retrieval, when they are required to relate an experience, reflects accurately what was stored. The fact that their account may not make sense to a listener is due to the incompleteness in the original perception rather than to an inability on their part to make sense of what occurred. Confirmation of this position is found clinically when I ask a caregiver to join a child during our sessions. When told by the child, the particular incident the child narrates is unintelligible; the account seems fragmented and disjointed. In the presence of the caregiver, who fills in the gaps, not only can I understand fully what occurred, but the child is able to confirm that understanding.

Self-Cohesion and Narrative Coherence

The sense of cohesion may be thought of as the experience that results from being in a context in which selfobject needs are satisfied and limitations that result from deficits are either complemented by others or compensated by the child. When associated with a coherent self-narrative, a sense of cohesion produces what may be described as a state of self-consolidation. Such a state is present in persons who can endure psychological stresses or narcissistic injuries without suffering from fragmentation, and who have sufficient resiliency, endurance, and strength to tolerate insults without major difficulties. The cohesive sense of self is reciprocally related to the sense of having a coherent self-narrative.

Narrative coherence results from the integration of life's occurrences into a set of meanings that are unique to each person. It is the product of the organization and integration of these meanings and their synthesis into preexisting meanings. The origins of these systems of meanings can be found in the dialogue with caregivers who provide selfobject functions and the factors contributed by the infant's endowment.

Psychologically, the human struggle is one of maintaining coherence and defending against the loss of the sense of self-cohesion (Cohler, 1993). Conflict results from the attempt to reconcile the irreconcilable, to bring opposites together in experience; it also stems from the difficulty of finding a unitary "truth" that is all-encompassing and coherent. We need not equate conflict with pathology, however. The level of incoherence or the disruption the conflict creates produces psychopathology.

Most children with NLD come to treatment with incoherent narratives. The incoherence may stem from their puzzlement at their lack of success or from their inability to come to grips with the limitations produced by their deficits. Some children, as noted, arrive at personal explanations that appear to satisfy them. These explanations may or may not conflict with the communal explanations for their difficulties. What stands out is that they have reached a satisfactory balance between the personal and shared meanings of their learning disorder.

The relationship between narrative coherence and self-cohesion is complex. There are several possible permutations: A person may be *cohesive and coherent, cohesive and incoherent, noncohesive and coherent*, and *noncohesive and incoherent*. The first is normative and does not require discussion, but the remaining three deserve further exploration, specifically with relation to children with NLD.

Mary, a child with an NLD, may feel cohesive because she is in a context that complements her deficits and because she has a coherent narrative in that she understands that she has a learning disorder that requires help from someone or some set of materials in order to function satisfactorily. She understands and accepts that she must use verbal mediation to process nonverbal communication in order to achieve understanding. Andy, in contrast, feels cohesive because of the support he gets from his family and tutors, but he does not understand the nature of his deficits. He would not be able to generate a coherent narrative to explain his difficulties. It is unlikely that Katy, who lacks a sense of cohesiveness, could simultaneously explain the reason for her lack of cohesiveness and the sources of her discomfort. Last we have Mark, a child who is both distressed and on the verge of fragmentation but has no idea of what is producing the distress. He lacks cohesiveness and does not have a coherent self-narrative.

Clearly, the relationship between self-cohesion and narrative coherence is complex, and one factor is not conditional for the other. Rather, it is an interactive relationship. Understanding may counteract the discomfort of an experience that is threatening, and an experience of being cared for may counteract the lack of understanding of what is occurring. However, loss of cohesion can also disrupt attempts at understanding. On the other hand, failure to comprehend a set of experiences can be countered by beliefs that help retain the sense of self-cohesion. It is also possible that a person can understand what is happening but still feel devastated by the occurrence. In other words, children with social difficulties due to NLD may understand the sources of their difficulties. This understanding can be either devastating to their sense of self or it can help them maintain their sense of self-cohesion. The same child can feel devastated by the treatment he or she receives at the hands of peers *and* possess the self-cohesion to turn to scholarly pursuits while discounting what others do to him or her.

Matt was a 9-year-old-boy at the time of referral. His parents asked for help because of his long history of problems in school. At this time they were having an increasingly difficult time managing his behavior, and the school was complaining that he was a serious behavior problem. They stated that everything revolves around him; everything has to be on his terms. He is rigid and will not bend on any aspect of his behavior, and he has no respect for authority. Teachers avoid confrontations with him because he "loses it" when caught in minor infractions of the rules, and then no amount of reasoning works. Academically, teachers complained that he seems inattentive (although he usually knows the answers), his handwriting is almost illegible, reading is a problem, and he has trouble in gym because his eye–hand coordination is so poor. In addition, he does not do well with peers, and when teased, does not understand.

Matt underwent his first evaluation by a neurologist at 4 years of age. The neurologist found that he had fine- and gross-motor delays, low muscle tone, low confidence level, fear of climbing, difficulty with rapid, alternating movements, mild choreoathetoses, and mild dystonia. In addition, his attention was poor, he "stared off," and was overactive and exuberant. He also was found to have a café-au-lait spot, a skin discoloration that, at times, indicates the presence of a neurological disorder. The diagnosis given at the time was ADHD. Occupational therapy was recommended. Multiple evaluations followed, and all came to similar conclusions. Trials of Ritalin produced no improvement. The occupational therapy, which lasted for 3 years, led to improved motor control in some areas.

At age 10, the latest psychoeducational testing revealed a 38-point discrepancy between his verbal and performance IQ on the WISC-III. His VIQ was 120, whereas his PIQ was 82. In nonverbal areas he had poor spatial relation, poor visual–motor integration, poor visual figure/ground discrimination, poor visual closure, and poor spatial construction. He was given a diagnosis of an NLD.

In the initial diagnostic sessions, Matt presented as a likable, verbal child who sat and talked the entire session. His eyes wandered all over the room while he talked; he made little eye contact. When asked a question he appeared not to be listening, but then would go on to answer it. His responses, however, had the quality of a monologue rather than a dialogue. As he talked, he revealed the following as his experience of the world: Kids at school pick on him constantly. However, he is used to it, so he tries to outsmart them to avoid their insults, and he gets back at them by tripping them up when they walk by him in class. The teachers are "unfair." They always punish him, but they overlook what other kids do to him. Sometimes he gets so mad that he gets into fights with kids. He does not like to do that because he is blamed for the fighting. The teachers do not notice that the other kids started it all. He has only one friend who sides with him and protects him from other kid's attacks. Otherwise, he likes school because *he does well in reading and math. The problem is that his handwriting is bad, so he ends up not doing well in his best subject: English.*

He gets mad at his parents because they are always limiting what he wants to do. He ends up screaming at them that they are not fair—but they do not listen. "They don't know the word 'Yes!' All they know is 'No, No, No!!'" They punish him by sending him to his room, and he ends up there "for hours." When asked whether the punishments were that severe, he acknowledged that they seemed so to him. Mostly, he argues with them about watching TV or playing video games. He loves basketball and wants to watch every game. They do not understand that; when they send him to bed before the game is over, he becomes furious at them.

Asked about some good experiences, he recalled going to Space Camp with his father. He loved the experience. He learned the names of every space mission, the rockets, the astronauts that manned them, and the dates they were launched. He had an overwhelming amount of information on the subject, which he eagerly shared. What was notable about Matt was that he was likeable and evoked positive responses in the therapist. He seemed hungry to be understood, and in spite of some of his difficult personality traits, he seemed to wish that he could behave differently.

Once-a-week therapy was recommended to interrupt the cycle of negative responses and help him gain a better understanding of the nature of his learning disabilities. Part of the treatment plan included an initial school conference with everyone involved with Matt, meetings with the mother every other week, as well as being available to her on the phone whenever management problems occurred. A recommendation was made to update his psychoeducational testing, and he was referred to a tutor who specializes in the educational problems of children with NLD.

Impressions: Matt's clinical presentation is typical of children with NLD's unstable sense of self-cohesion and incoherent self-narratives. He presents as a reasonably cohesive, likeable child who is distressed by how he feels others treat him. However, when stressed by events that reach a threshold, he becomes overwhelmed and loses his self-cohesion resulting in meltdowns. From the perspective of his self-narrative, he has no clue as to the sources of his social difficulties. He is able to use his cleverness to get back at the other kids, but does not see his contribution to the interactions. A primary source of compensation is his episodic memory, which provides him with reasons to feel proud and good about himself. At this time, he does not experience as helpful his parents efforts to provide him with complementary functions to regulate his behaviors. On the contrary, he perceives their interventions as intrusive and punitive. In sum, whereas

Matt feels cohesive most of the time, he cannot make sufficient sense of his world to construct a coherent self-narrative. His puzzlement constitutes a major vulnerability that serves to destabilize his sense of self.

Conclusion

To have a sense of self-cohesion and a coherent self-narrative is to have an intact sense of self. Children with NLD may lack a sense of self-cohesion or be unable to maintain a coherent self-narrative. To a degree, these capacities depend on the quality of their early attachment to caregivers and the degree of mindsharing that they can experience.

Children with NLD may be unable to maintain a sense of self-cohesion because of deficits in selfobject functions or because of the absence of adjunctive functions. These children may suffer from chronic, intense anxiety; they may be exposed to repeated narcissistic injuries; and they may have meltdowns that represent temporary fragmentations. Under those circumstances, a sense of fragility and vulnerability may pervade their experience. Such unavoidable vulnerabilities become integrated into emerging personality traits. Children with NLD may not only respond to stresses with a loss of cohesion but also may anticipate such a loss when confronting novel situations. A pattern of avoidance and isolation becomes a major defensive style, leading to a possible disorder of the self.

Implicit in coherent self-narratives are a sense of agency, the capacity for intentionality and volition, a sense of history, a sense of continuity of experience, a sense of integration and integrity that may be experienced as cohesiveness, as well as a sense of privacy within the context of intersubjective experiences.

Children with NLD face problems in integrating the meanings of their experiences into the themes within their self-narratives. They ask themselves: "Why am I having so much trouble in school?" "Why do my parents hate me? They keep criticizing me for not doing well in school." "Why don't I have any friends?" At a different level, they are aware of, and puzzled by, their own neuropsychological weaknesses as well as strengths. They ask themselves: "Why can't I be as good in sports as I am in math?" "Why am I so good in sports but can't read?" These questions set the stage for the enactment of themes that highlight a need for clinical intervention. Identification of these themes also provide an opportunity for revision or replacement.

10

Disorders of the Self in NLD

This chapter brings to a close the last of the three perspectives that organize the contents of this work. With the addition of the intrapersonal perspective, it becomes possible to assess the full dimensions of the social features of children with NLD. I have discussed the problems associated with nonlinguistic perception and those related to deficits in social cognition. By adding the disorders of the self to which these children are prone, it becomes possible to view the full range of constraints that these factors impose on children's development and the range of social difficulties that emerge within the broad spectrum of their personalities.

On completion of this chapter it will be possible to add another component to the definition of the social features of NLD given in Chapter 7: the disorders of the self associated with each of the four subtypes. As I emphasize in this chapter, there is no simple correlation between the neuropsychological deficits or impairments in social cognition of a specific subtype and the severity of a child's disorder of the self. Depending on the developmental factors at play, a child may have a mild to severe disorder of the self whether the neuropsychological deficits are mild or the social impairments severe. Each child's emotional state should be assessed in conjunction with the neuropsychological and social impairments. Protective factors such as resilience, compensations, and salutary environments may mitigate the effects of the deficits. Nevertheless, in general, the greater the neuropsychological deficits and social impairments, the greater the impact on the child's capacity to develop a cohesive sense of self or a coherent self-narrative.

Etiology and Psychodynamics

An important distinction must be drawn between *etiological* and *psychodynamic* explanations (Kohut, 1971) of the origins of the social–emotional problems of children with NLD. Neuropsychological theories offer hypotheses that explain the disorder as resulting from brain-based deficits. These theories explain the etiology of the disorder, whereas psychodynamic explanations provide insight into the motives that impel a child to act, think, or feel in certain ways. Psychodynamic explanations also provide an understanding of the processes through which a child encodes and stores experiences in implicit memory (Lyons-Ruth, 1998; Stern, 2004). Through the psychological structures formed by these implicit memories, the child reenacts situations when these memories are evoked. These reenactments reflect organizing principles that denote patterns of interactions the child has internalized. Although these two types of explanations, the neuropsychological and the psychodynamic, derive from different paradigms, they are compatible and enrich our understanding of the child.

From a psychodynamic perspective, a variety of contextual factors are seen as shaping children's personalities. Among these are the relational patterns to which children are exposed early in life, the type of attachment they form to significant caregivers, and the temperamental factors they bring to each context. These factors become the focus of attention in a discussion of the contributions that psychoanalytic theories make to our understanding of children's behaviors. A major assumption is that neuropsychological strengths and weaknesses set constraints on the extent to which the child can adapt to a particular context, and early experiences can, in turn, produce changes in brain development that may either mitigate or aggravate the effects of those constraints. Maturational factors influence the course of brain development, much as innate and contextual factors influence the development of personality.

It is a challenging task to identify which of these specific determinants produces a child's specific response. In fact, etiological and psychodynamic factors may lie along a continuum, or, as Freud stated, they may constitute they constitute a "complemental series" (Freud, 1916, pp. 361–362). By this term he meant that the effects of constitution and environment on psychopathology fall along a spectrum that includes cases in which constitutional factors predominate, whereas environmental factors play a minimal role, and at the other end of the spectrum, environmental factors predominate, whereas constitutional factors play a minimal role.

In any given case, it is difficult to distinguish between the *social–emotional problems* of children with NLD that result directly from the neuropsychological deficits or social impairments and the *disorders of the self* that result from the developmental disruptions that those deficits create. This is the case even if we set aside, for the moment, the effects of comorbid conditions or other factors that may impair functioning. Whether or not this distinction is theoretically possible, identifying which of the two causes produces the behaviors may not be possible. The threads of nature are interwoven with those of nurture; the embodied fabric of the child makes the differentiation of causal factors extremely difficult.

However, that does not mean that we cannot trace, through careful neuropsychological testing, *some* of the neuropsychological deficits. What is difficult to ferret out is the specific manner in which any of these deficits interact with other factors that shape the child's relational dysfunctional patterns. An attachment disorder may have originated in the child's inability to communicate nonverbally with the caregiver. Nevertheless, such a disorder develops a life of its own; difficulties in relating to others, intimacy problems, even distrust of others may all contribute to the outcomes of the early attachment problems.

What we confront here is the problem of origins. Trying to trace the specific origins of any behavioral pattern is a hazardous task. The origins are hidden within the interactions that occur from the first moment of birth. Caregivers, unaware of the child's neuropsychological deficits, may interact with the child expecting average or typical responses; they adapt to the infant's idiosyncrasies, attributing them to temperamental traits. They normalize the differences between this child and their other children, rationalizing these differences as inherent in the heritable aspects of the child's responses. "He looks and acts just like your father! He is going to have his personality," the concerned mother tells her husband. Nevertheless, temperamental traits may determine the outcomes, as Kagan has documented extensively (Kagan, 2004).

The unanswered question is, How many of those temperamental traits are entwined with neuropsychological strengths and weaknesses? We have to assume that both endowment and experience contribute to the final form that behavioral expressions take. Furthermore, we need not limit ourselves to behavioral expression, because behavior is an expression of feelings, thoughts, and motives as well. To say that the child's social–emotional problems result from the misperception of social situations is both inaccurate and simplistic. It is even reductionistic in that it attributes a single contributing cause to what is a highly complex set of determinants.

Including the concept of a disorder of the self in children with NLD addresses their subjective state. The presence of a disorder of the self would mean that the child's *sense of self lacks cohesiveness* and that *his or her self-narrative is incoherent or incomplete*. The absence of cohesion may be due to self-deficits that result from mismatched responses from caregivers—a mismatch that may be due to an absence of the capacity for mindsharing and/or to maladaptive responses from caregivers due to the interferences of neuropsychological deficits. The incoherences in the child's self-narrative may be due to the distorted or incomplete understanding the child has of his or her impairments and the history that contributes to how he or she experiences the world. In brief, selfobject or adjunctive deficits contribute to the lack of self-cohesion, whereas inaccurate or incomplete understanding of those deficits contributes to incoherent self-narratives.

It is worth emphasizing that disorders of the self in children with NLD are not always proportional to the nature and extent of the deficits. Although no simple correlation has been established, a relationship does exist between the subjective experience of the impairment and its effect on the child's development (Palombo, 1987b, 1991, 1992, 1993, 1995). Given the creative and adaptive capacities of children, we should guard against pathologizing any child's efforts at integrating his or her particular deficits and strengths into a coherent personality configuration.

In the discussion of disorders of the self in children with NLD that follows, I do not attempt to specify which disorders are associated with which NLD subtypes. Instead, I assume that all subtypes are susceptible to the range of disorders because it is the subjective experiences of the children that determine their responses. Children with mild NLD may develop severe disorders of the self, whereas those with more severe NLD impairments may develop less severe self-psychopathology. Little correlation exists between the two.

NLD and the Loss of Self-Cohesion

Disruptions in the sense of self may manifest as the loss of self-cohesion. Anxiety and defensive reactions are a general response to impending or actual loss of self-cohesion. Anxiety is an indicator of psychic pain and is analogous to physical pain. Physical pain signals a threat to one's physical integrity, whereas anxiety is a manifestation of a threat to one's psychological integrity. Primary anxieties that threaten the sense of self are the fear of loss of mindsharing functions (Hofer, 1995b). The result of such losses can range from momentary reversible losses of cohesion to feelings of inner disorganization, a loss of the sense of continuity in time and space, or the experience of disintegration. The child can experience the loss of cohesion in a precariously established sense of self as "disintegration anxiety." This form of anxiety results not from the fear of physical extinction but from the loss of the sense of humanity. We see disintegration anxiety in children whose sense of being different leads them to feel like aliens. Such a feeling is equivalent to a severe psychological injury. The overt symptoms a child may manifest include frequent meltdowns, chronic irritability or rage attacks with no apparent precipitant, severe oppositional behaviors or constant power struggles, or alternatively, withdrawal responses (e.g., apathy, lack of responsiveness) or a defeatist attitude toward any task that requires minimal effort.

Defenses are usually automatically instituted to deal with anxiety; they represent an effort at self-rescue from psychological harm. Defenses are mechanisms a child uses to survive psychologically or to avoid confrontation with intense psychic pain that can potentially lead to disintegration. Large differences in defenses and defensive styles exist due, in part, to developmental factors, in part to temperamental factors, and in part to the nature of the child's deficits. Some children will act out defensively, whereas others will withdraw. Some will develop fears, whereas others will engage in life-endangering activities. Some will lie to get out of the consequences they fear will result from their behaviors, whereas others will confess readily, enduring the punishments they anticipated. Some respond to these anxieties and injuries with uncontrolled rage; professionals label these children as having "behavioral problems" or a "conduct disorder." Other children may become withdrawn, turning to unexpressed fantasies of revenge, or fall back on the stance of infantile grandiosity. These labels lose much of their meaning when we understand the motives behind the defenses.

DISORDERS OF SELF-ESTEEM

Children with NLD experience a sense of isolation and loneliness that magnifies their feelings of anxiety. Not only do they feel the loss of contact with others, but they may also lack a sense of continuity with their own history. Disconnected from the network of their community, they experience a state in which no context exists to give them the support they need. At the most superficial level, children with NLD often develop an awareness of the differences between themselves and other children, and respond to the negative perceptions that others may have of them (Garber, 1988). Most often, these differences acquire a negative valence. The chil-

dren compare themselves to others and find themselves wanting, feel embarrassed, and quickly believe themselves to be inferior to others. This
awareness may emerge at a very early age—from the moment that a toddler finds him- or herself unable to perform a task he or she expects to be
able to perform or sees playmates demonstrate competencies that are beyond his or her reach. Teasing or criticism from other children can compound these feelings. At times, caregivers themselves are puzzled that the
child seems unable to perform some simple tasks and berate the child for
the shortcomings. The child experiences that realization of having shortcomings as an injury to his or her sense of self and may then feel imperfect or defective. The realization of lacking abilities diminishes the child's
view of self, resulting in shame, anxiety, depression, discouragement, or
feelings of incompetence. The loss of self-esteem leads to a destabilization
in the sense of self-cohesion.

The confusion these children feel about their strengths and weaknesses
introduces a further complexity into their psychodynamics. Some children, when confronted with the reality that they excel in some areas of
functioning but utterly fail in other areas, experience the disparity as a
source of puzzlement. On the one hand, they are often faced with tasks
that appear easy for others but are immensely difficult for them, whereas,
on the other hand, they see themselves excelling in tasks that appear difficult to others. In light of these experiences, they may conclude that there
is something terribly wrong with them or that the difficult tasks are not
worth the effort that goes into succeeding at them. These experiences reinforce a negative self-image.

UNSTABLE SENSE OF SELF-COHESION

Children who suffer from an unstable sense of cohesion manifest an er-
ratic and often unpredictable pattern of fragmentation and reintegration
that nevertheless appears to be predominantly cohesive in the overall adjustment. Although they are able to function at home and at school much
of the time, at times, their thoughts appear to be fragmented or discontin-
uous, their level of anxiety is overwhelming, their affects are intense and
unmanageable, and they lack the capacity for attunement to others. These
internal disruptions interfere with their capacity for self-regulation and
lead them to perceive the world as chaotic, overwhelming, and ungratify-
ing. Their ability to make sense of their environment appears impaired. In
their frustration and isolation, they feel enraged at those around them
who continue to make demands they cannot meet.

Attempts to deal with the overt symptoms through reward or punishment will generally fail. Caregivers or therapists must understand the un-

derlying dynamics that are motivating the behaviors if any interventions are to be successful. Teachers and caregivers often complain that these children do not seem to learn from past experience but keep responding with the same behaviors, no matter how often these have been labeled as unacceptable. What these caretakers do not appreciate is the fact that these children feel little control over their actions. They are impelled to behave as they do not because they are mean or determined to make life difficult for others but simply because they know of no other way to survive. It is difficult to feel empathy for children when their behavior is so disruptive, but only through empathy for their underlying motives will understanding come about and a successful intervention creatively devised. Through empathy, a mindsharing milieu may be fostered in which these children are to feel reconnected to their caregivers and more responsive to their interventions.

Although children's experiences vary widely, some of the elements of unstable self-cohesion may be summarized in a composite profile of a 9-year-old boy.

The child struggles to come to grips with an environment that he experiences as chaotic, ill defined, and poorly organized. He experiences an intolerable sense of frustrations and feels as though no one is able to understand his needs. He feels shut off from others, immured in himself.

The child experiences adults as demanding, badgering, and intrusive. Adult reactions seem bewildering and unrelated to his experiences. He feels constrained by their pressing demands and experiences them as imposing their will on him. He feels he must fight back against their efforts in order not to feel subjugated by them. To comply to their demands feels like a dangerous intrusion into his life.

His distress often escalates until he can respond only with rage and temper tantrums to the feelings of injury and devastation. In a diffuse, ill-directed manner, he attempts to get across to others the feeling of hopelessness and helplessness he experiences. He attacks others, often younger siblings, in the hope that somehow the discharge of tension would help relieve the distress and end the ceaseless intrusions. He feels it imperative to keep them out. He fights back with all his might; he kicks, bites, hits. The frenzy of his reactions seems to obliterate what actually triggered the outburst. All sense of time is lost.

Feeling exhausted following such bouts, he may withdraw or seek flight into fantasies, which provide much greater gratification than contact with others. Lost in fantasy, the child can experience a sense of omnipotent control, in contrast to the helplessness felt in the larger world. What started out as a simple frustration appears distant and meaningless. The child feels isolated and detached. He also feels surrounded by hostile, monstrous creatures that are intent on hurting him. He not only cannot trust them, he must not need anything from them. He must find ways to comfort and console himself.

The means for self-comforting are few and meager. He takes refuge in video games or watching TV, which he is restricted from doing; if discovered, he may be seriously reprimanded. Now he feels deprived of the one source of gratification he had found. Unable to escape into fantasy or gain comfort from closeness with another, he becomes overwhelmed by anxiety, which escalates and approaches fragmenting proportion. The child now experiences a variety of physical distresses: stomachaches, headaches, or other physical symptoms. Adults may address the physical ailments, not recognizing the psychological counterparts. The child may gain some minimal secondary comfort or may eventually withdraw into tearful isolation. His mother may attempt to comfort him; indeed, she may seem to go out of her way to please him. He is puzzled but gratified, and he tries to prolong the tender moment with her. It is as though he is caught between the sweet pleasure of her affection and the larger dangers of the world beyond her. When at school the ailments seem to intensify, and he yearns to be excused from attending. At first everyone seems to respond to him, and he feels they care. However, his parents soon decide that he is not really sick, that he is faking his illness, and that he must go to school anyway. How can they not understand? He now battles against being dragged to school, is forced to go, and is further immobilized by his fears. He becomes frantic and reckless.

He returns to brooding about his plight, craving satisfaction. This time he is diverted by thoughts of inflicting pain on others to redress the injustices he feels he has suffered. He may decide that his younger brother or sister, who are obviously not as unhappy as he is, are preferred by his parents. Why, he asks himself, should he be the one to suffer? He strikes out at them, gleefully hurting them and feeling vengefully satisfied. When they scream and call the parents to interdict him, he feels fully justified in what he has done and has no qualms about lying. They deserve what they got; he was the victim, not they.

The sweet taste of revenge is brief and the gloom returns as he again hears a voice reprimanding him to stop what he is doing. It is always so. Whenever he finds a source of satisfaction, it is taken away from him. He looks around for more distractions, spots his mother's purse, and remembers that he had asked for a toy—which she never bought him. He opens the purse, takes a bill out of the billfold, and runs out of the house. At first he feels frightened, hesitant, and unsure of whether he was seen or not. He is terrified that he will be caught. His heart is pounding as though he had committed a horrible crime. He soon discovers that his act went unnoticed. He runs to the store and feels thrilled at the enormous choices suddenly confronting him. He hardly knows where to start. He fills his pockets with candy and finds himself surround by friends eager to please him in exchange for what he has. He is now at center state and even seems to command the admiration of his peers. If he is not discovered, an avenue of greater satisfaction will have opened to him. If discovered, then that path would also be blocked, and he would have to find another.

School is his nemesis. There he can never do well, no matter how hard he tries. In fact, he stopped trying long ago. His work was never as good as that of his peers. His teachers were always critical of his best efforts. Math is a mystery he never solved. His writing seems fine to him, although he is always told that it is illegible. He can never find his homework, and can never keep track of all the stuff he has in his locker. In class he is the clown who draws attention to himself to defeat the teacher's efforts at making him feel bad. School is a huge waste of time. Recess and summer are his favorite times.

When night comes and he must go to bed, the feelings of gloom return, now heightened by the dark. He struggles against an overpowering feeling that untold horrors and inhuman figures lurk in every corner. He stays alert and awake to take flight, should he be attacked. The shadows he sees and the sounds he hears all signal the evil forces that are bent on his destruction. To call his parents now is to weaken and to give in to them, or to submit. Perhaps there is a lesser danger than that, but he cannot think of it. He finally goes to their bedroom and gets into bed with them. Now, at least, he feels some peace, cradled by his mother's body, feeling enveloped by her protectiveness. However, she awakens and screams at him to go back to his bed. He cries and pleads to no avail. He returns to his danger-filled room, as a drowning victim to a sea of sharks. Frozen by his terror, he drives himself to think of other things that would be distracting. His own mind now is the only source of salvation.

If by thinking he can reassure himself, then all is not lost. He mechanically repeats the same thoughts over and over and finds that in the mindless repeating of the thought, the anxiety can be momentarily blotted out. At first he simply repeats every new thought that comes to mind, but as he gets bored with that device, he creates a game in which he starts thinking in twos or threes. If he thinks of one monster, he must think of two others; if he hears one sound, he has to wait till he hears it twice more. He devises more complex combinations in sets so that his natural cognitive abilities are brought into play. By the time daylight breaks, he finally falls asleep, exhausted.

The next day this newly found game is continued. It now occupies a great deal of his time. His mother cannot interfere with it; she does not even know about it. If called to do something, he is too immersed in his thoughts to give any attention to other tasks. It is hard to tear himself away from this comforting activity; besides, he cannot be interrupted in the middle of a cycle because disaster would ensue. He has shaped his entire existence now around these rituals, which provide a modicum of comfort. However, to his dismay, he soon discovers that even this self-contained activity displeases his mother, to whom he has confided *his constant preoccupation. He is not allowed to reassure himself in any way. Every attempt he makes to maintain the internal security system he has devised is interfered with, and he must search elsewhere for an answer.*

Finally, he is convinced there is no avenue open to him for satisfaction. He must sacrifice himself if he is to survive. He must submit and pretend that all is well, hiding his fears and secretly living on two levels. On the surface, he will be the acquiescent and malleable child everyone wants him to be; inside, however, he will feel nothing. The gloom has turned to stone, and the sense of deadness displaces all feeling. This then becomes a way of life. To feel in touch with the tenderness and the pain would be unbearable. It is better to put these vulnerable feelings to the side and carry on as best one can. The alternative is to find a way to kill himself—in fact, he wishes he were dead.

NLD and Incoherent Self-Narratives

Child therapists have generally characterized the explanations that children give themselves for their difficulties as *fantasies*, because these explanations do not match the reality to which they refer. From this perspective, the goal of the therapeutic process is to help the child reveal these explanations, which the therapist then corrects so that the explanations match the probable reality at the time the child arrived at the explanations.

In relation to children with NLD, the question is whether it is correct to call their explanations of the reasons for their behavior, *fantasies*. It might be more correct to view these explanations as beliefs they have formed based on their limited knowledge of the world. Their explanations are based on the relationship they have established between their memories of actual events and their limited understanding of the causes of those events. Their autobiographical accounts are the product of connections they have made between those events as they experienced them. They may make use of memories or knowledge they have acquired to construct an elaborate story, knowing all along that the story is not veridical. The difference is between a fantasy—which is purely a product of their imagination—and a belief formed of memories thought to be accurate renditions of what actually happened.

Part of the problem in clarifying this distinction lies in the confusion between personal meanings and fantasies. In its restricted sense the concept of fantasy applies to imaginary or fictitious productions; consequently, the status of the events as nonexistent is not in question. The construct of personal meaning introduces a different form of discourse, however. Personal meanings reflect an interpretation of historical events, however idiosyncratic those interpretations might be. Nonetheless, the interpretations are of actual events. In the case of children with NLD whose narratives have elements of incoherence, the incoherences are due to the meanings that they have drawn from the events to which they were exposed, rather than their fantasies—although they may use their imaginations to elaborate on those explanations.

Incoherences in self-narratives can range from mild to severe. For example, at the milder end of the spectrum is the narrative of a child who is puzzled by his inability to achieve in spite of his conviction that he is smart. At the other extreme are the incoherences in the narrative of the child with Asperger's disorder, who has great difficulty integrating experiences into her sense of self. For such a child, creating a coherent narrative presents an insuperable task. When asked, she may attempt to give an account of her experiences, but her account would be either idiosyncratic or quite incoherent.

A common source of narrative incoherence in children with NLD is their failure to integrate aspects of their experiences. It is easier to understand how a person exposed to a traumatic experience is unable to integrate its full meaning than it is to understand how a person of average intelligence appears unable to integrate the meaning of relatively simple human interactions. However, that is what happens to some of these children, whose deficits impair their capacity to integrate day-to-day experiences. As we have seen, they have difficulty giving an accurate account of even simple transactions. The sequence of events is jumbled, the central point of the story appears to be missing, and the entire thread that ties the events together is tangled. Only through arduous questioning does an outline of what occurred take shape. Often the presence of a caregiver is required if one wants to elicit clear information about them and events in their lives. That is also the case for the explanations children create for their cognitive and social difficulties.

In summary, the coherence or incoherence of the self-narrative cannot be divorced from the correspondence between the account given in the self-narrative and the historical events. A fictitious self-narrative cannot carry the weight required to heal a child's disorder of the self. Shared meanings emerge from the sharing of personal memories of events, as understood within the context in which these occurred. The coherence of the narrative is related to those shared meanings and, by extension, to the view of reality as understood within the context. NLD often interferes with the creation of a coherent self-narrative, leading to personal meanings that are incomprehensible to others or at variance with the shared meanings of the culture. In some children, these incoherences lead to a disorder of the self.

Case Illustration

A young man whom I will call Paul was 16 years old when he first came into treatment. He provides an example of a person who struggled to make sense out of his life in order to arrive at a coherent self-narrative.

The school social worker referred him because of his poor school performance and a concern that he was running around with a crowd of delinquent kids. The fear was that he too might join them in some of their activities and start abusing drugs, much as they were. There was no indication that he had engaged in either of these activities.

Paul had been tested when he was 12 years old. However, the recommendations made by the examiner were not implemented, in part, because of Paul's resistance to acknowledging that he had a problem, and in part because the school system did not appreciate the significance of the findings. I did not have access to this report until Paul was well into his third year of treatment. He initially refused to let me see it. Portions of this report follow:

NEUROPSYCHOLOGICAL EVALUATION

Reason for referral: *Paul is a 12-year, 2-month-old Caucasian male who was reported by his parents and teachers to be forgetful, disorganized, slow completing work, and to have poor planning abilities. His mother also reported that he becomes upset easily and occasionally does not understand the subtleties of social situations. In general, Paul holds on to ideas rigidly, and in particular, tends to display rigid adherence to rules; when others violate these rules, he becomes enraged. These difficulties regulating his emotional display, plus insufficiently developed social skills, impede the development of friendships.*

Relevant history: *Paul was adopted at birth. His biological mother was 18 years old. The adoption was made privately through the family's attorney. Most of Paul's developmental milestones occurred within normal age limits. However, he did not walk alone until he was 16 months old. He was not fully bladder trained until he was between the ages of 4 and 4½ years old, and continued to show nocturnal enuresis for the next couple of years. She also reported that he speaks very softly and has some articulation difficulties. Finally, Paul showed precocious reading development, starting at the age of 4.*

His mother reported that *Paul was given to severe temper tantrums. These explosions tended to occur at school or when interacting with peers. Typically, he yelled and cried during these social explosions. His feeling that other children are not listening to him or that they have broken a rule usually precipitated these tantrums.*

At present, he adheres rigidly to concrete instructions from authority figures and has difficulty gleaning meaning from the intent of the rule and generalizing rules across situations. According to his mother, he sometimes feels that other children are violating rules when they are not. He then becomes very angry when he tries to tell the children that they have broken a rule and they respond by ignoring him. Furthermore, Paul does not have sufficiently developed social skills to initiate and develop friendships. He tends to gravitate toward younger children. The combination of soft voice, speech misarticulations, and gentle demeanor make him a target for teasing.

Behavioral observations: *Paul is tall and slim. He did not initially respond to the neuropsychologist's greetings. He tended to display mildly pleasant affect most of the time. He had difficulty making appropriate eye contact at nodal points in conversation and instead displayed a gaze with a wandering quality. He also blinked his eyes frequently. He showed little emotional responsivity to social cues and jokes but smiled and acted pleased with his performance on various assessment devices. When he did respond to humor, it was usually the kind of humor a 6-year-old child would appreciate but most 10 year olds would find childish and demeaning.*

Table 10.1 Results of WISC-III : Paul A

Verbal Tests	Scaled Scores	Performance Tests	Scaled Scores
Information	17	Picture Completion	10
Similarities	14	Coding	7
Arithmetic	15	Picture Arrangement	9
Vocabulary	17	Block Design	13
Comprehension	13	Object Assembly	5
Digit Span	(11)	Symbol Search	(10)

Verbal IQ   131   Performance IQ   93   Full Scale IQ   113

Verbal Comprehension	130
Perceptual Organization	96
Freedom from Distractibility	118
Processing Speed	93

His speech is high in pitch and has a sing-song quality. In general, Paul's interpersonal style and voice make him seem like a much younger child than he is. His language formulation was suitably communicative, and his verbal comprehension was intact.

Test findings: On the WISC-III, Paul obtained a VIQ of 131 (very superior range), a PIQ of 93 (average range), and a Full Scale IQ of 113 (high-average range). IQ and scale scores are presented below. Subtest standard scores have a mean of 10 and a standard deviation of 3.

Paul's verbal processing ability is significantly better developed and applied than his visuoperceptual and visuomotor problem-solving abilities. There is some variation within his verbal abilities as well. He possesses a great deal of factual knowledge; he is articulate and is able to formulate his ideas in a clear and concise manner. His responses frequently yielded significant intrasubtest variability, wherein he answered questions correctly up to the end of the subtest (i.e., 16-year-old items), but missed several earlier, easier items. Some of the missed responses seemed related to insufficient attention to the most relevant aspect of the response.

At a basic level, Paul does not always perceive and interpret situations in the manner that most others would. At times, his perceptions are accurate, but he focuses on details of situations that are less centrally relevant than others. At other times, when there are many aspects to a situation, he may develop an idiosyncratic interpretation of the occurrence, the factors leading up to the occurrence, and the meaning of the occurrence. His ideas about such situations are unusual at times, and his comments in peer social situations may seem unrelated to the conversation. He becomes easily confused, encounters a difficult time integrating ideas to develop a synthesized meaning, and when he is overwhelmed, may show a daydreaming, wide-eyed, or blank gaze, seemingly in a daze.

Paul cannot easily read facial or vocal emotional expressions, except for the most obvious of smiles. Therefore, he cannot make inferences or derive meaning from people's emotional reactions and motivations. He does not discuss his own feelings, which may suggest that he encounters difficulty identifying them. Not surprisingly, he does not ask about others' feelings, because this communicational language is not obvious to him. His voice is too loud at times, with an unusual vocal intonation, and his gestures, when present, seem awkward and stilted. He shows a high degree of depressive mood, anxiety, and fearfulness. His marked difficulty reading other people's emotional expressions leads him to understand poorly the impact of his behavior on others; consequently, he does not show interpersonal feelings such as guilt and empathy, which are predicated on the knowledge of others' feelings in relationship to self. Furthermore, Paul shows dramatic emotional lability, fluctuating between a quiet, gentle demeanor, and an extremely agitated response, which is often an overreaction to a minor situation, or resulting from a misinterpretation of a situation. His emotional agitation and self-blame have been so strong at times that he has threatened to kill himself.

Paul is resistant to changes in the environment and does not employ problem-solving skills to accommodate or alter those changes. He is overly attentive to the details of rules and their adherence and transgressions rather than understanding the meaning behind the rules. He does not always understand the role that he has played in interpersonal conflicts and tends to externalize blame and responsibility onto others. With adults, he needs continual reassurance and tends to display a dependent, clingy interpersonal demeanor. The neuropsychologist ended the report diagnosing Paul as having an NLD.

TREATMENT

In the initial session with me, Paul, who was 16 at the time, presented as a disheveled, long-haired, young man with a wild look in his eyes. He was tall for his age, thin and intense. He seemed on the verge of tears, although it was clear he would never allow himself to cry. He had a voice that seemed to be cracking under the stress and tension he felt. He had agreed to come to treatment on condition that I not speak with his mother about what transpired in our sessions—a condition which she and I accepted.

He began the session spontaneously and spoke of his impressions about what was happening to him. As an example he stated that on his way to the appointment, while he was walking on the sidewalk alongside the buildings, he began to feel the buildings pressing against him, as though they were about to topple on him. He found himself leaning in their direction so as to counteract the forces that they represented and to prevent their catastrophic fall. He gave this brief account in a broken, hesitant manner with many long pauses. He kept glancing at the door as though he were ready to spring out of his chair and leave at any moment. He spoke a little about the details of the referral and then lapsed into a vacant silence, out of which I occasionally stirred him with a question. His nonverbal responses suggested to me that he did not wish to communicate verbally, although he was quite desirous of accepting help. We agreed to meet once a week, and I found myself ending the session after half an hour, feeling that the stress of continuing would be intolerable for both of us.

For the first year of treatment, Paul kept his weekly appointments erratically, usually arriving 10–20 minutes late. He always manifested intense anxiety and an almost overwhelming feeling of desperation. His feelings, as far as I could detect, were ones of intense psychic pain. The sessions were often spent in silence; I felt that no words could possibly convey my empathic sense of what he felt. Words would either sound banal and trite or would evoke such emotion that he would flee. I could see no way in which to comfort him. After sitting a while he would, at times, decide that the feelings were too overwhelming and ask if it was *all right for him to leave. I sensed that he wished to stay but could not, and I allowed him to leave when he needed to. Often the sessions were no more than 10–20 minutes long, which I felt was all he could tolerate.*

We sat through these seemingly endless hours together until he began to feel freer to talk. He talked of his life as though he experienced it through a fog. I could detect the outlines of his reality, but felt that the true content of that reality still eluded me. It was not so much that he was vague, for he could be quite vivid in the descriptions of his feelings; it was more that his descriptions lacked coherence and meaning. His affect was flat, for the most part, although at times he would become excited and animated. He spontaneously talked about having tried some marijuana once and having had such a bad trip that it terrified him. He has since stayed away from it. It was clear that he wanted me to know that he was not on any drugs.

At first, I made some efforts to clarify what he was communicating to me by reflecting on his pain and the content of his verbalization, but I soon discovered that it was in error to do this. All he seemed to want of me was that I listen to the recitals of his experiences, giving him my undivided attention. He watched my face intently, scanning my reactions as though he were attempting to read into my empathic responses what he was experiencing.

I felt quite clearly that Paul had serious learning disabilities, which had remained unrecognized and for which he had received no help. I had just been introduced to the concept of NLD. However, his plight at this point was such that for me to introduce that topic would have been interpreted by him as a further injury.

During that first year he revealed indirectly that he lived with his divorced mother and an older sister. He made no mention of the whereabouts of his father, and I asked no questions to fill in the details of his history. That he was not a good student, I surmised from his references to school. His life seemed to center around the group of friends with whom he "hung around," although it was clear that he was peripheral to the group. He spoke disdainfully of their escapades and activities, seeing himself as superior to them and as uninterested in their childish pranks.

At the beginning of the second year I tried once more to make some efforts to clarify what he was communicating to me by reflecting on his pain and the content of his verbalizations. However, I soon discovered that I was in error again. He looked at me with utter puzzlement, seeming to have no comprehension of what I was talking about. I lapsed back into the silent presence he wished me to be. It soon became clear that my silent mirroring gave meaning to his self-reflections. My focused and accepting presence provided him with continuity and perhaps even a sense of his existence. Slowly the fragments of his life were beginning to be woven together by his reliving of them in our sessions.

At the end of the second year he spontaneously asked if he could come twice a week. I agreed. He was graduating from high school and had enrolled in a college, planning to live in a local dorm. He had not discussed his plans with me, so I knew little of the basis on which he had made his decision. He seemed exhilarated at the thought of moving away from home and being on his own. He saw himself as possibly finishing college in 3 years and moving on into a teaching career.

Up to this point, he had not experimented with alcohol, but once he moved into a dorm, he soon discovered the soothing effect drinking had for him. As he described drunken sprees with his roommate, it seemed to me that he wished to make up for lost time. In our sessions he was more animated and could tolerate a measure of dialogue. The depressive tone in his voice seemed to have dissipated somewhat, and he no longer appeared on the verge of tears. Although he was failing his classes, his plans for the future seemed unaffected by that detail. Because I did not see my role as one of defining reality for him, I continued to reflect his wishes and desires to get well and move ahead in his life. Pointing out the unrealistic nature of his plans would have devastated him and destroyed our relationship. I chose instead to support his healthy efforts at trying to find something in his life that could give him some satisfaction and that represented a meaningful goal toward which he could strive.

Reality itself intruded of its own accord soon enough as his grandiose schemes foundered. He was asked to take a leave of absence from school because he had not maintained the required "C" average. The painful moments that followed led to bouts of depression and to even heavier drinking. He began to use alcohol freely. At that point, I limited my interventions to reflecting his disappointment in himself and his disillusionment in his life, which had not turned out the way he wanted it to be. Because I never questioned him regarding his use of alcohol and drugs, I was never sure whether his condition was drug-induced or part of his enfeebled sense of self. I had the distinct impression at times that he was taking hallucinogens and only later discovered that he was not.

Toward the middle of the third year, he began to speak of feeling dissociated and of experiencing feelings of derealization. I grew very concerned about him and worried a great deal about him. His depression seemed profound, and I felt it necessary to suggest that perhaps a consultation for medication might be a better way to deal with what he was feeling than through alcohol and drugs. At first he resisted the idea but finally agreed to a consultation with a psychiatrist. Unfortunately, the experience turned out to be disastrous. The psychiatrist saw both the mother and Paul and diagnosed him as schizophrenic. He urged antipsychotic medication. Paul, upon being informed of the diagnosis, was outraged to be so classified, and he became enraged at me for making the referral. He refused the medication, disagreed with the diagnosis, and, much to my relief, continued his commitment to our sessions. At this point I offered to see him three times a week, to which he agreed.

During this period, he expressed a desire to find his biological parents. Because his grandparents had facilitated the adoption, he pressured them to give him whatever information they had. From that information he eventually pieced together the location of his biological father in a neighboring city. His father was a blue-collar worker from a small town outside the large metropolitan area in which Paul lived. Paul decided he wanted to track down his father to meet him and find out what he was really like. He seemed to feel a kinship with him, a fascination with the growing resemblance between his life and his father's life, as he had imagined it to be. With nothing more than an old photograph that he had found somewhere in his grandparents' home, he started frequenting the bars he guessed would be his father's favorite haunts. His preliminary efforts to find his father led nowhere, and he began to feel discouraged about ever finding him. Then, as he reported later to me, he found himself sitting down on the sidewalk of that small town, with a can of beer by his side, thinking deeply about how he might continue his search, when he spontaneously asked himself where he would be likely to be if he were his father. He took out a map of the city and located a section that was heavily populated with bars. He decided to resume his search there. He systematically visited bar after bar, showing the picture to the bartenders. Amazingly, he found a bartender who recognized the woman in the picture but not the man, who was his father. The woman was supposed to be a former girlfriend of his father. In any case, after a further 2-day search, he entered a bar, sat at the counter next to a man, spontaneously offered the man a drink, and then took a closer look—indeed it was the man in the picture, his father!

He identified himself, and a touching reunion followed in which both spent the rest of the week getting drunk and catching up on old times. His father was exactly as the mother had depicted him. However, this unfavorable depiction only endeared him to Paul, who could fully understand him. They became fast friends and drinking companions. After about a month, Paul decided that his quest was completed and decided to return home. His father made promises to keep in touch—promises that both knew could not be kept, and Paul never challenged his father about them.

Once back home Paul's depression deepened. The encounter with his father had produced a short-lived elation that was soon replaced with serious depression. He became actively suicidal. He felt that he had found what he had sought, but the prospect of his life following the same course as his father's was devastating. To add to the tragedy, a couple of months later he indirectly learned that his father had been killed in a car accident when the car he was driving, while intoxicated, went off the road.

Paul now felt convinced that life was not worth living and that suicide was the only course left for him. My anxiety at this point was immeasurable because I earnestly feared that he would take his life. Yet I, like him, felt that life had indeed lost all meaning for him. What was the point of living? I suggested hospitalization, which Paul turned down out-of-hand. He had returned to live with his mother, and while she was gone one day, he ingested a variety of medications that he found in a medicine cabinet and slashed one of his wrists. His mother returned sooner than expected, found him unconscious, and immediately rushed him to the emergency room. However, at the earliest opportunity, he walked out of the emergency room and refused to return home. His mother got in touch with me, hoping that I would have heard from him. She had no idea where he was.

The following morning Paul showed up for his appointment looking terrible. The fact that he had come to see me indicated that I represented for him the only thread of hope in life for him. It was as though a titanic struggle between the forces of life and those of death were at work within him. He wanted a reason to live but felt he had more to gain by dying. We spoke of his existential dilemma; of the fact that life without meaning may indeed not be worth living. Yet could it be that he had not found an answer for himself of the kind of life that he wished to pursue? What seemed remarkable at this point were both the clarity with which he saw his life and the starkness with which he perceived his limitations. There was no grandiosity, and there were no illusions. His perception of reality was absolutely clear. There was little self-deception and no attempt to defend against the immeasurable pain that he was experiencing.

The turning point came in the following session when I openly stated that I could accept his needing to kill himself if he felt he had no other choice. I spoke about the waste of a life, the finality of death, the sadness I would feel to no longer see him. He listened attentively to what I said, clearly taking in my words. The session ended in silence, but I somehow knew he would not harm himself.

A slow transformation then began to take place in his life. He decided to share the test report with me. As we were able to piece together the sources of his difficulties, he began to understand the course his life had taken. He decided to reenroll in the school from which he had dropped out, to begin to pursue the goal of finishing college. That goal became the central focus of his life for a time. Although he continued to medicate himself with alcohol, the drinking became more controlled and seemed to serve the purpose of permitting him to fall asleep at night.

At this juncture, his mother, who had remarried, decided to move out of town with her husband, who was being relocated by his firm. Paul faced a predicament: In part, he looked forward to a new start in a totally new environment; in part, he felt that he would lose the opportunity to continuing working with me. He decided that we had accomplished a good deal. He chose to move with his mother, saying that after a break, he would resume therapy with someone else.

This case illustrates some of the diagnostic issues that arise with an adolescent who has an NLD. Several questions come to the forefront regarding the contribution of his NLD to his condition, the effect of his impairments on his social relationships, and the disorder of the self that ensued. From a diagnostic perspective, I would say that Paul fits the criteria for NLD subtype IV. He clearly had nonlinguistic perceptual deficits, serious executive function problems, and a markedly impaired capacity to process social signs. Indeed, his condition could be labeled *severely impaired*. In the commentary that follows, I concentrate on Paul's efforts to maintain a sense of self-cohesion and construct a coherent self-narrative.

Self-Cohesion

Paul's initial confusion and bewilderment were due to several factors. A marked deterioration had occurred since his testing at age 12. Over the course of the 4 years since that testing, to the time of his referral, he had become more isolated from his peers. The unavailability of his father during the critical years of early adolescence, the erosive effects of his poor academic performance, and incipient depression all took their toll on his capacity to remain cohesive. Furthermore, his mother's preoccupation with events in her life and the unavailability of suitable objects for mind-sharing increased his sense of isolation and loneliness. He had to rely on his depleted inner resources to sustain him and to defend against fragmentation.

His refusal to accept the diagnostic findings from his neuropsychological testing and the mysteries that surrounded his adoption compounded his vulnerability to fragmentation. He confronted serious difficulties in attempting to formulate a coherent self-narrative. Such was his condition when he came to his first therapy session.

Given those dynamics, I decided that it was more important to keep the focus on Paul's inner experience rather than on external reality. I wanted to convey that understanding him would be more helpful than establishing the accuracy of the events he reported or of his historical recollections. As I struggled to understand his experience, I directed my efforts at helping him maintain a sense of cohesion. This goal was sustained through my attunement to his experience and his willingness to filter his experience through my responses to him. When I could make sense of those elements of his experience that I could grasp, he felt more cohesive. As he stated it at one point: "The question isn't 'What is the reason I feel this way?' The question is 'What is the feeling that leads me to reason this way?' " It is as though his faith in the coherence that I found in his existence gave him reasons to continue to share his experiences with me. I provided the organization through which his confusion could be dissipated. On the rare occasions when I could not be sufficiently attuned to him and failed to understand him, his annoyance seemed more related to his perception that my misunderstanding was evidence of my being disconnected from him, rather than just a failure to make sense of what he was saying.

I understood his grandiose schemes as weak efforts at coming to grips with tasks that he was poorly equipped to perform and that confounded him. My responses to his plans allowed him to experience me as mirroring his yearnings and thereby affirming him as a worthwhile person. A degree of mindsharing was established between us, which gave him the confidence to deal with the painful reality that confronted him. The corrections in his perception were the result of consolidation in his sense of self that occurred rather than from any confrontation with reality. Through most of the therapy, he retained the idealization of his father. The consequence was that he could not form an idealizing transference to me, even though my provision of those functions for him would have helped stabilize him further. His father's death, whether by accident or by intent, deprived Paul of the fantasized idealized selfobject.

Countertransference issues revolved primarily around not becoming overwhelmed by the intensity of the Paul's pain and not feeling panicked by the peremptory expression of his needs. The capacity to remain calm, to soothe, to convey a benign sense of strength helped anchor him and give him a feeling of control and cohesion.

The major countertransference challenge arose with his determination to commit suicide. A number of ethical, legal, and therapeutic issues converged around this problem. My choice in dealing with that threat was to convey to him that he faced a serious existential dilemma. He had lost the will to live, because he had nothing for which to live. By expressing my deep sorrow for his grief and stating clearly that I wanted him to live, I offered myself to him as a caring parent—someone he felt he had never had. His decision not to kill himself represented an expression of his attachment to me and of the emergence of a possible idealizing transference. It was this emerging transference that I believe helped him sustain a sense of self-cohesion and that enabled him to resume his academic career. Unfortunately, his having to move interrupted a process that might have eventually led to the establishment of a stable sense of self-cohesion. It would then have become possible to provide him with the parts that were missing from his self-narrative: those related to his NLD.

Self-Narrative

The major impediment to helping Paul develop a coherent self-narrative was his resistance to incorporating the findings of the testing into a view of himself. It is not unusual for a child or adolescent whose sense of self is fragile and vulnerable to refuse to confront or accept any fact that suggests that he or she is deficient or imperfect. The acknowledgment of such a fact is experienced as a narcissistic injury that is to be avoided, almost at any cost. Paul treated the least hint or suggestion that a neuropsychological deficit may lie at the root of his difficulties as an insult not to be tolerated. It was not possible, therefore, for me to construct explanations for his emotional responses and his behaviors that took into account his misperception of events or his incorrect interpretations of the reasons for others' responses.

His decision to search for his father seemed to me partly motivated by a desire to learn about his history but also partly based on the hope that an encounter with his father would help explain why he behaved as he did. The initial relief he felt after he met his father provided him with such an explanation. He saw himself as his father's son, someone who devalued many of society's expectations for achievement and valued instead the camaraderie found in the ambiance of bars.

The crash that followed was not totally unexpected. Not only did the encounter not provide satisfactory answers but it also led to the realization that his grandiose dreams of success could never be realized if he followed his father's example. The story could only have a tragic ending. His father's death, which may or may not have been accidental, only reinforced the sad ending of the self-narrative. Fortunately for both of us the thread that held us together was able to sustain the strain placed on it. My acceptance of his decision to be responsible for his life cleared the way for his acceptance of a different theme that could structure his self-narrative. It became possible to reconstruct his story along different lines—ones that were more consonant with the some of the factors that shaped who he was.

Expansion of the Definition of the Social Features of NLD

It is now possible to add a third component to the definition given in Chapter 7. In addition to the evaluation of the social features associated with the neuropsychological deficits and the social impairments, we may now add the assessment of whether the child has a disorder of the self. This assessment is the same regardless of the subtype to which the child belongs. A disorder of the self would exist if one or both of the following conditions are found to prevail:

1. *Sense of self cohesion.* The child has an unstable or vulnerable cohesive sense of self as demonstrated by:
   a. Being behaviorally prone to fragmentation, as evidenced by frequent tantrums and loss of control; having seriously low self-esteem, as evidenced by frequent self-criticism or unrealistic grandiosity; being consistently disrespectful of adults; and feeling a sense of alienation or disconnection from others that leads to a preference for isolation.
   b. Having a diminished capacity for mindsharing, as established by a detailed review of the developmental history.
   c. Having a tenuous or incomplete understanding of theory of mind functioning, as evaluated by the false-belief task or theory of relevance instruments.
2. *Coherence of the self-narrative.* Elements of the child's self-narrative lacks coherence as indicated by:
   a. a lack in the capacity for central coherence.
   b. a misattributribution of the reasons for his or her problems to factors other than those established to be caused by the neuropsychological and/or social impairments.

Comorbidity and NLD

Comorbidity, as used here, refers to the coexistence of one or more DSM-IV (American Psychiatric Association, 1994) diagnoses in a child with an NLD. NLD is not included among the DSM-IV diagnostic categories. However, there is clear clinical evidence that many children with NLD qualify for Axis I diagnoses of anxiety disorder, dysthymia, obsessive–compulsive disorder, or adjustment disorders. Little is known about the prevalence of these disorders among this population. As we have seen, many of the children are considered to have ADHD, although for the most part, they have elements of the condition but not necessarily the full disorder (Barkley, 1989, 1990). Many other neuropsychological deficits may also co-occur with an NLD. The one condition most commonly discussed in connection with NLD is Asperger's disorder. Given the importance of making a differentiation between this disorder and NLD, I devote the next chapter to that discussion.

Conclusion

The sense of self of the child with an NLD represents the convergence of all the elements that entered into its formation. From a developmental perspective, I have noted the constraints that neuropsychological factors impose on the child's social interactions as well as the capacity to achieve a sense of cohesion and a coherent self-narrative. During development, the effects of these constraints can be magnified or attenuated by the degree of severity of the deficits, the child's capacity to compensate for those deficits, and the capacity of those in the child's context to provide mindsharing functions.

The mindsharing and complementary functions that the context provides may serve as protective factors, immunizing the child from the development of a disorder of the self. Conversely, they may also accentuate the effects of the deficit by magnifying the sequelae. The child's sense of self provides the medium through which personal experiences are synthesized into a coherent whole. Alternatively, if the integrative capacities of the child are overwhelmed by the task, an incoherent self-narrative would result. The effects of the initial constraints leave their mark on children. These need not always be detrimental to ongoing development, although they often are. The "mark" may or may not be recognizable to those in the child's context; however, experienced clinicians may be able to identify some of the child's specific deficits provide a diagnosis and a treatment plan. The plethora of phenotypes is evidence of the multiple factors that contribute to each individual's identity and to the creative capacity of human beings to survive.

11

NLD and Asperger's Disorder

Controversy exists as to the relationship between NLD and Asperger's disorder. Some believe that at a minimum, children with Asperger's disorder have NLD but that few children with NLD have Asperger's disorder. An additional confound to diagnostic clarity is introduced by the concept of autistic spectrum disorder (ASDs). This disorder, along with diagnoses of pervasive developmental disorder (PDD) and PDD—NOS (not otherwise specified), blur the distinction between individuals with autism and those with higher-functioning autism, Asperger's disorder, or NLD. Furthermore, in a critical review of the construct of Asperger's disorder Klin and Volkmar (2003) found that, in their research, investigators have either modified the DSM-IV (American Psychiatric Association, 1994) criteria by treating Asperger's disorder and high functioning autism interchangeably or used altogether different criteria for their definition of the condition. They conclude that the anosologic status of AS (Asperger syndrome) is, therefore, extremely problematic, given that studies cannot be necessarily compared because of the adoption of different diagnostic definitions, and there has been no comparison across different diagnostic schemes with regard to the relative usefulness of each of the schemes (p. 8). Finally, confusion exists because the term Asperger syndrome rather that Asperger's disorder is used in many publications (e.g., Klin, 1994, 2004; Volkmar & Klin, 1998, 2000), the terms appear to be interchangeable. In this work, I use the term Asperger's disorder in conformity with the DSM-IV designation (American Psychiatric Association, 1994) except when I refer to investigators who use the term Asperger's syndrome instead.

If differentiations are to be drawn between NLD and Asperger's disorder, they must be made at the level of the three perspectives that we have discussed: the neurobehavioral, the social, and the intrapersonal. Although we may find an overlap among the neuropsychological deficits of both conditions, major demarcations exist between the social features and the intrapersonal dynamics of each.

We face several obstacles in our effort to differentiate NLD from Asperger's disorder. The first problem relates to the fact that different disciplines use different criteria in making a diagnosis. Neuropsychologists arrive at their diagnoses of NLD through a set of psychometric tests, with clear criteria and norms, that they administer to patients, whereas clinicians, i.e., psychiatrists, clinical psychologists, and clinical social workers, rely on their clinical impressions to arrive at a diagnosis. On the other hand, both psychiatrists and neuropsychologists make the diagnosis of Asperger's disorder, which is included in DSM-IV (American Psychiatric Association, 1994). Neuropsychologists and psychiatrists use different theoretical frameworks to arrive at their decisions. Each discipline considers different aspects of children's functioning to be diagnostically significant. Psychiatrists and psychotherapists are often unfamiliar with the diagnosis of NLD. Similarly, neuropsychologists often take little notice of motivational or psychodynamic issues in their assessment of a child's difficulties. Consequently, comparing diagnoses made by different disciplines is fraught with difficulties.

A second problem is fueled by the absence of agreement among researchers as to the core deficits that define each disorder. The issue centers on whether the neuropsychological deficits or the social impairments define the disorder. This viewpoint has led to the suggestion that we create a distinct label, such as SELD (social–emotional learning disability), to distinguish the problems of those children from children who have specific neurocognitive impairments. Current research on the neurobiology of social cognition may provide answers to these diagnostic problems. Borrowing from social and cognitive psychology, neuropsychologists and neurologists rely on constructs such as social cognition to identify domains of psychological function. The issue remains unresolved.

A third problem is that the use of a dimensional approach encourages the blurring of boundaries in an effort to underscore the fact that the children present with heterogeneous symptoms that vary in number, type, age of onset, and severity. The limits of this approach are reached when the dissimilarity between specific phenotypes raises questions as to whether two disorders belong within the same continuum. The choices as to which set of features is necessary for inclusion within the disorder, the level of severity of the symptoms, the level of cognitive impairment, and the age at which the diagnosis is made—all contribute to the inaccuracy of the diagnostic process.

The final obstacle is that of overcoming the limits of the perspective that each discipline brings to the diagnostic process. In this work I have advocated the use of multiple perspectives that are integrated to provide a developmental viewpoint that specifies the way in which each child's mental processes organize and integrate his or her experiences into a coherent whole.

The question we confront is whether NLD is a disorder that is distinct from Asperger's disorder, with its own social features, or whether it belongs within the autistic spectrum along with Asperger's disorder? I argue that NLD is distinct from Asperger's disorder and does not belong in the autistic spectrum. A further question relates to the construct of SELD, which encompasses many of the developmental deficits currently included under the diagnosis of PDD, and would include NLD. It does not appear wise to dismiss that construct at this time because researchers have not pursued it sufficiently. Eventually, it may have some value in making important differentiations.

Asperger's Disorder

In 1944 Hans Asperger published a paper describing a group of children whom he identified as suffering from "austistic psychopathy." These children closely resembled the children that Kanner (1943) had described earlier in his paper on autism, but with some significant differences. Asperger's work was not introduced to English speakers until Wing wrote about his work in 1981 and suggested the label "Asperger's disorder." Utah Frith eventually translated his original paper in 1991 (Asperger, 1991).

The children that Asperger described did not have the severe language impairments that characterized Kanner's children. The features of the syndrome, which was later given Asperger's name, included peculiarities in gaze, use of gesture, facial expressions, and vocal intonation. He described the children as original or creative in their ideas, and he found them to be accurate observers of other people, although they were also inattentive. Socially, they were capable of purposely hurting others and of generally negativistic and stereotypic behaviors. Their feelings did not match their intellectual level. They could not display affection toward others, and they maintained a distance that seemed to denote an inability to be intimate with others. Among their peculiar behaviors were their obsessions with objects, which they persisted in collecting. Finally, they lacked a sense of humor, having no understanding of jokes (Frith, 1991).

In her landmark contribution to the literature on autistic spectrum disorder, Wing (1988) suggested that "a necessary and sufficient condition for a diagnosis of a disorder in this continuum [autistic spectrum disorder] is an impairment in the development of the ability to engage in reciprocal social interactions" (p. 92). She added that children within the spectrum have social interaction impairments in (1) social recognition, (2) social communication, and (3) social imagination and understanding. An additional symptom is that of repetitive patterns of activity. Other psychological functions that are impaired include language (particularly, pragmatic language), motor coordination, responses to sensory stimuli, and cognitive skills. Wing considered the triad of impairments in social recognition, social communication, and imagination to constitute the core deficits in autism and in Asperger's disorder. She concluded that Kanner's and Asperger's disorder fell within a continuum of children having social impairments, although the profiles of Asperger's children differed from those of Kanner's (Wing, 1991).

Neuropsychological Features of NLD and Asperger's Disorder

Using Rourke's (1989a) profile of assets and deficits in NLD, Volkmar and Klin (1998; Klin, 1994; Klin, et al., 1995; Klin & Volkmar, 1997; Klin, Volkmar, 1994; Volkmar, Klin, Sebaltz, Rubin & Bronen, 2000) set out to differentiate Asperger syndrome from high-functioning autism (HFA). They found an overlap among some of the neurocognitive features of NLD and Asperger's disorder, but not with HFA. They concluded that Asperger Syndrome and HFA are different disorders. This conclusion left open the nature of the relationship between NLD and Asperger disorder, although they had found earlier that children with NLD do not exhibit the full clinical syndrome of Asperger disorder (Klin et al., 1995; Klin & Volkmar, 1997).

As we saw, Rourke's (1989a) theory proposed that the children's social behaviors are the product of their primary neuropsychological deficits. He interprets the results of the Klin and colleagues (1995) study as indicating that an "overwhelming concordance between AS (Asperger Syndrome) and NLD was obtained" (Rourke & Tsatsanis, 2000, p. 245; see also Gunter, Ghaziuddin, & Ellis, 2002). Rourke and Tsatsanis (2000) stated that "a "strikingly similar pattern of behavior and adaptive functioning" exists between NLD and Asperger Syndrome (p. 244). They concluded:

"[I]t is of note that there is convincing preliminary evidence to indicate a correspondence in the neuropsychological profiles of the two groups. The pattern of neuropsychological assets and deficits that is manifest in NLD seems also characteristic of AS [Asperger syndrome]" (p. 246).

In several publications Volkmar and Klin, who report on their extensive studies of autism and Asperger's disorder, concur that although the diagnoses of NLD and Asperger's disorder are derived from different disciplines—the former from neuropsychology and the latter from psychiatry—some features of the disorders overlap. In the discussion of a case, Klin stated that "Although AS and NLD are not mutually exclusive diagnoses (because they belong to different nosologies or classification systems) they often co-occur" (2004, p. 192). Children with Asperger's disorder have NLD, but many children with NLD do not have Asperger's disorder. Finally, Klin and Volkmar's (2003) review of current research leads them to conclude that "the state of discussions of the nosologic status of AS is . . . problematic, given that studies cannot be necessarily compared because of the adoption of different diagnostic definitions, and there has been no comparison across different diagnostic schemes with regard to the relative usefulness of each of the schemes" (pp. 7–8). Given the absence of clarity in the features that might characterize Asperger's disorder, the issue of its relationships to NLD presents difficult challenges.

It appears to me that the greatest overlap in symptomatology between NLD and Asperger's disorder lies in the *neuropsychological deficits*. Both groups of children have deficits in nonlinguistic perception and tend to have executive function difficulties. Were we to limit ourselves to this perspective in making a differentiation, we would find it difficult to demarcate the two disorders. This is not the case for the other two perspectives, the social and intrapersonal.

Social Features of NLD and Asperger's Disorder

Some researchers who focused their attention on the differentiation between Asperger's disorder and autism investigated the domain of social functioning. Ozonoff (Ozonoff, Rogers, & Pennington, 1991) and her associates found a basis for making a distinction between Asperger's disorder and high-functioning autism in the responses each group gave to theory of mind and executive function tasks. The latter group consistently performed more poorly than the former on those tasks. A defining feature of ASDs and Asperger's disorder for Pennington (1991) is the children's problems in social cognition. Children with social cognition problems present with difficulties in making social contact and understanding social contexts. Secondary problems for these children include pragmatic language problems, echolalia, stereotypies, and deficits in symbolic play. He suggests that children with autism have specific problems in the area of intersubjectivity, which he seems to equate with theory of mind functioning. Similar deficits may also be present in children with Asperger's disorder. The latter children have executive function difficulties, which suggest to him that the frontal lobes may be uniquely important in social and cognitive behaviors.

Although Pennington (1991) made a strong case for autism as associated with a deficit in social functioning and for the dissociability of social deficits and cognitive impairments, it is not clear that children with NLD belong within the autistic spectrum—although they too have similar, but not as severe, social impairments. An approach to resolving this issue is to contrast the social impairments of the two groups of children. Testing whether they are successful in passing the false-belief task would provide one source of data for making a differentiation. Two studies (Siegal et al, 1996; Siegal & Varley, 2002) conducted on young people and adults with Asperger's disorder to determine whether they could pass the false-belief test found that most of them could pass it. However, when asked to explain how they arrived at their answer, they did not use mental-state terms. The absence of these terms indicates that although they may have the capacity for first-order mental representation, they do not have second-order capacities. My clinical data suggest that children with NLD are capable of forming second-order mental representations. Furthermore, my clinical data suggests that the level of severity of problems with relevance theory appears to be far greater in children with Asperger's disorder than in children with NLD. Although children with NLD fail to contextualize fully their remarks, children with Asperger's disorder appear oblivious to their listeners' interest in the topics of their conversations. The pragmatic language difficulties of children with Asperger's disorder are also of a different order of severity from those of children with NLD.

At the level of reciprocal social interaction, as we have seen, children with NLD are capable of responding to, and interacting with, others at both the cognitive and affective levels. They are capable of sustaining a meaningful dialogue with others; they can appreciate another person's perspective; and they can engage in conversations that indicate an awareness of others as separate and independent beings. It is my clinical impression that most children with Asperger's disorder do not function at this level of complexity (see also Klin, 2004).

Finally, in the domain of the reception, expression, and processing of emotions, some sharp differences exist with regard to how the children feel about themselves and how they feel about others. In this domain the impairments of children with NLD are far less severe than those of children with Asperger's disorder. In contrast to children with NLD, the capacity to understand the meanings of some emotional communications seems much more limited in children with Asperger's disorder, as is their ability to communicate about their feeling states.

Intrapersonal Features of NLD and Asperger's Disorder

The differences between the two disorders are most marked in the intrapersonal domain. I alluded earlier to the differences in mindsharing capacities. It is sufficient here to reiterate that children with Asperger's disorder have serious limitations in those capacities. Although they are capable of using language to communicate, their capacities for imaginative play are limited, as is their appreciation of the feelings of others. They may be able to form secure attachments, but those appear based on their desire to have their needs satisfied. These constraints contrast with the capabilities of children with NLD for language communication and imaginative play, which are limited at times but remain functional.

The sense of self in children with Asperger's disorder lacks cohesion and central coherence, in contrast to children with NLD who are capable of varying degrees of self-cohesion. The evidence that children with Asperger's disorder can act as independent centers of initiative (see Atwood, 1998; Cassidy, 2004; Happe, 1991; Nesic-Vuckovik, 2004) is lacking. These children lack the ability to formulate life goals, to achieve those goals, and to participate in the transactions of their community. Most of all, they lack the ability to develop a coherent self-narrative. They have little sense of their history or of their place in their community. The tragedy of these children is that although they are not as seriously impaired as children with autism, they cannot fit comfortably into a society that demands competence, efficiency, and sophisticated social skills to survive psychologically.

NLD Contrasted with DSM-IV Criteria for Asperger's Disorder

In spite of the doubts cast on the validity of DSM-IV's criteria of Asperger's disorder (Klin & Volkmar, 2003), a comparison of the features of the four subtypes of NLD with the DSM-IV criteria for Asperger's disorder (see Table 11.1) would reveal clear-cut differences. There is little question as to the difference between NLD subtypes I and II, and Asperger's disorder. It is only when we consider children with the types of impairments in social cognition that are found in NLD subtypes III and IV that questions may be

Table 11.1. DSM-IV Criteria for Asperger's Disorder

A. Qualitative impairment in social interaction, as manifested by at least two of the following:
   (1) marked impairment in the use of multiple nonverbal behaviors such as eye-to-eye gaze, facial expression, body postures, and gestures to regulate social interaction
   (2) failure to develop peer relationships appropriate to development level
   (3) a lack of spontaneous seeking to share enjoyment, interests, or achievements with other people (e.g., by a lack of showing, bringing, or pointing out objects of interest to other people)
   (4) lack of social or emotional reciprocity

B. Restricted repetitive and stereotyped patterns of behavior, interests, and activities, as manifested by at least one of the following:
   (1) encompassing preoccupation with one or more stereotyped and restricted patterns of interest that is abnormal either in intensity or focus
   (2) apparently inflexible adherence to specific, nonfunctional routines or rituals
   (3) stereotyped and repetitive motor mannerisms (e.g., hand or finger flapping or twisting, or complex whole body movements)
   (4) persistent preoccupation with parts of objects.

C. The disturbance causes clinically significant impairment in social, occupation, or other important areas of functioning.

D. There is no clinically significant general delay in language (e.g., single words used by age 2 years, communicative phrases used by age 3 years).

E. There is no clinically significant delay in cognitive development or in the development of age-appropriate self-help skills, adaptive behavior (other than in social interaction), and curiosity about the environment in childhood.

F. Criteria are not met for another specific Pervasive Developmental Disorder or Schizophrenia.

raised as to whether they are distinct disorders or lie along a continuum. Perhaps making a differential diagnosis between a severe case of NLD subtype IV and Asperger's disorder would present the greatest challenge. I believe that we would then have to fall back on the clinical impression derived from the assessment of the child's intrapersonal status. The questions would center on whether the capacity for mindsharing confounds the diagnostic picture, whether the desire for isolation is defensive or essential to the child, whether the child's sense of self-cohesion is relatively stable, and finally, whether the child is capable of constructing a coherent self-narrative, with help.

If we were to contrast the features of severe NLD subtype IV with those of Asperger's disorder on DSM-IV criteria, we would find that the features listed in item A ("Qualitative impairment in social interaction") of the criteria for Asperger's disorder are identical to those for autistic disorder and are similar to many of the social impairments that are common in children with NLD subtype IV. What DSM-IV criteria leave unstated is the level of severity of those features. Taken alone, the criteria in item A would apply to many children with a variety of emotional disturbances who do not belong in the autistic spectrum (e.g., shy children, some children with social phobias or severe anxiety disorders).

The descriptions listed in item B ("restricted repetitive and stereotyped patterns of behavior, interest, and activities") are identical to those listed for autistic disorder in item C ("the disturbance causes clinically significant impairment in social, occupational, or other important areas of functioning"), with the possible exception of item B-1 ("encompassing preoccupation with one or more stereotyped and restricted patterns of interest that is abnormal either in intensity or focus"). These features are uncommon in children with NLD. However, because the criteria state that one feature would be sufficient to diagnose a child with the disorder, we must ask whether the characterization of "encompassing preoccupation with one or more stereotyped and restricted patterns of interest that is abnormal either in intensity or focus" is applicable to children with NLD subtype IV. I would argue that, in my clinical experience, some of the children have demonstrated unusual rote memory, but their interests were not all encompassing, nor were they of such intensity as to interfere with their relationships to others. Neither item B-2 ("apparently inflexible adherence to specific, nonfunctional routines or rituals") nor B-3 ("stereotyped and repetitive motor mannerisms [e.g., hand or finger flapping or twisting, or complex whole-boy movements]") applies to children with NLD.

Regarding item C ("the disturbance causes clinically significant impairment in social, occupational, or other important areas of functioning"), although the children's relationships with others are problematic and at times unsatisfactory, only in the severe cases of subtype IV do these cause "significant impairments . . . of functioning." Items D, E, and F would apply to children with NLD subtypes I or II. If applied to NLD subtypes III or IV, then making a valid differentiation would require more than a simple comparison among the children's symptoms. For each subtype we would need a developmental perspective that traces the path a child takes from birth on. It would also be essential to compare the mental processes that a child uses to organize his or her experience. Finally, the response of the child to clinical interventions is another important diagnostic determinant in that they may confirm or falsify a diagnosis.

We may now draw a sharp contrast between the profiles of children with Asperger's disorder and those with NLD. From a neurobehavioral perspective, most of the children with NLD have milder symptoms than those of children with Asperger's disorder. Their nonlinguistic perceptual deficits are not as severe and they may have attentional or executive function problems, but those do not necessarily interfere with their vocational adjustment. From the perspective of social cognition the capacity of children with NLD for reciprocal social relationships may be impaired but it does not preclude their ability to sustain a relationship with another person. They are capable of a degree of mindsharing functions and have theory of mind abilities, which is not true of children with Asperger's disorder. The pragmatic language problems of children with NLD are moderately severe and, at times, can interfere with their ability to communicate, but their strengths in verbal expression can help them compensate for that deficit. In contrast, children with Asperger's disorder have severe pragmatic language problems that often interfere with the possibility of sustaining a meaningful conversation with them. Their communications are centered on topics they wish to discuss, they disregard signals of disinterest from their listeners. Furthermore, their capacity to process affect states is similarly more impaired than that of children with NLD. For the latter group of children, processing affect states is problematic but for the former group it appears to constitute a foreign language. Finally, from an intrapersonal perspective the contrast between the two groups is greatest. Children with Asperger's disorder have critical deficits in mindsharing capacities. Their sense of self lacks cohesion and they are incapable of providing a coherent self-narrative. Children with NLD have an unstable sense of self-cohesion but can sustain that sense of cohesion when not under stress and can use the complementary functions that others provide to maintain that cohesion. Their self-narrative have lacunae caused by their deficits and their inability to understand the nature of their disorder. However, they are able to provide a reasonable account of their life stories even though these might be based on the personal meanings they have drawn from their experiences and might not make complete sense to others.

The contrast between the two disorders appears smallest in the severest cases of NLD (i.e., NLD subtype IV). In those cases, I believe that DSM-IV criteria come to the rescue in a making a differentiation. As I described above, many of item B's criteria and those of item C do not apply to children with NLD. Children with NLD can function independently; they formulate plans and goals to achieve vocationally. With assistance they are able to understand the nature of their deficits and arrive at coherent narratives of the effects those deficits have had on their development. My clinical experience with adults diagnosed with NLD confirms that impression. Some of these adults have achieved considerably in their chosen careers. They remain in successful relationships, have raised children, and given every indication of being good caretakers and providers. In contrast, adults with Asperger's disorder whom we have treated demonstrate impairments that limit severely both their careers and their relationships with others.

I conclude that NLD and Asperger's disorder are distinct diagnostic disorders.

NLD and Social–Emotional Learning Disabilities

As we have seen, Denckla (1983; 1991) advocated for a separate category called "social–emotional learning disability" (SELD) that is distinct from NLD. I could find no statement in her published work regarding her position on the issue of the relationship between NLD and Asperger's disorder or autistic spectrum disorders.

In an early paper, Voeller (1991) stated that "the core deficit linking AD [autistic disorder], AS [Asperger syndrome], and SELD is impaired social competence. The distinction is based on severity and associated features" (p. 739). A few years later Voeller (1997) noted that "the social deficits seen in SELD can be dissociated from the neuropsychological and academic deficits seen in nonverbal learning disability. A child can have nonverbal learning disability without the array of social deficits and the child with SELD can be quite competent in math and lack the visuoperceptual deficits that characterize nonverbal learning disability" (p. 796). Voeller is proposing two distinct disorders, one of which involves deficits in visual–spatial processing and the other in the ability to process social–emotional information and to make correct inferences about the meaning of social cues. She too suggests that the difficulties in the latter disorder may be related to primary deficits in theory of mind functioning. In addition, those children have pragmatic language problems and difficulties judging what is relevant or irrelevant in a given social situation. Finally, at the emotional level, children with SELD can have difficulty with the identification and processing of affects in some instances. Although she suggests that the symptoms of children with SELD can be "mapped onto" the symptoms of children with Asperger's disorder, she stops short of saying that the two are identical. I believe that this is due, in part, to her belief that Asperger's disorder is a psychiatric disorder, found in DSM-IV whereas SELD is a neurobehavioral entity suggested by neurologists and neuropsychologists. The labels are the creations of different disciplines.

In the absence of data from children diagnosed as having SELD, with no visual–perceptual, visual–spatial, or visual memory problems, we may only speculate as to their social–emotional profile. The hazard of introducing a new label for a disorder is that unless it is followed by research that justifies its introduction, it remains a pure academic exercise. With some justification, Denckla (2000) stated:

> Little progress has been made since 1993 in the clinical field of socio-emotional learning disabilities. . . . The clinician, therefore, is limited to recognition of the existence of a type of learning disability, an NVLD [nonverbal learning disability], that is characterized better by what is spared—well-developed linguistic elements, rote verbal memory, basic reading (i.e., decoding) and spelling skills—than by what is deficient. (p. 314)

In a personal communication with Lipton (February 14, 2005)[1], she suggested that a useful alternative is the creation of a category called social–emotional learning disorders (with the same acronym, SELD). She substitutes the term *disorders* for *disabilities* because of the problems associated with considering these disorders as "learning disabilities" rather than as neurobehavioral disorders. Such a category focuses on the child's social–emotional functioning. According to Lipton, the criteria used in an evaluation of a child's functioning would include (1) the extent of the child's social interests (desire for age-appropriate, reciprocal peer relationships), (2) the capacity for the comprehension of social–emotional communications, and (3) the ability to give expression to social–emotional behaviors required for effective peer relationships. The children who would be assessed through this algorithm would include all the children (with normal intellectual capacity) who are thought to have developmental brain-based difficulties with sociability as well as those who fall within the autistic spectrum and those currently diagnosed with NLD. The ra-

---

[1] Meryl Lipton is the Director of the Rush Neurobehavioral Center, Skokie, IL.

tionale for the category is that the symptoms of these children reflect core brain-based deficits in social–emotional cognition.

An advantage of this strategy would be the elimination of the variety of labels currently in use, which only confuses the diagnostic picture. The disadvantage is that, as a dimensional approach to disorders, it would not permit lines of demarcation to be drawn between different disorders. It would assume that the brain mechanisms of such diverse entities as autism and NLD are similar, unless we could specify the brain region in which the impairment that gives rise to the symptoms exists.

In the absence of supporting data, except that of children and adults with right hemisphere dysfunctions, the differentiation between NLD and SELD leaves open the question as to the differences between the two disorders. If we were to exclude the group of children with visual and visual–spatial deficits from the group diagnosed with NLD, would the residual group of children be diagnosed with Asperger's disorder or with an autistic spectrum disorder? In their 1997 paper Klin and Volkmar lump together SELD and other right hemisphere disorders, indicating that eventually the right hemisphere dysfunction may serve to differentiate among these disorders.

Neurobiology of Social Cognition

Current research on the neurobiology of social behavior and social cognition throws only indirect light on the social impairments of children with NLD. Most of the research is directed at establishing the linkages between specific brain processes and the representations we have of ourselves, of others, of the interrelationships among others and ourselves and others have among themselves. Major areas of research include the role of the amygdala in social behaviors, the mechanisms that subserve social and emotional information processing, and the regions involved in the selection of responses to social situations (Adolphs, 2001, 2003a, 2003b; Brothers, 1989, 1996, 1997).[2] A different line of investigation is pursued by researchers who are trying to establish linkages between neurobiology, personality development, and personality disorders (Gabbard, 2005; Grigsby & Stevens, 2000).

Furthermore, current research on the neurobiology of sociality may provide answers to some of the questions raised earlier. The lesson we learned from past research in neurobiology is that there are serious limitations to studies of patients with brain lesions (Amaral, Bauman, Capitanio,

[2] Cozolino (2002) stated that there does not appear to be a unitary module for social cognition within the brain; rather, there are a number of domains of sensory, cognitive, and emotional information processing that come together during normal development that result in social intelligence.

Lavenex, Mason, et. al., 2003; Anderson, Bechara, Damasio, Tranel, & Damasio, 1999; Bar-On, Tranel, Denburg, & Bechara, 2003; Mah, Arnold, & Grafman, 2004). One limitation is that examining something that is broken gives only a rough indication of the function that the broken component plays in the overall system. The strategy may be useful in narrowing the possibilities of the function of that component, because it does tell us what functions remain intact, but it fails to alert us to the interconnections between what fails to function and the other components of the system. A second limitation, which is even more relevant to this work, is the limitation imposed by the large gap that exists between the study of a developmental disorder and the study of intact systems that have been subsequently damaged. Developmental disorders follow their own path ontogenetically; they seldom affect discrete sectors of the brain. Often they are diffuse, affecting a broadband of systems. Significantly, during development such disorders affect how other systems also function, with the result that the symptoms the patients manifest are not simply those of the dysfunction in that region.

The promise of new technologies, such as computed tomography (CT) and functional magnetic resonance imaging (fMRI), is that these less intrusive methodologies can provide a more comprehensive understanding of what occurs in the brains of our children. This more comprehensive understanding will inevitably expose the greater complexity of the disorders—a complexity perhaps of a higher order then we currently imagine.

Conclusion

A close comparison of the features of NLD and Asperger's disorder along three different perspectives demonstrates that they are different disorders with different developmental trajectories driven by different constraints. Asperger's disorder appears to include some of the social features of NLD, although NLD does not share many of its features with Asperger's disorder. Even if we consider the shared features, there appears to be little basis for considering the two entities as part of a continuum of disorders. There are clear demarcations between the two. The fact that questions exist as to the viability of Asperger's disorder as a separate diagnostic entity is a complicating factor in making the differentiation.

The proposal of a separate label, SELD, for the entire class of disorders is an interesting one. By assuming that a set of brain functions undergirds all social–cognitive functions, it promises to provide a basis for establishing a continuum of disorders. We must await further research to substantiate this proposal. Even then, the SELD conceptualization may not answer the question regarding the distinctiveness of the disorders.

Part IV

TREATMENT

12

Restoring Self-Cohesion and Narrative Coherence

Therapists with a psychodynamic orientation face the challenge of integrating the emerging knowledge from the neurosciences into their perspective. The tension between a point of view that is rooted in the perspective that nurture (caregivers, in particular) is responsible for psychopathology and our understanding of the contributions of neuropsychological factors to most disorders is greatest in the psychotherapeutic encounter. Some therapists believe that if they incorporate a neurobiological perspective into their practice, they will be less effective because they cannot change the patient's nature. Others—for example, psychoanalytic purists—resist because they claim that matters biological are not in their purview, and they would rather let others deal with such issues. I would argue against both of these positions and insist that the neglect of neuropsychological factors leads to misleading diagnoses and ineffective treatment (Caroll, 2003; Mace, 2003; Palombo, 1987b, 1991, 1992, 1993, 1994, 1995, 1996, 2001a, 2001b; Palombo & Berenberg, 1997).

Before instituting a treatment plan for a child with an NLD, it is essential that a clear diagnosis be made through psychoeducational and/or neuropsychological testing. Although it is possible to arrive at a clinical diagnosis from neurological or behavioral observations, these alone do not establish a definitive diagnosis. In addition, it is most helpful for therapists to have a clear idea of the specific areas of a child's strengths and deficits, which such testing can provide. If available, projective testing also can be very helpful, provided the examiner appreciates the fact that the child's visual–spatial problems will affect his or her perceptions and responses to visually presented projective materials such as Rorschach and Thematic Apperception Test (TAT) cards. An examiner who does not consider these problems often interprets the protocols as presenting a much more pathological picture of the child than might actually be the case.

Recommendations must take into account the range of possible interventions the child may require. An assessment must be made of the domains that may be impaired, and a list of priorities must then be drawn. In the neuropsychological domain, sensory and motor deficits would benefit from occupational therapy intervention. Attentional problems may require medication, whereas executive function difficulties would benefit from specific tutoring to accommodate for the child's organizational problems. In the social domain, social skills training may be helpful, and speech and language therapy directed toward the child's pragmatic language difficulties may enhance his or her communicative competence. Finally, in the intrapersonal domain, individual psychotherapy directed at helping the child attain an optimal level of self-cohesion and develop an understanding of the nature of his or her problems would enhance the coherence of his or her self-narrative. Two added interventions would be academic tutoring and family therapy (or some type of work with parents around the child's issues). In this chapter, I consider only the provision of individual psychotherapy for the child; in the next chapter we turn to working with caregivers.

Individual Psychotherapy with a Child with an NLD

Treatment of children with NLD,[1] which follows the general principles of child psychotherapy, consists in the creation of a context within which the children can experience and share their feelings and thoughts with the therapist. The goal of treatment is twofold: (1) to strengthen their sense of self sufficiently so that they feel stable and cohesive in the face of the stresses to which they are exposed and (2) to provide them with an understanding of the nature and sources of their problems so that they can gain a sense of history and a coherent self-narrative.

A primary concern during the initial phases of treatment is to provide the support necessary for the child to maintain a sense of self-cohesion. If

[1] For a more extended discussion of treatment of children with learning disorders, see Palombo (2001b).

the stresses the child confronts lead to fragmenting incidents in which he or she has meltdowns, those stresses must be alleviated for a viable therapeutic milieu to be instituted. This alleviation may take the form of support provided by a therapist who is sufficiently attuned to the child to be touched by what he or she experienced or is experiencing. The therapist may be able to articulate the child's feelings and thoughts and thereby give new and more coherent meanings to his or her experiences. The medium through which the therapist conducts the dialogue varies with the age of the child. Activities such as fantasy, play, or drawings may be used with a young child, verbal exchanges may be used with an adolescent. The therapist becomes the "container" for the feelings and experiences the child shares, resonating with the affects and the contents of what the child divulges. As the child reveals more of him- or herself, it becomes clear that there are past experiences that he or she has not fully integrated. These become the focus of the treatment.

Children often construe events to reflect private meanings that are unique to them. The problematic nature of the meanings is revealed when contrasted with the shared meanings within the community. The therapist attempts to create a setting in which these children can experience some of the unintegrated emotions that remain problematic. They may then begin to feel hope that a meaningful coherent narrative will emerge (i.e., they will make sense to themselves) to serve as a point of orientation around which they can understand what happened historically. A tension is created between their "story" about their problems and the therapist's hypothesis of what is central to their distress. This tension reveals itself when they feel misunderstood by the therapist. The tension between children's personal meanings and the therapist's views begins to resolve when both share a set of positive experiences (e.g., 6-year-old Allan was constantly criticized for misbehaving in art class. In therapy, he maintained that drawing was dumb; it's for babies. During one session, he asked the therapist to draw something he wanted to communicate. To Allan's relief, the therapist complied saying I'm not good at art either. Allan smiled warmly as he picked up the crayon to draw). Because children see aspects of the present through the lens of their past experiences—a perspective the therapist initially does not share—it is necessary for the therapist to enter empathically into that past to understand fully their current experience.

At times, the mere fact of sharing a meaningful experience with the therapist can provide relief for children. The sense of isolation and loneliness that surrounded the experience in its first occurrence is broken. Having originally experienced the events in the absence of others who could be responsive, these children lived alone with their pain. The opportunity to share those events with a person who is able to resonate with their meanings is potentially curative. Such experiences can facilitate the integration of the affects associated with hurtful experiences and lend meaning to them.

In part, the suffering of these children is related to their inability to retain a sense of self-cohesion or to an incoherent self-narrative. Their yearning for responses to their distress lead them to expect the therapist to create a context in which mindsharing can occur. At the same time, they are wary of expressing their vulnerabilities, having felt repeatedly rebuffed or injured in the past when seeking comfort from others.

The process through which the goals of therapy are attained occurs at two levels. At one level is the positive transference, which creates the conditions in which the dialogue occurs that may make it possible for these children to regain a sense of well-being. Such experiences are integral to any eventual healing that is to occur. At another level is the negative transference, during which children see the therapist as instrumental in the rearousal of past painful events and as representing painful figures from the past.

The Therapeutic Process

It is possible to describe some aspects of the therapeutic process as a series of experiences that recreate the early caregiver/infant setting. Viewed from this perspective we may draw a parallel between Stern's (1983) description of what constitutes "being with" and the therapeutic process. Stern described three types of "being with": 1) self-other complementing, 2) mental state sharing, and 3) state transforming. Translated into terms that apply to therapy, *self-other complementing* refers to the children's need for complementarity to which I referred in an earlier chapter. It consists in the provision of selfobject and adjunctive functions to assist in the restoration of a sense of self-cohesion. *Mental state sharing* is equivalent to mindsharing, which is produced by the therapist's empathy for the child's subjective experience. It is intended to help the child feel understood and to reduce the sense of isolation into which the child had withdrawn. Finally, these two interventions, added to other interventions the therapist might use, produce a transformation of the child's affect state, i.e., *state transforming*. The child moves from conditions of uncertainty, anxiety, or depression to feeling reassured, comforted, and at peace. However, the therapeutic process is far more than the simple recreation of the experiences between the mother/infant dyad. Reversing the established pathological patterns requires in addition other interventions which I discuss in what follows.

CLINICAL PRESENTATION

In many respects the techniques used with children with NLD are no different from those used in therapy with children with other disorders. What is different is the therapist's awareness of the child's strengths and deficits, the impact these have had on the child's development and on relationships to others. This awareness permits the therapist to empathize with the child's distress while being aware of its sources. On beginning therapy, the clinical presentation of the latency-age child with an NLD leaves a distinctive and lasting impression. Although that impression is not as haunting as that left by a child with autism, it nevertheless sets a pattern of expectations that carries over to the identification of other children with the disorder.

Most often these children prefer to sit and talk rather than play. They make little or no eye contact, giving the impression of being distracted or not interested in what the therapist has to say. Many children seem to flop around on their chairs; they may choose to lie on the floor, looking up at the ceiling, while talking to the therapist. The impression is that they are marginally appropriate in their behavior, appearing discourteous rather than overtly disrespectful. They respond to questions and participate in the dialogue with the therapist but seldom spontaneously initiate topics for discussion.

Nevertheless, they are highly verbal in their responses, using sophisticated vocabularies. They appear much more mature in their thinking than would be expected of children that age. However, this appearance is misleading, and they quickly give evidence of having little insight into the nature and causes of their problem. If questioned directly about their problems at school or home, they minimize their difficulties, blaming a sibling or caregiver.

Most evident is their avoidance of discussing feelings, except for references to anger and frustration. They seldom refer to their anxieties; these are detected only indirectly from references they make to fears they have or to their avoidance of certain situations. They may refer to "liking" to spend time playing video games or enjoying some activities, but they display little emotion when speaking of these activities. Mention of feelings about themselves and others is particularly absent. If asked directly about how they feel about coming to therapy, their response is one of neutral indifference. They give the impression of complying with caregivers' directions rather than being actively engaged in the decision to participate in the process.

When asked about peers, they respond that they do have friends, although close questioning reveals that these are acquaintances with whom they have only peripheral contact. They may complain of being teased at school but appear dismissive of these interactions.

Given this presentation, therapists generally find themselves having few handles to grab unto for therapeutic leverage. Engaging these children in the process presents a challenge that must be met if they are to benefit from being in therapy. A large part of the challenge is that of empathizing with their inner states, that is, their feelings. Because their ability to communicate nonverbally is limited, the therapist cannot gain access to their feelings through this channel. The obstacle is not simply that they are resistant to becoming involved or reluctant to establish an intimate rapport with the therapist; these factors may be at work, but the real obstacles are related to the unavailability of a common language through which emotions and feelings can be communicated. The therapist must find a medium through which interchanges can occur that allow access to their inner world and can help them feel truly understood.

I have found the following techniques helpful in this work. First, because most children with NLD tend to miss subtle social cures, verbal mediation takes on an important role in conveying the therapist's meaning. The therapist must pay close attention to all nonverbal channels to make sure that the children understand the meanings the therapist intends to convey. Gestures often need to be made with broader strokes than usual. It may be necessary to ask them tactfully, so as not to embarrass them, to make eye contact so as not to miss facial expressions. Because they have difficulty reading between the lines, making inferences, and understanding humor and the double meaning of expressions, the therapist needs to clarify these with specific examples from each child's experience. Sometimes the therapist will need to explain verbally his or her nonverbal communications to the child. This is an opportunity for the impaired child to learn this new language. Similarly, many children benefit from having their own nonverbal signals labeled verbally so that they know what their faces and bodies are communicating to others. Sometimes a child will express surprise at the disparity between what he or she meant and what the therapist understood him or her to be conveying.

Second, even when giving a verbal account of an event, children with NLD are not always reliable informants as to what transpires in their lives. Nevertheless, it is most important to convey belief in what they describe. Often they have missed so much of the interaction with others that it may be impossible to get a clear picture of what occurred from the account given. The account is likely to be disconnected, fragmentary, and confused, and the recital may be devoid of feeling. Alternatively, their expressions of feeling are likely to be exaggerated or unmodulated, leaving the impression of a dissynchrony between the feelings and the content. Often they cannot pick out the main point from the supporting details, the relevant from the irrelevant, or cannot organize a coherent narrative; they may grasp one aspect of the total picture and miss the broader gestalt. This narrative incoherence presents a difficult problem to therapist, who must rely on the children's communication to learn about day-to-day events. The experience of those who work with these children is that it wise to remain in constant contact with the caregivers and to bring them into sessions as often as necessary to have them clarify significant events, if they can.

Some children with strong verbal skills and severe nonverbal disabilities may be able to relate the *verbal* aspects of their social interchanges with considerable accuracy, but simply fail to take note of the relevant *nonverbal* cues—an omission that probably led them astray in the original interaction. The therapist can replay the scene, using different tones of voice, facial expressions, gestures, and interpersonal distance to help the children fill in the picture. The therapist can also uncover the set of overly rigid rules they may have acquired to cope with their confusion about the world. Often these children feel injured when they dutifully apply these rules, only to find them unhelpful. The therapist can create an atmosphere in which these rules are examined jointly and are playfully modified, an activity that enhances the children's communicative skills and fluid reasoning.

Third, although play, a nonverbal mode of expression, occupies a central position in the therapeutic process with most latency-age children, this is not generally true of children with NLD. There are multiple reasons for their lack of interest in play—or their inability to play. It is not clear that this lack of interest or inability is due to their lack of capacity for imaginative play. Some cannot play because of the rigidity or concreteness of their approach to situations, or they may not be able to engage in unstructured imaginative interactions that are nonverbal in content. Other children prefer to use their strengths in verbalization to relate to the therapist. The therapy can take on an adult-like character that may lead the therapist to overestimate children's capacity to work through their problems verbally. Keeping in mind that this is their preferred mode of communication, the therapist must beware of the dangers of intellectualization at the expense of dealing with their feelings. On the one hand, the therapist can reframe issues through verbal interchanges to introduce some flexibility in the children's way of thinking. Because most children with NLD are not used to considering that several options for understanding their experiences exist, learning to do so in the safety of the relationship with the therapist can produce significant shifts in the way they approach the world. On the other hand, because they are unable to deal with feelings at the verbal level, the introduction of imaginative play or fantasy may give them a channel for their expression. An indication of progress would then be their ability to participate in imaginative play. However, some children go through the whole course of successful treatment without taking this step.

Fourth, demonstrations of the children's strengths and affirmations of their capacities are essential to their self-esteem. When children report instances of frustration or failure in school or social settings, the therapist can help them understand those in terms of their learning difficulties and assets. They may need similar help in understanding successful instances, too. The goal for many children is to provide them with acceptance and a clear enough understanding that they can become self-advocates, helping to structure their learning situations in a manner that is suitable to them. As self-confident children who are clear about their learning styles, they can become active participants in planning their own educational and social interventions.

Transference Motifs

Transference refers to the phenomenon through which we reshape our perceptions of current situations and of others with whom we interact in such a way that they conform to our past experiences (see Palombo, 2001a, p. 48). Transference reflects the fact that past experiences structure our personalities into organizing principles that lead us to expect that the past will be repeated in the present. During treatment, the therapist's anonymity leads children to have two sets of expectations of how the therapist will respond: one positive and one negative. In the positive transference, children expect the therapist to respond to their unfulfilled longings for nurture, in contrast to how they have experienced others responding to them. In the negative transference, children expect the therapist to be unresponsive, that is, to replicate how they experienced others' treatment of them. The therapist, therefore, represents both the hoped-for curative agent who may undo past traumas and the retraumatizing agent who will repeat what occurred in the past.

Whereas these two sets of transferences are central to the treatment of children with NLD, a third pattern of interactions plays a significant role in the relationship. That pattern, which is not a transference motif, is forged by the child's neuropsychological deficits. This pattern is the imprint left on the children's personality by their assets and deficits. Although it is the source of social and emotional difficulties for the children, it must be distinguished and addressed differently from the transference motifs (see Palombo, 2001b). These positive and negative transference themes are intertwined with the children's sense of self; indeed, they are at the core of their identity. Consequently, the transference during treatment will reflect the state of the children's self-cohesion and the themes that organize their self-narrative.

POSITIVE TRANSFERENCE

In the positive transference, the therapeutic process evokes in the children the wish for complementary or mindsharing responses from the therapist. Their longings for missing selfobject functions are activated. These may be wishes for affirmation, for soothing reassurance, or for a connection with another who values and validates their experiences. The priority for a response by the therapist is set by the children's needs, by which of these longings is primary for them. A child who suffers from meltdowns because he or she is poorly regulated needs to experience the therapist as a strong, kind, and comforting presence who is capable of bringing about a "state-transforming" outcome that allows the child to feel in control. A child who has felt dehumanized by the teasing and ridicule to which he or she is exposed needs to experience a connection with the therapist whose depth of understanding allows the child to feel that there is another human being with whom he or she can share the daily distress.

When the positive transference is in the foreground, the therapist may also be able to complement the children's social and cognitive deficits by providing missing adjunctive functions related to the neuropsychological deficits. The provision of these adjunctive functions activates the children's hope that someone is there who understands. At other times, the therapist may wish to demonstrate to the child that he or she is not like the others in the child's milieu who got angry, set impossible expectations, or inflict punishment for nonconformity. The therapist then provides a corrective experience for the children. The positive transference is instrumental in helping these children maintain a sense of self-cohesion. Through the therapist's empathy for the distress, the therapist creates a context within which the children feel a sense of connection and complementarity with someone who cares.

Mary, 7½ years old, made fortune-tellers and paper airplanes with her therapist.[2] These activities were popular with Mary's peer group and hence very important to her. The fortune-tellers were complicated and particularly difficult for Mary. She could not follow the numerous steps involved in making them. The

---

[2] A female therapist treated this child.

task was challenging to both the therapist and to Mary, who became confused when the therapist had trouble remembering how to make them. The therapist remained calm, again serving as a container for Mary's anxiety. The therapist modeled a problem-solving approach, reframing the task as one in which both were experimenters trying to solve a problem. The therapist hoped to undo Mary's expectation that the only possible outcomes were immediate success or no hope for success whatsoever. Once they figured out how to make the fortune-tellers, the therapist accompanied the task with a running verbal commentary while Mary tried to make them herself. The intent was to provide her with a compensatory strategy that she could subsequently use herself. In the next session the therapist asked Mary to show her how to make the fortune-tellers and verbalized, once again, each step as Mary performed the task. At times, the therapist had to provide verbal instruction prior to a step Mary had forgotten. The therapist felt she was consciously reinforcing an image of Mary as someone who could perform the task, while also reinforcing the strategy of verbal mediation. As they turned to making and flying the paper airplanes, the therapist used that activity to provide Mary with a metaphor that she could carry with her in working on other challenges. She interpreted the activity as one in which Mary and she were experimenters who tried things out to see which approaches would work.

By responding differently from the way others have, the therapist generates a new set of experiences for these children. This new set of experiences lays the groundwork for what is to be curative in the process. The children's incomplete or faulty processing of others' responses leads to responses that others, in turn, cannot understand; others respond to the children's *faulty* responses. Finally, the children respond to others' responses with what seem to be inappropriate behaviors. A vicious circle occurs in which it is impossible to conduct a dialogue. In treatment, children experience patterns that are different from those to which they resorted in the past, and they gain an understanding of the old patterns through the therapist's interpretations. The children are then in a position to compensate for their deficits. They not only create a new theme or motif in their self-narrative, but they also look upon the narrative in a different light. The new patterns include the meanings of past experiences and the new meanings gained through the relationship with the therapist. The understanding the children acquire through this set of shared experiences with the therapist serves to break through their former isolation. Patterns and motifs that were central in the configuration of the narrative are reshaped. New motifs come into play and the children's expectations are modified. These new motifs give the children greater hope for success.

Another goal of treatment is to produce a shift in the themes or motifs—the patterns that guide the children's conduct, provide the motives for much of their behavior, and are part of the plot of their narratives. For some children a theme or motif might be, "Everybody hates me!" or "I can't do it, it's too hard!" or "I'm scared, don't leave me!" or "Everybody thinks I'm dumb, I can't do anything right!" By replacing such motifs with more positive ones, the children can begin to dialogue with others, to experience a greater sense of self-cohesion, and to achieve a more integrated self-narrative. Only through such a shift, accomplished via educational, corrective, or interpretive means, can permanent changes in psychodynamics occur.

The younger the child, the less likely it is that he or she would be able to gain insights into his or her psychodynamics or relationship patterns or even gain cognitive understanding of the neurocognitive deficits. In that case, the goals are to alleviate the child's symptoms of overwhelming anxiety, negatively toned interactions with others, and poor self-esteem. Accomplishing these goals is possible through the help the child receives to develop compensatory strategies, the enhancement of complementarity or mindsharing with others, medication, or other means. It is possible to work toward these goals simultaneously.

Therapy with children who have NLD usually must include helping them come to some type of useful understanding of their disabilities. This understanding occurs through a gradual process of "working through." Although simple didactic explanations may be helpful for some children, they are often not sufficient. The issue must be revisited at different stages in the treatment, with different goals for each step. The evidence for the greater integration of the children's experiences occurs in the greater coherence of their self-narrative. Themes that formerly reflected the construal of personal meanings now encompass a set of shared meanings that grew out of the children's maturation and experiences in therapy. It is difficult to point to specific events or interventions that produce this greater sense of coherence; it usually results from the cumulative effects of the implementation of the broad treatment plan. Rehabilitation and restoration to achieve higher levels of functioning can be credited to the combination of greater parental understanding, appropriate school programming, improved social functioning, and the therapist's educative, corrective, and interpretive efforts.

Most children enter therapy having had numerous experiences of frustration in relation to their learning disabilities. If they had received no explanations as to why they have had so much trouble or why they were receiving special help in school, they are in the dark as to the source of their difficulties. Even if they were told about their NLD, they often come away with the feeling that they have been told that something is wrong with them; they do not have a clear cognitive grasp of the nature of their difficulties. In part, this is because the explanations themselves may have constituted injuries to which they responded by "not hearing" what was said. In larger part, it is because the words alone are difficult for the children to translate into an integrated understanding of the deficits. With the assistance of the test results and direct experience with the children, the therapist is able to "educate" them about the nature of their difficulties. Such explanations occur in the context of the therapeutic relationship. The most powerful explanations come when the therapist can concretely demonstrate to the child how the deficits impede what is happening in the clinical setting. This can occur through the construction of a project, the child's recital of an event at school, or processing a failed communication between the therapist and child.

Robert, age 9, came into therapy convinced he was stupid.[3] He struggled in school, particularly in math and writing, and found himself severely wanting when he compared himself to other kids in his class. Other kids noticed his embarrassment and sensed a good target for teasing. He had a vague idea that he had been labeled with a problem but did not understand what "learning disability" meant, nor was he able to identify his own disabilities.

Once an alliance was established, the therapist approached the subject of his disability. Robert listened with growing interest when his therapist told him that he had many strengths, such as a good vocabulary and a good ability to remember what he had heard. Robert was then able to give examples of instances when he had used those strengths. He listened with considerable discomfort, but also considerable recognition, when his therapist talked about the things that were hard for him, such as making sense of what he saw or making his hand move a pencil the way he wanted when writing. The therapist talked with Robert about ways in which he had used verbal explanations to make sense of visual experiences and reminded him, "When you said the numbers out loud, you remembered them better than when you just saw them on paper." Although it was clear that this didactic explanation only touched the surface, Robert showed a measure of relief at gaining that understanding.

Whenever an opportunity arose, the therapist helped Robert work on both the receptive and the expressive aspects of nonverbal communication that interfered with Robert feeling understood and understanding other people. For example, when his gestures and facial expression in the therapy room did not match what he was saying, she gently and tactfully pointed that out to him, gradually raising his level of consciousness about these nonverbal indicators. The explanation was given that these were harder for him to observe and he had to think about them

---

[3] A female therapist treated this child.

more explicitly if he wanted to be sure people understood him. The discussion could then move on to talking about his puzzlement when he felt the teacher's facial expressions did not match her words.

Over the next year, as he talked about his school experiences, the discussions focused on how his disabilities specifically fit into the ways he learned from school materials. When he spoke of his struggles with handwriting, the therapist could convey easy acceptance, acknowledging that the task was harder for him than he would wish, then pointing out that the question was how to help him find ways to manage the task. They worked at separating out his experience of frustration over the process of writing from his experience of having good ideas he wished to communicate. The therapist helped him think about compensations, such as use of the computer. She followed up these discussions with contacts with teachers and parents to make sure that her suggestions were implemented successfully. She legitimized his feelings that math speed tests were painful, because they did not provide a good measure of his competency. Because his math teacher required all students to take such tests weekly, the therapist helped Robert develop a defensive stance that allowed him to survive those tests without feeling responsible that he could not demonstrate how well he could do. Eventually, his parents provided him with a math tutor to help shore up his skills. When Robert was ready to enter middle school, he was given a voice in deciding which math class he would take. He chose a slower-paced class in which the teacher used a systematic approach that was more suitable for him.

When he found himself disciplined by a teacher for an infraction he did not understand, Robert discussed the problem with his therapist, concluding, "I'd do better if the teacher would give me a warning first, telling me what I'm doing wrong!" The therapist agreed to call the teacher to lay the groundwork for Robert to talk with her. This phone call became an opportunity for the therapist to discuss NLD with the teacher and to point out the importance of verbal cues in communicating with Robert. The teacher and Robert then talked, agreeing that the teacher would give Robert verbal signals when he was doing something wrong and when he was doing something right. Robert felt greatly empowered by this negotiation. He felt that it provided him with an avenue for problem solving that had not been available to him previously.

NEGATIVE TRANSFERENCE

There are times, particularly early in the treatment, when the negative transference dominates the interaction. During such moments, the therapist must keep in mind that the child is experiencing the therapist in the way that the child has experienced others in his or her context. The child attempts to create a complementarity between his or her own expectations and the therapist's responses, based on the child's experiences with others in the past. The child's despair will be mobilized only if the therapist actually replicates past experiences with the child. If that occurs, the stage is set for a rupture in the relationship, a derailment of the dialogue or a disjunction in the treatment. Otherwise, these moments provide an opportunity for the therapist to alter deliberately the patterns in which the child felt trapped by responding to the child in a different fashion. The child is then in a position to develop compensatory strategies to deal with the deficits that caused the problems.

The child brings to the therapy a set of expectations about the world based on previous experience; this set of expectations contains the organizing motifs in the child's narrative. The child expects the therapist to feel as anxious and helpless as he or she feels. When a firm alliance with the child exists, it is possible to help the child begin to look at his or her own contribution to the derailed dialogue. By taking examples from the treatment relationship, the therapist can illustrate how the child missed cues and distorted a shared experience. Depending on the cognitive capacities and age of the child, he or she may begin to take in such interpretations and understand some of the reasons for the confusion.

Alternatively, the child may expect the therapist to take over, but then, no matter how the therapist responds, the child may experience the therapist as being unhelpful. The child's ultimate fear is one of abandonment. The child enacts in treatment situations that recreate this theme. When the therapist responds differently to this negative transference, a powerful opportunity emerges to shift the child's narrative motif from one of helplessness to one in which the child becomes a proactive explorer and experimenter in a world that is exciting and potentially gratifying. This shift may occur through the metaphor of the play that the child enacts in the sessions. Through these activities the therapist not only models for the child ways in which to approach problem solving, but also presents alternative experiences that could help the child conceive of him- or herself as experimenting rather than fumbling and as exploring rather than being disoriented. These issues are worked through when the child recreates moments in his or her life that are reminiscent of the motifs that organized his or her sense of helplessness.

Countertransference Motifs

It is useful to review some of the kinds of countertransference problems that occur when working with children who have NLD. Therapists at times experience extreme frustration at what they perceive to be children's resistance to treatment. They may then resort to power struggles or to punitive measures in an attempt to engage the children in the therapeutic process.

What therapists must keep in mind is that, from the perspective of these children, the environment has felt so hostile that they fear retraumatization. The children may resist coming to therapy, or they may come and be silent and uncommunicative, or they may depreciate or be contemptuous of the therapist. For example, it is not uncommon for such children to accuse the therapist that he or she is only interested in getting paid, not in helping. The therapist may respond with anger or may take an authoritarian stance, feeling his or her competence challenged. Such countertransference responses only lead to the very circumstance that should be avoided, the repetition for the children of what they experienced from those who failed to understand them (Palombo, 1985).

Another possible source of countertransference can be the therapist's theoretical orientation. Some therapists do not believe that learning disabilities are neurologically based conditions that have a heritable or constitutional basis. Such therapists cannot fully understand these children's view of the world and often inadvertently recreate disjunctions similar to the ones the children have experienced already—the consequence being that a stalemate occurs in the treatment. I believe that if some improvement does not occur from individual treatment within 9 months to a year of once- or twice-a-week therapy, the therapist must take responsibility for the lack of progress. It is not enough to say that the child's problems are severe, the parents are sabotaging the treatment, or the environment is not conducive to change. The therapist must consider that diagnostically some important aspect is missing. It may be that individual therapy is not indicated, that the match between the child and therapist is not optimal, or that the deficits have not been accurately identified. The stalemate must be brought to a resolution or the therapy interrupted. Referral for interventions through other modalities, such as educational therapy or tutoring, may be indicated.

What follows is a summary of the treatment of Jason, whom we met in Chapter 1, and who was about to start first grade when treatment began.[4]

Case Illustration

This case illustrates what long-term treatment of a child with NLD can accomplish by a therapist who was willing to be flexible, persevering, and creative in his approach.

With the parents' full endorsement, the diagnostic sessions were followed immediately by regular weekly sessions with Jason. I also met with Jason's parents in

---

[4] As noted earlier, this case was treated by Josh Mark.

separate sessions every 4–6 weeks. During those sessions, I continued to hear about the many behavioral problems at school and home. However, Jason was not aggressive or difficult to manage in his sessions. He continued to use some of the time during each appointment to draw. These drawings consisted of objects or buildings. His main concern was "getting it right." Periodically, I would comment on what he was drawing, although he seldom responded to those comments. This type of active observation was not easy for me, and I struggled to attune myself to him. He would usually criticize me for not seeing his drawing correctly. "Can't you see that that's a door, not a box?" If I asked him to describe what he was drawing, he would usually scoff, saying, "You'll see in a minute." I pulled back and made fewer comments. "Jason, I think I'll just watch you and comment less, because I seem to be bothering you." There was no response. "Do I bother you with my comments?" Jason then said, "I don't know, I'm just trying to make a drawing, and it's hard to get it right." "You're a hard worker," I added. "Thank you," he said gruffly without looking up.

Jason did not tell me much about his life at school or home. He did provide some stories about his soccer games. He was on his first soccer team and was proud of his accomplishments. This new interest seemed to translate into more ball playing in my office. Jason wanted to kick the ball around my office, which proved impractical, so we began going outside to play at the nearby park—an arrangement that continued periodically for many years. Jason seemed less agitated and more able to talk as we walked. During the 5-minute walk to and from the park, Jason would give me glimpses of events at school, at home, and at his synagogue. At the park, Jason and I would kick or throw around a ball. Despite my attempts to give Jason feedback, the ball would usually go sailing over my head. There continued to be very little reciprocity in the physical communication. What began to develop further in our relationship was a "Look, Ma, no hands!" or mirroring form of interaction. Jason enjoyed my positive comments about his throws and kicks. It was refreshing to experience his upbeat affect and the positive aspect of his vitality. The development of reciprocity would be a long-term project for us, but finding a reprieve from his irritable mood was a welcome development.

I began working with the parents on behavioral management strategies, particularly the systematic approach developed by Ross Greene (1998) to help manage explosive episodes. The parents seemed to appreciate this pragmatic support. Six months into treatment, I asked his parents, the teacher, and the nanny to fill out a behavioral checklist form. At school the behavior problems were continuing. The kindergarten teacher at the day school reported that earlier in the week, a substitute had asked the kids to sit in a line instead of in a circle—and Jason had exploded in a 20-minute rage attack; the principal had to come to help. I spoke to the teacher on the phone after her lengthy note on the back of the checklist form that alerted me to what had occurred. She reported that Jason had great difficulty sitting in his chair and insisted on aligning it with the table in front of him. He fidgeted constantly. She tried to be as flexible as she could, but he kept bothering other children so that she had to intervene. Finally, she was worried that he would not be able to manage the dual curriculum (secular and religious) that began in first grade.

The nanny also wrote a long note, and because she often brought Jason to appointments, we too developed a rapport. She reported frequent problems dealing with Jason hitting his sister, as the sister struggled to manage his bossiness, rigidity, and irritability. The nanny arranged play dates, noting that "Jason enjoys the companionship until the child wants to do something that Jason doesn't want to do. I have to supervise the play closely or else . . ." If Jason did not get his way, he would have an uncontrollable rage attack that would last 20–30 minutes. "He touches others a lot but doesn't like to be touched." She added, "He can be loving and delightful, too."

The parents' reports echoed the school's and nanny's; both parents commented on the hyperactivity, irritability, severe temper outbursts, and struggles with disruptions in routines. They also offered several poignant accounts of Jason's struggles. Before he went to bed, he had to make sure that the items on his desk were perfectly in order. He recently had a tantrum at bedtime because he wanted his shoes in bed with him. Another meltdown occurred because he wanted a certain spoon to eat with, and that spoon was in the dishwasher. Another meltdown occurred because he had to be restrained from walking on the furniture. A recent family trip was "a complete disaster."

Jason's dejected parents were not surprised by the outcome of the questionnaires and the agreement across the spheres of his life. Nor were they surprised by my recommendation for a psychiatric evaluation.

While we waited several months for the psychiatric evaluation, because the psychiatrist I recommended was not immediately available, Jason began to complain about coming to see me. Several times, as he and the parent or nanny were leaving for my office, he precipitated a meltdown. I witnessed one such episode on their arrival, which I can only describe as a full-blown, roaring display of rage. To help him settle, we began to gently bounce a soft balloon back and forth, after which he slowly calmed down. He made no comment about the incident, and I finally said, "That was a rough one." Jason responded, "I wanted to stop crying, but I couldn't do it." He began to cry again, this time mournfully. I stopped tossing the ball and walked over to put my hand on his shoulder. He recoiled and looked at me with angry eyes. I said, "Let's just play catch then"—which we did for the remainder of the hour.

Several months later, after the completion of the evaluation, the psychiatrist called me with his concerns. He described Jason's depressed mood, hyperactivity and impulse control problems, and high-level anxiety. He also reported that Jason appeared to meet the criteria for obsessive–compulsive disorder as well. He prescribed stimulant medication for the ADHD, from which there was immediate, noticeable improvement. The morning routine proved to be less volatile and Jason seemed more in control at school. He was not able to tell me that he felt any differently with the medication, but his parents felt somewhat encouraged at this development.

Jason and I continued with our weekly appointments. The main change I noticed was that he was less fidgety. The mood variability continued, however. Some days he would walk into the office in a very dour mood, whereas at other times he would bounce on his toes with a smile on his face. During these sessions he never chose symbolic play, despite the option of puppets, play figures, and so on. He still drew occasionally, but he told me that he really did not like how his drawings turned out. The ball play continued. His favorite activity was catching the nerf football while diving onto my couch. We walked to the park, weather permitting, and Jason would then be able to talk about first grade, home, sports, and some of the family's religious activities. He experienced the teachers at school as strict and could not understand "why they are always on my case." He was proud of his schoolwork and he loved recess.

Our game of catch at the park was still a work in progress. He loved making spectacular catches and was often upset with me for not throwing the ball in just the right place so he could "look like a football star on ESPN." His tosses to me continued to sail over my head. I spent time each session offering verbal feedback about his overthrows, trying to help him understand his role in my difficulty catching the ball. When I threw a ball off course, I made a point of saying something like, "I'm sorry, Jason, I threw that one too much to the right." Occasionally Jason would say "my bad" when he messed up a throw. This was really a break in his perspective taking ability. I praised his self-observation in every way I could and incorporated his language, which he picked up at recess. "My bad," I would say when my throw went off course.

Other small successes occurred at home. The parents began to reduce their expectations of Jason during such regular events as the Sabbath meal. The meltdowns continued, but with somewhat less frequency.

As the second half of the school year rolled in, Jason's behavior at school worsened. Perhaps the first-grade teacher was somewhat less structured than last year's teacher. In addition to Jason's impulse control problems, there were many more "power struggles" in the classroom. Jason's stubborn presentation was experienced as willful and belligerent—and was not well tolerated; he spent more and more time in the principal's office. He also struggled with learning tasks as well, such as writing. Eventually, a tutor was added in the spring of first grade.

The addition of the tutor led to problems with his coming to therapy. Jason did not think it was fair that he should have two appointments after school. He became more resistant to his appointments with the tutor and with me as well. In our sessions I could not help but notice his nervous behaviors. Beyond his perfectionism and the related compulsions, his anxiety seemed to express itself or overflow into various repetitive behaviors such as nose picking, nail biting, and most notably when we played ball, hand licking. I reported this behavior to the parents, who had been noticing these symptoms for some time. I consulted with the psychiatrist. Later that year the psychiatrist added an antidepressant to Jason's medication regime. The result was observable but not dramatic. The repetitive behaviors, except the hand licking, diminished. Jason's mood was still often irritable and volatile.

I recommended to the parents that they follow through with the neuropsychological evaluation, which I had recommended for Jason when I first saw him. He was now old enough for the test to have some validity. In addition to the mood,

Table 12.1. Results of Jason's Testing on the Wechsler Intelligence Scale for Children—Third Edition (WISC-III)

Subtests	Standard Score	Percentile	Description
Verbal Tests			
Information	125	95	Superior
Similarities	90	25	Average
Arithmetic	115	85	High Average
Vocabulary	130	97	Very Superior
Comprehension	125	95	Superior
Digit Span—Total Score	130	97	Very Superior
Digit Span—Forward	10	97	Very Superior
Digit Span—Backward	100	50	Average
Performance Tests			
Picture Completion	100	50	Average
Coding	120	92	Superior
Picture Arrangement	90	25	Average
Block Design	106	63	Average
Object Assembly	95	37	Average
Mazes	125	95	Superior
Symbol Search	125	95	Superior
Full Scale IQ	113	81	High Average
Verbal Scale IQ	121	92	Superior
Performance or Nonverbal IQ	103	58	Average
Verbal Comprehension Factor Index	120	91	Superior
Perceptual Organization Factor Index	97	42	Average
Freedom from Distractibility Factor Index	126	96	Superior
Processing Speed Factor Index`	124	95	Superior

anxiety, impulse, and attentional problems, Jason appeared to struggle academically as well. A more complete picture of Jason's strengths and difficulties would help in the ongoing treatment and remediation planning.

The findings from the neuropsychological report were initially too complicated for the parents to fully absorb, but ultimately were useful for both them and me. A distillation of the 18-page report showed that Jason's global cognitive functioning was within the high-average range, with significantly stronger and superior verbal capabilities compared to average nonverbal skills. He showed strengths in the areas of general knowledge, verbal ability, practical comprehension, reading, and spelling. He demonstrated difficulty in attention, working memory and executive functioning, automatic language, social and cognitive processing, auditory processing, and fine-motor dexterity. Social–cognitive and pragmatic processing weaknesses were pronounced. The psychologist also was concerned about Jason's attentional problems and his anxiety and mood, which were evident during the testing and in the questionnaires that he administered. Table 12.1 lists the results of Jason's WISC-III.

The psychologist gave Jason several diagnoses, beginning with NLD, ADHD, and OCD. His moodiness and explosiveness, although observed and reported, were not formally diagnosed at this time.

The report indicated that many of Jason's difficulties were, in fact, rooted in brain-based deficits that affected his ability to understand and negotiate in the social world. The psychologist worked with the parents and the school to help them understand the complicated report. I gave my support to these efforts in an ongoing way. I found an appropriate social group for Jason at a local center for children with learning disabilities. In this time-limited group, Jason worked on the basic mechanics of sending and receiving social communications. I continued the weekly individual sessions and made every attempt to support Jason's pragmatic social development.

Jason wanted to make friends, but he was resistant to the group. He received some rewards at home to encourage his attendance, and I agreed to reduce my sessions to every other week as part of the deal. The time-limited group was not useful for Jason in any way that I could detect. His attitude about the group was negative, because he thought the other kids in the group were "stupid geeks." He dismissed the skill training as "baby stuff." In addition, the group's therapists were not able to address many things Jason did to interfere with his own social success. The group's focus was on teaching prosocial skills—about which he was not open to receiving feedback.

As we moved into the spring of second grade, the classroom disruptions continued. The religious school, despite their best efforts, had great difficulty meeting Jason's needs both behaviorally and academically. I hesitated before talking with the parents about changing to the public school where special education resources were available for both his social and academic needs. I was relieved *that they were open to the suggestion of exploring the neighborhood public school, which we began to do. "We see the writing on the wall," they told me.*

I recognized, though, that removing their child from the religious school was a significant loss for the parents. I discussed the potential school change with Jason. As expected, his focus was on the concrete details, such as dismissal times, recess, gym, etc. Feelings about leaving the school and classmates or concerns about acceptance were not an immediate issue for him. He did express some anxiety as to whether anyone else would be wearing a yarmulke at the school. We talked over everything. Jason could discuss his feelings with me, but it was up to me, at this point in the process, to probe specifically about his feelings— and to do so when I judged that he was not overwhelmed with other thoughts and feelings. This kind of therapeutic intervention was a critical part of my usefulness in expanding the depth of his personal narrative and helping him understand more of his feelings. I could help him negotiate his world with less disruption. He was not capable of bringing these issues forth on his own. Understandably, he focused more on finding some immediate relief from his distress. He wanted to avoid any painful feelings. The times we spent walking to and from the park or bouncing a ball back and forth in my office were usually the times when I would bring up these sensitive topics. For example: "You're going to be the new kid in the class. What has it been like when new kids came in the middle of the year at your school? Have you thought about what this might be like for you?"

During many sessions, such work could not be accomplished. Jason's mood would commonly overflow, usually with anger, about something that was "done to" him at school or home. On some days, having to come to therapy was sometimes enough to put Jason over the edge and precipitate a meltdown. Jason could explain this to me when he was not overwhelmed by his mood. "It's not that being here is so bad, it's having to leave what I'm doing that's bad. I need time to relax—and besides, it's not fair!" I attempted to empathize with Jason's need to relax, understanding his need to consolidate his inner state and gain some feeling of self-regulation as he changed gears.

During this period, the psychiatrist began a trial of mood stabilizing medication in addition to the stimulant and the antidepressant. The psychiatrist provisionally diagnosed Jason as having a bipolar disorder to explain his often volatile, irritable moods. He was hesitant to use this label, because he did not want to overpathologize the already complicated diagnosis, but we agreed that the persistent irritability and meltdowns were causing daily problems.

In the month preceding the school change, Jason's irritable moods, although still high, were less extreme, and there were more "good days." The full-fledged meltdowns diminished as well. The medication change proved helpful and provided a sturdier platform on which to make the school change.

Jason, who was now 9 years old, liked his new school and became invested in "making it" there. Our work together soon focused on a goal that was clearly his: "I want friends!" A building block to this awareness was the concrete fact of changing schools. He noticed that "no one really calls me from my old school." He also could clearly observe that there was a lot of social interaction at the new school, of which he wanted to be a part. He was extremely enthusiastic about the sports and games at recess. I was more optimistic about his chances of experiencing some social success. His motivation for social activities was more clearly present, and articulated by him. He was more willing to talk these issues over with me. His mood swings, although still present, were better controlled with the mood stabilizing medication. His special education team was available to him during the day to help him navigate the social world as well as the academic world. The school staff actively collaborated with me and his parents to meet Jason's complex needs. Additionally, I received reports from school and home that kept me specifically informed about how Jason was doing and added depth and detail to Jason's own narrative.

There were many problems on the playground, but I framed these as "positive stress." At least he was in the midst of the social interaction. However, Jason often still did not know what to do to initiate and maintain interaction with his peers.

During the period when Jason was in the third through fifth grades, we focused on "how to make friends and get along with people." We discussed his current dilemmas, which usually involved some form of exclusion from the group. "I wonder why they did that," I might say, trying to help him with the basics of perspective taking. We would then try to reconstruct what happened sequentially— a task that was difficult for Jason. Despite his often negative affect, I realized that Jason trusted me with very personal stories.

I also became more skilled in helping Jason consolidate his mood when he arrived. He was usually shutdown and negative when he arrived. I found that he could best utilize me if I did not engage his negative mood. I did acknowledge his moodiness, and I tried to respect his present disposition as I helped him soothe himself and transition to being more fully with me. I would greet him but not talk too much at first. He would often remain silent, as if he was "on strike." He would then rant about some recent injustice or about being mad at his mother for making him come. I would commonly bounce a soft ball to him, beginning to connect this way, and then comment on the here-and-now aspects of the play, saying such things as "nice one, good catch, my bad." I think Jason experienced my confidence in him and my steadiness as enabling him to right himself and be more in control. I could then "strike when the iron was cold," to probe a problem about which he had complained, or about which he had fumed as he walked into the office. I shared this strategy with Jason's parents, teachers, and tutors and tried to help them adapt it to their setting.

As Jason approached his next transition to junior high school, a positive shift occurred in the treatment. Jason came to the appointments with topics to discuss.

He would begin, commonly sitting in my chair, and bring up an issue for us to address. Several narrative themes emerged that we discussed and to which we referred from week to week. Dealing with a particularly troublesome and aggressive kid on the playground was one such theme. We discussed how to understand where this kid was coming from, and how to manage being ridiculed and excluded. More depth and thickness were added to the narrative as Jason came to realize that he admired this boy's toughness but resented the fact that when he acted this way, people seemed to reject him. This topic led into an increasing awareness on Jason's part of how his special needs set him apart from other kids. Jason began the process of working through his identity issues, which included the complications of being an Orthodox Jew and a special ed student in a public school.

Even as these welcomed developments occurred in therapy, Jason continued to struggle with his mood and self-control. I saw Jason one day after he had experienced a severe episode of loss of control at a sixth grade school meeting that I had attended. He explained his frustration: "What people don't understand about me is that I wanted to stop crying, but I just couldn't. It's like a force inside me sometimes, and I just can't stop." This lifelong problem was controlled somewhat by medication, but not totally, as the episode indicated. However, Jason was better able to communicate with words what was going on within him. His expanding self-awareness and ego capability allowed him to share this isolating experience, and to share his agony—which perhaps lessened his burden.

Jason has continued to matriculate through school, and despite his learning disabilities, he is on track academically. He has had a successful summer session at a school for children with special needs. For the first time in many years, Jason had a birthday party at his home, for his 12th birthday, with a large group of children. He recently ushered at a play series at the local community center. Next year will be his bar mitzvah, for which he is well prepared. He is growing up. However, it is still never easy.

There has been maturation, paralleling the many interventions, including his ongoing therapy with me. The therapy has evolved, but the neuropsychological based difficulties remain. Jason's mood swings, impulsivity, anxiety, rigidity, and inflexibility amplify the difficulties he has understanding others' intentions and the nuances of social meaning. Helping Jason achieve a stable mood has always been the cornerstone to his availability to the work. When his mood is sufficiently stable, I can connect with Jason as someone who will struggle to understand his inner world and act as a guide for him in navigating the social world.

COMMENTARY ON CASE ILLUSTRATION

At the beginning of treatment, Jason presented as a child with a typical case of NLD subtype IV, in the moderately severe range. Aside from his evident visual–spatial deficits, he had clear limitations in his ability to process nonlinguistic perceptual information. This deficit resulted in his misreading of others' responses and led to social difficulties from an early age. He was also found to have attentional and executive function difficulties, with all the many effects these have on social adjustment and academic performance. In addition, he had clear deficits in the domain of social cognition. His capacity for theory of mind functioning appeared limited too, which impaired his capacity for reciprocal social relationships. In the language domain there was evidence that his capacity for nonverbal communication was quite limited, and his verbal communication provided evidence of a failure to contextualize his remarks, which led to difficulties in understanding precisely what he was trying to convey. We may say that his capacity for theory of relevance functioning was impaired. In his emotional functioning, he clearly had problems identifying and expressing his feelings, and his capacity to modulate his own affect states was seriously impaired. Furthermore, the presence of comorbid conditions (ADHD, OCD and possible bipolar disorder), which were identified later, greatly compounded the complexity of his social, emotional, and behavioral difficulties. Lastly, he suffered from a disorder of the self. He had limited capacity for mindsharing, and his sense of self-cohesion was unstable, as evidenced by his frequent meltdowns. Finally, he had little idea of the motives for his behaviors or the ways in which his NLD affected his conduct.

Having said all of this, we do not do justice to a child by simply cataloging his or her problems, difficulties, deficits, and impairments. The completion of the picture requires that we also comment on assets and positive qualities. These may be hard to find, especially when the focus is turned so acutely on the management difficulties that the child's caregivers face on a day-to-day basis. Yet, if we are to build on those assets and competencies, we are required to credit the child with the positive qualities that may be hidden behind the façade he or she presents.

In Jason's case, first there was something likable about him to which his therapist was drawn. In spite of the barriers the child placed to experiencing a connection with his therapist, the latter was not put off or discouraged. In fact, he seemed to find behind the barriers a vulnerable, immature, and potentially lovable child who craved contact but did not quite know how to elicit or receive it. Second, Jason gave indications that he was not so totally alienated by the negative experiences to which he had been exposed. He still seemed to hope that someone would be able to understand and help him. He came to sessions willingly, if not eagerly. He was willing to engage the therapist and was even forgiving of the therapist's eagerness to intrude into his psychological space. Jason conveyed in clear nonverbal messages when he wished to be left alone and when he could tolerate feeling connected. Third, Jason demonstrated a quality that will serve him well in the long run: the capacity for perseverance. Clinical experience has convinced me that this quality, which not all children possess, can help a child to overcome many of his or her limitations. It is a quality that demonstrates the child's resilience and ultimately the capacity to endure and overcome adversity. In Jason, it speaks well for his potential to make a reasonably good adjustment in the long run.

Turning to the themes that emerged in the treatment, I limit myself to a discussion of three threads among the many that were present. Two of these relate to Jason's vulnerable sense of self-cohesion, and the third addresses the incoherencies in his self-narrative. With regard to the vulnerable sense of self-cohesion, the therapist experienced considerable pressure to "do something" about Jason's meltdowns, which not surprisingly, caused considerable disruption at home and at school. Yet the meltdowns were not a priority for Jason himself. The longings he expressed were for admiration and affirmation. He seemed to wish for the adulation of a football quarterback on the playing field. His sense of self had been battered by the criticisms to which he had been exposed. Whether justified from an objective point of view, from his perspective those criticisms only meant that he was not "a good kid" or worse that he was "a bad kid." These negative feelings were reinforced by his lack of success in peer relationships. He often felt bad because he believed he was being treated unfairly.

In my perception, repairing those injuries to Jason's sense of self was an imperative without which there could be no relationship. The therapist's willingness to participate in the "football games" that Jason set up conveyed a message that the therapist understood what was important. To have focused on the whys and wherefores of the meltdowns had the potential of evoking a negative transference. The therapist would then be experienced as no different from other critical adults who had berated Jason for his bad behavior.

A related aspect to the complex transference was the fact that, indirectly, the therapist was addressing the issue of the meltdowns. Jason's inability to regulate and modulate his own affect states was related to two factors, as mentioned in earlier discussions of this topic. These were the developmental deficits and the failure to internalize the caregivers' functions. Whereas medication could modify the former, to a degree, the latter required therapeutic intervention. The missing selfobject function related to Jason's deficit was the internalization of an "idealized other"—that is, experiencing the other as a powerful, yet reassuring and soothing presence who could calm Jason by his very demeanor. As the relationship developed and the therapist learned to "strike while the iron is cold," that was precisely what happened. Jason acquired a capacity to control himself by evoking the reassuring presence of someone he admired, felt close to, and who could be comforting.

The second major component of the therapy was engaged when Jason matured sufficiently to be able to discuss the nature of his deficits and their effects on his behavior. Making sense of his responses became the focus of the therapy during its later stages. Jason's curiosity was stimulated and his intelligence engaged in processing what was occurring on a day-to-day basis. The prospect for the development of a coherent self-narrative strengthened his relationship with his therapist.

Obviously, the work in therapy continues. The future remains somewhat uncertain, in that Jason still must confront the many obstacles that lie ahead on the path to adulthood. His therapy, the many other sources of support and intervention he has received, and the presence of devoted parents who have stood by him during those difficult times, have all contributed to his progress and portend well for his future.

Psychotherapy with these children involves several strategies. First, it is essential to work with parents on a regular basis, making them active partners in the therapeutic process. Although the focus with them is primarily educational, the process parallels the child's treatment. When the therapist makes empathic connection with the parents and resonates with their experiences, they feel relieved, and their anxiety and rage are better contained. When they are helped to go back over interactions that had gone awry, identifying the patterns and figuring out new ways of handling situations based on what is now known about the child, positive transference with them is dominant, and they usually leave these sessions feeling calmer and empowered. At other times, however, disjunctions occur when their helplessness overwhelms them and they feel the therapist was not sufficiently available to them or could not concretely help them with specific interventions they could use with the child. However, if the therapist can manage these periodic disjunctions, the connection with the parents can be maintained and eventually they feel positive and pleased with the successes their child encounters.

Second, visits to the school and telephone contacts with teachers and other professionals are essential to create a context in which the child can begin to perceive him- or herself differently, to act differently, and to make efforts in areas where he or she had given up previously. The direct work on skills that is done through the teachers, such as the pairing of verbal cues with nonverbal signals, helps to diminish the child's confusion and frustration. The child's self-esteem is also assisted when the teacher stops telling him or her to "be more careful" and begins to give specific, repeated guidelines, such as how to align the work on the paper, as well as encouraging the child to ask for help when becoming confused.

Conclusion

Children with NLD present with a wide spectrum of disabilities from mild to severe. Children who function in the moderately to severely impaired range are unable to carry out the normal routines of children their ages. A primary goal of therapy is to help the child modify the themes that organize his or her self-narrative. Two major factors influence the modification of the child's narrative motifs: the corrective aspects of the relationship with the therapist, and the understanding the child gains about the influence of those themes on his or her conduct and relationships. The themes that emerge in therapy are metaphors for—expressions of—the motifs that have organized his or her narrative. As changes occur in the relationship to the therapist, shifts in the metaphor occur. The therapist may also actively introduce shifts in the metaphor that reframe for the child's view of the world. The child may then be able to view him- or herself differently, as an adventurous experimenter rather than as an ineffectual bumbler. Although this may be a primary goal in the treatment of any child, what is specific to the treatment of children with NLD is the way in which the process is conceptualized. Viewing the process as a series of moments in which the therapist addresses issues as they arise avoids framing the process as one in which the sole aim is to resolve a set of transference reenactments. The larger aim is also to help the child develop compensations for his or her cognitive deficits.

In this chapter I have attempted to illustrate a treatment approach to children with NLD that specifically addresses some of the emotional problems that result from the neurocognitive deficits. I have emphasized that, for such children, the neurocognitive deficits shape their experience of, and their responses to, the world. Every child lives within a context, and each child's responses to the context are based on his or her own experiences. In addition, the response of the context to the child cannot be minimized. Thus, the family setting, the school setting, and peer relationships all contribute to the child's ultimate integration of his or her experiences.

Treatment is an encounter between a child, who brings in a personal narrative that organizes his or her responses to the world, and a therapist, who attempts to understand and modify the child's narrative. This goal is achievable only through a process in which the child feels understood and validated. Once a set of shared experiences has occurred, it becomes possible for the child to experience the differences between the therapist's responses and those of others. This process assists in the creation of a set of shared meanings with the therapist that can help the child reframe his or her understanding of the problems.

13

Attending to Caregivers

As we enter the context of the child's family, we are drawn into the child's relationships with family members.[1] Earlier, I alluded to some of the caregivers' responses to the infant. Being unlike their older children, caregivers take note of the differences with a sense of puzzlement. At first, they may question their parenting skills, wondering whether their failures are producing the child's difficulties. This tendency may be especially true of first-time parents. Soon the differences noted between their infant and others take on a life of their own. The caregivers' adaptive capacities are strained as they wonder what is wrong. The disrupted dialogue contributes to the gap that begins to widen between the infant and the caregiver. At this point, there is no direct evidence of the precise nature of the infant's deficits that the caregivers can detect. A vulnerable period is heralded as the caregivers react to the child. If they feel rejected by the child, frustrated by their own failures to accommodate to the child, or injured by those failures, then the polarity in their feelings may match those of the child—a matching that only reinforces the negative interactions. They label the infant as difficult, consider parenting unsatisfying (at least), and resent the increasing disruption caused by the presence of the "stranger in

[1] Several worthwhile resources for caregivers are now available. Unfortunately, some of them address the concerns of caregivers of children with Asperger's disorder in conjunction with those of children with NLD. See Appendix 2.

their midst." In fact, these first signs of disruption are only the harbingers of what is to come, as chronic disruptions invade the family system.

The positive or negative responses that exist between the child and the family members may distort the family's dynamics. No longer will that child be an equal citizen among the other citizens within the family. Instead, the child with an NLD will increasingly consume more and more of the family's resources and energies. Some couples give up plans to have more children; some fathers find that the attention required by the child detracts from the marital intimacy; and some of those fathers may decide to leave the family rather than withstand the strains the child imposes. Mothers often feel that they have to fend for themselves and to manage the child's existence with little support. Siblings within the family feel shortchanged by the attention given to the child. Rivalries become inflamed, adding to the disruption already present.

As the child grows older, the developmental deficits become more evident, and caregivers find themselves criticized by well-meaning relatives. Grandparents may suggest that the child is not being disciplined properly. Aunts and uncles may stop inviting the family's children to family functions because the disruptions that occur when the child is present detract from the atmosphere they wish to create. Friends of the family may remain loyal and supportive but their critical eyes are fixed on the child.

If the family is fortunate enough to have the child's deficits identified by a professional, a new era begins. Now the family confronts the task of integrating the knowledge of having a child with an NLD. That knowledge is accompanied by an imperative: that the family begin to channel some of its resources into interventions and remediation for the child. Some caregivers make that task their mission in life. They become more knowledgeable and expert about the disorder than some of the professionals toward whom they turned for help. Some caregivers take on the job of advocacy for their child and for children with similar disorders. Many of these families have had to reposition their lives, a fact that it is not lost to outsiders who observe how far the family's path has strayed from the direction in which it began prior to the arrival of the child.

If the family had not obtained the diagnosis prior to the beginning of formal schooling, which often is the case, they may be unprepared for what awaits them. Depending on the sophistication of the school system and its resources, the family now has to contend with a complex system that expects conventionalized behavior from the students enrolled in its classes. Children who do not fit in will be subject to critical appraisal first by teachers and the support personnel in the school and finally by the school's administration. Many experienced and competent teachers have a repertoire of techniques for dealing with children whom they do not understand. They may be familiar with the problems of children who have reading problems, or they may know how to deal with children who have poor handwriting and require assistance for their fine-motor skills; they may even be familiar with the challenges of children who are impulsive and who cannot stay seated. But children with NLD present a different and somewhat baffling challenge. These children appear impulsive, they have poor handwriting, but they have excellent reading skills and appear to be quite bright. Furthermore, their relationships to other children are practically nonexistent. Peers shun them, they are not invited to parties, and a disturbing pattern emerges in which other children tease and scape-goat them. During recess and lunchtime, these children find no place for themselves, and they frequently respond to what they experience as as-saults by becoming assaultive themselves. At this point teachers and school personnel label them as behaviorally disordered. The children re-sist those labels and argue with the teachers, maintaining that they are not at fault; they are soon labeled as oppositional and defiant. The course is set for these children to experience a negative engagement with the school system.

Working with Caregivers

By the time parents come for assistance, they may have had prior consul-tations or assessments and experienced the contacts with those profes-sionals as blaming them for their child's problems. If the disabilities were not diagnosed correctly, the impression could have been conveyed that the child's behaviors are the result of the family dynamics or inadvertent trauma to which the child was exposed. As a result, many parents ap-proach the new evaluation with suspicion and defensiveness. They come prepared for criticism, ready to resist suggestions for testing, viewing the process either as unnecessary or as endangering because it would expose their own vulnerabilities. Some parents are so guilt ridden that they antic-ipate the worst from the diagnostician. At times, they may feel they have contributed to the child's problems because they suspect that they have similar problems (Palombo, 1999).

The approach that I find most helpful is to offer respectful compassion to each parent. Children with disabilities are difficult to parent. Conveying to parents an attitude of concern for a troubled child best characterizes the basis for the emerging alliance. Treating parents as one would a colleague or a close friend who asks for counsel helps parents feel that they are not part of the problem; rather, that their help will be solicited in finding bet-ter ways of coping with their child. Before they can begin to re-appreciate the positive aspects and strengths their child possesses, they may need to express the full weight of the sadness they feel at the disruption that having such a child creates. They will need some preparation for the fact that, even though help is now at hand, the chronicity of the child's disorder ensures that problems will arise at every turn. They will continue to face the constant frustration of never being able to anticipate precisely when a problem will arise. Often it will occur when they least expect it. Crises may develop at the least opportune moment or when the family should be joyously celebrating an event. The effort it takes to stabilize situations or avoid emergencies often drains much of their energies. As the child grows, the nature of the difficulties will change. A plethora of new challenges accompanies each developmental step. Although these declarations may sound overly pessimistic, their effect is to convey a deep understanding of what parents confront, thus forming a bond of empathy with them in their distress. This bond serves as a model for the empathy they will later be able to feel for their distressed child and for the alliance the therapist will form with all of them.

Sometimes the downward cycle of disappointment and despair has taken such a toll that considerable work is necessary to help parents identify and respond to their child's positive qualities. Often, because of the pervasiveness of the child's problems, they have been completely preoccupied with managing the child's weaknesses as best they can. For them to come to the point where they can value, once more, the child and nurture his or her strengths requires a change in the way they view their child. Once that change occurs, they can then begin the process of building a positive relationship. As the cycle is broken and the disruptions diminish, parents can then express their love of, and devotion to, their child. The child's qualities that at one time were irritants can now be appreciated for their adaptive qualities. A child's perseverance, or wonderful memory for facts, or love of music, which the child may have used defensively to keep people at a distance, now can be put to good service in achieving desirable goals.

Educational Focus

I conceive of work with parents of children with NLD as a partnership between therapist and parents in which the goals are as follows: (1) to give parents the necessary support to feel that they are not alone in dealing with their difficult child; (2) to provide them with information that will allow them to understand the reasons behind their child's behaviors; and (3) to equip them with a set of specific strategies to use when confronted with difficult behaviors. The aim of these goals is to create conditions that will permit parents to form complementary relationships with their child, enhance the child's capacity to form compensatory structures, and ultimately increase the child's capacity to cope with his or her environment. Parents are encouraged to cultivate positive feelings for their child and to maximize the child's strengths.

Parents are entitled to the best explanation available of their child's problem. To the extent possible, it is desirable to give the parents general advice on the management of the child and on ways to provide the child with positive experiences (Garber, 1991; Rourke, 1995a; Vigilante, 1983). Once parents gain an understanding of the nature of their child's deficits and the ways in which these deficits affect the child's life, they often experience considerable relief at finally having answers to their questions. They begin to make connections between situations and their child's deficits. Often they will seek to educate themselves further about the disorder. If they feel comfortable in joining a group of parents of children with the same problems, they may find support in learning that they are not alone in their struggles with this kind of child. Sharing their experiences and learning from others can alleviate their anxieties and dispel their confusions. It can also help them learn different strategies for dealing with some of their child's difficult behaviors.

Providing parents with information about their child's deficits also involves the larger task of refraining their understanding of their child's behaviors. Parents come with many different views as to why their child behaves as he or she does. Some parents have tried to deal with their challenging child by using the same child-rearing methods they use with their other children—only to find that these do not work. They feel frustration and confusion as their expectations that this child is no different from their other children crumble. They feel caught by the need to treat one child differently, and they fear that their other children will interpret their interventions as favoritism. For these parents it is important to convey that their child is different from their other children and requires special management because of his or her impairment. The specifics of the deficits can be interpreted with examples from the results of the testing as well as by giving them materials to read about the disorder.

Other parents, caught up in the vicious cycle of oppositional behavior, may believe that their child is responding as he or she does because of inadequate socialization or out of simple meanness. For these parents, reframing the child's difficulties involves a slow and systematic demonstration of the ways in which the child's impairment leads to failures in communication, which the child has interpreted as lack of caring. Changing this type of interaction presents one of the more challenging tasks in working with parents.

It is important to help parents realize the scope of their child's difficulties—difficulties that often permeate every aspect of the child's life, from the time the child gets up in the morning until bedtime. For example, as the child tries to judge how much toothpaste to put on the toothbrush, visual–spatial problems interfere with the task. Problems intrude in the classroom, where he or she may struggle with math or the nuances of fiction reading comprehension. At recess, the child is bewildered by the experience of 20-odd moving bodies rapidly giving off multiple social cues. At the dinner table, negotiating the crosscurrents of family signals presents its own challenges. Every step in the developmental path presents new challenges for the child, as he or she displays different behaviors and variations on old themes.

Once parents grasp how pervasively the disabilities affect their child's life, they can be helped to hone in on the particulars of their child's experience. It is usually productive to examine their child's everyday life with an eye to the demands made upon the child for nonverbal competencies. Much as the parents of a physically challenged child need to assess the environment to identify potential obstacles to their child's functioning, so too must the parents of a child with an NLD identify the impediments in his or her world. Parents can then introduce appropriate modifications. They can begin by asking themselves questions, such as what is entailed for the child to be able to walk to school? Older siblings may have easily managed the task at this age, but is it realistic to expect this child to manage on his or her own? On written work, does the child always get mixed up when there are too many math problems on a page? When school is over, is there a large group of neighborhood children with which the child must cope? Or is the child enrolled in a loosely run after-school care program that overtaxes the his or her meager social resources? Is the child expected to manage playing with more than one peer at a time on play dates? Even when limited to playing with one friend, does the child need some planned activities and adult input to keep things running smoothly? Such a careful inventory helps to identify the stress points for this particular child in this particular family and enables the therapist and parents to find starting points for specific interventions.

As parents talk about the difficulties and challenges their child presents, it sometimes becomes apparent that over the years their patience has worn thin. They may have become irritated by the child's inability to modify his or her behaviors in spite of numerous attempts at getting the child to alter the dysfunctional patterns. When the therapist and caregivers review those difficulties to see what went wrong, they find that by reinterpreting their meanings, solutions become available. For example, when parents understand that if a child puts up a fuss and resists going to relatives they have not seen in great while it is not because the child is being oppositional but rather is anxious about facing a new situation, their attitude toward the child changes and they may be able to intervene to minimize the child's anxiety. The contributions of the child's deficits to the interaction can be highlighted in a way that has not been apparent to the parents. Then the problems can be seen as arising from a failure in communication rather than being solely attributable to a willful child who is defiant.

It is essential to nurture the positives in the parents' relationship to, and interactions with, their child. This nurturance occurs on two different levels. As therapist and parents discuss the child's difficulties, it is always important to draw attention, at some point, to other aspects of the child that they value and cherish. Parents may admire their child's capacities for verbal expression; they may take pleasure in the child's theater performances once he or she has learned to gesture appropriately or use proper vocal expression to give emphasis to a set of feelings. Even some things about the child that are irritating, such as perseveration at seemingly pointless tasks, may contain within them the seeds of something positive, such as perseverance. These kinds of positive expressions provide the foundation for building the child's self-esteem.

In any set of interventions with a child, it is important to build on success. The child needs to know what he or she is doing right each step of the way. For the children with an NLD, it is particularly important to verbalize an appreciation of the gains—no matter how minor—in order to solidify them. When the child finally looks the caregiver in the eye while saying "Hello," he or she needs to know what a difference that has made. Empty praise, such as the mindless "That's great!" in response to every drawing the child makes, is not useful because it cheapens real praise and because it is not specific enough to foster strengths or accomplishments. Indeed, it is only confusing. Commenting on the use of different colors or the added detail in the drawing, however, nurtures the child's growth. Genuine positive responses keep the child moving forward. In addition, as the parents notice what is going right, they can begin to feel better about their own parenting.

In offering specific interventions for parents, I keep two goals in mind: one is to increase the child's coping capacities and the other is to enhance the child's self-esteem. An awareness of the issues facing this child in this family situation will guide the therapist and parents as to where to begin. Some strategies will be more useful for some children than for others. The order in which caregivers introduce them will vary from child to child. The therapist tailors the interventions in accordance with what is required by the problematic situation. And while the therapist provides information to parents, he or she is also mindful of the parallel process through which he or she is using similar interventions with the parents to help model the strategies being discussed. Bringing the parallel process to parents' awareness often helps them integrate the intervention (see also Burger, 2004; Duke & Nowicki, 1996; Klass & Costello, 2003; Nowicki & Duke, 1992; Rourke, 1995a; Rubenstein, 2005; Tanguay, 2001; Whitney, 2002).

The interventions that follow are not discrete techniques that apply to children or situations without regard to the total context. Many of these interventions are applicable simultaneously or in combination with others. Of greater importance than the interventions as strategies is the mindset from which they arise. Parents who are immersed in their child's modes of functioning will find themselves using these techniques flexibly and creatively. Their sense of oneness with their child will lead to the establishment of a sense of complementarity.

Interventions

The interventions that follow are organized according to the three perspectives used in the work: the neuropsychological deficits, the social impairments, and the intrapersonal constraints.

NONLINGUISTIC PERCEPTUAL DEFICITS/ATTENTION AND EXECUTIVE FUNCTION DISORDERS

Teaching the Child about Nonverbal Communication
In this section, I discuss some of the interventions that are useful in dealing with the neuropsychological assets and deficits of children with NLD. The nonverbal domain in human communication involves the ability to decode other's nonverbal messages, to use nonverbal signals to convey messages to others, and to process the meanings associated with each component of the nonverbal domain. Among the most common components of this domain are facial expressions, gestures, gaze (eye-to-eye contact), body posture, vocal intonation, tactile communication (the use of touch), and proximics (the awareness of the appropriate social distance to use in different social contexts). Most children do not require formal instruction in the use of these modalities; they appear to absorb them through observation of others. However, children with NLD have deficits in one or more of these components or in the capacity to encode, decode, or process messages in this domain. As noted, Nowicki and Duke (1992; Duke, Nowicki, and Martin, 1996) use the term *dyssemia* to characterize the difficulties children generally have in the use of this channel of com-

munication. They believe that it is necessary to instruct all children more formally in its use. We believe that for the children with whom we are concerned, such instruction is critical for them to compensate for their deficits. This instruction should be undertaken as if one were to teach the child a foreign language. It requires breaking down tasks and actively demonstrating to the child what is involved.

Caregivers then should consider the demands upon the child to read nonverbal social cues. They can ask themselves questions such as:

> How do people in their family communicate?
> Are there frequently given signals the child can be taught to recognize?
> Can family members modify their nonverbal communication by pairing their nonverbal signs with words the child can understand?
> Is the child regularly exposed to situations that demand problems-solving abilities or flexibility in thinking skills that may be over his or her head?

Such questions will heighten the parents' awareness of their own modes of nonverbal communication as well as the child's deficits in nonverbal ways of communicating.

Once parents have formed a solid picture in their minds of the problematic areas, the task of remediation can begin. The means through which this remediation can be given is complex. Demonstration alone cannot accomplish the task. What is required is the use of *verbal mediation*, that is, the use of words, to translate for the child what is being taught. Language is an area of strength for children with NLD. Although they may have articulation problems early on, they soon demonstrate verbal skills beyond their years. Caregivers must both demonstrate and translate nonverbal messages into verbal forms to enable the child to negotiate situations successfully. The task for parents is to develop the means through which to instruct patiently the child, for example, to look a person in the eyes when speaking to him or her, to notice whether the person is smiling or frowning, to listen to the tone of voice. At first, the child will be puzzled and bewildered, not knowing what to look for, but eventually a sensitization process will lead to the acquisition of a rudimentary vocabulary upon which the child and parent can enlarge.

Jane, age 12, has had chronic problems acquiring and retaining friends. She either overwhelms new friends, which pushes them away, or she is so inappropriate in groups that they shy away from contact with her. In one of her sessions with her therapist, she brought a series of pictures from her birthday party to which she had managed to attract a few friends. In one of the pictures Jane is holding on to the shoulder of one of the girls, having pulled her toward her to have their picture taken. The friend looked clearly uncomfortable, forcing herself to smile for the camera. The therapist first praised Jane for her success in attracting the friends to the party and then gently pointed out the girl's discomfort in the picture. Jane responded by saying that the girl was smiling. The therapist noted that it looked like a forced smile. Jane said, "How did you know that? My teacher said the same thing!" The therapist then made a face that should have appeared as a forced smile and contrasted it with a genuine smile. Jane detected no difference. They then both went to a mirror and started making faces. It was clear that the various expressions were indistinguishable for Jane. Finally, the therapist brought out a Polaroid camera, asking Jane to pretend she was smiling and to make a genuine smile. Pictures were taken of both. She examined them carefully and began to notice some of the difference. The point was to teach Jane about a domain of communication of which she had no awareness. Pointing it out helped introduce the concept and illustrate for her an area of weakness.

When the therapist later met with Jane's parents, she went over the incident, which they quickly recognized because they, too, had reacted the same way to the picture. The therapist explained what she had done and explained the need for Jane to be tutored in the reading of different facial expressions. The therapist or parents must point out the visual cues and reinforce the connection to help Jane decode them and make then part of her vocabulary.

Preparing the Child for New Situations

When children enter a new situation, they have to change their mind-set or frame of reference so as to contextualize themselves within the new environment. The shift in attitude that such recontextualization requires is most difficult for children with NLD. It is unclear whether this difficulty is due to the anxiety new situations create for them, to their inability to process the visual information with which they feel bombarded in a new environment, or both. What is clear is that the child needs help in assimilating even the most pleasurable elements of new situations. Structuring the child's day, making it as predictable as possible, can help him or her anticipate what is to come well in advance of the change. However, there are always events that are not part of the child's daily routine, with which parents have to contend. Going to a new place in town, visiting relatives that the child had not seen in while, starting in a new school, going on vacation—each of these is fraught with anxieties that lead to defensive responses by the child. Counteracting these anxieties requires patience and special strategies tailored to each child. Parents should be reminded that they often take for granted changes that present no problems for them and their other children. Some children can use verbal mediation alone, but most children with NLD will require more scaffolding. At the minimum, the child requires an *anticipatory rehearsal* of the events he or she is about to encounter. Optimally, a *full dress rehearsal* of the event should be conducted. A child will feel most comfortable only if he or she can actually visit the setting prior to the event itself with a parent who is skilled in providing complementary support and guidance.

Knowing that the child needs to be prepared provides parents with an opportunity to teach the child to deal with his or her anticipatory anxiety. Some children with NLD have not made the connection between the butterflies in their stomach and the fact that it is a signal that they are anxious. By making the connection parents not only help the child read his or her body signals but also begin to interpret the meanings these signal have. The child is then ready to struggle with the feeling and find ways to accommodate the situation.

Robert, 8 years old, was to begin a soccer program at the local park. Knowing his difficulties with new situations, his parents needed to take a proactive approach to anticipate the problems Robert might encounter. They first walked to the park with Robert several times, helping him identify landmarks on the way so that later he could orient himself through them. Once at the park, they helped him become familiar with the field, locating the goals, the sidelines, the centerline, and other essential markers. To compensate further for his confusion about left and right, they discussed his wearing a sweatband on his left wrist. They helped him practice putting on his shin guards and discussed with him the possibility that he might feel what he called "that jumpy feeling" in his stomach. They told him that meant that he was nervous and excited about doing something new, and he could use it as a signal to remember what they had practiced. In addition, the parents met with the coach before the first practice session to inform him of Robert's enthusiasm about playing but also to alert him to his difficulties with directionality and his need to receive verbal instructions to supplement any demonstration of physical activities. They also let the coach know that they did not expect him to turn Robert into a star player. These strategies were instrumental in making the experience a successful one for Robert.

Reinforcing Thinking about Part–Whole Relationships
When caregivers ask children with NLD to report an incident in which they have been involved, their narrative is disjointed, fragmented, and often unintelligible. It is difficult for the listener to get a sense of what occurred, even from the child's own perspective. The sequence in which events occurred is unclear, the child does not highlight significant elements, important details are left out, and the child's involvement is ob-

scure. Not only is the sense of the sequence missing in the child's recital, but also the relationship of the significant elements to other elements in the story is not clearly delineated. The foreground components are meshed with background components so that no gestalt appears. Part of the difficulty seems to be related to the child's inability to see the whole and relate the elements to each other.

The strategy parents can use to help correct for this difficulty is much like the one tutors use in teaching a child to outline an essay; we call it *weaving a narrative*. A good story has a number of identifiable elements: (1) a beginning, a middle, and an end, which describe the sequence in which the events in the story occurred; (2) a "protagonist" who is the hero or main focus of the story; (3) a theme or plot around which the elements are woven; (4) a specific time and setting in which the action occurred; and (5) a coherent account into which its elements are organized. To deal with the deficit in seeing part–whole relationships, the child must learn to tell a good story. One place where parents can begin with this task is by drawing the analogy between a story and a school essay. The parents should patiently ask about "the main point" of the story, just as the child was taught to identify the main point of an essay. This process could be reinforced by writing down what the child says, so as to provide a different channel for the integration of the material. Next parents can ask about the other events and, even though the child may not be able to give them sequentially, he or she should write them down to reorder at a later point. Finally, once they have gained a sufficient understanding of what occurred, the parents should reward the child with their approval for the effort put into the process of telling the story, praising the child for helping them "get" what had upset him or her. Other strategies involve roleplaying the scene of the occurrence with the child. With a young child, this can be done either directly or using dolls or hand puppets. The child may be able to enact behaviorally what he or she could not relate verbally.

Once the child learns to tell his or her story in a coherent fashion, the next task is to help him or her modify dysfunctional behaviors by *rewriting the narrative* of the problematic interactions. The child can then conceive of different outcomes than those to which he or she has become accustomed. Part of the child's inability to respond differently is due to the rigidity in the way he or she thinks about other's responses. To the child with an NLD there appears to be no other way to react. However, once the child has learned to perceive and comprehend clearly the problematic interactions, he or she can then be guided through a series of steps to change the plot of the narrative so that a different outcome takes place. The characters in the story can change from being all-powerful tormentors to insecure children who scapegoat to assert control over situations. The child with an NLD can then imagine a different response and outcome than what previously occurred.

Ten-year-old Matthew came home from school at least once a week with a jumbled set of complaints about kids being "mean" to him. The only clear communications his parents could get from him were statements such as "He keeps teasing me!", "He laughed at me!", "He chased me!", and "He hit me!" Clearly, he was having trouble with his peers. Neither he nor his parents had any idea as to why.

Matthew's parents and his therapist began to help him use an outline for his tales of woe, similar to the outlines he was learning to use in school to write stories. First, Matthew was asked to set the scene: where was he, who else was there, what were they doing before the painful part of the incident began? Next, his parents asked Matthew to recount the first thing the other child said or did, followed by Matthew's response: What did he say, how did he say it, how did he move? Next, how did the other child respond to him? and so forth. At first, he found it very difficult and frustrating to structure his story as requested. He insisted that the process was not helping him, and he could not see the long-term benefits. After several months of friendly coaching, he got the idea of setting the stage before describing what occurred. Knowing that his parents were interested in talking with him about these incidents also helped him to become more alert to the events as they took place. In the early months, when Matthew had no idea of how to describe the nonverbal aspects of the interaction, the therapist encouraged the parents to act out different tones of voice, facial expressions, or gestures. Matthew began to pick the ones that best matched the way the classmate had looked or sounded. Finally, Matthew's accounts began to approach a coherent narrative. The parents encouraged his efforts through their genuine interest. They found that by clearly restating his story, as they understood it, he could focus more on the essentials.

Even after the pattern was identified, Matthew could see no alternatives to his actions. The next challenge was to get Matthew to consider the possibility that there might be other ways to respond. He came up with and rejected the idea of telling the teacher, because it would bring about more teasing. Matthew's interest was captured, however, by an idea put forth by his therapist: the real problem was how to keep Tim from having so much power over Matthew. Tim was "making" Matthew chase him. How could Matthew take away that power? Matthew was able to be curious about how he could keep Tim from having that power. Although he had repeatedly rejected the idea of doing nothing as "wimpy," now he decided to experiment with choosing not to chase Tim. He came back from the next incident grinning. He had avoided chasing Tim. Meanwhile Tim, who expected the usual pattern, kept lying in wait for Matthew until he ended up being late for class. Matthew could see that by making an active de-

cision not to allow himself to be goaded into following Tim, he had rewritten the narrative. Later, Matthew would entertain the notion that he could similarly make an active choice to respond to name-calling by looking steadily at the other child but not being drawn into arguing defensively. Practicing this new behavior with his parents before trying it out with other kids helped him to use it in peer situations. Matthew was getting the idea that he could change the course of his stories about peer incidents by trying out alternative actions.

Enhancing Problem-Solving Capacities

Children with NLD have problems in flexibly applying what they learned in different contexts to new situations. The result is that they appear to butt their heads perseveratively against a wall when confronted with situations that they had not previously encountered or that are even slightly different from one they had previously negotiated successfully. They seem incapable of getting around the barriers they perceive to be in their way, even when a simple shift in strategies would lead to a resolution of the situation. What seems to happen is that once they seize upon a rule derived from a previous situation, they generalize from that rule and indiscriminately apply it to all situations that bear any similarly to the original one. The sources of their inflexibility are probably multiple; what is relevant here is their inability to problem solve. Discussions of problems are circular, and suggestions and alternatives proposed to the child are met with resistance or discouragement that they would not work. Children with NLD often feel a sense of hopelessness about their lives that leaves them completely unmotivated to try different approaches. It is as though they are convinced that people will generally be unresponsive to them, no matter how much effort they make, or that the world is simply not a friendly place that would welcome their attempt at being successful. Parents become disheartened by their failures to negotiate resolutions to situation. Helping these children develop patterns through which problems can be resolved is central to dealing with this issue.

One approach is to teach the child systematically about *negotiation*. This technique should be introduced around some fun activity that makes the process enjoyable. At times, some children can engage in strategy games that offer opportunities for negotiation. These games can become a model through which the child can learn to apply similar tactics to life situations. An important point to convey to the child is that negotiations can be structured so that they become "win/win" situations, rather than there having to be a winner and loser. Both sides can be seen to gain from a successful negotiation; one side need not humiliate the other by claiming victory. Some parents who have taught the technique to their child initially feel that they have created a monster. The child insists on applying the approach to every situation, no matter how inappropriate it may be from the parent's point of view. Parents should not despair; they have simply encountered another aspect of the child's deficit—the inability to contextualize responses—with which we will deal in the next section. The skills a child acquires when he or she learns to negotiate can be extended to broader problem-solving strategies that enlarge the child's repertoire of coping mechanisms.

Kevin was a 12½-year-old youngster whom his classmates teased mercilessly. They found endless ways to torment him: They held the gym door closed so he could not get in, they took his hat and tossed it around so that he could not get it back, they falsely accused him of cruelty to pets, and so on. Kevin invariably responded with screaming protests, hoping teachers would hear and come to his rescue—which, at times, they did. However, Kevin had also taken to screaming out in the middle of class when kids took his pencils, snatched his books, or even simply laughed in his face. The teachers did not appreciate the ensuing disruptions. They asked Kevin to come talk to them privately at the end of class so that they could correct the situation. In spite of numerous conversations with teachers about finding alternative ways of dealing with these occurrences, Kevin persisted in using the same pattern. He, in turn, was convinced that the teachers were against him and were unwilling to protect him or side with him. The parents reported similar responses from Kevin around sharing the television with his sister, choosing activities on family vacations, or involving himself in any task that required his cooperation to attain a goal. His parents felt that he insisted on having his way, rigidly sticking to old patterns and not compromising.

What became clear during these discussions is that Kevin's rigid thinking style did not permit him to see that there are different ways of dealing with situations and that unless he could modify his approach, he would end up frustrated. The task for these parents was to offer several alternative ways of solving the problem from which he could choose. Although there would be times when he would be unable to make a shift, the fact remained that the notion that there is more than one way to manage a problem situation would be central to his learning new patterns. An opening occurred when Kevin reported an incident to his tutor that occurred in one of the science labs when another child provoked him; Kevin responded by throwing a book at the boy. The teacher got furious and marched him to the principal's office to be severely reprimanded. Kevin was furious; he felt unfairly created, especially because nothing was done to the boy who had instigated the disturbance.

In trying to debrief him around this incident, Kevin's tutor patiently listened to what had happened. She had been through similar incidents many times and knew that unless she listened to his side of it, she would get nowhere with helping him with his responses. She had also talked to the teacher and heard the con-

cerns the teacher had about the possible disastrous effects of a book flying across a room containing lab equipment and lit Bunsen burners on top of counters. The teacher feared for the safety of the class and the school.

Rather than address Kevin's indignation, the tutor talked with him about his inability to appreciate the fear he had induced in the teacher, and the concern the teacher felt for the safety of the children in the class. She asked if he noticed her expression as being more than just anger at him for what he had done. Slowly it dawned on Kevin that what he had done was dangerous—it had never occurred to him that his action would frighten the teacher. He felt guilty and contrite that he had acted so impulsively and expressed a desire to apologize to the teacher for his thoughtless behavior. The tutor then rehearsed with Kevin a strategy through which he could negotiate with the teacher as to how further incidents should be handled. The tutor knew that he was a participant in a model United Nations session being held at school to discuss how nations negotiate with each other. She drew a parallel between him, the teacher, and other children as each representing different countries. Kevin, who was excellent in geography (not because he could visually locate regions on the map but because of his astonishing memory for facts) and had recently won a geography contest, loved the idea. At first he playfully imagined himself using nuclear weapons to wipe out "the enemy." Then he was able to find more peaceful approaches to problem solving. Together they drew up a scenario in which he would have a "summit meeting" with his teacher to discuss his plight. The pride with which Kevin was able to engage in this process led the parents to take up the idea and generalize the practice to other situations.

SOCIAL COGNITION IMPAIRMENTS

As we have seen, three major areas require attention in this domain: reciprocal social interaction, social communication, and affective communication. I suggest interventions for each by discussing: teaching social skills, using verbal mediation, and dealing with feelings.

Teaching Social Skills
We spoke earlier of the value of teaching children with NLD strategies to understand nonverbal communications. However, social interactions involve more that just the ability to read or understand social cues. Social skills must be taught in conjunction with an understanding of mindsharing functions. A beginning can be made by discussing with the child, in simple terms, theory of mind modes of thinking. The child could be asked if she understands what made her respond in a particular way to a situation. She is then invited to be curious about the motives behind her actions and those of others. The concept of having a motive for a response

underlies such a discussion. If asked in a way that does not elicit a defensive reaction, the child can begin to think psychologically about him- or herself and others.

Such discussions set the stage for speculation about why people act the way they do. The therapist engages the child in a game by picking neutral topics and asking questions such as, "Why do you think that your dad bought the car he did rather than another?" "Why do you think your mom stays on her cell phone so much?" "What makes you want to watch so much TV?" The child is encouraged to use his or her imagination to guess at motives. Because research supports the view that such discussions enhance the capacity for theory of mind functioning it is advisable to scaffold the child's thinking with them and open a repertoire of possible reasons for other's responses.

The move to the broader issue of mindsharing can occur through an extension of these discussions into the realm of empathy. Such interventions lay the foundation for teaching the pragmatics of social communication through which social skills are integrated.

A "pragmatics" dimension parallels the pragmatics in verbal language usage that must also be learned. We might distinguish this area by identifying it as that of *social functioning, in* contrast to the area of *social interactions.* Social skills are the competencies required to become assimilated into a social milieu. The inability to read or understand social cues leads the child to appear inept in social situations. Unable to function smoothly, the child withdraws, becomes socially isolated, or acts in a manner that appears perplexing to peers. In contrast, the elements in successful social functioning involve a variety of qualities that our culture values; for example, those of appearing "polite," "courteous," "considerate" or "thoughtful." For the child with an NLD, these qualities seem as difficult to acquire as calculus is for a first grader. Yet that does not mean that this area should be written off. As mentioned, simply pointing out the correct behavior is not helpful to the child. Instead, the effective strategy for teaching some of these qualities is *systematic modeling and identification.* The process of socialization often occurs silently as the child observes adults' behaviors and assimilates what is proper and what is not. For children with NLD this process must not only be made explicit but it must also be rehearsed, reinforced, and rewarded until the behaviors become habitual. The child may never achieve the kind of naturalness of other children without this problem, but he or she can achieve a good approximation.

Ten-year-old Tiffany's family had dinner with her grandparents every month. Although the grandparents cared very much about the three children, they were becoming estranged from Tiffany because they felt she was insolent and rude.

They faulted their daughter-in-law for not raising her properly. When the grandparents made an effort to talk to Tiffany at the table, she looked bored, made no eye contact, did not respond the their questions, and gave little indication of even listening to what they were saying. When she did talk to them, she usually looked at her plate, her voice seemed expressionless, and what she said was difficult to follow. Tiffany's experience of these visits was that her grandparents were nagging her.

As her parents discussed this situation with the therapist, they realized that the poor eye contact and lack of appropriate expressiveness were symptoms of her recently identified NLD. They had come to overlook these traits, attributing them to Tiffany's personality. They knew that she was listening because she retained information and later gave evidence that she was quite aware of what transpired. After alerting the grandparents to Tiffany's problems, they went about actively teaching her some of the social skills she needed in order to act appropriately in social settings. They instructed her to look at people's eyes periodically while speaking to them or when spoken to, even though that felt uncomfortable to her. At first her efforts seemed mechanical and unnatural, but after a time, she developed a style that fit her overall demeanor, eventually finding pleasure in her grandparents' positive responses to her. However, one of her parents often had to sit next to her to gently remind and signal her as to what she needed to do. The parents who had a positive relationship with her became responsible for extending the teaching to other areas, facilitating for Tiffany her interactions with others.

Using Verbal Mediation

In the prior section I introduced the concept of verbal mediation as an important tool to help children compensate for their nonverbal deficits. I find it necessary to elaborate on this concept so as to help parents avoid feeling defeated when they begin using this approach and find themselves not being successful, even after repeated efforts. Although the idea of using an alternative channel of communication—one in which the children appear to be quite fluent—seems commonsensical, in reality the process through which these children learn is much more complex. We can draw an analogy with the difficulties that children who make letter reversals have when they begin writing. At first, it seems easy to think that by simply pointing out the error to the child, he or she will be able to correct it. However, the fact that the child's neurological immaturity does not permit him or her to see the letter correctly may escape the inexperienced adult. A parent might simply think that the child was inattentive. In reality, the child does not see the letter as others see it. Simply pointing out the correct form of the letter does not lead the child to learn the proper configuration.

This phenomenon of nonrecognition of letters is quite similar to the one we encounter in children with NLD. If they do not perceive as others do, it is not because they are inattentive or unmotivated but rather because their brains process that kind of information differently. Consequently, pointing out visual cues verbally does not necessarily lead the child to perceive those cues as others do. The child is made aware that something is wrong but cannot at first fathom what it is. Verbal explanations, given with empathy and understanding rather than with criticism, will begin to help the child narrow the range of stimuli to which to attend and process. The child can learn to vocalize, rehearsing verbally, what he or she has been taught so as to reinforce the procedure. What often occurs is that the child begins to notice the visual cues but does not use the information attached to those cues in an integrated fashion. By *pairing the verbal explanation with the nonverbal activity*, the child will learn to associate the words with the cue. For example, simply telling a child to look directly at a person when talking is insufficient. Demonstration of what the child must do should accompany the explanation given. At first, the child will look the person in the eyes, but the stare is penetrating and expressionless. Further explanations and demonstrations can make the child aware of the content of the communication and the appropriate feeling that should accompany this content. Eventually, it is possible that the meanings we attach to these modes of expression will also be learned, so that the verbal explanations given the child will lead to a deeper understanding and a better integration of those signals.

John, age 10, had another boy over to play. He was having a wonderful time making up rhymes with the other boy's name. John's mother could see that the other boy was becoming progressively more uncomfortable. Because she did not want to embarrass her son by chastising him in front of his friend, she resorted to signaling him to stop the behavior by raising her eyebrows or shaking her head. However, these signals went unheeded. She became increasingly distressed by what she experienced as John ignoring her or defying her by continuing to tease his friend. She thought she was escalating her communication by raising her finger, indicating clearly (to her, that is) that he should stop—all to no avail. Now she got angry. Raising her voice, she told John that because he was being rude, had to stop playing with his friend and instead go to his room and think about his poor behavior. Bewildered by his mother's response, he cried out that she was being mean for no reason. By this time the situation had deteriorated to the point that the friend asked to go home. The mother felt defeated: once again, her son had ruined a chance to develop a friendship.

As the therapist reviewed the incident with John and his mother, John maintained that his friend was having fun and enjoyed the teasing, "He was smiling,

Mom. He must have liked it!" Obviously, John had misread his friend's facial expression, misinterpreting the grimace of discomfort for a grin. From his perspective, Mother's anger was unexpected; he felt he had no warning. For her part, Mother did not realize that her attempts to spare him embarrassment through her nonverbal signals were totally lost on him. She learned that nonverbal signals must be accompanied by clear verbal comments if John is to understand her communications.

Dealing with Feelings

The area of feelings requires special attention. Frequently, children with NLD have particular difficulties in identifying and expressing their feelings. Many of these children find it hard to read other's feelings, to express their own feelings, or to understand the common meanings attached to some feelings. At times, the problems take the form of understanding or expressing feelings only when these reach a significant level of intensity. It is as though their feeling "volume knobs" are either turned down or fully on, so that they either have little or no awareness of subtle feelings states or attend to intense feelings. At times, the children have problems regulating their feelings; they may have serious outbursts or cannot calm down once they become excited. Consequently, there are two distinct areas in which parents can assist these children with their feelings: helping them learn to identify feeling states in themselves and others, and instructing them in ways to regulate their frustrations and affect states.

The display of feelings is a highly culture-bound activity, guided by rules children learn at an early age. These display rules are also largely gender determined; what is proper for a girl to express may not be proper for a boy, and vice versa. However, before a child can learn display rules, he or she must first be able to experience and identify the feelings. Later, through attunement to others, the child can learn to read how others feel. The task for children with NLD is that of first being able to identify their own feelings; they can then develop the capacity to identify others' feelings. This task is not just a cognitive one, for it involves the capacity to process the meaning associated with emotions generally.

I spoke earlier of the child who had difficulty identifying whether or not her friend was displaying a genuine smile. The cognitive component of the task involves simply recognizing the facial features that are indicative of a smile. Beyond that is the meaning associated with that display and the message the display conveys to the recipient of the smile. This latter task involves a capacity to attune to the other person's feeling state, resonate with that state, recognize the feeling in oneself, and translate it as a friendly, receptive gesture. Some children with NLD may be able to perform the cognitive component of the task but not have a clue as to how to process the signal. Others may be able to process the signal but not be able to give expression to the affective message they wish to convey. Understanding the specific nature of the child's problem in this area is therefore critical to the introduction of an intervention.

Generally, I approach parents by asking that they test whether the child appears to display a range of feelings. They can ask themselves whether they notice their child appropriately displaying feelings of joy, sadness, anger, or fear, or whether the child's responses are undifferentiated and indistinguishable from one another. If they establish that the child's responses are difficult to differentiate, then we can move on to distinguishing whether the child has difficulty with reception, expression, or processing elements. The strategy is to ask the child to *stop and listen* to him- or herself. It may sound artificial at first to require a child to stop in the middle of a social transaction and listen to his or her feelings. However, once the initial embarrassment is overcome, the technique becomes automatic and gets smoothly integrated into the repertoire of day-to-day transactions. Eventually the child incorporates the strategy into his or her life.

The task for children who appear not to experience any feelings is much more difficult than it is for those children who give indications of the presence of feelings but have communication impairments. Parents of children who have a severe NLD struggle to teach them about feelings. Some of them have done so through children's books, movies, music, or dance. The medium chosen is usually one the child enjoys. At first, a child with a good memory learns to identify feelings in others by rote. Once that occurs, the parents identify similar feelings within the child. It is a moving experience to hear a parent report his or her success in getting a child to say "I am sad!" or "I feel happy!" in an appropriate context.

Activities such as art therapy, dance or movement therapy, and theater can be very useful in helping these children learn to express or recognize feelings. We also find that occupational therapy, especially if instituted at an early age, can be especially beneficial for children's coordination or other motor problems, thereby helping to build self-esteem and also loosen their capacity to experience their affect states.

The issue of the regulation of feelings in children with NLD is one that often looms large in parents' mind. They often refer to what we have come to identify as "affective meltdowns." Children dissolve in tears, have tantrums that last for prolonged periods, lash out impulsively and unexpectedly at siblings or adults, and seem generally unable to contain their frustrations. What seems characteristic of these children is that these outbursts are not always predictable, and parents are often unprepared for their appearance. This unpredictability makes it almost impossible to anticipate their emergence or to institute measures to prevent their occurrence. In addition, the problem of dealing with these explosions is complicated by the child's inability or unwillingness to process what happened, once the eruption has subsided.

The counterpart of this phenomenon is the children's response to other people's feelings. Parents report that their child will appear either not to pay attention to their requests unless the volume of their voices is raised to the level of a scream, or they will be accused of screaming when they speak in their usual tone of voice. In other words, the children's perception of how others regulate their own feelings appears to be distorted.

In discussing these issues with parents, therapists must first try to determine whether the failures in regulation might be attributable to depression, ADHD, or an overload of anxiety. If any of these conditions coexist with the NLD, it is possible that a regimen of medication will alleviate some of the problems. However, if the child does not have these conditions or if the medications are ineffective in containing the outbursts, then the parents will need professional help in learning how to function as regulators for the child.

It is probably correct to say that there are no *good* ways for parents to contain a child's emotional storms, there are only responses that are less destructive than others. When parents try to control the child who is out of control, verbal means are least effective. Generally, the child is too upset to hear what is said, much less benefit from the words. Soothing words may be effective if the child can discriminate between different vocal intonations, but if he or she cannot, then the balm does not heal the wound or minimize the pain. Physically restraining a child, when done improperly, can be hazardous, because it creates a pattern in which the child experiences the adult as more powerful but not necessarily as providing safety or empathy. Some children can experience this type of restraint as abusive. However, when a child is in the midst of a meltdown, he or she must be protected from doing harm to self or others. The child may need to be physically removed from the situation and isolated in a protective environment. Isolating the child has its own limitations, in that it distances the child from those who should be available as nurturing selfobjects. Remaining in the presence of the child may attenuate that aspect.

Parents often find themselves running out of options and lapsing into helplessness under these conditions. The child, seeing that the adults are helpless, becomes even more anxious and escalates to higher levels of despair. It is that helplessness that parents must avoid if the family is not to be robbed of all sense of rationality. The parents must remain sufficiently calm to weather the storm and be available to put back the pieces of their disintegrated child again.

The strategy in helping a child become more regulated is to institute some form of *time-outs*. The time-outs we recommend are not meant to be a *consequence for the child's behavior but rather a time to "chill out,"* until calm is restored. The time-out technique is widely used, though parents often find it difficult to implement. In part, this difficulty arises because the definition of what constitutes a time-out may be unreasonable; in part, because absolute consistency in implementation is essential to its success—something that parents often find difficult to employ. The time to use this technique is not when the child is in the midst of a meltdown; rather, it should be introduced when the child is beginning to get worked up but is still sufficiently calm to be able to benefit. At its first introduction, the child is asked to stop, pay attention to what is being said, and sit quietly for 10–15 seconds. For a child who has difficulty with self-control, sitting quietly is a monumental task. Parents must be sensitive enough to request only what they are certain will succeed. They will be able to build upon success, not upon the child's failure to use the technique. The lesson the child learns is that he or she can indeed contain the feelings for a brief period. As the child demonstrates success in controlling outbursts, parents can reinforce the desired behavior by acknowledging the child's efforts and praising the child's growing ability to control him- or herself. Parents are then challenged to take on bigger incidents. However, the technique should only be used if there is some assurance of success; otherwise a negative pattern sets in and both parents and child will feel discouraged and defeated.

Gary, a 10½-year-old boy with a severe NLD, was an only child given to terrible tantrums. Most often he would fall apart at home, but the tantrums would also occur in extended family situations, in public places, and at school. The family felt controlled by their child because they could not face the embarrassment he would cause them whenever they went out of the house. Added to their humiliation was the criticism that teachers and close family member directed at them, attributing Jason "misbehaviors" to the parents' indulgence of him. They could barely reveal to the therapist that in their efforts to control the boy, they felt they were abusive to him. Whenever they tried to intervene in his tantrums, he would become assaultive. An escalating cycle would evolve in which he would become out of control, pursuing his mother around the house, challenging her to control him. When the father was present, he would physically remove the boy and lock him in his room. However, Jason would start throwing everything on which he could lay his hands out the window and threaten to jump out himself.

Whereas Gary's behavior appeared to be intentional and manipulative, this was only partly true. Behind the theatrics was a boy who truly feared his own impulsivity and rage. Jason was placed on an antidepressant that significantly

diminished the tantrums. The parents were amazed at the transformation pro-
duced by the medication. They became convinced that the behavior was more
neurologically driven than the product of their mismanagement. However, as
undesirable side effects appeared, they had to discontinue the medication. They
were then able to mobilize themselves to obtain counseling for the boy and to
display less reactive behavior to his eruptions. At that point it became possible to
introduce time-outs to Gary, to begin to help him acquire some of the internal
controls he did not have.

INTRAPERSONAL CONSTRAINTS

The goal of the interventions in this domain is three-fold: (1) to engage in
activities that enhance the child's capacity for mindsharing, (2) to help the
child sustain self-cohesion, and (3) to encourage the development of a coherent self-narrative. Because there is much overlap in the interventions in
this and the previous domains, some of the interventions discussed previously are applicable to this goal.

Debriefing the Child to Encourage Compensations

The interventions I have discussed so far place the parents in positions in
which they are complementing the child's deficits. However, at the same
time, it is important that they encourage the child to be less reliant on
these complementary functions, i.e., external sources of support, by learning ways to compensate for his or her own deficits. Each child possesses
strengths that come into service when this process begins. However, it is
often difficult to predict the specific ways in which a child will use these
strengths for purposes of compensation. Through debriefing the child
about incidents, both positive and negative, he or she is encouraged to
process dimensions and aspects of social interactions of which he or she
was previously unaware. The child thereby learns much through the debriefing.

Many parents find that it takes a great deal of effort to engage a child in
the aftermath of an outburst. The child is either unresponsive or
adamantly opposed to any discussion. Under these circumstances it is important to remember that the child probably thinks the parents intend to
punish or reprimand him or her for what occurred. Furthermore, children's awareness of their deficits leads them to experience facing these issues as blows to their self-esteem. It is humiliating to them to realize that
there are interferences in their capacities to deal with complex events that
are beyond their control. The parent should approach the matter sensi-
tively while the child's resistances to discussing the outburst are at an ebb.
If possible, a dispassionate problem-solving attitude would help establish

a working relationship so that the child feels that the parents are his or her allies. The debriefing also serves the purpose of helping the parents work through and manage their own frustrations at the problems the child has created.

An important aspect of these debriefings is that they provide the means through which parents help the child learn from the troublesome incidents. First, parents must understand that the fact that they have gone over a series of incidents many times does not necessarily mean that the child will avoid such incidents in the future. The manner in which children with NLD learn from life events is unlike that of other children. Even if the child is helped to deal with the feelings that result from the episode, the conceptual task of drawing a set of rules of conduct that will guide future behaviors remains complex. The child may be able to indicate that he or she has abstracted a rule but still be mystified as to when the rule should be applied. Unable to see the bigger picture, the child may rigidly take an element from a previous discussion with the parents, misapply it to a context that appears appropriate to him or her, only to experience a consequence that is no better than prior instances. The child may then bitterly complain that he or she did indeed do what was agreed to in the discussions. Because none of the strategies I am offering can be applied singly or piecemeal, parents must resort to complementing the child's deficits by bringing in other aspects the child misses. The important point to remember is to help the child draw a simple lesson from what occurred and to build on what the child has learned from past instances of similar occurrences. *Contextualizing the child's role* by pointing to elements of the situation the child has overlooked may help the child enhance his or her own ability to apply a rule appropriately. Having the child learn to take responsibility for his or her contribution can be a major achievement toward the goal of modifying behavior. Debriefing the child after he or she has successfully handled all or part of a problematic situation and verbalizing what actions the child took helps to solidify the gains as well as bolster the child's self-esteem.

Larry refused to get ready for bed by himself, saying he was scared. His parents felt it was ridiculous for an 8-year-old to be afraid of being upstairs by himself, and they attributed his stalling to manipulation and disobedience. He was supposed to start getting ready for bed by 8:00: take a shower, put his dirty clothes in the hamper, brush his teeth, and get in bed by 8:30. Things never went smoothly. In a detailed discussion with the therapist of the steps Larry had to take, his parents figured out some of the major pitfalls in their plan for him. They realized that Robert was confused about how to regulate the water temperature in the shower. He could never remember which was the hot and which the cold faucet. He could not keep in mind which direction to turn the faucet to get more or less water flowing. His father developed a strategy to help him through the process. First, they marked the hot water faucet with red nail polish. Then Larry learned to say "lefty loosey, righty tighty." This jingle also helped remind him that screwing and unscrewing bottles was similar to turning on and off faucet handles. Step by step, Larry learned to master what for him was the intricate task of running his own shower, compensating for his perceptual deficits by using his good rote memory. What was a simple matter for other family members required detailed instruction for Larry. This type of debriefing after encountering a problem became a pattern between the parents and Larry. They learned that rather than get upset and critical of him, they needed to go over the crises to discover the sources of the difficulties. The family's interactions became much more pleasant subsequently.

Managing the Anxiety Generated by NLD

It is often impossible to appreciate the level of the child's anxiety, given the child's outward, masked appearance. In our experience, most children with NLD live with chronic fears that pervade their lives. They take those feelings for granted, not realizing that most people do not feel the same way. The children often overtly display their fears in circumstances that appear reasonable to parents. A grandparent's illness or death, an unexpected traumatic separation, a change in housing arrangements may suddenly bring on overt signs of severe anxiety. However, less overt may be the severe night fears, apprehension about thunder or storms, fears that a parent will die, the somatic complaints, or the nightmares. It is easy for a child to associate an emerging anxiety state with an external triggering event. However, my observations have led me to conclude that the triggering circumstances provide the child with a rationale for the overt expression of feelings that were there to begin with. It is as though the child has been given an opportunity to express the mysterious and unexplainable feelings that have accompanied him or her for years. The child will then tenaciously cling to the triggering event as the explanatory factor justifying the presence of the fears. The events give a concrete focus around which the child can organize the vague and chaotic feelings with which she or he is chronically buffeted.

Adults will then often respond by trying the help the child work through the presumed cause but find that no amount of reassurance or discussion is effective. For children with NLD, the world is a dangerous place—as they have repeatedly found from their experiences. From early childhood, their efforts at negotiating circumstances around them have led to failures or disastrous outcomes. Their perceptions are that their parents did not respond in predictable ways, and their judgments were never accurate enough for the children to feel assured that undesirable consequences would not follow. It is as though the children became conditioned to associating *failure* with *relationships*. Consequently, they substituted vigilance and wariness for spontaneity and lightheartedness.

This understanding of the sources of the child's anxiety allows an appreciation of what it would take to calm the child's fears. Fundamentally, what appear to motivate this pervasive anxiety are the repeated experiences of failure to engage in favorable interactions with others. The child lives with a conviction that the world is an unfriendly or even dangerous place. To undo this conviction, the parents must work at replacing it with *a view of the world as, on the whole, a benevolent and predictable place*. The message to the child is that it is possible to discriminate between those who can be trusted and those who cannot. The message is also that by using areas of strength, the child can find successes and satisfactions that are growth producing.

At times, medication might diminish the extent of the anxiety. The relief the medication provides can permit the child to use more cognitive strategies for dealing with the remaining anxiety. It is helpful for a child to learn to label bodily cues as related to anxiety states. Recognition of the somatic equivalents can then alert the child to situations that magnify the anxiety and signal that it is time to use the strategies he or she has learned for dealing with that situation. Eventually an antidote to the anxiety is found in the growing confidence a child feels in negotiating the world successfully. Through the efforts of parents who, at first, provide complementary functions for the child, and who then enhance the child's compensatory strategies as he or she matures, the child can eventually find the self-assurance that will pull him or her through the difficulties that lie ahead.

Dennis is an 11½-year-old who has been in once-a-week individual therapy for 2 years. His parents became quite knowledgeable about his problems and were very adept at developing strategies to avoid serious disruptions. One day they came to his session with him to discuss some school issues. In the course of the session the mother noted that she was anxious about turning in a school form that would give permission for Dennis to go on an out-of-town trip with members of his class. They had discussed it together, but she felt unresolved as to whether it was best for him to go. Dennis immediately protested that he really very much wanted to be part of this trip. As she talked about the pros and cons of going, his mother, who is very attuned to his problems, stated that part of the trip involved going to an amusement park. He had never been to one, and she feared that it would be totally disorienting, overstimulating, and ultimately upsetting to him. She wanted at least to rehearse how he would manage such an environment in order to anticipate any problems. She hoped that he could learn to avoid situations he could not handle. Dennis immediately started complaining that she must not want him to go. When the mother responded that she wanted him to be able to go and enjoy himself, he retorted that she then must want him to decide not to go! His anxiety kept escalating, his voice got louder, and he gestured wildly, writhing in his chair. It became evident to the therapist that Dennis had now displaced the anxiety about the trip onto the fear that he would not be able to go. The therapist felt that it would be impossible to process the anxiety associated with the trip until Dennis was reassured that he would be going, and only then would he be able sit still enough to think about what he would face when he got there. The therapist interpreted his understanding to the parents, who agreed and then told Dennis they would allow him to go. Dennis insisted that they sign the form right then and there, which they did. Even then, Dennis was too anxious and overstimulated to be able to listen, and the rehearsal of what he should anticipate had to be postponed to another session. In this example, Dennis's anticipatory anxiety was itself a barrier to processing the events he was to face later. Only after some days had passed and he had become used to the idea that he would indeed be going on the trip were his parents able to process with him what he was to face on the trip.

Encouraging the Development of a Sense of Humor

In spite of their excellent verbal skills, children with NLD have difficulties understanding humor. They take humorous remarks concretely and cannot appreciate the lightness that comes from levity or joking. Teasing is interpreted as aggression rather than as tenderness or a reaching out for closeness. Yet humor is a remarkable facilitator of human interaction. It can serve as a vehicle to bring to a child's attention mannerisms that interfere with communication; it can help overcome the narcissistic injury a child might feel from learning about a deficit, or it can convey feelings that a child might otherwise miss. We ordinarily do not think of humor as something that is deliberately taught to a child. However, because children with NLD do not seem to have that natural capacity, a studied approach to instructing them in the art of wit is indicated. The lesson the child learns is that there is *a place for joy and fun in this world.*

When Eric's parents met with their child's therapist, they reported a novel development. The child had developed a quirky sense of humor that delighted them and his teachers at school. Situations that were previously fraught with anger or anxiety seemed not to affect him as intensely. He could joke about them, even making fun of some of his idiosyncrasies. Adults and peers were responding to him much more positively than they had done previously. The parents were curious as to how the therapist had accomplished this feat.

Eager to help the parents with a new strategy, the therapist described how he had begun by making some outlandish remark related to the activities in which they would engage. Eric, 12 years old, was at first totally bewildered by the therapist's remarks. The therapist would point out that Eric had not noticed the therapist's smile that indicated he was joking. After many repetitions of this interaction, Eric began to peer into the therapist's face to decode an expression that indicated a smile. Eventually, he responded with funny comments of his own, and both would laugh. The enjoyment they both derived from these exchanges were indicative of the bond that existed between them. Eric felt comfortable, accepted, and strengthened. His first attempts at humor in other settings were not successful. As he talked about them, it was evident that what was funny to him was not to others. Fortunately, others began to appreciate his efforts and joined him in laughter. His parents were encouraged to use that approach to defuse tense situations. Eric's father, who may have had a problem similar to his son, himself had a distinctive sense of humor that fit in with his son's. He felt that they could enjoy each other's sense of the comical, bonding together around their common wit.

"What Is in Store for My Child?"

Parents often raise concerns for their child's future, wanting to know whether the condition will handicap him or her permanently. Except in cases of extreme deficits, the answers to these questions should be framed in the most optimistic light. Children's capacities for adaptation, compensation, and maturation must be emphasized. The younger the child at the point of diagnosis and the more aggressive the interventions, the more optimistic the outcome. We have seen many children who at a young age appeared so vulnerable or disadvantaged by their deficits that there seemed little hope that they could become well-functioning adults. Although systematic follow-up research remains to be done in this area, our clinical experience leads us to take a hopeful attitude.

There appear to be nodal points in the course of maturation that offer opportunities for forward leaps to occur. It is unclear whether these leaps occur because of neurological maturation or because a greater integration occurs when the child attains the stage of formal operational thought, or for some other reason. One nodal point appears at around age 17, when the adolescent is a junior in high school. At that point the motivation to achieve academically drives some adolescents forward, and successes bring greater self-confidence and a different perspective on social relationships. For others, a similar point is reached in the sophomore or junior year in college. A sudden flowering of the personality appears to occur. The awkwardness diminishes, the young adult becomes more self-directed toward a goal, a career choice is made, and all the elements of the personality appear to join together to make for personal success. Others are really late bloomers; these are children whose parents truly despair that they will ever make it. Yet at around the age of 27 or 28, a transformation occurs. New possibilities open up for the young adult. If the parents have not totally given up and if they have not alienated the young man or woman by taking a "tough-love" approach, he or she may become open to receiving support to find his or her way to a constructive path. What is paramount is that the parents make every effort to maintain a positive relationship with their child. No matter how alienating the child's behavior may be, if the bond is maintained, hope is kept alive and the child will eventually respond. That is the message we try to convey to the parents of these children.

14

Conclusion
The Challenges Ahead

As often happens in science, an early discovery or set of observations raises high hopes that an answer may be found to a complex problem. A conjecture is put forth that crystallizes the findings into a hypothesis. Attempts at confirmation of the hypothesis are pursued zealously. However, researchers soon encounter unexplained anomalies. As they try to fit the hypothesis into a larger theory, inconsistencies emerge. What at first appeared simple and straightforward is now understood to be highly complex. As the initial hypothesis acquires disciples, who at times have institutional support for their position, it also acquires unwarranted devotion and is seldom set aside completely. The hypothesis may even be taken as fact. In time, the scientific community sorts out the wheat from the chaff, and researchers modify their hypotheses. What emerges, while bearing some resemblance to the original hypothesis, is quite different. The cycle that began with the discovery may be repeated as paradigm shifts disrupt scientists' most carefully laid plans. Such is the story of NLD.

We may compare our understanding of NLD and of brain function at this time to the understanding we had of the universe during medieval times. The Ptolemaic view, with its Earth-centered perspective, required a complex set of epicycles to explain the motion of the planets. The system accounted for all of the astronomical observations of that day but required the planets, as spheres, to be attached to spherical circles, which themselves were attached to circles around which they orbited. The shift in perspective that came with the Copernican view put the sun at the center of the universe, with the Earth as no more than one of its satellites. Once that shift was made, much of the complexity of the old system fell away and an elegant solution was found. Now, in spite of the great advances made in the neurosciences, we still lack a unified view of brain function. We have piecemeal explanations but no coherent overarching scheme. Until that happens, the puzzle of NLD, and of other disorders, may remain unsolved.

This work has focused on the factors that contribute to the social features of NLD. Given the multiplicity of brain functions that contribute to sociability, we faced the challenge of finding a common denominator that would constitute a primary core deficit for all phenotypes. Second, as we considered the contributions of specific deficits—their number, types, and severity—we saw that each contributes to qualitative differences that make the separate behavioral expressions distinct from one another. The cumulative effects of several dysfunctions necessarily lead to different forms of expression. This diversity suggested that a set of subtypes, around which to organize the symptoms, would provide a partial solution to the problem.

The constellation of symptoms originally identified by Johnson and Myklebust has endured as the core set of social impairments that characterize this group of children. The initial hypothesis conjectured that a right hemisphere dysfunction was the cause of the disorder. Rourke proposed his white matter hypothesis to explain the phenomena, and some neurologists found support for right hemisphere dysfunction in patients with brain lesions and hypothesized that the social features were directly associated with the neuropsychological deficits. Denckla, Pennington, and Voeller made a convincing case for the dissociability of spatial cognition from social cognition. This position laid the foundation for the exploration of the neurobiology of sociability as distinct from the neuropsychological deficits associated with NLD.

My contribution in this area of research has been to enlarge the dialogue by suggesting that a comprehensive understanding of any child must include not only the neurobiological factors that contribute to the child's behavior, but also the social and intrapersonal factors. I proposed a developmental viewpoint that specifies the way in which three sets of factors organize the child's experience: the neuropsychological, the social, and the intrapersonal. Limiting the causes of the children's social–emotional problems to deficits in brain function appears to me to be too restrictive a criterion. It neglects the role that processing social information contributes, and it neglects to consider the fact that children are agents of their own behaviors and that they are motivated by inner factors, such as their emotions, the meanings they attach to their experiences, the relationships they have with others, and the coherence of their view of reality.

Pennington's proposal that the problems in social cognition belong within the autistic spectrum raises serious difficulties. The social–emotional problems of children with NLD are different from those children with Asperger's disorder and very different from those of children with autism. The suggestion that we create a new category of disorders to be labeled *SELD* (social–emotional learning disability [or disorder]) has some merits but several problems. One of the merits is that it would dovetail with recent work on the neurobiology of sociality. If these explorations turn out to provide a sound basis for the understanding of social behavior, then the label would have some meaning. It would provide a unitary foundation for all dysfunctions. One problem with the label is that of delineating the inclusion and exclusion criteria for the definition of the disorder. Given the heterogeneity of the symptoms of NLD, a dimensional approach, which would define a spectrum of symptoms, would only compound our difficulties. Such an approach would be so inclusive as to make the label difficult to apply.

A FULL RESEARCH AGENDA AWAITS INVESTIGATORS. FIRST, several problems require our attention regarding the theories of NLD. Although we have data that support the existence of a condition that investigators call a *nonverbal learning disability*, much debate exists as to the definition of this construct. Does the term refer to a categorical entity with an identifiable etiology? If such a syndrome exists, does it lie within a spectrum of conditions with loosely demarcated borders? Does it refer to a syndrome with identifiable subtypes? Do the symptoms represent a set of disconnected signs that do not reflect an underlying syndrome? These questions go to the heart of what researchers call *construct validity*. A construct has validity if it satisfies two sets of conditions: internal validity and external validity. Szatmari (1992) explained:

> A diagnostic category should have internal validity, that is, it should be possible to measure, or operationalize the category in the first place, and use measures such as inter-rater and test–retest reliability, internal consistency, and convergent and discriminant validity. Moreover, a disorder should have external validity, that is, it should differ from related disorders on attributes other than the behavioral descriptors by which the disorder was originally defined. The external parameters include associated (i.e., nondiagnostic) behaviors;

possible markers of etiology; clinical course or outcome; and finally, response to treatment or treatment needs. (p. 584)

Given that there are now competing theories that explain the children's symptoms, neither the external nor the internal validity of the NLD construct has been established clearly. Validating the construct requires the development of techniques to measure social competence in children (Voeller, 1994). We encounter a bewildering array of nomenclatures in the literature. The names given to the condition appear to apply to a set of symptoms that have some commonalities. Whether any of these commonalities satisfies the criteria of construct validity is questionable. The establishment of the validity of the construct remains a work in progress whose completion will occur when researchers uncover a specific set of etiological determinants.

Second, the establishment of a construct should be followed by demographic studies to determine the prevalence rates and sex ratios of the disorder in the school-age population. Without such rates, it would be difficult to advocate for support and interventions for those children.

Third, the three perspectives—the neurobehavioral, the social, and the intrapersonal—generate questions that are fruitful to pursue. Study of the neurobehavioral domain raises questions: Why do some children with nonlinguistic perceptual deficits develop social imperception problems, whereas other do not? What is the relationship between the children's attentional and executive function problems and their nonlinguistic perceptual deficits? Are they comorbid conditions, or does their co-occurrence reflect a more general right hemisphere dysfunction? What evidence can we gather about right hemisphere dysfunctions from postmortem studies of patients diagnosed with NLD?

The domain of social cognition also opens a wide array of topics for study. How would children with NLD respond to the false-belief test? What can we learn about those children's use of theory of relevance? In the domain of affect processing, much remains to be learned about the sources of the children's anxiety, their dispositional states, and their problems with affect regulation.

In the intrapersonal domain, the concept of mindsharing requires further elucidation. Furthermore, we have an insufficient understanding of the protective factors that immunize children from disorders of the self. We also know little about the factors that make it possible for some children to compensate for their deficits, whereas other children seem unable to develop such compensations.

Fourth, although many clinicians have contributed to the creation of a body of techniques for the remediation of the disorder, insufficient research has been conducted to determine the indications for, and effectiveness of, psychotherapy for children with NLD. Outcome studies of modalities of psychotherapy, frequency of contact, and nature of the transference would enhance our ability to use such modalities effectively.

Finally, although this book focused on children, consideration must be given to the complexities that adolescent and adult development introduce (Johnson, 1987b; Palombo, 2000b). We assume that many of the social features of children with NLD are developmentally continuous with adolescence and adulthood; however, the data for such an assumption are absent, and only longitudinal studies would confirm that hypothesis. If we take seriously the proposition that with maturation modifications in the sense of self occurs, we may find discontinuities in the development of these patients. In fact, the clinical evidence from the observation of children confirms this view. We have seen children who were diagnosed as PDD or with autism early in childhood, only to find that by the age of 12 they are diagnosed with NLD. There is no doubt that adolescent changes bring with them modification in children's behaviors. These modifications may either mitigate or aggravate the effects of the deficits. The social context may impel the changes in either direction. New experiences may present challenges which, if met, can enhance self-cohesion and permit the person to overcome inhibitions formerly imposed by the deficits, or they may lead to compensations in unexpected areas of competence. The consolidation in the sense of self that comes about in late adolescence may also permit achievements that were formerly unanticipated.

In adulthood, finding a partner who can complement the individual's deficits may permit that person to lead a rich and productive life. This is not to say that the deficits will not impose constraints on that person, and that when situations arise in which the person confronts those deficits, crises would not occur. My clinical impression, derived from the observation of the parents of children with these deficits, who themselves appear to have similar deficits and to have had similar histories, is that some of these parents succeeded in finding rewarding careers, in having satisfying relationships with their partners, in having families and children, and in developing a cohesive sense of self.

What is also true is that as clinicians we encounter adolescents and adults whose lives are less successful and more disrupted by their deficits. However, these individuals were not diagnosed at an early age or did not receive timely interventions that might have mitigated the effects of their deficits. The self-imposed isolation of these patients is not simply the result of their deficits but is also due to the injuries and victimization they have suffered at the hands of those who failed to understand the origins of the social dysfunctions.

In summary, when we consider the social and emotional behaviors of children with NLD, we must take into account genetic factors, the child's specific neuropsychological strengths and deficits, the child's stage of development, the family's dynamics, the effect of caregivers' responses, the child's own reaction to his or her neuropsychological deficits, the effects of peer rejection/teasing/bullying, and the effects of comorbid conditions with which the child may be affected (cf. Hynd, 1988). In contrast to lesion-based neurological conditions in which a direct relationship may exist between the specific brain dysfunction and the presenting symptom, such a direct relationship eludes us in our examination of the social and emotional problems of children with NLD. We are left with the challenge to find measures to assess the weight to be given to each factor that contributes to the manifest behavior.

APPENDICES

Appendix 1

Summary of NLD Social–Emotional Symptoms

Social Domain

Eye contact: Generally averts eyes; eye contact is fleeting (e.g., steals glances), fluctuating, variable, minimal, inconsistent, gaze-like, inappropriate, not well-timed; makes insufficient use of eye contact or does not accommodate to others' eye contact in conversation.

Facial expression: Limited, strained, grimaced, muted, neutral, adult-like or flat; does not reflect or is not congruent with emotional experience; is insufficiently communicative, does not convey underlying emotions, or may even suggest contrary emotions than those felt; is not well-modulated; comes across as awkward, stilted, exaggerated, or out of proportion to situation.

Prosody: Flat, not well-modulated; unusual, exaggerated, or dramatized; either too loud or too soft; "sing-songy" in quality; does not express the child's feelings; comes across as awkward, stilted, exaggerated, or out of proportion to situation.

Gestures: Uses few bodily or hand gestures; these may be muted or neutral, fail to match verbal output (i.e., nods head to indicate "yes" but says "no"), are insufficiently communicative, they show little emotion; or if they do show emotion, they seem awkward, stilted, exaggerated, or out of proportion to situation.

Social cues: Does not understand nonverbal cues (e.g., appears not to notice that other children are annoyed with, or may not like, him or her; persists in talking about own interests, not noticing that others are no longer interested); has difficulty understanding, or misinterprets, social contexts; does not use nonverbal communication effectively; reads social situations poorly, thus experiencing the world as puzzling, surprising or antagonistic; does not know how to go about getting the information necessary to read and anticipate occurrences in the world.

ADAPTABILITY

Transitions: Exhibits difficulty managing behavior when making a transition from one task to another; becomes easily frustrated, disinhibited, anxious, oppositional, aggressive, or disruptive gets upset with changes in routine; accommodates best when given a warning of a change in routine.

Novel situations: Has difficulty applying academic skills to new situations; has difficulty accommodating or adapting to contextual aspects of novel or unpredictable situations; responds to novel situations with distress or anxiety; becomes oppositional or aggressive when faced with new tasks; encounters difficulty organizing elements of new or unpredictable situations.

Problem solving: Has difficulty maintaining a consistent problem-solving approach throughout a task; tends to lose track of goal and problem-solving process during task; shows significantly better reasoning with verbal information alone than when social and pragmatic problem solving is required; oppositionality and intellectualizing behaviors impede problem-solving efforts.

PEER RELATIONSHIPS

Peer relations: Has relational problems with peers; does not have good friends; has difficulty forming and keeping positive peer relationships; is bossy, aggressive, and defensive with peers; relies on rules in interactions with peers; relates better one-to-one than in groups of peers; has trouble fitting in groups.

Rejection: Neglected or rejected by peers.

RECIPROCAL SOCIAL INTERACTION

Social disconnection: Avoids social engagement; has difficulty negotiating the reciprocal nature of social interactions; has difficulty initiating and maintaining conversations; is unresponsive to others when spoken to; makes comments unrelated to the topic of conversation; poorly understands the impact of own behavior on others; isolates self; is inattentive to others' interests or nonverbal cues; remains on the periphery of groups; is "spacey" in interactions with others; prefers to be alone; shows little emotional responsivity.

Social clumsiness: Is socially awkward, inappropriate, or maladroit; applies learned rules of behavior mechanically; asks personal questions or makes inappropriate or irrelevant comments that make others uncomfortable; seems unaware of others' emotions; does not pick up or use social interactional norms; interprets social situations idiosyncratically or in an overpersonalized way; is offensive, intrusive, or hurtful in comments or behaviors, without awareness of impact he or she is having on others.

Poor interpreter of social cues: Is poor interpreter of social situations; has difficulty integrating important aspects of situations or focuses on details that are less relevant, missing the main point; is unsure why own behavior is perceived as disturbing to others; tends to overgeneralize or misapply rules derived from dissimilar situations; poor at deriving social rules when he does derive a rule he encounters difficulty translating the information into his own actions.

Social immaturity: Relies on socially immature ways of problem solving; needs more frequent reassurance than other children of same age; over reliant on approval from others; is clingy and dependent; needs affection, nuturance, and/or structure typical of younger children.

Behavioral dysfunction: Is argumentative, oppositional, provocative, bossy, aggressive toward others; blames others, failing to take responsibility for own actions; is quarrelsome, disobedient or noncompliant, hostile, annoying, and irritating; behaves disruptively, circumvents rules, and acts antisocially; is inappropriately mischievous; modulates aggressive behavior poorly.

Poor humor: Has difficulty understanding the implicit meaning of jokes or humorous remarks or gestures; takes jokes or sarcastic remarks too literally; misinterprets friendly teasing as critical or derogatory.

Emotional Domain

SELF-STATE

Self-evaluation: Is self-critical, perfectionistic, lacking in self confidence; feels inadequate; has low self-esteem; feels unworthy or undeserving; has a poor sense of self-efficacy.

Sensitivity: Is touchy and becomes tearful easily; feels neglected or rejected easily (e.g., is easily hurt by minor critical comments); feels vulnerable or helpless; interprets others' responses as victimizing or scapegoating; expresses feeling different from other children.

Sensory overload: Feels overwhelmed and overstimulated easily; experiences the world as too complicated to read and understand; becomes easily confused or disorganized in thinking when confronted with difficult situations; has difficulty integrating ideas and stimuli.

AFFECT STATE

Anxiety: Appears worried (e.g., flushed face, eyes wide open), uncomfortable, and fidgety; is wary of situations in general; manifests signs of nervousness; appears distraught; is fearful; complains of stomachaches; expresses worries about bad things happening to beloved people (e.g., family members); fears hurting others; is overly concerned about performance on tasks; is hesitant on tasks for fear of failure.

Anger: Expresses irritation; responds aggressively or with hostility; displays frustration; blames for difficulties; is provocative in responses.

Sadness: Expresses unhappiness or sadness; appears depressed, distressed, or dysphoric.

AFFECT MODULATION

Has difficulty modulating affect states; Expressions of affect are overly intense, poorly controlled, disinhibited, dramatic, exaggerated; moods fluctuate or, if suppressed, result in intense and poorly regulated displays of emotions or "meltdowns"; is emotionally labile.

AFFECT PROCESSING

Affect reception: Has difficulty identifying or recognizing others' emotional expressions through facial expressions, gestures, vocal intonations, or other nonverbal social cues; seems unaware of others' emotions; has difficulty understanding and interpreting others' feelings or the conventional meanings that feelings have for others; recognizes feelings in others only if they are expressed with intensity; has similar difficulties identifying feelings in self.

Affect expression: Appears unable to display affect states; does not display feelings through eye contact on facial or gestural expressions; facial or gestural expressions appear to convey the contrary emotions to those felt; seldom discusses own feelings.

APPENDIX 2

Helpful Resources

Many of these works also address the problems of children with Asperger's disorder.

Books

Atwood, T. (1998). *Asperger's disorder: A guide for parents and professionals*. London: Jessica Kingsley.

Burger, N. R. (2004). *A special kind of brain: Living with nonverbal learning disabilities*. London: Jessica Kingsley.

Casey, J. E., & Strang, J. D. (1994). The neuropsychology of nonverbal learning disabilities: A practical guide for the clinical practitioners. Koziol, L. F. & Stout, J. D. (Ed.), *The neuropsychology of mental disorders: A practical guide* (pp. 187–201). Springfield, IL: Thomas.

Duke, M. P., Nowicki, S. & Martin, E. A. (1996). *Teaching your child the language of social success*. Atlanta, GA: Peachtree.

Klass, P., & Costello, E. (2003). *Quirky kids: Understanding and helping your child who doesn't fit in—when to worry and when not to worry*. New York: Balantine.

Molenaar-Klumper, M. (2002). *Non-verbal learning disabilities: Diagnosis and treatment within an educational setting*. London: Jessica Kingsley.

Nowicki, S., & Duke, M. P. (1992). *Helping the child who doesn't fit in*. Atlanta, GA: Peachtree.

Nowicki, S., & Duke, M. P. (2003). *Will I ever fit in?: The breakthrough program for conquering adult dyssemia*. Atlanta, GA: Peachtree.

Rubinstein, M. B. (2005). *Raising NLD superstars: What families with nonverbal learning disabilities need to know about nurturing confident, competent kids*. London: Jessica Kingsley.

Stanford, A. (2003). *Asperger's disorder and long-term relationships*. Philadelphia: Jessica Kingsley.

Stewart, K. (2002). *Helping a child with nonverbal learning disorder or Asperger's disorder: A parent's guide*. Oakland, CA: New Harbinger.

Tanguay, P. B. (2003). *Nonverbal learning disabilities at school: Educating students with NLD, Asperger's disorder, and related conditions*. London: Jessica Kingsley.

Tanguay, P. B. (2001). *Nonverbal learning disabilities at home: A parent's guide*. Philadelphia: Jessica Kingsley.

Thompson, S. (1997). *The source for nonverbal disorders*. East Moline, IL: LinguiSystems.

Whitney, R. V. (2002). *Bridging the gap: Raising a child with nonverbal disorder*. New York: Berkeley Publishing Group.

Websites

ATTENTION DEFICIT/HYPERACTIVITY DISORDERS

Children and Adults with Attention Deficit Disorder (CHADD):
http://www.chadd.org
National Attention Deficit Disorder Association
http://www.add.org

EXECUTIVE FUNCTION DISORDERS

Yale Medical School
http://info.med.yale.edu/chldstdy/ plomdevelop/genetics/00auggen.htm
National Academy of Neuropsychology
http://nanonline.org/nandistance/mtbi/ClinNeuro/executive.html#top

NONVERBAL LEARNING DISABILITIES

Nonverbal learning disabilities
http://www.nldline.com
NLD on the Web
http://www.nldontheweb.org

ASPERGER'S DISORDER

ASPEN (Asperger Syndrome Education Network)
http://www.aspennj.org
Tony Attwood (Attwood is author of guide for parents & professionals.)
http://www.tonyattwood.com

GENERAL RESOURCES

Office of Special Education and Rehabilitative Services, U.S. Department of Education
http://www.ed.gov/offices/OSERS/
Rush Neurobehavioral Center (Center specializes in and conducts research on the assessment and treatment of NLD)
http://www.Rush.edu/patients/RNB C
The Schwab Foundation for Learning (Provides helpful information for parents of children with L.D.)
http://www.schwablearning.org
Joseph Palombo
www.josephpalombo.com

References

Adolphs, R. (2001). The neurobiology of social cognition. *Current Opinion in Neurobiology, 11*(2): 231–239.

Adolphs, R. (2003a). Cognitive neuroscience of human social behavior. *Nature Reviews: Neuroscience, 4*(3): 165–178.

Adolphs, R. (2003b). Investigating the cognitive neuroscience of social behavior. *Neuropsychologia, 41,* 119–126.

Amaral, D. G., Bauman, M. D., Capitanio, J. P., Lavenex, P., Mason, W.A., Maulding-Jourdain, M. L., & Mendoza, S. P. (2003). The amygdala: Is it an essential component of the neural network of social cognition? *Neuropsychologia, 41,* 517–522.

American Psychiatric Association. (1994). *Diagnostic and statistical manual of mental disorders—Fourth Edition.* Washington, DC: Author.

Amini, F., Lewis, T., Rannon, R., Louis, A., Baumbacher, G., McGuiness, T., & Schiff, E. Z. (1996). Affect, attachment, memory: Contributions toward psychobiologic integration. *Psychiatry, 59*(3), 213–239.

Anderson, S. W., Bechara, A., Damasio, H., Tranel, D., & Damasio, A. R. (1999). Impairment of social and moral behavior related to early damage in human prefrontal cortex. *Nature Neuroscience, 2*(11), 1032–1037.

Anthony, E. J. (1987). Risk, vulnerability, and resilience: An overview. In E. J. Anthony & B. J. Cohler (Eds.), *The invulnerable child* (pp. 3–48). New York: Guilford Press.

Asperger, H. (1991). "Autistic psychopathy" in childhood. In *Autism and Asperger's disorder*, translated and annotated by U. Frith (pp. 37–92). Cambridge, UK: Cambridge University Press.

Astington, J. W. (1990). Narrative and the child's theory of mind. In B. K. Britton & A. D. Pellegrine (Eds.), *Narrative thought and narrative language* (pp. 151–172). Mahwah, NJ: Erlbaum.

Atwood, T. (1998). *Asperger's disorder: A guide for parents and professionals.* London: Jessica Kingsley.

Baddeley, A. D. (1988). Cognitive psychology and human memory. *Trends in Neurosciences, 11*(4), 176–181.

Badian, N. A. (1986). Nonverbal disorders of learning: The reverse of Dyslexia? *Annals of Dyslexia, 36,* 253–269.

Badian, N. A. (1992). Nonverbal learning disability, school behavior, and Dyslexia. *Annals of Dyslexia, 42,* 159–178.

Barkley, R. A. (1989). Attention deficit-hyperactivity disorder. In E. J. Mosh & R. A. Barkley (Eds.), *Treatment of childhood disorders* (pp. 39–72). New York: Guilford Press.

Barkley, R. A. (1990). *Attention-deficit hyperactivity disorder: A handbook for diagnosis and treatment*. New York: Guilford Press.

Barkley, R. A. (1996). Linkages between attention and executive function. In G. R. Lyon & N. A. Krasnegor (Eds.), *Attention, memory, and executive function* (pp. 307–325). Baltimore: H Brookes.

Bar-On, R., Tranel, D., Denburg, N. L., Bechara, A. (2003). Exploring the neurological substrate of emotional and social intelligence. *Brain, 126*, 1790–1800.

Baron-Cohen, S. (1993). From attention–goal psychology to belief–desire psychology: The development of a theory of mind, and its dysfunction. In S. Baron-Cohen, H. Tager-Flusberg, & D. J. Cohen (Eds.), *Understanding other minds* (pp. 59–82). Oxford, UK: Oxford University Press.

Baron-Cohen, S. (1997). *Mindblindness: An essay on autism and theory of mind*. Cambridge, MA: MIT Press.

Baron-Cohen, S., & Swettenham, J. (1997). Theory of mind in autism: Its relationship to executive function and central coherence. In D. J. Cohen & F. R. Volkmar (Eds.), *Handbook of autism and pervasive developmental disorders* (pp. 880–893). New York: Wiley.

Baron-Cohen, S., Tager-Flusberg, H., & Cohen, D. J. (Eds.). (1993). *Understanding other minds: Perspectives from Autism* (pp. 3–55). Oxford, UK: Oxford University Press.

Barton, S. (1994). Chaos, self-organization, and psychology. *American Psychologist, 49*(1), 5–14.

Basch, M. F. (1974). *Piaget and Freud*. Unpublished manuscript.

Bauminger, N., Edelsztein, H. S., Morash, J., (2005). Social information processing and emotional understanding in children with LD. *Journal of Learning Disabilities, 38*(1), 45–61.

Beebe, B. (1986). Mother–infant mutual influence and precursors of self- and object representation. In J. Masling (Ed.), *Empirical studies of psychoanalytic theories* (vol. 2, pp. 27–48). Hillsdale, NJ: Analytic Press.

Beebe, B., & Lachmann, F. M. (1988). Mother–infant mutual influence and precursors of psychic structure. In A. Goldberg (Ed.), *Progress in self psychology* (vol. 3, pp. 3–25). Hillsdale, NJ: Analytic Press.

Beebe, B., & Lachmann, F. M. (1998). Co-constructing inner and relational processes: Self- and mutual regulation in infant research and adult treatment. *Psychoanalytic Psychology, 15*(4), 480–516.

Beeman, M., & Chiarello, C. (Eds.). (1998a). *Right hemisphere language comprehension: Perspectives from cognitive neuroscience*. Mahwah, NJ: Erlbaum.

Beeman, M. & Chiarello, C. (1998b). Concluding remarks: Getting the whole story right. In M. Beeman & C. Chiarello (Eds.), *Right hemisphere language comprehension: Perspective from cognitive neuroscience* (pp. 377–389). Mahwah, NJ: Erlbaum.

Benowitz, L. I., Moya, K. L., & Kevin, D.N. (1990). Impaired verbal reasoning and constructional apraxia in subjects with right hemisphere damage. *Neuropsychologia, 38*(3), 231–241.

Bezuidenhout, A., & Sroda, M. S. (1998). Children's use of contextual cues to resolve referential ambiguity: An application of Relevance Theory. *Pragmatics and Cognition, 6*(1/2), 265–299.

Bishop, D. V. M. (1989). Autism, Asperger's disorder and semantic–pragmatic disorder: Where are the boundaries? *British Journal of Disorders of Communication, 24*, 107–121.

Blair, C. (2002). School readiness: Integrating cognition and emotion in a neurobiological conceptualization of children's functioning at school entry. *American Psychologist, 57*(2), 111–127.

Borod, J. C., Bloom, R. L., & Haywood, C.S. (1998). Verbal aspects of emotional communication. In M. Beeman & C. Chiarello (Eds.), *Right hemisphere language comprehension: Perspectives from cognitive neuroscience* (pp. 285–307). Mahwah, NJ: Erlbaum.

Borod, J. C., & Madigan, N. K. (2000). Neuropsychology of emotion and emotional disorders: An overview and research directions. In J. C., Borod (Ed.), *The neuropsychology of emotion* (pp. 3–30). Oxford, UK: Oxford University Press.

Bowers, D., Bauer, R. M., & Heilman, K. M. (1993). The nonverbal affect lexicon: Theoretical perspectives from neuropsychological studies of affect perception. *Neurology, 7*(4), 433–444.

Bowlby, J. (1969). *Attachment and loss. Vol. I Attachment.* New York: Basic Books.

Bowlby, J. (1973). *Attachment and loss. Vol. II. Separation: Anxiety and anger.* New York: Basic Books.

Brandell, J. R. (1984). Storytelling in child psychotherapy. *Psychotherapy, 21,* 154–162.

Brandell, J. R. (2000). *Of mice and metaphors: Therapeutic story telling in children.* New York: Basic Books.

Bretherton, I., Ridgeway, D., & Cassidi, J. (1990). Assessing internal working models of the attachment relationship. In M. T. Greenberg, D. Cicchetti, & E. M. (Eds), *Attachment in the preschool years* (pp. 273–308). Chicago: University of Chicago Press.

Brothers, L. (1989). A biological perspective on empathy. *American Journal of Psychiatry, 146*(1), 10–19.

Brothers, L. (1996). Brain mechanisms of social cognition. *Journal of Psychopharmacology, 10*(1), 2–8.

Brothers, L. (1997). *Friday's footprint: How society shapes the human mind.* New York: Oxford University Press.

Brothers, L., & Ring, B. (1992). A neuroethological framework for the representation of minds. *Journal of Cognitive Neuroscience, 4*(2), 107–118.

Brownell, H., & Martino, G. (1998). Deficits in inference and social cognition: The effects of right hemisphere brain damage on discourse. In M. C. Beeman, (Ed.), *Right hemisphere language comprehension: Perspectives from cognitive neuroscience* (pp. 309–337). Mahwah, NJ: Erlbaum.

Bruner, J. S. (1984). *In search of mind: Essays in autobiography.* New York: Harper & Row.

Bruner, J. S. (1987). Life as Narrative. *Social Research, 54*(1), 11–32.

Bruner, J. S. (1990). *Acts of meaning.* Cambridge, MA: Harvard University Press.

Bruner, J. (2002). *Making stories: Law, literature, life.* New York: Farrar, Straus & Giroux.

Bryan, T. (1990). Assessment of social cognition: Review of research in learning disabilities. In H. L. Swanson (Ed.), *Handbook on the assessment of learning disabilities: Theory, research, and practice* (pp. 285–311). Austin, TX: PRO-ED.

Bryan, T., Burstein, K., & Ergul, C., (2004). The social–emotional side of learning disabilities: A science-based presentation of the state of the art. *Learning Disabilities Quarterly, 27*(1), 43–51.

Buchler, J. (1939). *Charles Peirce's empiricism.* London: Kegan Paul, Trench, Trubner.

Burger, N. R. (2004). *A special kind of brain: Living with nonverbal learning disabilities.* London: Jessica Kingsley.

Calarge, C., Andreason, N. C., & O'Leary, D. S., (2003). Visualizing how one brain understands another: A PET study of theory of mind. *American Journal of Psychiatry, 160*, 1954–1964.

Carey, M. E., Barakat, L. P., Foley, B., Gyato, K., & Phyllips, P. C. (2001). Neuropsychological functioning and social functioning of survivors of pediatric brain tumors: Evidence of nonverbal learning disability. *Child Neuropsychology, 2*(4), 265–272.

Caroll, R. (2003). "At the border between chaos and order": What psychotherapy and neuroscience have in common. In J. Corrigall & H. Wilkinson (Eds.), *Revolutionary connections: Psychotherapy and neuroscience* (pp. 191–212). New York: Karnac.

Cassidy, J. (2004). "I need my scripts": A bosy with Asperger's disorder entering adolescence. In M. Rhode & T. Klauber (Eds.), *The Many Faces of Asperger's Disorder* (pp. 21–233) London: Karnac.

Chess, S. and A. Thomas (1977). Temperamental individuality: from childhood to adolescence. *Journal of the American Academy of Child & Adolescent Psychiatry, 16*(2), 218–226.

Cohler, B. J. (1987). Adversity, resilience, and the study of lives. In E. J. Anthony & B. J. Cohler (Eds.), *The invulnerable child* (pp. 363–424). New York: Guilford Press.

Cohler, B. J. (1993). Aging, morale, and meaning: The nexus of narrative. In T. R. Cole & W. A. Achenbaum (Eds.), *Voices and visions of aging: Toward a clinical gerontology* (pp. 107–133). New York: Springer.

Cooper, A. M. (1985). Will neurobiology influence psychoanalysis? *American Journal of Psychiatry, 142*(12), 1395–1402.

Coplin, J. W., & Morgan, S. B. (1988). Learning disabilities: A multidimensional perspective. *Journal of Learning Disabilities, 21*(10), 614–622.

Cornelius, R. R. (1996). *The science of emotion: Research and tradition in the psychology of emotion*. Upper Saddle River, NJ: Prentice Hall.

Cornoldi, C., Rigoni, F., Tressoleti, P. E., & Vio, C. (1999). Imagery deficits in nonverbal learning disabilities. *Journal of Learning Disabilities, 32*(1), 48–57.

Cozolino, L. (2002). *The neuroscience of psychotherapy: Building and rebuilding the brain*. New York: Norton.

Damasio, A. R. (1994). *Descartes' error: Emotion, reason, and the human brain*. New York: Putnam.

Damasio, A. R. (2003). *Looking for Spinoza: Joy, sorrow, and the feeling brain*. New York: Harcourt.

Davidson, R. J. (1993). The neuropsychology of emotion and affective style. In M. Lewis & J. M. Haviland (Eds.), *Handbook of emotions* (pp. 143–154). New York: Guilford Press.

Davidson, R. J. (1994). Temperament, affective style, and frontal lobe asymmetry. In G. Dawson, K. W. Fischer (Ed.), *Human behavior and the developing brain* (pp. 518–536). New York: Guilford Press.

Davidson, R. J. (2000). The functional neuroanatomy of affective style. In R. D. Lane & N. Lynn (Eds.), *Cognitive neuroscience of emotion* (pp. 371–388). London: Oxfrod University Press.

Davidson, R. J. (2003a). Affective neuroscience: A case for interdisciplinary research. In F. Kessel & P. L. Rosenfield (Eds.), *Expanding boundaries and social science: Case studies in interdisciplinary innovation* (pp. 99–121). London: Oxford University Press.

Davidson, R. J. (2003b). Affective neuroscience. In F. Kessel & P. L. Rosenfield

(Eds.), *Expanding the boundaries of health and social sciences: Case studies in interdisciplinary innovation* (pp. 99–121). London: Oxford University Press.

Davidson, R. J. (2003c). Affective neuroscience and psychophysiology: Toward a synthesis. *Psychophysiology, 40*, 655–665.

Davidson, R. J. (2003d). Seven sins in the study of emotion: Correctives from affective neuroscience. *Brain and Cognition, 52*, 129–132.

Denckla, M. B. (1978). Minimal brain dysfunction. In J. S. Chall & A. F. Mirsky (Eds.), *Education and the brain* (pp. 223–268). Chicago: University of Chicago Press.

Denckla, M. B. (1983). The neuropsychology of social–emotional learning disabilities. *Archives of Neurology, 40*, 461–462.

Denckla, M. B. (1991). Academic and extracurricular aspects of nonverbal learning disabilities. *Psychiatric Annals, 21*(12), 717–724.

Denckla, M. B. (1994). Measurement of executive function. In G. R. Lyon (Ed.), *Frames of reference for the assessment of learning disabilities* (pp. 117–142). Baltimore: Brookes.

Denckla, M. B. (1996). A theory and model of executive function: A neuropsychological perspective. In G. R. Lyon & N. A. Krasnegor (Eds.), *Attention, memory, and executive function* (pp. 263–278). Baltimore, MD: Brookes.

Denckla, M. B. (2000). Learning disabilities and Attention-Deficit/Hyperactivity Disorder in adults: Overlap with executive dysfunction. In T. E. Brown (Ed.), *Attention-deficit disorders and comorbities in children, adolescents, and adults* (pp. 297–318). Washington, DC: American Psychiatric Press.

Diamond, D., & Blatt, S. J. (1994). Internal working models and the representational world in attachment and psychoanalytic theories. In M. B. Sperling & W. H. Berman (Ed.), *Attachment in adults: Clinical and developmental perspectives* (pp. 72–97). New York: Guilford Press.

Dimitrovsky, L., Spector, H., Terry-Schiff, R., & Valik, E. (1998). Interpretation of facial expressions of affect in children with learning disabilities with verbal or nonverbal deficits. *Journal of Learning Disabilities, 31*(3), 286–312.

Douglas, W. (2000). The dialogue between psychoanalysis and neuroscience: Alienation and reparation. *Neuro-Psychoanalysis, 2*(2), 183–192.

Drummond, C. R., Ahmad, S. A., & Rourke, B. P. (2005). Rules of the classification of younger children with nonverbal learning disabilities and basic phonological processing disabilities. *Archives of Clinical Neuropsychology, 20*, 171–182.

Duke, M. P., Nowicki, S., & Martin, E. A. (1996). *Teaching your child the language of social success.* Atlanta, GA: Peachtree.

Elksnin, L. K., & Elksnin, N. (2004). The social–emotional side of learning disabilities. *Learning Disabilities Quarterly, 27*(1), 3–8.

Ellenberg, L. (1999). Executive functions in children with learning disabilities and attention deficit disorder. In J. A. Incorvia, B. S. Mark-Goldstein, & D. Tessmer (Eds.), *Understanding, diagnosing, and treating AD/HD in children and adolescents: An integrative approach* (pp. 197–219). Northdale, NJ: Jason Aronson.

Feldman, R. S., Philoppot, P., & Custrini, R. J. (1991). Social competence and nonverbal behavior. In R. S. R. Feldman & B. Cambridge (Eds.), *Fundamentals of nonverbal behavior* (pp. 329–350). Cambridge, UK: Cambridge University Press.

Filley, C. M. (2005). Why the white brain matters. *Cerebrum, 7*(1), 53–66.

Fletcher, J. M. (1989). Nonverbal learning disabilities and suicide: Classification leads to prevention. *Journal of Learning Disabilities, 22*(3), 176–179.

Fonagy, P. (2001). *Attachment theory and psychoanalysis.* New York: Other Press.

Fraiberg, S. H. (1971). Separation crisis in two blind children. *Psychoanalytic Study of the Child, 26,* 355–371.

Fraiberg, S. H., Siegel, B. L., & Gibson, R. (1966). The role of sound in the search behavior of a blind infant. *Psychoanalytic Study of the Child, 21,* 327–357.

Franco, F. (1997). The development of meaning in infancy: Early communication and understanding people. In S. Hala (Ed.), *The development of social cognition* (pp. 95–188). East Sussex, UK: Psychology Press.

Freud, S. (1960). *Introductory lectures on psychoanalysis.* J. Strachey (Ed. & Trans.) The *standard edition of the complete psychological works of Sigmund Freud* (vol. 16, pp. 243–463). London: Hogarth Press. (Original work published 1916.)

Frith, C. D., & Frith, U. (2001). Interacting minds—a biological basis. *Current Directions in Psychological Science, 10*(5), 151–155.

Frith, U. (1989a). Autism and theory of mind. In C. Gillberg (Ed.), *Diagnosis and treatment of autism* (pp. 32–52). New York: Plenum Press.

Frith, U. (1989b). *Autism: Explaining the enigma.* Cambridge, UK: Backwell.

Frith, U. (Ed.). (1991). *Autism and Asperger's disorder.* Cambridge, UK: Cambridge University Press.

Fuerst, K. B., & Rourke, B. P. (1995). White matter physiology and pathology. In B. Rourke (Ed.), *Syndrome of nonverbal learning disability* (pp. 27–44). New York: Guilford Press.

Gabbard, G. O. (2005). Mind, brain, and personality disorders. *American Journal of Psychiatry, 162,* 648–655.

Galatzer-Levy, R. M. (1995). Psychoanalysis and chaos theory. *Journal of the American Psychoanalytic Association, 43*(4), 1085–1112.

Garber, B. (1988). The emotional implications of learning disabilities: A theoretical integration. In G. H. Pollard (Ed.), *The annual of psychoanalysis* (vol. 16, pp. 111–128). Madison, CT: International Universities Press.

Garber, B. (1991). The Analysis of a learning-disabled child. In A. Goldberg (Ed.), *The annual of psychoanalysis* (vol. 19, pp. 127–150). Hillsdale, N.J., The Analytic Press.

Gazzaniga, M. S. (1988). *Mind matters: How mind and brain interact to create our conscious lives.* Boston: Houghton Mifflin.

Gazzaniga, M. S., Ivry, R. B., & Mangun, G. R. (2002). *Cognitive neuroscience: The biology of the mind* (2nd ed.). New York: Norton.

Geschwind, N., & Galaburda, A. M. (1985). Cerebral lateralization: Biological mechanisms, association and pathology: I. A hypothesis and a program for research. *Archives of Neurology, 42,* 428–457.

Gilger, J. W., Ho, H., Whipple, A. D., & Spitz, R. (2001). Genotype–environment correlations for language-related abilities: Implications for typical and atypical learners. *Journal of Learning Disabilities, 34*(6), 492–502.

Gilkerson, L. (2001). Integrating an understanding of brain development into early childhood education. *Infant Mental Health Journal, 22*(1–2), 174–187.

Ginsburg, H., & Opper, S. (1988). *Piaget's theory of intellectual development* (3rd ed.). Englewood Cliffs, NJ: Prentice-Hall.

Gleick, J. (1987). *Chaos: Making a new science.* New York: Viking.

Goldberg, E. (2001). *The executive brain: Frontal lobes and the civilized mind.* New York: Oxford University Press.

Goldberg, E., & Costa, L. D. (1981). Hemisphere differences in the acquisition and use of descriptive systems. *Brain and Language, 14,* 144–173.

Green, R. W. (1998). *The explosive child: A new approach for understanding and parenting easily frustrated, "chronically inflexible" children*. New York: Harper Collins.

Greenspan, S. I. (1979). *Intelligence and adaptation: An integration of psychoanalytic and Piagetian developmental psychology*. New York: International Universities Press.

Greenspan, S. I. (1988). The development of the ego: Insights from clinical work with infants and young children. *Journal of the American Psychoanalytic Association, 36*(1), 3–55.

Greenspan, S. I. (1989a). *The development of the ego: Implications for personality theory, psychopathology, and the psychotherapeutic process*. Madison, CT: International Universities Press.

Greenspan, S. I. (1989b). The development of the ego: Biological and environmental specificity in the psychopathological developmental process and the selection and construction of ego defenses. *Journal of the American Psychoanalytic Association, 37*(3), 639–686.

Greenspan, S. I. (1997). *The growth of mind and the endangered origins of intelligence*. Reading, MA: Addison-Wesley.

Greenspan, S. I., & Wieder, S. (1997). Developmental patterns and outcomes in infant and children with disorders in relating and communicating: A chart review of 200 cases of children with autistic spectrum diagnosis. *Journal of Developmental and Learning Disorders, 1*(1), 87–141.

Greenspan, S. I., & Shanker, S. G. (2004). *The first idea: How symbols, language, and intelligence evolved from our primate ancestors to modern humans*. Cambridge, MA: Da Capo Press.

Greenspan, S. I. & Wieder, S. (2000). Asperger's Disorder: The developmental individual-difference, relationship-based (DIR) approach to diagnosis and intervention. *The Journal of Developmental and Learning Disorders, 4*(1), 59–82.

Grigsby, J., & Stevens, D. (2000). *Neurodynamics of personality*. New York: Guilford Press.

Gross-Tsur, V., Shalev, R. S., Manor, O., & Amir, N. (1995). Developmental right-hemisphere syndrome: Clinical spectrum of the nonverbal learning disability. *Journal of Learning Disabilities, 28*(2), 80–86.

Gunter, H. L., Ghaziuddin, M., & Ellis, H. D. (2002). Asperger's disorder: Test of and interhemispheric space communication. *Journal of Autism and Developmental Disorders, 32*(4), 263–281.

Hala, S. (Ed.). (1997). *The development of social cognition*. Howe, East Sussex, UK: Psychology Press.

Hanley, M. F. (1996). "Narrative," now and then: A critical realist approach. *International Journal of Psycho-Analysis, 77*, 445–457.

Happe, F. G. E. (1991). The autobiographical writings of three Asperger's disorder adults: Problems of interpretation and implications for theory. In U. Frith (Ed.), *Autism and Asperger's disorder* (pp. 207–241). Cambridge, UK: Cambridge University Press.

Happe, F. G. E. (1993). Communicative competence and theory of mind in autism: A test of relevance theory. *Cognition, 48*, 101–119.

Harding, C. G. (1982). Development of the intention to communicate. *Human Development, 25*, 140–151.

Harnadek, C. S., & Rourke, B. P. (1993). Principal identifying features of the syndrome of nonverbal learning disabilities in children. *Journal of Learning Disabilities, 27*(3), 144–154.

Harris, P. L., & Saarni, C. (1989). Children's understanding of emotion: An introduction. In P. L. Harris (Ed.), *Children's understanding of emotion* (pp. 3–24). Cambridge, UK: Cambridge University Press.

Heilman, K. M. (2002). *Matter of mind: A neurologist's view of brain–behavior relationships*. Oxford, UK: Oxford University press.

Hofer, M. (1984). Relationships as regulators: A psychobiologic perspective on bereavement. *Psychosomatic Medicine, 46*(3), 183–197.

Hofer, M. (1990). Early symbiotic processes: Hard evidence from a soft place. In. R. A. Glick & S. Bone (Eds.), *Pleasure beyond the pleasure principle: The role of affect in motivation, development, and adaptation* (pp. 55–78). New Haven, CT: Yale University Press.

Hofer, M. (1995a). Hidden regulators: Implication for a new understanding of attachment, separation, and loss. In S. Goldberg, R. Muir, & Kerr, J. (Eds.), *Attachment theory: Social, developmental, and clinical perspectives* (pp. 203–230). Hillsdale, NJ: Analytic Press.

Hofer, M. (1995b). An evolutionary perspective on anxiety. In S. P. Roose & R. A. Glick (Eds.), *Anxiety as symptom and signal* (pp. 17–38). Hillsdale, NJ: Analytic Press.

Hofer, M. (1996). On the nature and consequences of early loss. *Psychosomatic Medicine, 58*, 570–581.

Hofer, M. (2003). The emerging neurobiology of attachment and separation: How parents shape their infant's brain and behavior. In S. W. Coates, J. L. Rosenthal, & D. S. Schechter (Eds.), *Trauma and human bonds* (pp. 191–209). Hilldale, NJ: Analytic Press.

Holmes, J. (1996). *Attachment, intimacy, autonomy: Using attachment theory in adult psychotherapy*. Northdale, NJ: Jason Aronson.

Hynd, G. W. (1988). *Neuropsychological assessment in clinical child psychology*. Dewberry Park: CA, Sage.

Hynd, G. W., & Hooper, S. R. (1992). *Neurological basis of childhood psychopathology*. Newbury Park, CA: Sage.

Innis, R. E. (Ed.) (1985). *Semiotics: An introductory anthology*. Bloomington, In: Indiana University Press.

Izard, C. E. (1991). *The psychology of emotion*. New York: Plenum Press.

Izard, C. E. (1997). Emotions and facial expressions: A perspective from differential emotions theory. In J. A. Russell & J. M. Fernandez-Dols (Eds.), *The psychology of facial expression: Studies in emotion and social interaction* (pp. 57–77). New York: Cambridge University Press.

Jakobson, R. (1985). Closing statement: Linguistics and poetics. In R. E. Innis (Ed.), *Semiotics: An introductory anthology* (pp. 145–175). Bloomington: Indiana University Press.

Johnson, D. J. (1987a). Nonverbal learning disabilities. *Pediatric Annals, 16*(2), 133–141.

Johnson, D. J. (1987b). *Adults with learning disabilities: Clinical studies*. New York: Grune & Stratton.

Johnson, D. J., & Myklebust, H. R. (1967). *Learning disabilities: Educational principles and practices*. New York: Grune & Stratton.

Kagan, J. (2004). New insights into temperament. *Cerebrum, 6*(1), 51–66.

Kandel, E. R. (1998). A new intellectual framework for psychiatry. *American Journal of Psychiatry, 155*(4), 457–469.

Kandel, E. R. (1999). Biology and the future of psychoanalysis: A new intellectual framework for psychiatry revised. *American Journal of Psychiatry, 156*(4), 505–524.

Kanner, L. (1943). Autistic disturbances of affective contact. *Nervous Child, 2,* 217–250.

Klass, P., & Costello, E. (2003). *Quirky kids: Understanding and helping your child who doesn't fit in-when to worry and when not to worry.* New York: Balantine.

Klin, A. (1994). Asperger's disorder. *Child and Adolescent Psychiatric Clinics of North America, 3*(1), 131.

Klin, A. (2004). When Asperger's disorder and a nonverbal learning disability look alike. *Developmental and Behavioral Pediatrics, 25*(3), 190–193.

Klin, A., Sparrow, S. S., Volkmar, F. R., Cicchetti, D. V., & Rourke, B. P. (1995). Asperger's disorder. In B. P. Rourke (Ed.), *Syndrome of nonverbal learning disabilities: Neurodevelopmental manifestations* (pp. 93–118). New York: Guilford Press.

Klin, A., & Volkmar, F. R. (1997). Asperger's disorder. In D. Cohen & F. R. Volkmar (Eds.), *Handbook of autism and pervasive developmental disorders* (pp. 94–122). New York: J. Wiley.

Klin, A., & Volkmar, F. (2003). Asperger's disorder: Diagnosis and external validity. *Child and Adolescent Psychiatric Clinics of North America, 12,* 1–13.

Klitzing, K. V. (2000). Gender-specific characteristics of 5-year-olds' play narratives and associations with behavior ratings. *Journal of the American Academy of Child and Adolescent Psychiatry, 39*(8), 1017–1023.

Kohut, H. (1959). Introspection, empathy and psychoanalysis. *Journal of the American Psychoanalytic Association, 7,* 459–483.

Kohut, H. (1971). *The analysis of the self.* New York: International Universities Press.

Kohut, H. (1978). Remarks about the formation of the self: Letter to a student regarding some principles of psychoanalytic research. In P. H. Ornstein (Ed.), *The search for the self: Selected writings of Heinz Kohut 1950–78* (pp. 737–770). New York: International Universities Press.

Kohut, H. (1991). Four basic concepts in self psychology (1979). In P. H. Ornstein (Ed.), *The search for the self: Selected writings of Heinz Kohut: 1978–1981,* (vol. 4, pp. 447–470). Madison, CT: International Universities Press.

Kolb, B., & Whishaw, I. Q. (2001). *Fundamentals of human neuropsychology* (4th Ed.). New York: Freedman.

Kraemer, G. W. (1992). A psychobiology theory of attachment. *Behavioral and Brain Sciences, 15,* 493–541.

Kraemer, G. W. (1995). Significance of social attachment in primate infants: The infant–caregiver relations and volition. In C. R. Pryce, R. D. Martin, & D. Skuse (Eds.), *Motherhood in human and nonhuman primates* (pp. 152–161). Basel, Switzerland: Karger.

Kunda, Z. (2000). *Social cognition: Making sense of people.* Cambridge, MA: MIT Press.

Leckman, J. E., & Lombroso, P. J. (1998). Introduction: Why should a child and adolescent psychiatrist care about genetics and neuroscience? *Journal of the American Academy of Child and Adolescent Psychiatry, 37*(1), 115.

LeDoux, L. (1996). *The emotional brain: The mysterious underpinnings of emotional life.* New York: Simon & Schuster.

LeDoux, L. (2002). *Synaptic self: How our brains become who we are.* New York: Viking.

Leinonen, E., & Kerbel, D. (1999). Relevance theory and pragmatic impairment. *International Journal of Language and Communication Disorders, 34*(4), 367–390.

Leslie, A. M. (1987). Pretence and representation: The origin of a "theory of mind". *Psychological Review, 94*, 412–426.

Leslie, A. M., & Roth, D. (1993). What autism teaches us about metarepresentation. In S. Baron-Cohen, H. Tager-Flusgerg, & D. J. Cohen (Eds.), *Understanding other minds: Perspectives from autism* (pp. 83–111). Oxford, UK: Oxford University Press.

Levin, F. M. (1991). *Mapping the mind*. Hillsdale, NJ: Analytic Press.

Little, S. S. (1993). Nonverbal learning disabilities and socioemotional functioning: A review of the recent literature. *Journal of Learning Disabilities, 26*(10), 653–665.

Loveland, K. A., Fletcher, J. M., & Bailey, V. (1990). Verbal and nonverbal communication of events in learning-disability subtypes. *Journal of Clinical and Experimental Neuropsychology, 12*(4), 433–447.

Luria, A. R. (1973). *The working brain: An introduction to neuropsychology*. New York: Basic Books.

Lyons-Ruth, K. (1998). Implicit relational knowing: Its role in development and psychoanalytic treatment. *Infant Mental Health Journal, 19*(3), 282–289.

Mace, C. (2003). Psychotherapy and neuroscience: How close can they get? In J. Corrigall & H. Wilkinson (Eds.), *Revolutionary connections: Psychotherapy and neuroscience* (pp. 163–174). NY: Karnac.

Mah, L., Arnold, M. C., & Grafman, J. (2004). Impairment of social perception associated with lesions of the prefrontal cortex. *American Journal of Psychiatry, 161*(7), 1247–1255.

Mahler, M. S. (1968). *On human symbiosis and the vicissitudes of individuation*. New York: International Universities Press.

Mahler, M. S. (1975). *The psychological birth of the human infant*. New York: Basic Books.

Manoach, D. S., Sandson, T. A., & Weentraub, S. (1995). The developmental social–emotional processing disorder is associated with right hemisphere abnormalities. *Neuropsychiatry, Neuropsychology, and Behavioral Neurology, 8*(1), 99–105.

Martin, I., & McDonald, S. (2003). Weak coherence, no theory of mind, or executive dysfunction? Solving the puzzle of pragmatic language disorders. *Brain and Language, 85*, 451–466.

Mesulam, M. (2000). *Principles of behavioral and cognitive neurology*. New York: Oxford University Press.

Miller, L. (1991). Psychotherapy of the brain-injured patient: Principles and practices. *Journal of Cognitive Rehabilitation 9*(2) 24–30.

Miller, L. (1992). Cognitive rehabilitation, cognitive therapy, and cognitive style: Toward an integrative model of personality and psychotherapy. *Journal of Cognitive Rehabilitation, 10*(1) 18–29.

Morrison, S. R., & Siegel, L. S. (1991). Learning disabilities: A critical review of definitional and assessment issues. In J. S. Obrzut & G. W. Hynd, *Neuropsychological foundations of learning disabilities* (pp. 79–97). San Diego, CA: Academic Press.

Myklebust, H. R. (1975). Nonverbal learning disabilities: Assessment and intervention. In H. R. Myklebust (Ed.), *Progress in learning disabilities* (vol. 3, pp. 85–121). New York: Grune & Stratton.

Nass, R., Petersen, H. D., & Koch, D. (1989). Differential effects of congenital left and right brain injury on intelligence. *Brain and Cognition, 9*, 258–266.

National Center for Education Statistics (2003). *Digest of Education Statistics, 2003*. Washington, DC: Institute of Education Services.

Nelson, K., & Gruendel, J. (1986). Children's scripts. In K. Nelson (Ed.), *Event knowledge* (pp. 21–46). Hillsdale, NJ: Erlbaum.

Nesic-Vuckovic, T. (2004). Out of the nightmare: the treatment of a 5-year-old girl with Asperger's disorder. In M. Rhode & T. Klauber, (Eds.), *The Many Faces of Asperger's Disorder* (pp. 168–182). London: Karnac.

Noth, W. (1990). *Handbook of semiotics*. Bloomington: Indiana University Press.

Nowicki, S., & Duke, M. P. (1992). *Helping the child who doesn't fit in*. Atlanta, GA: Peachtree.

Nowicki, S., & Duke, M. P. (1992). *Helping the child who doesn't fit in*. Atlanta, GA: Peachtree.

Nowicki, S., & Duke, M. P. (1994). Individual differences in the nonverbal communication of affect: The diagnostic analysis of nonverbal accuracy scale. *Journal of Nonverbal Behavior, 18*(1), 9–35.

Nowicki, S., & Duke, M. P. (2003). *Will I ever fit in?: The breakthrough program for conquering adult dyssemia*. Atlanta, GA: Peachtree.

O'Connor, T. G., & Pianta, R. C. (1999). Psychosocial factors in the aetiology and course of specific learning disabilities. In K. Whitmore, H. Hart, & G. Willems (Eds.), *A neurodevelopmental approach to specific learning disorders* (pp. 211–226). London, Cambridge University Press.

Olds, D. D., (1994). Connectionism and psychoanalysis. *Journal of the American Psychoanalytic Association, 42*(2), 581–611.

Olds, D. D., & Cooper, A. M. (1997). Dialogue with other sciences: Opportunities for mutual gain [Editorial]. *International Journal of Psycho-Analysis, 78*, 219–225.

Ozonoff, S., Rogers, S. J., & Pennington, B., (1991). Asperger's disorder: Evidence of an empirical distinction from high-functioning austism. *Journal of Child Psychology and Psychiatry, 32*(7), 1107–1122.

Pally, R. (1998). Bilaterality: Hemispheric specialization and integration. *International Journal of Psycho-analysis, 79*, 565–578.

Pally, R. (2001). A primary role for nonverbal communication in psychoanalysis. *Psychoanalytic Inquiry, 21*(1), 71–93.

Palombo, J. (1985). The borderline child: Approaches to etiology, diagnosis and treatment [Book review]. *Child and Adolescent Social Work Journal, 2*(4), 272–273.

Palombo, J. (1987a). Clinical issues in self psychology. In P. Caroff & M. Gottesfeld (Eds.), *Psychosocial Studies* (pp. 54–83). New York: Gardner Press.

Palombo, J. (1987b). Selfobject transferences in the treatment of borderline neurocognitively impaired children. In J. S. Grotstein, M. F. Solomon, & J. Lang (Eds.), *The borderline patient* (pp. 317–346). Hillsdale, NJ: Analytic Press.

Palombo, J. (1991). Neurocognitive differences, self cohesion, and incoherent self narratives. *Child and Adolescent Social Work Journal, 8*(6), 449–472.

Palombo, J. (1992, April). *Learning disabilities in children: Developmental, diagnostic and treatment considerations*. Fourth National Health Policy Forum. Washington, DC.

Palombo, J. (1993). Neurocognitive deficits, developmental distortions, and incoherent narratives. *Psychoanalytic Inquiry, 13*(1), 85–102.

Palombo, J. (1994). Incoherent self-narratives and disorders of the self in children with learning disabilities. *Smith College Studies in Social Work, 64*(2), 129–152.

Palombo, J. (1995). Psychodynamic and relational problems of children with nonverbal learning disabilities. In B. S. Mark & J. A. Incorvaia (Eds.), *The handbook of infant, child, and adolescent psychotherapy: A guide to diagnosis and treatment* (vol. 1, pp. 147–176). Hillsdale, NJ: Jason Aronson.

Palombo, J. (1996). The diagnosis and treatment of children with nonverbal learning disabilities. *Child and Adolescent Social Work Journal, 13*(4), 311–332.

Palombo, J. (2000a). Psychoanalysis: A house divided. *Psychoanalytic Social Work, 7*(1), 7–26.

Palombo, J. (2000b). A disorder of the self in an adult with a nonverbal learning disability. In A. Goldberg (Ed.), *Progress in self psychology* (vol. 16, pp. 311–335). New York: Analytic Press.

Palombo, J. (2001a). *Learning disorders and disorders of the self in children and adolescents.* New York: Norton.

Palombo, J. (2001b). The therapeutic process with children with learning disorders. *Psychoanalytic Social Work, 8*(3/4), 143–168.

Palombo, J., & Berenberg, A. H. (1997). Psychotherapy for children with nonverbal learning disabilities. In B. S. Mark, & J. A. Incorvaia, (Eds.), *The Handbook of infant, child and adolescent psychotherapy: New directions in integrative treatment* (vol. 2, pp. 25–68). Northvale, NJ: Jason Aronson.

Palombo, J., & Berenberg, A. H. (1999). Working with parents of children with nonverbal learning disabilities: A conceptual and intervention model. In J. A. Incorvia, B. S. Mark-Goldstein, & D. Tessmer (Eds.), *Understanding, diagnosing, and treating AD/HD in children and adolescents: An integrative approach* (pp. 389–441). Northvale, NJ: Jason Aronson: 389–441.

Palombo, S. R. (1999). *The emergent ego: Complexity and coevolution in the psychoanalytic process.* Madison, CT: International Universities Press.

Panksepp, J. (2001). The long-term psychobiological consequences of infant emotions: Prescriptions for the twenty-first century. *Infant Mental Health Journal, 22*(1–2), 132–173.

Peirce, C. S. (1940). *Philosophical writings of Peirce.* New York: Dover.

Peirce, C. S. (1958). *Selected writings of Charles S. Peirce: Values in a universe of change.* Garden City, NY: Doubleday Anchor Books.

Peirce, C. S. (1991). *Peirce on signs: Writings on semiotics by Charles Sanders Peirce.* Chapel Hill: University of North Carolina Press.

Pelletier, P. M., Ahmad, S. A., & Rourka, B. P. (2001). Classification rules for basic phonological processing disabilities and nonverbal learning disabilities: Formulation and external validity. *Child Neuropsychology, 7*(2), 84–98.

Pennington, B. F. (1991). *Diagnosing learning disorders: A neuropsychological framework.* New York: Guilford Press.

Pennington, B. F., Bennetto, L., McAlees, O., & Roberts, R. J. (1996). Executive functions and working memory. In Krasnegor (Ed.), *Attention, memory, and executive function* (pp. 327–348). Baltimore: Paul H. Brookes.

Petti, V. L., Voelker, Shore D. L., & Nayman-Abello, S. E., (2003). Perception of nonverbal emotion cues by children with nonverbal learning disabilities. *Journal of Developmental and Physical Disabilities, 15*(1), 23–36.

Pinkham, A. E., Penn, D. L., Perkins, D. O., & Lieberman, J. (2003). Implications of neural basis of social cognition for the study of schizophrenia. *American Journal of Psychiatry, 160*(5), 815–824.

Plante, E., Boliek, C., Mahendra, N., Story, J., Glaspey, K. (2001). Right hemisphere contribution to developmental language disorder: Neuroanatomical and behavioral evidence. *Journal of Communication Disorders, 34,* 415–436.

Ramos, F. Y. (1998). A decade of relevance theory. *Journal of Pragmatics, 30,* 304–345.

Rass, E. (2002). *Kindliches Erleben bei Wahrnehmungsproblem*. Berlin, Peter Lang.

Reiser, M. F. (1984). *Mind, brain, body: Toward a convergence of psychoanalysis and neurobiology*. New York: Basic Books.

Rogers, L. J. (2003). Seeking the right answers about right brain–left brain. *Cerebrum, 5*(4), 55–68.

Ross, E. D. (1981). The aprosodia: Functional–anatomic organization of the affective components of language in the right hemisphere. *Archives of Neurology, 38*, 561–569.

Ross, E. D. (2000). Affective prosody and the aprosodias. In M. M. Mesulam (Ed.), *Principles of behavior and cognitive neurology* (pp. 316–331). Oxford, UK: Oxford University Press.

Ross, E. D., & Mesulam, M. (1979). Dominant language functions of the right hemisphere?: Prosody and emotional gesturing. *Archives of Neurology, 36*, 144–148.

Rothstein, A., Benjamin, A., Crosby, M., & Eisenstadt, K. (1988). *Learning disorders: An integration of neuropsychological and psychoanalytic considerations*. Madison, CT: International Universities Press.

Rothstein, A. A., & Glenn, J. (1999). *Learning disabilities and psychic conflict: A psychoanalytic casebook*. Madison, CT: International Universities Press.

Rourke, B. P. (1982). Central processing deficiencies in children: Toward a developmental neuropsychological model. *Journal of Clinical Neuropsychology, 4*(1), 1–18.

Rourke, B. P. (Ed.). (1985). *Neuropsychology of learning disabilities: Essentials of subtype analysis*. New York: Guilford Press.

Rourke, B. P. (1989a). *Nonverbal learning disabilities: The syndrome and the model*. New York: Guilford Press.

Rourke, B. P. (1989b). Nonverbal learning disabilities, socioemotional disturbance, and suicide: A reply to Fletcher, Kowalchuk, and Bigler. *Journal of Learning Disabilities, 22*(3), 186–187.

Rourke, B. P. (1993). Arithmetic disabilities, specific and otherwise: A neuropsychological perspective. *Journal of Learning Disabilities, 26*(4), 214–226.

Rourke, B. P. (1995a). Appendix: Treatment program for the child with NLD. In B. P. Rourke (Ed.), *Syndrome of nonverbal learning disabilities: Neurodevelopmental manifestations* (pp. 497–508). New York: Guilford Press.

Rourke, B. P. (1995b). Introduction: The NLD syndrome and the white matter model. In B. P. Rourke (Ed.), *Syndrome of nonverbal learning disabilities: Neurodevelopmental manifestations* (pp. 1–26). New York: Guilford Press.

Rourke, B. P. (Ed.). (1995c). *Syndrome of nonverbal learning disabilities: Neurodevelopmental manifestations*. New York: Guilford Press.

Rourke, B. P. (2000). Neuropsychological and psychosocial subtyping: A review of investigations within the University of Windsor laboratory. *Canadian Psychology, 41*(1), 34–51.

Rourke, B. P., & Fuerst, D. R. (1991). *Learning disabilities and psychosocial functions: A neuropsychological perspective*. New York: Guilford Press.

Rourke, B. P., & Fuerst, D. R. (1994). Cognitive processing, academic achievement, and psychosocial functioning: A neurodevelopmental perspective. In D. Cocchetti & D. J. Cohen (Eds.), *Developmental psychopathology* (pp. 391–432). New York: Wiley.

Rourke, B. P., & Tsatsanis, K. D. (1996). Syndrome of nonverbal learning disabilities: Psycholinguistic assets and deficits. *Topics in Language Disorders, 16*(2), 30–44.

Rourke, B. P., & Tsatsanis, K. D. (2000). Nonverbal learning disabilities and Asperger's disorder. In A. Klin, F. R. Volkmar, & S. S. Sparrow (Eds.), *Asperger's disorder* (pp. 231–233). New York, Guilford Press.

Rourke, B. P., Young, G. C., & Leenaars, A. A. (1989). A childhood learning disability that predisposes those afflicted to adolescent and adult depression and suicide risk. *Journal of Learning Disabilities, 22*(3), 169–175.

Rubinstein, M. B. (2005). *Raising NLD superstars: What families with nonverbal learning disabilities need to know about nurturing confident, competent kids.* London: Jessica Kingsley.

Schacter, D. L. (1996). *Searching for memory: The brain, the mind, and the past.* New York: Basic Books.

Schacter, D. L., & Scarry, E. (Eds.). (2000). *Memory, brain, and belief.* Cambridge, MA: Harvard University Press.

Schore, A. N. (1994). *Affect regulation and the origin of the self: The neurobiology of emotional development.* Hillsdale, NJ: Erlbaum.

Schore, A. N. (1997). A century after Freud's Project: Is a rapproachement between psychoanalysis and neurobiology at hand? *Journal of the American Psychoanalytic Association, 45*(3), 807–840.

Schore, A. N. (2001). Effects of a secure attachment relationship on right brain development, affect regulation, and infant mental health. *Infant Mental Health Journal, 22*(1–2), 7–66.

Schore, A. N. (2002). Advances in neuropsychoanalysis, attachment theory, and trauma research: Implications for self psychology. *Psychoanalytic Inquiry, 22*(3), 433–484.

Schore, A. N. (2003a). Minds in the making: Attachment, the self-organizing brain, and developmentally-oriented psychoanalytic psychotherapy. In J. Corrigall & H. Wlinkinson (Eds.), *Revolutionary connections: Psychotherapy and neuroscience* (pp. 7–51). London: Karnac.

Schore, A. N. (2003b). Attachment and the regulation of the right brain. *Attachment and Human Development, 2*(1), 23–47.

Semrud-Clikeman, M., & Hynd, G. W. (1990). Right hemisphere dysfunction in nonverbal learning disabilities: Social, academic and adaptive functioning in adults and children. *Psychological Bulletin, 107*(2), 196–209.

Semrud-Clikeman, M., & Hynd, G. W. (1991). Specific nonverbal and social-skills deficits in children with learning disabilities. In J. E. Obrzut & G. W. Hynde (Eds.), *Neuropsychological foundations of learning disabilities: A handbook of issues, methods and practices* (pp. 603–629). San Diego, CA: Academic Press.

Shapiro, J. R., & Applegate, J. S. (2000). Cognitive neuroscience, neurobiology and affect regulation: Implications for clinical social work. *Clinical Social Work Journal, 28*(1): 9–21.

Shields, J. (1991). The semantics—pragmatic disorder: A right-hemisphere syndrome? *British Journal of Disorders of Communication, 26,* 383–392.

Siegal, M., Carrington, J., & Radel, M. (1996). Theory of mind and pragmatic understanding following right hemisphere damage. *Brain and Language, 53,* 40–50.

Siegal, M., & Varley, R. (2002). Neural systems involved in "Theory of Mind." *Nature Reviews: Neuroscience, 3,* 463–471.

Sodian, B., & U. Frith (1993). The theory of mind deficit in autism: evidence from deception. In S. Baron-Cohen, H. Tager-Flusberg, & D. J. Cohen. *Understanding other minds: Perspectives from autism* (pp. 158–180). Oxford, UK: Oxford University Press.

Solms, M. (2000). Preliminaries for an integration of psychoanalysis and neuroscience. *Annual of Psychoanalysis, 28,* 179–200.

Solms, M., & Turnbull, O. (2002). *The brain and the inner world: An introduction to the neuroscience of subjective experience.* New York: Other Press.

Springer, S. P., & Deutsch, G. (1989). *Left brain, right brain* (3rd ed.). New York: Freedman.

Squire, L. R., & Kandel, E. R. (1999). *Memory: From mind to molecules.* New York: Scientific American Library.

Sroufe, L. A. (1995). *Emotional development: The organization of emotional life in the early years.* Cambridge, UK: Cambridge University Press.

Starkstein, A. E., Federoff, J. P., Price, T. R., Leiguarda, R. C., & Robinson, R. G. (1994). Neuropsychological and neuroradiologic correlates of emotional prosody comprehension. *Neurology, 44,* 515–522.

Stern, D. N. (1983). The early development of schemas of self, other, and "self with other." In J. D. K. Lichtenberg & S. Kaplan, (Eds.), *Reflections on Self Psychology* (pp. 49–84). Hillsdale, NJ: Analytic Press.

Stern, D. N. (1985). *The interpersonal world of the infant.* New York: Basic Books.

Stern, D. N. (2004). *The present moment in psychotherapy and everyday life.* New York: Norton.

Stolorow, R. D., Brandchaft, B., & Atwood, G. E., (1987). *Psychoanalytic treatment: An intersubjective approach.* Hillsdale, NJ: Analytic Press.

Szatmari, P. (1992). The validity of autistic specutrum disorders: A literature review. *Journal of Autism and Developmental Disorders, 22*(4), 583–600.

Tager-Flusberg, H. (1996). Language acquisition and theory of mind: Contributions from the study of autism. In L. B. Adamson & M. A. Romski (Eds.), *Communication and language acquisition: Discoveries from atypical development* (pp. 135–160). Baltimore, MD; Paul H. Brookes.

Tager-Flusberg, H., & Baron-Cohen, S. (1993). An introduction to the debate. In S. Baron-Cohen, H. Tager-Flusgerg, & D. J. Cohen (Eds), *Understanding otherminds* (pp. 3–9). Oxford, UK: Oxford University Press.

Tanguay, P. B. (2001). *Nonverbal learning disabilities at home: A parent's guide.* Philadelphia: Jessica Kingsley.

Tanguay, P. B. (2003). *Nonverbal learning disabilities at school: Educating students with NLDs, Asperger's Disorder, and related conditions.* London: Jessica Kingsley.

Teglasi, H., A. Cohn, & Meshbesher, N. (2004). Temperament and learning disability. *Learning Disabilities Quarterly, 27*(1), 9–20.

Teicholz, J. G. (2001). The many meanings of intersubjectivity and their implications for analyst self-expression and self-disclosure. In A. Goldberg (Ed.), *Progress in self psychology: The narcissistic pateint revisited* (pp. 9–42). Hillsdale, NJ: Analytic Press.

Tomasello, M. (1999). *The cultural origins of human cognition.* Cambridge, MA: Harvard University Press.

Tomkins, S. S. (1962). *Affects, imagery, consciousness. Vol. I: The positive affects.* New York: Springer.

Tomkins, S. S. (1963). *Affect, Imagery, Consciousness. Vol. II: The negative affects.* New York: Springer.

Tomkins, S. S. (1979). Script theory: Differential magnification of affects. In H. E. Howe & R. A. Dienstbier (Eds.), *Nebraska symposium on motivation* (vol. 36, pp. 201–236). Lincoln: University of Nebraska Press.

Tomkins, S. S. (1981). The quest for primary motives: Biography and autobiography of an idea. *Journal of Personality and Social Psychology, 41*, 306–329.

Tomkins, S. S. (1987). Script theory. In J. Aronogg, A. I. Rabin, & R. A. Zucker (Eds.), *The emergence of personality* (pp. 147–215). New York: Springer.

Torgesen, J. K. (1986). Learning disabilities theory: Its current state and future prospects. *Journal of Learning Disabilities, 19*(7), 399–407.

Torgesen, J. K. (1994). Issues in the assessment of executive function: An information-processing perspective. In G. R. Lyon (Ed.), *Frames of reference for the assessment of learning disabilities: New views on measurement issues* (pp. 143–162). Baltimore, MD: Brookes.

Torgesen, J. K. (1996). A model of memory from an information processing perspective: The special case of phonological memory. In G. R. Lyon & N.A. Krasnegor, (Eds.), *Attention, memory, and executive function* (pp. 157–184). Baltimore, MD: Brookes.

Trevarthen, C. (2003). Neuroscience and intrinsic psychodynamics: Current knowledge and potential for therapy. In J Corrigall & H. Wilkinson (Eds.), *Revolutionary connections: Psychotherapy and neuroscience* (pp. 53–78). New York: Karnac.

Tsatsanis, K. D., & Rourke, B. P. (1995). Conclusions and future directions. In B. P. Rourke (Ed.), *Syndrome of nonverbal learning disabilities: Neurodevelopmental manifestations* (pp. 476–796). New York: Guilford Press.

Tur-Kaspa, H., & Bryan, T. (1994). Social information-processing skills of students with learning disabilities. *Learning Disabilities Research and Practice, 9*(1), 12–23.

Vigilante, F. W. (1983). Working with families of learning disabled children. *Child Welfare 65*(5); 429–436.

Voeller, K. K. S. (1986). Right-hemisphere deficits syndrome in children. *American Journal of Psychiatry, 143*(8), 1004–1009.

Voeller, K. K. S. (1991). Social–emotional learning disabilities. *Psychiatric Annals, 21*(12), 735–741.

Voeller, K. K. S. (1994). Techniques for measuring social competence in children. In G. R. Lyon (Ed.), *Frames of reference for the assessment of learning disabilities: New views on measurement issues* (pp. 523–554). Baltimore, MD: Brookes.

Voeller, K. K. S. (1997). Social and emotional learning disabilities. In T. E. Feinburg & M. J. Farah (Eds.), *Behavioral neurology and neuropsychology* (pp. 795–801). New York: McGraw Hill.

Volkmar, F., & Klin, A. (1998). Asperger's disorder and nonverbal learning disabilities. In E. Schopler, G. B. Mesibov, & L. J. Kunce (Eds.), *Asperger's disorder or high-functioning autismm?* (pp. 107–121). New York: Plenum Press.

Volkmar, F. R., Klin, A., Schultz, R. T., Rubon, E., & Bronen, R. (2000). Asperger's disorder. *American Journal of Psychiatry, 157*(2), 262–267.

Vygotsky, L. (1986). *Thought and language.* (A. Korzulin, Trans.). Cambridge, MA: MIT Press.

Watt, D. (2000). The dialogue between psychoanalysis and neuroscience: Alienation and reparation. *Neuro-Psychoanalysis, 2*(2), 183–192.

Weintraub, S., & Mesulam M. (1982). Developmental learning disabilities of the right hemisphere: Emotional, interpersonal and cognitive components. *Archives of Neurology, 40*, 463–468.

Wellman, H. M. (1993). Early understanding of mind: The normal case. In S. Baron-Cohen, H. Tager-Flusberg, D. J. Cohen, Caparulo, B. K., & H., Wetstone

(Eds.), *Understanding other minds: Perspectives from autism* (pp. 10–39). Oxford, UK: Oxford University Press.

Westen, D. (1998). The scientific legacy of Sigmund Freud: Toward a psychodynamically informed psychological science. *Psychological Bulletin, 124*(3), 333–371.

Whitney, R. V. (2002). *Bridging the gap: Raising a child with nonverbal disorder.* New York: Berkeley.

Wing, L. (1988). The continuum of autistic characteristics. In E. Schopler & G. Mesibov (Eds.), *Diagnosis and assessment in autism* (pp. 91–110). New York: Plenum Press.

Wing, L. (1991). The relationship between Asperger's disorder and Kanners' Autism. In U. Frith (Ed.), *Autism and Asperger's disorder* (pp. 93–121). Cambridge, UK: Cambridge University Press.

Winnicott, D. W. (1953). Transitional objects and transitional phenomena. *International Journal of Psycho-Analysis, 34,* 89–97.

Winnicott, D. W. (1971). *Playing and reality.* New York: Basic Books.

Wolf, E. S. (1988). *Treating the self: Elements of clinical self psychology.* New York: Guilford Press.

.

Index